EVERYTHING IS
UNDER CONTROL

EVERYTHING IS

UNDER CONTROL

Conspiracies, Cults, and Cover-ups

ROBERT ANTON WILSON

WITH MIRIAM JOAN HILL

HarperResource
An Imprint of HarperCollinsPublishers

HarperCollins books may be purchased for educational, business, or sales promotional use. For information please write: Special Markets Department, HarperCollins Publishers, Inc., 10 East 53rd Street, New York, NY 10022.

FIRST EDITION

Designed by Jessica Shatan

Library of Congress Cataloging-in-Publication Data

Wilson, Robert Anton.
    Everything is under control : conspiracies, cults, and cover-ups / by Robert Anton Wilson with Miriam Joan Hill. — 1st ed.
      p.   cm.
    Includes bibliographical references.
    ISBN 0-06-273417-2
    1. Conspiracies.   I. Hill, Miriam, Joan.   II. Title.
HV6275.W55   1998   98-3332
909—dc21

06 07 08 09 ❖/RRD 20 19 18 17 16 15

DEDICATION

to
Mimi Hill
one wonderfully efficient Websearcher

and to
Valerie and Barry and Christina and Alexandra and Maureen
and Jennifer and Jeremie and Brahm and Richard and Paula

and to
Arlen
"semper in te glorior"

A characteristic common to all intelligence officers,
East and West, is that they have
a special open-mindedness.
For them nothing is impossible
just because it is improbable.

from http://www.livelinks.com/sumeria/politics/supermol.html

EVERYTHING IS

UNDER CONTROL

INTRODUCTION

*Just because you're not paranoid doesn't mean they're
not plotting against you.*

—Popular proverb of the 1990s

A random telephone survey of 800 American adults in
September 1996 found that 74 percent—virtually three out of
four citizens—believe that the U.S. government regularly
engages in conspiratorial and clandestine operations. This does
not necessarily indicate increasing flight to fantasy, or confusing
TV with reality: The same study found that only 29 percent
believe in witchcraft, and a mere 10 percent believe Elvis Presley
is still alive.[1]

If three out of four of our citizens—a much greater majority
than that won by any president of the U.S. in our lifetimes—suspect the government of felonious and nefarious activities, that
means that quite ordinary people now believe what only embit-

[1] Survey published by *George* magazine (November 1996), cited in *Fortean
Times*, February 1997, p. 21.

tered left-wing radicals believed a century ago, in the 1890s (and only professional cynics like H.L. Mencken believed as late as the 1920s). Now, not just the far left and the cynics see all manner of double-dealing in Washington: The far-right wing has even more dire suspicions than all the galoots ahoof in the Republic added together. *Nobody* in the U.S. today has the sort of blind faith in our rulers that they taught us in grade school, and the above-mentioned three out of four of us hardly trust them at all.

But the government does not have any monopoly on the low end of the confidence curve. We live in an age in which humans distrust other humans more than ever before. One can hardly think of any subset of the species, Homo Sap, that has not become an object of uneasy suspicion by some other subset. The professions all belong to the criminal classes, according to popular opinion: TV repairpersons cheat us regularly, and so do auto mechanics. Doctors, merchants, the clergy, and alleged "experts" of all sorts have a dark smog of similar suspicions floating almost visibly around them. We all know that "experts" can be hired to testify to any side of any case. (See *Elmyr.*) Other groups also appear fungible and nefarious to many.

Even Academia has its own brands of conspiracy theory, or something much like it. The two leading schools of art/culture criticism, known as Deconstructionism and Post-Modernism, amount to seeking, and usually finding, ulterior motives in anybody's "model" or "narrative" about the human situation, whether that "narrative" appears as a play by a genius such as Shakespeare or just a TV sitcom; or as a novel, a film, a documentary film, a sculpture, a grand opera, a painting; or as an alleged "finding" of social science, or even an ordained law in the hard sciences; or as a political or religious faith. Basing their skeptical method on both the best and worst zetetic tendencies from Freud to

Buddhism, the Deconstructionists leave one feeling that no communication can be trusted to say what it means or to mean what it says. The Post-Modernists often seem to refuse to communicate at all. (I say that without malice, because I myself have been called a Post-Modernist.)

Maybe dogs are the only people around who still trust human beings, and I have even noted that some dogs seem dubious about us lately.

Strange Narratives

When I first developed a taste for books (around age 8 or 9, I guess) one of the first I read had the daunting title *Believe It or Not!* and contained hundreds of almost unbelievable but allegedly factual yarns about strange doings on this planet. The author, a popular cartoonist of the time named Robert Ripley, began with a section on oddities of human religion, under the classical-looking headline, "Strange is man when he seeks after his gods." Even at this age, I do not know if Mr. Ripley invented that aphorism or found it in some real classic; but it lingered in my memory for more than half a century.

Men (and women) indeed become strange when seeking gods. As the present work will show, however, they become even stranger when seeking devils. And the narratives they invent have all the sinister charm and eerie cornball poetry of Bela Lugosi at his best moments. It almost seems that the human mind works like a giant magnifying glass: If you turn it to Positive Thoughts, it will enlarge them and multiply positivity endlessly, as it does for Christian Scientists and disciples of Rev. Norman Vincent Peale; but if you turn it upon Evil, it will soon show you everything you most fear lurking with slavering jaws and green tentacles right outside your front door.

Not since the heyday of St. Paul and St. Augustine have so many people felt obliged to look at everything with an Evil magnifying glass and howled in such despair at the magnified Evil they then saw in this "fallen" world. Neither the government nor medicine nor commerce has a monopoly on popular anxiety. Most right-wing Catholics fear the Freemasons, and most Freemasons have worrying anxieties about the Vatican and all its minions. Many Euro-American citizens have taken to the hills (in Idaho and elsewhere) believing that our Afro-American citizens are determined to exterminate the white race (either in revenge for slavery, or because some other, more fiendish conspiracy has deliberately misled them). Probably a much higher percentage of Afro-American citizens believes that the Euro-American ruling class intends to exterminate *them*; see *Tuskegee Syphilis Study* and its links to other entries in the main text of this volume.

Black helicopters hover above our rural areas, and only potheads think the helicopters are part of the Drug Enforcement Administration, seeking taboo herbs (so that the multibillion-dollar pharmaceutical industry can go on gouging us with less reliable medicines at higher prices, according to the most popular theory); others have darker fears. Some believe the helicopters work hand-in-glove with a Satanic consortium of cattle mutilators, child abusers, demented preschool teachers, and punk rockers; and many citizens believe these sinister aircraft serve an alleged UN/New World Order conspiracy, which intends to invade us any day now.

And, of course, nobody trusts the advertisements. Not even people who write them. . .

Perhaps such generalized uneasiness about other members of our own species became inevitable after Auschwitz and Hiroshima. Indeed, anybody who doesn't share some of the "misanthropy" of

Swift, Bierce, Twain, and the like must have missed most of the news since 1944—or earlier. (Both Freud and Yeats, a great psychologist and a great poet, became increasingly uneasy about human beings after the horrors of World War I, which now seem meager compared to more recent atrocities.)

Finding the Guilty Parties

In this "Demonic Dictionary" we deal only with theories that proclaim that *some* persons or groups, whom the theorist can specify, often with front names, hind names, and addresses, deserve all the blame for the horrors that afflict the rest of us—from ecological imbalance to economic hardship, from war to poverty, from drug cartels to the fact you can't even get a plumber on weekends anymore. Those who want to blame all of us equally do not have a Conspiracy Theory but an Original Sin Theory.

The malign subsets of humanity in Conspiracy Theory almost always appear as fungible or homogeneous. When a conspiracy theory posits that the members of the Conspiracy do not share equally in the conscious evil of their leaders, that theory has become somewhat more sophisticated and a good deal more realistic than most such "scapegoat" theories. For instance, in Canto 52, *Ezra Pound* writes:

sin drawing vengeance, poor yitts paying for

——

paying for a few big jews vendetta on goyim[2]

(The —— represents "Rothschild," a name removed by Pound's publisher on advice of counsel. Pound insisted on leaving the —— as evidence that his text had undergone expurgation.)

[2] *The Cantos of Ezra Pound*, New Directions, 1975, p. 257.

Whatever one thinks of Pound's use of vernacular, his words represent one of the rare non-fungible conspiracy theories. A few big (i.e., rich) Jews deserve all the blame, he says, and the poor Jews pay for it unjustly. Such theories, containing a smidgen of rationality, do not usually last very long in conspiriological circles, or even in the minds of individual conspiracy hunters. A few years after writing those lines, Pound began raving and ranting on Rome radio about "the Jews" as a homogeneous group responsible for all bad economics. A similar dynamic appears in the evolution of *almost* all conspiracy theorists (except me and my friends, and, of course, the readers of this book).

The fungible groups dreaded by ardent conspiriologists cannot, of course, exist in reality, because all groups consist of individuals, each of whom differs in some respects from all others. (No two brains are totally alike, just as no two fingerprints are.) Nonetheless, most existing conspiracy theories *tend* to move toward the hypothesis of the fungibility of the devil-group, and this seems to result from both the "paranoid" (or "Mr. District Attorney") *style* of the conspiracy hunter's mind and from the structure of our language, which makes it easy to talk about the Jews, the Catholics, the legal profession, the medical profession, the bankers, the Freemasons, the politicians, the males of our species, etc., as fungible and uniformly evil.

As Nietzsche pointed out, after humanity got tired saying "this leaf" and "that leaf" and "the next leaf," etc., we invented the grammatical/mystic category "the leaf," of which all individual leaves become specific cases. But "the leaf" exists nowhere outside *grammar and Platonic philosophy*—and thus *our language tends to promote neo-Platonism by populating the world with grammatical abstractions. Any conspiracy theory that moves toward fungibility evolves also toward Platonic Idealism.* This "linguistic hypnosis" seems so widespread that Count Alfred

Korzybski invented the science of general semantics as an attempted cure for it.[3]

In other words, because we can say "the Jews" or "the New World Order" or "the Patriarchy," we can believe, or almost believe, that these grammatical abstractions have the same kind of reality as basketballs, barking dogs, and baked beans. Individuals, with all their hair and fingernails and ideals and delusions and funky smells, disappear, as it were, and the world becomes haunted by collective nouns. (See *Hawthorne Abendsen.*)

Americans in particular seem to have a passion for theories that explain that everything bad results from the machinations of an evil group who have no more morals than SPECTRE in the James Bond novels. Perhaps, instead of dividing our citizens into those who believe in some such conspiracy theory and those who do not, we should divide ourselves into those who blame one of the better-known conspiracies—the CIA, the *Protocols of the Elders of Zion*, the *Freemasons*—and those who have given their faith and allegiance to more recondite theories, placing the blame on secretive and clandestine groups most ordinary people have never even heard of, such as the *Gnomes of Zurich*, the *Knights of Malta,* or the *Insiders.*

Those who deny all possibility of conspiracy anywhere must eventually decide, like Voltaire, that the extent of human stupidity is roughly equal to what mathematicians contemplate when they speak of The Infinite. Others, who cannot believe stupidity reaches such transcendent proportions, perforce believe in some kind of conspiracy, or conspiracies, at least part of the time. Stupidity, we mostly believe, cannot explain *everything* wrong with this planet. . . .

[3] Students of Korzybski's school of semantics learn to say $leaf_1$, $leaf_2$, etc., Jew_1, Jew_2, etc., instead of "the leaf" or "the Jew." Most conspiracy theories could not survive this reform. Imagine an edition of *MS. Magazine* in which "the male" did not appear but only $male_1$, $male_2$, etc.

Indeed, those who think "conspiracy theories" never contain anything but paranoid fantasy should remember that our government itself and all advanced governments believe in conspiracies and have laws against them. Special branches of the police power have the job of investigating possible conspiracies in various areas—the SEC looks for bank swindles, the Red Squad of every police department looks for subversive ideas, district attorneys hunt for books so evil they are not protected by the First Amendment (which radicals like the late Justice Brennan believed was intended to protect all books), even the CIA (when it can spare the time from its profitable cocaine business) looks for external conspiracies, etc. If we (or three out of four of us) don't trust the people who govern us, they don't trust us, either.

And no other country lacks some criminal conspiracy laws or agencies charged with seeking them out and prosecuting them. This, for instance, explains how the Italian government in the 1980s discovered the *P2 conspiracy,* which had placed over 950 of its agents in top government positions. Similarly, the U.S. government has recently found evidence of a conspiracy of deception by the tobacco industry. Such facts should warn us again dismissing *all* conspiracy theories as the pastime of dingbats and cranks.

None of the investigative agencies charged with bringing hard evidence into court, however, have ever found traces of any of the Really Big Conspiracies that most "conspiracy buffs" believe in. This, of course, only proves one thing to the true conspiriologist: The major conspiracies really do have almost universal power, because the investigating agencies themselves "are part of the cover-up." Against that kind of logic, the gods themselves contend in vain.

But, of course, a truly powerful and truly intelligent conspiracy would never get "exposed" or even suspected, as Mel Gibson says in the popular film *Conspiracy Theory.*

Thus nobody can totally refute any truly crazy conspiracy theory, because all such theories have a Strange Loop in their construction. Any evidence against them also functions as evidence to support them, if you want to look at it that way. Thus, like its cousin, theology, the pop demonology of conspiracy theory survives any and all criticisms. *People do not believe theological or demonological models of the world for logical or scientific reasons, but for "artistic" or at least emotional reasons.* These models or narratives provide harmonious, coherent, and starkly simple explanations of events that otherwise seem chaotic and beyond human comprehension. That's why I believe in so many of them myself.

Cultic Twilight

Conspiracy theories therefore flourish in times and places of anxiety and uncertainty; but they come to full flower in those times when the government also fears conspiracies, i.e., does not trust the people. We here enter a truly murky area, where many people are presently under surveillance precisely because they once thought and said that the government might spy on them.

"If the government doesn't trust the people, why doesn't it dissolve them and elect a new people?" playwright Bert Brecht once asked. A government afraid of its people cannot "dissolve" them so easily, or replace them with a people seized and imported from somewhere else, so it simply spies on the people it has and probes into their privacy even more than usual.

"Superstitions like bats fly most at twilight," Sir Francis Bacon wrote. Similarly, after studying conspiracy theory for nearly 30 years, I think that I have found that batty conspiracy theories and modern folklore in general thrive best in an environment of uncertainty and anxiety. When people do not know what will happen next, any wild yarn will travel very rapidly through the population; it appears humans need any narrative, even a nonsense narrative, rather than having no explanation at all about their predicament. And the essence of any good story is, as in conspiracy theory, the *plot*.

If the people do not trust the government, it does not trust them. If the government does not trust the people, they do not trust it. This merry-go-round is almost a perpetual motion machine. (See *"Every Knee Shall Bow."*)

In a nation where even one's urine is not private, where the Power Elite sends its snoopers to search into your very innards—your bladder, no less—what man or woman can feel any sense of freedom or security?

Hence, the people grow more hostile and "paranoid" about the government, and the government, noting this, grows more nervous about "militias" or "cults" or "hippies" or "extremists" or some other anti-governmental minority that might live *anywhere* and might secretly plot *anything*. It therefore hires more eavesdroppers, installs more wiretaps, and spies on the people with greater vigor. This Strange Loop quickly becomes a Vicious Circle, since governmental paranoia about people and people's paranoia about government each reinforce the other. (See *The War on Some Drugs*.)

This cycle continues until the system collapses, until the funding runs out, or until, due to Divine Intervention, sanity reappears. In the interlude, endless and labyrinthine conspiracy theory flourishes, among both the government and the governed, as each becomes more frightened of the other. (See *James Jesus Angleton*.)

The Cold War has left us a legacy of spying, snooping, and paranoia that no longer serves any rational function (if it ever did). This continues even after the Cold War has ended, because politics like Newtonian mechanics has a *Law of Inertia whereby a political crusade in motion continues in motion in the same direction until some outside force interrupts it*. No such outside force has yet slowed our general drift toward a Kafka–Orwell world where the worst fantasies seem more and more plausible to more and more people.

Another factor tending to multiply conspiracy theories beyond necessity lies in the fact that all intelligence agencies have two functions, viz.:

1. *Collection of accurate information.*
2. *Planting and encouraging inaccurate information.*

An intelligence agency, in other words, needs to know "what the hell is really going on" for the same reason a bank or a grocer or you and I need that kind of factual input. Hence, the huge budgets for item 1 above.

Intelligence agencies, however, also need to keep ahead of their competitors, the rival intelligence agencies of other and, hence, perfidious governments. They therefore engage in frenetic efforts of spreading misinformation, "disinformation" (a euphemism for the former), "cover stories," "cover-ups," etc. In order to deceive whoever currently functions as "the enemy," these fantasies must have enough facts mixed into them, and enough general plausibility, that they will deceive many others not yet defined as "enemy." Always, they *must* deceive persons of average intelligence and average education or they just don't work. The best disinformation should also deceive persons of more-than-average wit and know-how, for a while at least.

In brief, modern secret-police work functions much like poker. All players try to send false signals at least part of the time, and all players try to detect "the real truth" behind the false signals sent by the others.[4] In a world where nations relate to each other in

---

[4] A detailed analysis of this Strange Loop appears in *Theory of Games and Economic Behavior*, by John von Neumann and Oskar Morgenstern, Princeton University Press, 1948.

this manner, conspiracy models flourish like bacteria in a sewage system. As *Henry Kissinger* allegedly said, "Anybody in Washington who isn't paranoid must be crazy." Indeed, any citizen in a world run like that who doesn't have some "paranoid" suspicions must have suffered brain damage in childhood.

When the government engages in extensive (well-publicized) snooping and spying on the public, this paranoia escalates rapidly. Where there exists a secret police agency of any sort, in any nation, the people soon learn to suspect those who suspect them. Concretely, many Americans fear that any part of government, or even any organization not admittedly part of the government, may function as a front for the CIA, the FBI, the BATF, the National Security Agency, or groups even more esoteric and manipulative.

Thus, the more omnipresent the government's "control," the more suspicious and uneasy the people become. And the more people indicate a lack of faith of such government, the more such government will need to spy on them, to feel absolutely sure they have not become alienated enough to hatch rebellion or set off more homemade bombs of the Oklahoma City variety. The government will therefore increase its spying and snooping, and the people will become more "careful." As a crude kind of survey, I have asked audiences in hundreds of lectures and seminars if any of them ever willingly tell the *whole truth about anything* to a government official. Nobody has ever held up their hand and claimed that degree of faith and tractability.

No man or woman in the United States today wants the Feds to know too much about what he or she is really doing. Since the government long ago passed the point of "anything not forbidden is compulsory" and now also wishes to enforce "anything not compulsory is forbidden," we all suspect that we are technical criminals at least, although like Kafka's hero we are never quite sure which statute or statutes we may have violated.

We thus arrive at a situation that in the Army is called Optimum Snafu. Those at the top are never told what might cause them to punish the informant, and those at the bottom keep their mouths shut about more and more of what they actually see, hear, smell, taste, or otherwise sense of the environment. In the long run, the top people in the pyramid are attempting to regulate things they know nothing about, based on reports that have been invented by liars and flatterers to prevent them from using their awful powers too destructively.

But if most people always lie a little in dealing with the State, the State must have a very weird and inaccurate picture of who the people are and what they really think and want. Laws will therefore direct themselves to a fictitious citizenry, not to the people we really are. Thus, the laws increasingly make no sense to the folk who have to endure them, and more hostility to government appears.

All these cycles make up a set of Strange Loops and Vicious Circles from which there presently appears no exit. Unless, as suggested before, the funding runs out or Divine Intervention occurs, conspiracy theories will flourish, both among the increasingly anxiety-ridden citizenry and among the politicos and bureaucrats who try to command them. And every voice that tries, or pretends, to tell the truth in this schizoid situation immediately comes under suspicion as another possible Deceiver and Manipulator whose yarn has to be looked at as critically as any Post-Modernist would look at the Declaration of Independence or the Second Law of Thermodynamics.

We are all Deconstructionists now, whether we ever heard the word before or not.

The Age of Uncertainty

In case anybody thinks the above picture exaggerated or merely satirical, let us point out that two recent surveys show that public confidence in the media, which allegedly "inform" us, has sunk to what must be an all-time low. A *Wall Street Journal*/NBC poll found that only 21 percent of the respondents rated the news media "very" or "mostly" honest. That means that nearly 80 percent of us don't trust the media (TV, radio, print) quite as much as we used to. Similarly, a Gallup poll found that only 29 percent of us express "a great deal" of confidence in the newspapers specifically. About seven out of ten, then, have growing doubts and suspicions about the medium where we once looked to find the facts behind the incoherent sound bytes of radio and TV "news."[5]

But since most people need some narrative or model to explain the world, if they don't trust the media, who can they trust? Nobody. Then how can they make decisions? More and more, they reactively assume reality is precisely the opposite of whatever they are being told by the Voice of Authority.

Personally, I view all this from a unique vantage point. Circumstances have combined to place me in a rather singular position in the conspiracy-literature spectrum. In 1969–71, I wrote *Illuminatus!* with the late Robert Shea. This book parodied popular conspiracy theories of the '60s but in a deliberately off-kilter way: The perspective was "Post-Joycean," in that the reader was not told what to believe by the Omniscient Narrator of traditional fiction, but rather was left to decide for himself/herself how much or how little to take seriously of the models of the world (or "tall tales") offered by many wildly conflicting and sometimes wacko

[5] Both studies were cited in the *Christian Science Monitor*, 16 April 1997.

narrators. (The theory of Joyce's Uncertainty Principle is more recondite and labyrinthine than explained in this short note, but in general when I use the term I mean the kind of book, like *Ulysses*, that does not present itself as a Puzzle Solved but as a Puzzle to Be Worked On.)

Illuminatus! remains in print 23 years after it first appeared in 1975. It has been translated into several languages and performed as a stage play in Liverpool, London, Amsterdam, Cambridge University, Frankfurt, and Seattle, Washington. As a result, I *never* stop receiving mail or press clippings from people who hold a variety of weird opinions about me. Some think I believe that all the conspiracies in that wild and crazy book really exist and want to keep me informed about the latest swindles. Some think that I believe in none of them and write only as a satirist of unconventional people (and therefore a sly defender of the Establishment), and they want to straighten me out.

Many believe I am deliberately engaged in confusing (or, as spokespersons for Generation X say, "screwing with the heads of") the more serious, or more solemn, conspiracy theorists; several have carried this to the point of identifying (to their own satisfaction) which conspiracy I really work for. Many think it's the CIA, but *Lyndon LaRouche* thinks it's the original *Illuminati*. The late Mae Brussel, more originally, claimed I worked for the Rockefellers. I cheerfully confessed to the last, adding that David Rockefeller personally comes around once a month to deliver the filthy lucre in gold bars, which I keep stacked in my basement. I thought that would improve my credit rating, but evidently nobody but Mae believed it.

You see, I have never denied any of these charges, since flat denial wouldn't convince anybody with a truly suspicious mind. You are free to believe any or all of them. To quote *The X Files*, the Bible of Those Who Doubt, *Trust no one*. Maybe I'm an

Illuminated Judeo-Masonic Pot-Smoking Homosexual Satanist from Planet X after all.

Researching the present book has renewed my faith in the power of what William Blake called poetic imagination. (Psychiatrists sometimes call it flight from reality.) I did a lot of similar research in co-authoring *Illuminatus!,* and I thought most of this book would consist of revisiting familiar ground. To my astonishment and delight, my collaborator/research associate, Miriam Joan Hill, found more conspiracy theories than I ever dreamed possible. If we didn't stop and deliver this manuscript to the publisher, we could seemingly go on for years and produce a work with as many volumes as the *Britannica.* You simply cannot invent any conspiracy theory so ridiculous and so obviously satirical that some people somewhere don't already believe it.

To those who complain that their favorite conspiracy isn't here, I can only plead that space and time are not infinite, especially at my age. But go ahead and complain anyway. Maybe I'll get a contract to write a sequel.

"Ah, time! cash! art! and patience!" as Melville wrote.

A final word: I have found that nobody can dive very deeply into these infested waters without having at least occasional flashes of true paranoia—that is, not just entertaining the idea that *some* of the more plausible theories here *may* be true, but worrying about even the silliest of them. As an example, Mike Reynolds, a writer I knew back in the 1970s, after being hired to do an article about "cattle mutilations" for a slick men's magazine, had his house ransacked and burglarized just before sending in his final draft. He came to me to discuss his fears, and I assure you he was a very sane and skeptical person. Nonetheless, he suffered from a bout of that anxious uncertainty I can only call Conspiracy Coincidence Syndrome: When you look into this kind of material long enough, any nastiness that happens to you—not just a burglary, which disturbs anybody, because it reminds us of our vulnerability, but even "small" things such as strange phone noises, damaged (opened?) mail, or **men in black** hanging around your corner—can make you wonder: Are They *really* real, after all? And are They just checking me out or preparing a preemptive strike? What is that sound in the backyard?

Don't let it bother you. It happens to all of us. Besides, if you do let it bother you, you will become as paranoid as most of the full-time conspiracy researchers I have met.

Of course, if I am an agent of the CIA or the Rockefellers or somebody like that, I would try to keep you from getting too alarmed about all this, wouldn't I?

Just because you're not paranoid doesn't mean they're not plotting against you. . . .

Or did I quote that already?
Well, it's worth remembering. . . .

A-Albionic Consulting and Research

The most plausible of the multiconspiracy theories—i.e., those scenarios that do not claim that one supersecret criminal gang rules this planet, but rather that *at least* two such "gangs" exist, at war with each other—comes forth from an outfit styling itself A-Albionic Consulting and Research, in Ferndale, Michigan.

A-Albionic began in 1985 with a common or garden-variety uniconspiracy theory, blaming everything on the British royal family—rather like *Lyndon LaRouche,* who may have served as their original inspiration. In 1989, however, A-Albionic revised their model of the world (yes, they actually use the scientific word "model" and show other signs of some technical education). The post–1989 A-Albionic scenario holds that, in their own words (capitals included), "The Overt and Covert Organs of the Vatican and the British Empire are Locked in Mortal Combat for Control of the World."

A-Albionic traces this Mortal Combat back to the reign of the first Queen Elizabeth, when Protestant-Catholic warfare raged all over Europe—the time when the English, typically, made their pioneer scientific rationalist, Sir Francis Bacon, a high government official, while the Vatican took *their* pioneer scientific rationalist, *Giordano Bruno,* and burned him at the stake. The British Crown and the Throne of Peter have continued to make war on each other ever since, in this model, and every other "interest group," "trade union," "association of manufacturers," *Mafia* family, international bank or intelligence agency—everything that might qualify as a conspiracy in anybody's mind—have all become puppets, unknowingly, in this megastruggle.

Thus, the Windsor Family Mega-Conspiracy manipulates a motley crew, which A-Albionic sums up as "Comsymp–International Banker-Judeo–Masonic–Labour Party–British Intelligence–Socialist International–Social Democrat–Fabian–AFL–CIO–UAW–KGB"—the same unlikely bedfellows that appear in many anti-*Illuminati* theories. The Vatican, on the opposite side of the world power struggle, controls an assembly of "CIA–Fascist International–Georgetown Jesuits–McCarthyite–Buckleyite–Knights of Malta." (See *Knights of Malta* and *P2*.)

Duoconspiracy theories, like uniconspiracy theories, often lead to logical conclusions that seem bizarre to outsiders. Thus, the late *Carroll Quigley,* professor of history at Georgetown University, appears as a member of the *Insiders* in the *John Birch Society* theory, and these alleged Insiders, who sound a lot like the Illuminati, all belong to the British Royal Family Jumbo Conspiracy in A-Albionic's system. In fact, many right-wing theories become compatible if one identifies Insiders with Illuminati and both with international bankers (Jewish, Dutch, or whichever suspects you prefer). . . . Ergo, Quigley was an agent of the Windsor Gang.

But Prof. Quiqley taught at Georgetown, which the Jesuits own, so this makes him actually a tool of the Vatican conspiracy according to A-Albionic. He had entered the Windsor–Insider–International Banker–Illuminati conspiracy, A-Albionic says, but only to expose it. Quigley's book, *Tragedy and Hope,* usually cited by right-wingers as "inadvertently" revealing the Insider's plot for world government, had nothing inadvertent about it at all. The Jesuits sent Quigley to spy out the enemy and publish their secrets, according to A-Albionic.

This minor detail in the conspiratorial mosaic became a matter of passionate debate among conspiriologists during the 1992 presidential race, because *Bill Clinton,* in one speech, mentioned Prof. Quigley as a teacher who had vastly inspired him in his youth. To the majority of right-wing conspiracy buffs, this "proved" that Clinton worked for the Insiders, or the Illuminati or at least the international bankers. But A-Albionic insisted on their own analysis. If President Clinton really received inspiration from a Jesuit school, they claim, then he has become a tool of the Vatican/CIA, or anti-Illuminati, conspiracy.

See also:

The Con, Princess Di's Death, *Terra Papers, Yankee and Cowboy War*

Reference:

http://a-albionic.com/a-albionic.html

A∴A∴

> *The A∴A∴ is the Supreme and Eternal Inner School of initiates who have in all times overseen the evolution of consciousness on this planet (and, presumably, elsewhere). This order has assumed various forms and names throughout history.*
>
> —from the A∴ A∴ web page:
>
> http://www.crl.com/~thelema/aa.html

The A∴A∴ must rank as the most secretive secret society in the world. Perhaps nobody, not even the few writers who have discussed it, knows for sure when the A∴A∴ began, which group claiming to be the A∴A∴ at present is the *real* A∴A∴, or even what the symbols A∴A∴ stand for—although many claim to know all these things, of course.

The best documented form of this secret society dates from ca. 1906 and already claimed a long underground history. It advertised itself as a "magick" society for advanced adepts of the occult. (Magick, pronounced mage-ick, as in Magus or the Three Magi, deals with altering consciousness and enlarging perception, using chants, rituals, drugs, jewels, symbols such as the penta-gram, and special exercises to strengthen will and imagination.) The leader, known only by the initials V.V.V.V.V., also claimed that the A∴A∴ held the rank of "higher order" above the G∴.D∴ (*Hermetic Order of the Golden Dawn*), then the most "advanced" *Freemasonic* or pseudo-Freemasonic order in England, at least in its own judgment. Thus, by claiming a higher rank, the A∴A∴ guaranteed itself a curious audience, at least among those who really take occultism seriously. Just as the Golden Dawn had ten degrees, so did the A∴A∴, but you needed to have graduated from the tenth degree of the Golden Dawn to begin the first degree of the A∴A∴.

Occult historians generally agree that V.V.V.V.V. signified *Vi Veri Vniversum Vivus Vici* ("By the force of truth I have con-quered the universe"), one of the eleven magick mottoes of *Aleister Crowley*. It also appears that Crowley set the standards for admission to the A∴A∴ a bit too high—the candidate not only had to be an advanced Golden Dawn adept but also expert at the most difficult yoga postures to even qualify to take the examination for the first of the ten degrees—and therefore he got few recruits he considered worthy; Crowley therefore devoted most of his subsequent energies to promoting and managing the *Ordo Templi Orientis*, a somewhat less advanced occult lodge.

In the 1970s both *Kenneth Grant* and a person named Michael Mota insisted that the A∴A∴ still exists, although they differed on all else, especially on the "real" head of the order, each claim-ing that position for himself. The order currently on the Internet does not seem to recognize either Grant or Mota as its head.

John Symonds, a hostile critic of occultism in general and Crowley in particular, claimed to have evidence that A∴A∴ stands for "Atlantean Adepts"; Grant claimed it means Argentum Astrum ("Silver Star"), which he identifies with *Sirius* and the occult traditions about certain advanced adepts on this planet who allegedly communicate telepathically with even more advanced adepts in that double star system.

Right-wing Christian conspiriologists generally identify the A∴A∴ and Sirius with the *Illuminati*, and, usually, with Satanism. Curiously, the same years in which Crowley began promoting the A∴A∴ he also began using the title Epopt of the Illuminati and publishing a journal, *The Equinox,* which announced itself on the cover of each issue as a "journal of Scientific Illuminism."

See also:

The Con, Gerard de Sede, George I. Gurdjieff, Insiders, Merovingians, Robert Morning Sky, *Sirius Mystery*

References:

http://www.crl.com/~thelema/aa.html

Portable Darkness, ed. by Scott Michaelson, Harmony Books, New York, 1989

Cults of the Shadow, by Kenneth Grant, Samuel Weiser Books, New York, 1976

Light on Freemasonry, David Bernard, Vonnieda and Sowers, Washington, D.C., 1858

Abductees Anonymous

This organization serves as a support group for persons who believe that extraterrestrials have kidnapped and sexually molested them—one of the largest subgroups in the *recovered memory* community, trailing behind only the *incest survivors* and the *Satanic abuse* survivors. While the whole theory and therapy of the "recovered memory" movement has come under increasing criticism in recent years, it still has many believers, who sincerely think that their therapists helped them remember (not fantasize) incidents of incest, cannibalism, coprophilia, sadomasochism, rape, infant sacrifice, and/or evil *Greys*—a race of detached scientific investigators and/or sexual monsters who come from outer space and have engaged in genetic experiments or sexual assault or both on helpless humans.

AbAnon says nothing about the incest and Satanism yarns, also created or discovered by the same hypnotic techniques, but insists that "many millions" have had the abduction experience and even if you personally can't remember it—or *especially* if you can't remember it—this interstellar rape may have happened to you. They have a list of 52 symptoms that will help you decide if indeed it did happen to you. A few significant signs from this list:

- *Have unusual scars or marks with no possible explanation on how you received them, especially if you have an emotional reaction to them (i.e., small scoop indentation, straight line scar, scars in roof of mouth, in nose, behind or in ears, or genitals, etc.).*

- *Have a cosmic awareness, an interest in ecology, environment, or vegetarianism, or are very socially conscious.*

- *Have inexplicably strong fears or phobias (i.e., heights, snakes, spiders, large insects, certain sounds, bright lights, your personal security, or being alone).*

- *Have the feeling of being watched much of the time, especially at night.*

- *Have awoken with soreness in your genitals, which cannot be explained.*

- *Have seen a hooded figure in or near your home, especially next to your bed.*

- *Have had frequent or sporadic ringing in your ears, especially in one ear.*

- *Have insomnia or sleep disorders that are puzzling to you.*

- *Have the feeling that you are going crazy for even thinking about these sorts of things.*

- *Have a difficult time trusting other people, especially author-ity figures.*

- *Have had dreams of destruction or catastrophe.*

- *Have many of these traits but can't remember anything about an abduction or alien encounter.*

Those who have these stigmata or most of them might contact Abductees Anonymous through the website below.

On the other hand, many of the same (or similar) signs may indicate that you are another incest survivor or Satanic abuse survivor; better consult those entries, too. Can't be too careful these days.

See also:

Demonic Duck, Greys, National Association for Consumer Protection in Mental Health Practices

Reference:

http://www.CyberGate.com/~ufonline

Abel

As the first murder victim in the world (according to Judeo-Christian scriptures) Abel should feature in some conspiracy theory, and, in fact, he appears in two.

According to Henry Bailey Stevens, the Cain-Abel story represents lying propaganda by the carnivores against the vegetarians. In Stevens' construction (or deconstruction) of Genesis, Cain, the tiller of the soil, represents simple, honest, nonviolent humanity in its vegetarian stage—Stevens' version of Rousseau's Noble Savage. The Good People, in other words.

Abel, the butcher of cattle, then represents the corrupt meat-eating humanity who have dominated the last several thousand years, introducing such vices as war, slavery, and general criminality. The Bad People.

The Bible myth, by unjustly pinning the murder rap on the kindly Cain, the good or primary man, represents the decadent meat-eaters attempt to defame the vegetarians, according to Stevens, who staunchly insists that meat-eaters have historically shown more inclination to murder than vegetarians have.

We don't know how Stevens would react to the current Californian bumper sticker:

I'm a Vegetarian
But I Don't Love Animals—
I Just Hate Plants

A sharply different version of the Cain-Abel myth comes from John Steinbacher, who claims that Cain did not spring from the holy matrimonial union of Adam and Eve but from an unholy bestial union of Eve and the Serpent. The snaky Cain then fathered the reptilian *Illuminati*, the vile secret society that forever plots to corrupt and enslave the rest of humanity. The worst of the current plots of these Children of Cain, according to Steinbacher, are the **Federal Reserve Bank** and the **Internal Revenue Service.**

See also:

AYA, Eye on the Pyramid, Illuminati, Robert Morning Sky, *Terra Papers*

References:

The Recovery of Culture, by Henry Bailey Stevens, Harper and Brothers, New York, 1949

Steinbacher—

Los Angeles Free Press, July 26, 1968, quoting his book, *Novus Ordo Seclorum*

Hawthorne Abendsen

Hawthorne Abendsen (dates unknown; probably a pseudonym) has offered us the most hair-raising form of the Feminist conspiracy theory of the Patriarchy.

Inside the "Men's Club": Secrets of the Patriarchy, by Abendsen, traces the Conspiracy back to the first all-male secret societies of the first Stone Age tribes. (Some students of occultism want to trace **Freemasonry** that far back, too. . . .) According to Abendsen, at the beginning of the Bronze Age, when both war and trade shook up many remotely deployed societies and brought them into frequent contact, these magick brotherhoods began to amalgamate, and today they have all joined together into the **Priory of Sion.**

The basic "secrets" of the Priory—the mystical doctrines underlying THE PATRIARCHY—Abendsen tells us, consists chiefly of two long-guarded secrets:

1. *The Priory identifies the True God of Judaism, Christianity, and Islam as the God who appeared to Abraham and gave his name as Al-Shaddai, "the Lord of Battles." In other words, the Priory serves a bloodthirsty divinity cognate with the Roman Mars, the Egyptian Ra-Hoor-Khuit, the Greek Ares, and the Teutonic Wotan—a god of war and gore, pure and simple.*

    *Worship of this god consists of making war (what does a war god most desire?) and of various grisly human and animal sacrifices of the type Protestant Fundamentalists and "**MS. Magazine**" have attributed to a Satanic conspiracy. Satanists actually have nothing to do with it, according to Abendsen: Holy war and ritual bloodshed represent the earliest and truest form of the Judeo-Christian-Islamic faith. Later, more humane images of divinity—i.e., the "god of love"—represent conscious fraud, intended to keep the majority from knowing the true purpose and meaning of what our rulers do. The priest is a shill for the tyrant, in a more radical and horrible way than Voltaire or Marx ever imagined.*

2. *A central part of the cult of Al-Shaddai, god of war, consists of homosexual rituals, affirming male bonding and maintaining the magick subjugation of women as second-class citizens. (In this context, see* **Christians Awake AIDs Theory.***)*

"Hawthorne Abendsen" was originally the name of the character who wrote the novel within the novel in *The Man in the High Tower*, by *Philip K. Dick.*

See also:

Abdul Alhazred, Committee to Protect the Rights and Privileges of Low-Cost Housing, The Con, Gerard de Sede, Feminist Conspiracy Theories, Charles Fort, *Gods of Eden,* Illuminati, Insiders, Robert Morning Sky, *MS. Magazine,* The Red Serpent

Reference:

Inside the "Men's Club," by Hawthorne Abendsen, A-Albionic Consulting and Research, Ferndale, Mich., n.d.

Hiram Abiff

The central character in *Freemasonic* lore is Hiram Abiff, a widow's son, builder of Solomon's temple—an edifice that occultists believe contains in its structure the key to all mystic and secret matters. After completing this work of gnostic architecture, Hiram was killed by three ruffians named Jubela, Jubelo, and Jubelum. The names alone suggest that the story is allegorical, and Albert Pike, in many respects the creator of modern Freemasonry, informs us they contain two names of God, Ju and Bel, repeated three times. The three endings of Ju-Bel, *A-O-UM,* represent a variation on the *OM* or *AUM* used by Hindic peoples to attain meditative consciousness

Every Freemason to pass the Third Degree—a term that has entered everyday speech with a similar, but different, meaning—must re-enact and re-experience the martyrdom of Hiram, and then rises reborn as a Brother in the Craft.

(In the *Ordo Templi Orientis*, which regards itself as the only true Masonic order, and is regarded as pseudo-Masonic by more conventional lodges, Hiram is replaced by the Sufi martyr Mansur al-Hallaj, who was stoned to death for crying out in mystic rapture, "I am the Truth and there is nothing within my turban but God!")

Hiram built Solomon's temple without noise of hammering, making each piece of brass interlock with the others, and this also is symbolic. His death also has many meanings: The three ruffians killed him for refusing to tell them the *Mason Word*. Pike also provides the useful hint that the three wounds of Hiram—to the head, the throat, and the heart—represent the spiritual *death* imposed on humanity by Tyranny and Superstition: The head wound signifies the death of thought (mind control), the throat wound represents the suppression of free speech (censorship), and the stab to the heart means that normal human feeling atrophies and dies when people are not allowed to think or speak their thoughts (narcissism or sociopathy, in clinical jargon). The goal of Freemasonry, in Pike's account, is to combat these three wounds of the human spirit and recapture freedom of thought, word, and conscience.

See also:

Great Seal of the United States, Men in Black

References:

Conspiracies, Cover-Ups and Crimes, by Jonathan Vankin, Paragon, N.Y., 1992

Morals and Dogma of the Ancient and Accepted Scottish Rite of Freemasonry, by Albert Pike, Supreme Council of the Southern Jurisdiction, Washington, D.C., 1871

Abuse, Satanic

See:

Abductees Anonymous, *Ms. Magazine*, Recovered Memory Therapy

Lord Acton

Baron John Emerich Edward Dalberg-Acton (1834–1902), generally called simply Lord Acton, led the liberal Roman Catholic minority that rejected the doctrine of papal infallibility. A learned historian, Acton also wrote one of the most famous aphorisms of all time: "All power tends to corrupt, and absolute power corrupts absolutely."

Acton's terse aphorism serves as the (conscious or unconscious) motto of all skeptics of government power, whether they develop conspiracy theories or not. Cognate sentiments appear in H.L. Mencken, *Benjamin R. Tucker,* I.F. Stone, and even in Leo Tolstoy ("In order to get power and retain it, it is necessary to love power; but love of power is not connected with goodness, but with qualities which are the opposite of goodness, such as pride, cunning and cruelty"). Such views usually motivate libertarian conspiriologists.

A modern variation on Acton's rule comes from Boston University historian Carl Oglesby, who has written, "Conspiracy is the normal continuation of normal politics by normal means" and "Conspiratorial play is a universal of power politics, and where there is no limit to power, there is no limit to conspiracy."

All of these notions are implicit in a recent Clint Eastwood movie, which in its title refers directly to Acton: *Absolute Power.*

See also:

Government as Criminal Conspiracy, Great Pirates, Internal Revenue Service

References:

The Heretic's Handbook of Quotations, edited by Charles Bufe, Sea Sharp Press, San Francisco, 1988—Acton, p. 1, Tolstoy p. 37

The Yankee and Cowboy War, by Carl Oglesby, Berkley Medallion Books, New York, 1977, pp. 25, 26

John Adams on Banking

John Adams (1735–1826), lawyer, farmer, the first member of the Continental Congress to propose independence from England, later an ambassador and diplomat, then vice president for eight years under George Washington, president for four years, and generally considered a pragmatic conservative, had strong opinions about banks and banking and, in fact, sounds shockingly like some modern conspiracy theorists and money cranks.

In a letter to Benjamin Rush of 9 February 1811, Adams writes: "Funds and banks I never approved, or was satisfied with our funding system; it was founded on no consistent principle; it was contrived to enrich particular individuals at the public expense. Our whole banking system I ever abhorred, I continue to abhor, and I shall die abhorring. . .

"I am not an enemy of funding systems. . . . But every bank of discount, every bank by which interest is to be paid or profit of any kind made by the deponent, is downright corruption. It is taxing the public for the benefit and profit of individuals; it is worse than the old tenor, continental currency, or any other paper money. . .

"My opinion is, that a circulating medium of gold and silver only ought to be introduced and established; that a national bank only, with a branch in each state, should be allowed; that every bank in the Union ought to be annihilated, and every bank of discount prohibited to all eternity."

Adams adds that if he published this view both the Federalists and the Republicans would say he should be confined to Dr. Rush's "tranquilizing chair." (Rush was a pioneer psychiatrist.)

See also:

Saint Ambrose, Bank of England, Thomas Hart Benton, Federal Reserve Bank, R. Buckminster Fuller, Gnomes of Zurich, Ezra Pound

Reference:

Selected Writings of John and John Quincy Adams, Greenwood Press, Westport, Conn., 1946, pp. 162–63

Aeon of Horus

The next stage of history is called the Aeon of Horus by *Aleister Crowley*—as others call it the Age of Aquarius, the New Age, the *New World Order*, etc. In Crowley's prophecies, as aided by an angel or extraterrestrial or some superhuman being named *Aiwass*, humanity has passed through the Age of Isis (roughly, early Matriarchy) and the Age of Osiris (Patriarchy) and after 1904 stands at the dawn of the Age of Horus, the Crowned and Conquering Child, i.e., an age ushered in by wars and revolutions and then followed by an aeon of "love, light and liberty" much like Rabelais' hedonic Abbey of *Thelema* extended to the whole planet.

The post–1904 wars and other violence represent the aspect of Horus called Ra-Hoor-Khuit, a war god of the bloodiest sort. The age of love and liberty represents Hoor-Par-Krat, the god of silence and of illumination. Horus was called "the Lord of Two Horizons" because he contains these opposite aspects, and because he symbolizes both the rising and the setting sun, East and West. Crowley often identifies Horus also with the Chinese union of *yin and yang*.

See also:

Hawthorne Abendsen, Illuminati, Joachim of Floris, *Liber Al*, Sacred Chao

References:

http://www.crl.com/~thelema

The Eye in the Triangle, by Israel Regardie, New Falcon Press, Phoenix, 1970

Portable Darkness, ed. by Scott Michaelson, Harmony Books, New York, 1989

AIDS Conspiracy Theories

Fort Detrick, Maryland, houses a research laboratory that has long investigated plagues and other forms of biological warfare— to protect us against them, of course. Nonetheless, according to one theory, Fort Detrick produced the HIV virus, which escaped accidentally and began infecting people in Washington and New York before becoming the international AIDS epidemic.

Critics of the Fort Detrick theory of the origin of AIDS point out that AIDS appeared in Africa before it was found in Washington or New York, but Dr. *Peter Duesberg* has complicated matters by arguing, with some plausibility, that African AIDS is a different disease from American AIDS, neither of them caused by HIV: The African variety, he says, results from malnutrition and the American strain from overuse of stimulant drugs (crack, crank, and poppers). All of these compounds increase sensation during sex and tend to produce more undulating and prolonged orgasms, but they have a strong addiction potential and have been statistically linked with paranoia and heart attacks even before Dr. Duesberg blamed them for AIDS.

It seems worth noting that ending the AIDS controversy and finding a real diagnosis and cure that all can agree upon becomes more urgent every day: There are now 30,000,000 AIDS victims worldwide.

Thirty million.

See also:

Aspirin/AIDS Conspiracy, AZT/AIDS Conspiracy, Christians Awake, Cloned Out of Existence?, Leonard Horowitz, Iatrogenic AIDS Theory, John Lauritsen, D.M. McArtor, New York Subway Experiment, Our Lady of the Roses, Jon Rappoport, Salk Vaccine and AIDS, Soviet AIDS Theory, Robert Strecker, and see especially El Salvador: Germ Warfare and Haitian experiment Claim

Reference:

30,000,000 victims—

KPIG, 107.5 FM, Freedom, Calif., November 26, 1997

AIDS Incorporated

See:

Jon Rappoport

AIDS War, The

See:

John Lauritsen

Aiwass

An alleged superhuman intelligence contacted by *Aleister Crowley* in 1904, Aiwass dictated to Crowley a work called *"Liber Al"* or the *"Book of the Law,"* which prophesied wars and revolutions leading to the collapse of Christian civilizations and the dawn of the *Aeon of Horus*. *Liber Al* also proclaims the Law of *Thelema,* usually summed up in three mantra-like aphorisms: "Do what thou wilt shall be the whole of the law," "Love is the law, love under will," and "Every man and every woman is a star."

According to former Crowley student Dr. *Israel Regardie*, a Reichian psychotherapist and occultist, Aiwass represented the deepest, most abysmal part of Crowley's own mind, which is common to all life, mammal, insect, and all, deeper than either the Freudian or Jungian unconscious. According to another Crowley student, *Kenneth Grant*, Aiwass is an extraterrestrial from *Sirius*.

Members of the *Ordo Templi Orientis* begin important rituals with the Hebrew words, *"Atoh Aiwass Malkuth ve Geburah ve Gedullah le olahm. Amen."* (For thine, Aiwass, is the kingdom, the power, and the glory forever. So be it.)

See also:

Philip K. Dick, George I. Gurdjieff, Robert Morning Sky, *Sirius Mystery*

References:

Confessions of Aleister Crowley, Bantam, New York, 1971

The Eye in the Triangle, by Israel Regardie, New Falcon Press, Phoenix, 1970

Aleister Crowley and the Hidden God, by Kenneth Grant, Samuel Weiser, New York, 1974

Abdul Alhazred

The semi-legendary Abdul Alhazred allegedly wrote the infamous *"Al Azif"* ca. 750 in Damascus. Aside from this singular (if dubious) achievement, little else about Alhazred seems undisputed, and some even claim that he and his book are both mythic. What we do know about him largely derives from the small amount of biographical information in *Al Azif* itself. His birth appears to have occurred in Sana'a in the Yemen, and he traveled widely from Alexandria to the Punjab, learning many languages and studying many odd old books. (He boasts often of his ability to read and translate ancient manuscripts that remained inscrutable to lesser scholars.)

Basically, the doctrine of *Al Azif* holds that entities far greater than mankind once roamed this earth and still remain present and potent "not in the spaces we know but *between* them," because "Past, present, future: all are one in **Yog Sothoth**." (Such intimations of modern physics are common in Alhazred.) Alliances with Yog Sothoth or similar stellar entities, who have charming titles such as Cthulhu, Azathoth, Nyarlathotop, and He Who Is Not to Be Named, Alhazred alleges, produce wonderful results—"starry wisdom" in the words of one of his admirers; critics claim that these cosmic mind-melds usually culminate in madness, violent death, or even worse. *Much* worse.

Alhazred's own demise, as reported by contemporaries, seems incredible and probably derives from legend and folklore, since he allegedly came apart in bloody fragments, as if devoured by an invisible monster, in the marketplace of Damascus.

Al Azif, translated by Olaus Wormius into Latin under the title *"Necronomicon,"* had a long and colorful history and increasingly influences modern occultism and conspiriology, no small feat for a book some claim never really existed.

See also:

Dr. John Dee, Elmyr, Charles Fort, H.P. Lovecraft, Merovingians, Noon Blue Apples

Reference:

http://www.primenet.com/~sothoth/NecroFAQ.htm

Alien Autopsy

A film called *Alien Autopsy*, in which the viewer plainly sees an alleged female extraterrestrial sawed open and taken apart, has added further controversy to the already heated debate about what did or did not happen in Roswell, New Mexico, in summer 1947. This film, distributed by one Ray Santilli of London, either proves that aliens did land (and the U.S. Army cut one of the females up, to see what was inside her) or that old films in black and white can contain as many special effects as a George Lucas space opera. The *Fortean Times* suggests that the most "realistic" details (i.e., the gory parts) use the same techniques as *Snuff*, a 1960s porn film that ended with the (faked) murder of the female lead. (*Snuff*, in turn, appears to have been created *after* rumors about such a film, including a real murder, had circulated widely for two or three years.)

Skeptics point out that Santilli has never given a convincing explanation of how he got this film, but believers insist, heatedly, that you can actually *see* the dead extraterrestrial and the doctor actually cutting her up and removing internal organs.

See also:

Bisociation, Crop Circles, Elmyr, Men in Black, Noon Blue Apples, Roswell UFO Crash

Reference:

Fortean Times, April 1997

Alien Photos

The *"Alien Autopsy"* film is not the only photographic evidence of weird critters among us. Early in 1997, Bob Guccione, sophisticated publisher of the sexy *Penthouse* and the brainy *Omni*, paid between $50,000 and $100,000 (reports differ) for a photo of an alleged extraterrestrial. This turned out to be a photo of a dummy in the International UFO Museum in Roswell.

In 1991, a book called *UFO Crash Secrets at Wright-Patterson Air Force Base*, a re-issue of an earlier (1970) book more simply called *The Wright Field Story*, included new material—and two photos of alleged aliens recovered from a UFO crash in Russia. Jim Moseley, co-author of the original 1970 version, revealed recently that the editor of the new edition added the photos, which are depictions of a statue exhibited from 1978 to 1981 at an art show in Montreal. The sculptor, Linda Corriveau, who simply calls the odd, vaguely Oriental chap "the man of my dreams," describes herself as "amused" at what has become of her artistic creation.

See also:

Hono Intelligence Service 1901, *Mothman Prophecies,* Noon Blue Apples, OM, Roswell UFO Crash, Ummo Letters

Reference:

Saucer Smear, Vol. 45, No. 1, January 1998 (Box 1709, Key West, FL 33041)

Saint Ambrose of Milan

Saint Ambrose (ca. 339–397) was a major figure in the development of Christian theology and political ethics. Appointed Bishop of Milan in 374, he became famous as both orator and scholar and established the official Church teaching on *usury,* which remained the orthodox view until the Renaissance.

In Ambrose's view (based on Aristotle and the Old Testament) usury signifies not the charge of excessive interest on loans, but the charge of *any* interest at all. His view therefore condemns the entire structure of modern finance capitalism, and indeed capitalism as we know it did not arise until Saint Ambrose's ideas were rejected, first by John Calvin and other Protestants and later by the Vatican itself.

Ambrose condemned money-lending at interest as "against nature" as nature was understood in the Aristotelian physics of his time: Cows are sentient and fertile, in this view, so they can birth other cows, but insensate, infertile money cannot produce other money, except by some species of swindle or counterfeiting. He also denounced usurers as "hoggers of the harvest" and the main cause of poverty and starvation.

Views similar to these appear in such modern social critics and/or conspiriologists as **Benjamin R. Tucker, Lyndon LaRouche,** and **Ezra Pound.** Ironically, Ambrose's name also lives on in the title of the scandal-ridden **Banco Ambrosiano** in Milan.

See also:

R. Buckminster Fuller, Federal Reserve Bank, P2 Conspiracy

References:

Webster's Family Encyclopedia, Vol. I, p. 87

Patriologia Latina, Vol. XVII, Paris, 1845

American Dynasty

Of the 37 presidents of the United States before Jimmy Carter, at least 18 or 21 (depending on which source you believe) were close relatives. That comes to somewhere between 48.6 percent and 56.7 percent—far too much to be a coincidence, as any conspiriologist (or mathematician) would tell you.

Not only was *John Adams*, who helped design the *Great Seal*, related to F.D. Roosevelt, who put it on the dollar bill, but even a seeming outsider such as Richard Nixon was related to James Monroe; three presidents were cousins (Franklin Pierce, James Garfield, and Grover Cleveland); and William Henry Harrison was related to Jefferson, Jackson, Tyler, and Benjamin Harrison (his grandson). Calvin Coolidge, Harry Truman, and Lyndon Johnson were more distantly related to Jefferson, Jackson, and the Harrisons.

The Roosevelt and *Delano* families, who gave us the only president to get elected to four terms, were related to Grant, Washington, van Buren, and Taft. Of the 224 ancestors in the family tree of 21 presidents, we find 13 Roosevelts, 16 Coolidges, and 14 Tylers. Another source manages to relate 60 percent of the presidents and link most of them to the super-rich Astor family.

This data does not include genealogies of the four most recent presidents, Carter, *Reagan, Bush,* and *Clinton,* which we have not found; but Clinton is related to the Rockefellers, according to a source in our *Princess Diana* entry.

Psychologist G. William Domhoff claims that a large part of America's ruling elite, just like that of Europe, are related by marriage.

See also:

A-Albionic, Carroll Quigley, *Yankee and Cowboy War*

References:

The Illuminoids, by Neal Wilgus, Sun Books, Albuquerque, N.Mex., 1978, pp. 37–39, citing *Yipster Times,* Fall-Winter 1975

Takeover, November 1976

American Hero

American Hero, a novel by Larry Beinhart, is based on the premise that the Gulf War was entirely a Hollywood production. According to this revisionist history, Lee Atwater, Republican "dirty tricks" expert, left a memo at the time of his death, to be opened only if **President George Bush** began to lose popularity. The memo outlined how to use Hollywood experts to produce a "good" war—a war that would be popular, that would have very few American casualties, and that would be over too quickly for organized opposition to begin to undermine public enthusiasm for the enterprise. Beinhart even suggested that the Hollywood people picked a desert locale because desert battles are especially photogenic, and that Saddam was bribed to cooperate and play a convincingly Hitler-like villain.

This novel has many flat statements that it is entirely a work of fiction, but these are constantly undermined by footnotes documenting that many of the details are in fact true; and the ending leaves it up to the reader to decide if the book exposes a real conspiracy or is just a cleverly crafted hoax.

Beinhart includes 39 questions that make the official version of the war seem less plausible than his "fiction." Among them:

". . . Why did we stop when we could have driven into Baghdad?. . . What happened to Saddam's threats to unleash terrorists on the West?. . . What happened to Saddam's threats to use biological and chemical warfare?. . . How come, if Saddam was another Hitler, we let him stay in power?"

Publishers Weekly said *American Hero* "makes more sense than the actual war itself"; *Kirkus Reviews* called it "plausible"; and Marshall Brickman said it was "probably true."

See also:

Elmyr, Gulf War Syndrome, Holocaust Deniers, Clifford Irving, Pearl
Harbor, World War II Deniers

References:

American Hero, by Larry Beinhart, Ballantine Books, New York, 1993

Reviewer's quotes from the front matter of the novel itself

Yigil and Geula Amir

Yigil Amir allegedly shot Israeli prime minister Yitzhak Rabin
because of Rabin's "liberal" attitudes toward the Palestinian
Arabs. That's not the real story, according to Yigil's mother, Geula.
Yigil actually thought he was participating in a fake assassination
with blank bullets.

Mrs. Amir also claims that the U.S. Embassy in Tel Aviv has not
provided her with a visa to travel and lecture in the U.S. and
hasn't even given her a reason for the delay. Israeli Foreign
Ministry spokesman Danny Shek said that Israel was not consulted by the U.S. Embassy. "This has nothing to do with us," he
said. "This is purely a U.S. matter."

See Also:

John F. Kennedy Assassination, Robert Kennedy Assassination, MMAO,
Octopus, Marina Oswald

Reference:

Jerusalem Post, February 18, 1997

James Jesus Angleton

James Jesus Angleton served as director of counterintelligence
for the CIA from 1954 to 1974 when he was removed for illegal activities. He was a strange, brilliant, and paranoid person,

obsessed with the search for Soviet moles within the CIA and suspicious of almost everybody. Apparently, he never did abandon his beliefs that Tito was a Soviet mole and that the chief Soviet mole in the CIA has reached a rank at least as high as his own.

As we hinted in the introduction, behavior that would rank as clinical paranoia in ordinary life becomes pragmatic caution in the world of "Intelligence." The KGB would love to have an agent high in the CIA, Angleton knew; they were clever and tireless, he also knew; ergo, they would eventually have a mole in the Company, and maybe they had one already. He never stopped hunting that Russian mole, and he operated with even more secrecy than was normal in the CIA.

A.J. Weberman believes that Angleton masterminded the assassination of John Kennedy, using an agent to implicate and frame *Lee Harvey Oswald.* Most of the evidence for this hypothesis will be found in the Weberman website cited below; but see also *E. Howard Hunt, Marina Oswald, The Three Tramps,* and links therefrom. If Angleton really did it, he probably believed Kennedy was the "top Soviet mole" he'd been hunting so many years.

Angleton's obsession with this ambiguous Russian "mole" code-named *Sasha* led him to shred documents totally, long before that practice became common, fearing that the mole might ransack his office at night.

Another CIA officer, Edward Petty, stated of Angleton, "He was strictly a lone wolf, a strange bird. The man was doing all sorts of things on his own that nobody ever told him to do. . . . What an Angleton operation was, nobody really knows."

Angleton helped form the *P2 conspiracy* in Rome, which used drug dealing to finance anti-communist and pro-fascist activities, sometimes using over 200 real and imaginary banks to launder the money.

See also:

Roberto Calvi, David Ferrie, *In Banks We Trust,* Knights of Malta, Octopus, General Robert C. Richardson III, *Scandals of the Priory of Sion,* World Finance Corporation

References:

Angleton's paranoia—

http://www.forbes.com/tool/html/97/aug/cool0802/feature.htm

http://www.nd.edu/~astrouni/zhiwriter/spool/95121704.htm

http://www.worldmedia.com/caq/articles/gladio.html

Angleton and JFK assassination—

http://www.weberman.com/htdocs

Angleton and P2—

http://www.worldmedia.com/caq/articles/gladio.html

The Anti-"Bob"

The Anti-"Bob" is the evil twin of J.R. "Bob" Dobbs, the founder and CEO of the *Church of the Sub-Genius.* According to Sub-Genius prophecy, the Anti-"Bob" will appear in the last days—i.e., shortly before "X Day" (July 5, 1998)—and will deceive millions. These dupes will stop tithing 10 percent of their earnings to "Bob" and begin sending their money to the Anti-"Bob" instead, but they will all be destroyed with atomic death rays when the *Xists* arrive from *Planet X.* Those who remain faithful to "Bob," however, will be spared and richly rewarded.

See also:

"Bob," Discordianism, Slack

Reference:

http://www.subgenius.com/

The Antichrist

The Antichrist is usually considered a person who will appear in the days of apocalypse, leading many away from the Christian religion to their eternal doom. The *Catholic Encyclopedia* accepts this as one possible view but adds that there is "no specific one person or thing indicated by the term," i.e., the Antichrist may be a mass movement or a series of events.

Sign Ministries gives a more literal or fundamentalist reading, telling us that the Antichrist will also be known as the man of lawlessness, Gog, the son of destruction, and the abomination of desolation. He will rule over "the final beast empire of Satan," set up his throne in Jerusalem, and demand worship by the whole world. He will die at the battle of Armageddon, thirty days after the end of the seventieth week of his reign. (See *"Every Knee Shall Bow."*)

Historically, many persons have been identified as the Antichrist by their critics, including Nero, Martin Luther, and *Aleister Crowley* (who had the initials for the job). In this present decade various writers have identified the Antichrist as Bill Gates (president of Microsoft), Mickey Mouse, computers as a social force, and even Barney the Dinosaur. In the film *Who's That Girl?*, Madonna is asked if she is the Antichrist but evades a direct answer.

In *Naming the Antichrist,* Professor Robert Fuller argues that Americans have a greater obsession with identifying the Antichrist than any other people in history. He suggests that this results from our national habit of mythologizing life and seeing Biblical metaphors behind the surface appearance of events. He mentions a long list of other candidates for Antichrist who have been nominated by various theologians, professional and amateur: among them are Yasir Arafat, the *Illuminati* as a group, *Prince Bernhard,* Jimmy Carter, the Catholic Church, Communism, England, Saddam Hussein, *freemasons,* the New Deal, the Susan B. Anthony dollar, and Teenage Mutant Ninja Turtles.

The Antichrist has his/her/its own website and sounds very happy about how the world is progressing. Anti says that he or she last appeared as John Lennon but is now back stronger and more popular than Lennon and will lead the world to end Christian "repression" and achieve total freedom in the year 2000. She or he also brags extensively about total control over the media (see *Media criticized*).

See also:

Anti-"Bob", Lucent Technologies, 666, UFO/Satanic Conspiracy

References:

Naming the Antichrist: The History of an American Obsession, by Robert Fuller, Oxford University Press, 1995, pp. 5, 227–8

Catholic Encyclopedia—

http://www.aloha.net/~mikesch/cath.htm

Bill Gates as Antichrist—

http://www.west-teq.net/~graben/gates.htm

Mickey Mouse as Antichrist—

http://www.concentric.net/~Chocker/v1i5/baptist.htm

Computers as Antichrist—

http://www.parascope.com/other/wwwboard/general/messages/1240.htm

Barney as Antichrist—

http://www.sydney.socialchange.net.au/CinemaConnection/Tv_Shows/Other _Shows/3776.html

Sign Ministries—

http://www.signministries.org/glos/glos011_ant.html

Antichrist's own website—

http://www.ANTICHRIST.com/acim.htm

AOL4Free

Even in the murky domain between conspiracy and prank, AOL4Free occupies an unusually ambiguous area. First, it began as a typical "hacker's" joke, judged criminal by those who suffered its sting: AOL4FREE.COM was a program written deliberately to provide illegal access to America Online (AOL), one of our largest computer networks. The creator may have considered himself/herself a rebel against capitalism or just a clever young joker having some fun, but the program circulated widely enough to allow "hundreds" of other rebels or funsters to get into the AOL system for free; AOL estimated its loss as between $40,000 and $70,000. The culprit, a former Yale computer science student, pled guilty when brought to trial.

Ever since then a fake AOL4Free document has circulated on the net saying (condensed):

VIRUS ALERT!!!
DON'T OPEN E-MAIL NOTING "AOL4FREE"
Anyone who receives this must sent [sic] it to as many people as you can. It is essential that this problem be reconciled as soon as possible. A few hours ago, I opened an E-mail that had the subject heading "AOL4FREE.COM." Within seconds of opening it, a window appeared and began display [sic] my files that were being deleted. I immediately shut down my computer, but it was too late. The virus wiped me out. It ate the Anti-Virus Software that comes with the Windows '95 Program. . .

Since *ladder conspiracies* have no organization or leader, each member acting spontaneously in accord with his/her own mischievous or felonious temperament, they may last as long as the spirit of anarchy exists in some human hearts.

See also:

CIAC

Reference:

http://ciac.llnl.gov/ciac/CIACHoaxes.html

Ardennes Forest

A hilly forest in northeast France that has an average height of around 1,650 feet, the Ardennes was the site of heavy fighting in both World War I and World War II, but occupies conspiracy researchers for other reasons.

It was while hunting in the Ardennes that the mysterious *Dagobert II,* last king of the *Merovingian* dynasty, was murdered on December 23, 679; and it was also in the Ardennes that the even more mysterious "Marquis de B." was murdered on December 23, 1972, after informing *Gerard de Sede* that the Merovingians were partly descended from extraterrestrials from *Sirius*.

See also:

Princess Di's Death, Robert Morning Sky, Noon Blue Apples, 23 Enigma

References:

Webster's *Family Encyclopedia,* Vol. I (A-BEI)

La Race fabuleuse, by Gerard de Sede, Editions J'ai Lui, Paris, 1973

Holy Blood, Holy Grail, by Michael Baigent, Henry Lincoln, and Richard Leigh, Delacorte, New York, 1982

Area 51

Groom Lake Air Force Base, better known as Area 51 (a grid map reference number), has the most sinister reputation of any U.S. government facility known to the general public; only *Fort Detrick* has a worse reputation, and that is known only to Gays and Leftists. The rumors, legends, and "disclosures" about Area 51 are so wild and numerous that it has even earned a third name—Dreamland.

Groom Lake/Area 51/Dreamland is a very secret U.S. military operation, so no horror story about it can absolutely be denied or refuted. The government is hiding *something* there: The only open questions are what are they hiding from us this time, and why are they hiding it? Your answers to those questions depend on many factors, chiefly (1) your own mix of credulity and suspiciousness and (2) which sources of "information" you regard as trustworthy.

Here are a few undisputed facts (we think): Area 51 has been in operation for more than 40 years. It lies 120 miles northwest of Las Vegas in the remote desert/mountain lands of Nevada. It has the longest aircraft runway in the world. Ordinary citizens can never get closer than 25 miles from the base without being stopped and sent away.

The rumors and legends began with pilot *John Lear*, who has asserted for some time that friends in the intelligence community have confided that the U.S. government made a treaty with the aliens ca. 1969–71, involving an exchange of their technology for government cooperation in what the aliens called "research," which involved both mutilation of cattle and sexual/genetic molestation of humans. Others have given different dates for this treaty (1947, 1957, etc.), but all agree with Lear that Groom Lake/Area 51 plays a key role in government/alien experimentation of some sort.

A survey on the web (from a site mostly dedicated to science-fiction fandom) found that, of 1,700 respondents thus far, 77 percent believe there are alien spacecraft or technology in Area 51, 75 percent believe live aliens are or have been there, 95 percent believe secret Air Force projects are tested there, and 59 percent will venture only that the secrecy is based on "valid national security reasons."

The Art Bell radio show has a standing invitation to employees or former employees of Dreamland to call in and tell what they know, anonymously. This led to a very interesting and decidedly sinister phone call about Area 51 on September 11, 1997. The transcript runs as follows:

MALE CALLER: Hello, Art?

ART: Yes.

CALLER [*SOUNDS FRIGHTENED*]: I don't have a whole lot of time.

ART: Well, look, let's begin by finding out if you're using this line properly or not.

CALLER: OK, in Area 51?

ART: Yes. Are *[sic]* you an employee or are you now?

CALLER: I'm a former employee. I, I was let go on a medical discharge about a week ago and, and . . . (*chokes*) I kind been running across the country. Damn, I don't know where to start, they're, they're gonna, they'll triangulate on this position real soon.

ART: So you can't spend a lot of time on the phone, so give us something quick.

CALLER [*VOICE BREAKING UP WITH APPARENT SUPPRESSED CRYING*]: OK, um, um, OK, what we're thinking of as aliens, Art, they're extradimensional beings, that an earlier precurser of the space program they made contact with. They are not what they claim to be. They've infiltrated a lot of aspects of, of, of the military establishment, particularly the Area 51. The disasters that are coming, they, the military, I'm sorry, the government knows about them. And there's a lot of safe areas in the world that they could begin moving the population to now, Art.

ART: So they're not doing, not doing anything.

CALLER: They are not. They want those major population centers wiped out so that the few that are left will be more easily controllable. . . .

ART [*FRAGMENT*]: . . . discharged . . .

CALLER [*SOBBING, THEN FRAGMENT*]: I say we g . . . .

At this point the show went off the air. (Listeners must have felt like those in 1938 when *Orson Welles'* famous drama about Martian invasion went off the air for one very long minute. . . .)

An old show was then replayed (an interview with Los Angeles policeman Mark Furhman). It was later explained that a technical failure was responsible for the loss of the rest of the phone call, but a lot of people still don't believe that. . . .

See also:

William Cooper, Phillip J. Corso, *NASA, Nazis and JFK,* Mothman Prophecies, UMMO Letters

References:

General—

http://wkweb4.cableinet.co.uk/jdickie/area51.htm

Revelations: Alien Contact and Human Deception, by Jacques Vallee, Ballantine Books, New York, 1991

Survey—

http://www.nauticom.net/users/ata/area51results.html

Art Bell call—

http://www.artbell.com/satoutage.html

"Ask About the Cocaine!"

During the Senate hearings on Iran-Contra, three members of the audience stood up and shouted, "Ask about the cocaine!" They were arrested, charged with contempt of Congress, convicted, and sentenced to one year in prison each.

The senators never did ask about the cocaine.

See also:

Cisalpine Bank, John Hull, Gladio, Octopus, World Finance Corporation

Reference:

Coverup: Behind the Iran-Contra Affair, 72-minute color video documentary, directed by Barbara Trent, Empowerment Project, 1988

Aspirin/AIDS Conspiracy

Howard Armistead of West Hollywood believes that aspirin can serve as a very useful adjunct to other AIDS therapies. He has presented a peer-reviewed study on this therapy to the Eighth International Conference on AIDS in Amsterdam in 1992, addressed the California Ryan White Committee on AIDS, and distributed nearly 1,500 copies of his papers on aspirin's effects on HIV reproduction at the AIDS Conference in Yokohama in 1996. Nonetheless, he finds a notable lack of interest among both doctors and the Gay community, which he attributes merely to the usual combination of conservatism and skepticism that greets all new or alternative therapies; nevertheless his work was called to our attention by an e-mailer who evidently thinks there may be some commercial conspiracy blocking research and discussion of Armistead's ideas.

The American Foundation for AIDS Research Treatment Directory warns that aspirin can cause stomach ulcers, especially in high doses.

Mr. Armistead has been taking seven aspirin a day along with conventional AZT therapy since 1990 and is executive director of the Project for Aspirin Research and Education (PARE) at (310) 659–6965. He believes his HIV dates from around 1982, but it has not yet developed into AIDS.

See also:

AIDS Conspiracy Theories

Reference:

http://www.apla.org/apla/9509/aspirin.html

The Assassins

"Assassins" is an old European name for the Ismaeli sect of Islam of which the Aga Khan is the current ruler. The name "assassin" derives either from Hassan i Sabbah, the founder of this order, or from "hashish," which the Ismaelis evidently used in those days (c. 1100 A.D.) in combination with Sufi dancing. Anyone who has tried fast (very fast) dancing while stoned on strong cannabis will assure you that the altered state achieved can easily reach mystic ecstasy, unless the novice falls into a panic attack first.

Hassan i Sabbah, according to other accounts, did not use hashish this way, but slipped it into the food of prospective recruits (usually teenage boys) for his defense forces. When thoroughly intoxicated, these candidates would be taken to the Garden of Delights for sweet dalliance with the houris promised to the faithful when they arrive in Paradise. Those who came out of this trip convinced that Lord Hassan indeed had the keys to Heaven became assassins, in the modern sense, and the first sleeper agents in history. They would enter the court of some shah or king who might have ill will toward the Ismaelis; they would work hard and honestly for years, sometimes many years; but at the first sign of preparation for war against Hassan, they would slit the throat of their master. This made everybody nervous about starting hostilities against Hassan i Sabbah.

Hassan's alleged last words were "Nothing is true, all is permitted." Due to William S. Burroughs, this has become something of a mantra and something of a koan to the literary counterculture of our time.

See also:

Abbe Barruel, Ewige Blumenkraft, *History of Secret Societies,* Sex Magick, War on Some Drugs

References:

http://home.fireplug.net/~rshand/streams/masons/assassins.html

History of Secret Societies, by Akron Daraul, Citadel Press, New York, 1961

Association for Ontological Anarchy

The Association for Ontological Anarchy, largely the product of *Hakim Bey* and his friends, aims to provide, and we quote, "a sound irrational basis, a strange philosophy if you like, for ... the Free Religions, including the Psychedelic & Discordian currents, non-hierarchical neo-paganism, antinomian heresies, chaos & Kaos Magik, revolutionary HooDoo, 'unchurched' & anarchist Christians, Magical Judaism, the Moorish Orthodox Church, *Church of the Sub-Genius*, etc., etc." (Kaos Magik, the product of English mathematician/mystic Peter Carroll, combines ideas from *Aleister Crowley, Discordianism,* and chaos mathematics. For details on the Moorish Orthodox Church, see *Noble Drew Ali.*)

The AOA also rejects the verb forms of "is" and "be" (see *Language as Conspiracy*), sponsors *poetic terrorism,* and has a long philosophic pedigree, in addition to the religious affiliations above, recognizing affinity with Max Stirner, Nietzsche, surrealism, and situationism. They have their own *hollow Earth* theory, too, claiming psychic contact with "Kallikaks of the Hollow Earth, Lovecraftian renegades, hermits, skulking incestuous smugglers, runaway criminals, anarchists forced into hiding after the Entropy Wars, fugitives from Genetic Puritanism, dissident Chinese Tongs & Yellow Turban fanatics, lascar cave-pirates, pale, shiftless whitetrash from the prolewarrens of the industrial domes along Thwait's Tongue & the Walgreen Coast & Edsel-Ford-Land—the Trogs have kept alive for over 200 years the folk-memory of the Autonomous Zone, the myth that someday it will appear again."

Although not yet discovered and vulgarized by the major media, the AOA has about as much underground influence on the counterculture as the Beats did before they became famous.

See also:

The Con, Elmyr, H.P. Lovecraft, *Necronomicon,* OM

Reference:

http://www.unicorn.com/lib/commun.html

AYA

According to researcher **Robert Morning Sky**, a queen named AYA (or in some tongues AA) was the model for all the Great Mother Goddesses of "primitive" humanity. AYA was not a metaphor or a myth or even a symbol of Earth, Morning Sky writes, but an actual female—queen of a serpentine race from the region of Orion, who have had a long, long battle with a wolf-like race from *Sirius,* during which Earth was conquered first by AYA and her snake-like warriors and later by the wolfish folk from the Dog Star.

Morning Sky, who studied linguistics at the University of Arizona, bases this theory on traditional Hopi legends, his own analysis of the linguistic roots of goddess names in Egypt, Babylon, Greece, etc., and his grandfather's encounter with an extraterrestrial who survived the 1947 *Roswell UFO crash.*

See also:

Philip J. Corso, *Guardians of the Grail, Terra Papers,* UFO Conspiracies

References:

http://www.xroads.com/~rms/welcome.html

Guardians of the Grail, by Robert Morning Sky, Morning Sky Books, Phoenix, Ariz., n.d.

Al Azif

Usually called "the book of the Mad Arab," *Al Azif* was allegedly composed by *Abdul Alhazred* in the eighth century and contains the most astounding metaphysics ever presented to humanity, urging us to worship or at least form alliances with interstellar beings of ill repute. This book is better known under the title of its Latin translation, *Necronomicon,* and Robert M. Price has argued that the familiar label—or libel—used by most modern commentators on Alhazred, "the Mad Arab," misses the point: In classic Arabic, "madman," "poet," and "prophet" all had much the same meanings.

The title *Al Azif* means roughly the "book of buzzings," but this means more than English-speaking readers realize, since *azif* signified the kind of buzzing or humming heard in the desert at night when the djinn are allegedly active. Similar buzzing/humming noises frequently accompany modern UFO sightings.

See also:

Campus Crusade for Cthulhu, Charles Fort, H.P. Lovecraft

References:

Critical Commentary on the Necronomicon, by Roger M. Price, Cryptic
   Publications, Mount Olive, N.C., 1988

http://www.primenet.com/~sothoth/

AZT/AIDS Conspiracy

The Food and Drug Administration (FDA) allegedly hid old
AZT data in order to get it approved in 1987 for AIDS
patients. According to this assertion, an FDA drug analyst had
recommended that AZT not be approved because of its serious
side effects, including anemia, but he was overruled. Some Gay
theorists therefore contend that the hurried manner in which
the medical profession and the news media promoted and still
promote AZT is actually part of a planned campaign to kill off
the homosexual community worldwide.

Critics of AZT claim it is highly toxic, severely damages the
kidneys and the liver, blocks DNA synthesis, provokes nausea and
violent vomiting, and even causes cancer.

See also:

AIDS Conspiracy Theories, Chicago Malaria Study, Tuskegee Syphilis
   Study

Reference:

http://www.pnc.com.au/~cafmr/newsl/azt.html

Baby Poison

The baby-formula industry, a multibillion dollar enterprise,
allegedly causes tremendous numbers of children to die of diar-
rhea and malnutrition every year. This happens, critics say,
because most of these concoctions have to be diluted with water

and the majority of the victims are poverty stricken Third World citizens who have access only to unsanitary water supplies; they mix the formula with tainted water, and it turns lethal. Many illiterate parents also inadvertently kill their infants by misusing the formula because they cannot read the instructions.

The problem is compounded by aggressive marketing campaigns that target poor and often undernourished women who believe that formula feeding will ensure the survival of their child better than their own breast milk, though critics claim just the opposite.

See also:

AIDS Conspiracy Theories, Dr. Wilhelm Reich, Tuskegee Syphilis Study

Reference:

http://www.disinfo.com

Banco Ambrosiano

The Banco Ambrosiano in Milan served as a major part of the *P2 conspiracy* in Italy during the 1970s–1980s. In 1982, the president of the bank, *Roberto Calvi*, was accused of laundering drug money, embezzlement, and conspiring in a long list of political and financial crimes with *Michele "The Shark" Sindona* and Archbishop *Paul "The Gorilla" Marcinkus*; the former being president of *Franklin National Bank* and the latter president of the Vatican Bank. Calvi immediately disappeared but on June 18, 1982, was found hanging from a bridge in London with his pockets full of bricks. The same day, Calvi's secretary, Graziella Corrocher, plunged to her death from a window of the bank in Milan. Both deaths have been called suicides, and both have been called murders.

In investigations of Banco Ambrosiano's irregularities, magistrates found that Calvi and some associates had created over 200 "ghost banks," financial institutions that had no existence outside his ledgers but served to create a labyrinth of confusion for those trying to get to the heart of the conspiracy. One real bank, *Cisalpine* in the Bahamas, which Calvi and Archbishop Marcinkus administrate, was seemingly deeply involved in laundering cocaine money from Latin America in collaboration with the *World Finance Corporation* in Miami.

See also:

James Jesus Angleton, Licio Gelli, John Hull, MMAO, Ezra Pound

References:

The Calvi Affair, by Larry Gurwin, Pan Books, London, 1984

In Banks We Trust, by Penny Lernoux, Doubleday/Anchor, New York, 1984

In God's Name, by David Yallop, Jonathan Cape, London, 1984

Bank of England

Founded by William P. Paterson (1658–1719) in 1692, the Bank of England was the first privately owned institution to issue the currency for a nation. Critics of our current monetary system regard this date, 1692, as the end of the *rule by governments* and the beginning of *rule by bankers*, unelected by and usually unknown to the general public. *Ezra Pound* dates what he calls the Age of Usury from 1692 for this reason, and the only lines underlined in his epic poem *The Cantos* are a quote (somewhat condensed) from Paterson in a letter to potential investors:

Hath benefit of interest on all
the moneys which it, the bank, creates out of nothing.

That banks of issue do, seemingly, create money "out of nothing" and make the nation's taxpayers pay interest on it remains a major complaint of all major critics of modern banking. (See *Federal Reserve Bank*.)

See also:

Saint Ambrose, John Adams, Bank of the United States, Thomas Hart Benton, GRUNCH

References:

The Two Nations, by Christopher Hollis, Routledge, London, 1937, chap. 2

The Cantos, by Ezra Pound, New Directions, New York, 13th printing 1995, p. 233

Bank of the United States

The first privately owned institution to issue national currency in the United States, the Bank of the United States was founded by Alexander Hamilton in 1791 and abolished by Andrew Jackson in 1833. That the bank masterminded the attempted assassination of President Jackson is proclaimed by the Conspiracy Museum in Dallas, Texas (right around the corner from Dealey Plaza), which finds bankers behind every other assassination or attempted assassination in our history.

See also:

Bank of England, Thomas Hart Benton, MMAO, Marina Oswald, Rosicrucianism

References:

Conspiracy Museum, Dallas, Tex.

Thirty Years' View: The Working of Government for Thirty Years, 1820–1850, by Thomas Hart Benton, New York, 1854

Abbe Barruel: Jumbo Conspiracy Theory

In 1797, an embittered French Jesuit, Abbe Barruel, set down in print his theory of why the French Revolution had occurred. Where other historians would attribute that social explosion to the sufferings of the poor, or the ambitions of the rising merchant class, or the alienation of the nobility (who mostly despised their king and called him "the fat boy" behind his back), or some combination of these forces aided by the new ideas of Reason and Democracy, the angry priest had a simpler theory: The revolution had resulted from the machinations of a literally Diabolical Conspiracy.

The notions of this extremely reactionary priest might seem a matter of only historical interest, except that his Jumbo Conspiracy Theory, as developed ca. 1797–1808, gradually grew to include so much that it has directly or indirectly influenced almost all the conspiracy buffs who have written since Barruel's day.

First of all, the Abbe blamed the Revolution on the Bavarian *Illuminati,* a secret society that had existed between 1776 and 1786, when the Bavarian government banned them; it did not take too much of a leap of speculation to consider that maybe the Illuminati had not disappeared when condemned in '86. Maybe they had lingered, under other names, and had indeed played a role in the uprising of '89. This thesis appeared around the same time in another book, *"Proofs of a Conspiracy,"* by an earnest Scotch academic (and former Mason) named John Robison, who claimed the Illuminati had infiltrated most Continental Masonic lodges and warned his Scotch, Irish, and English brethren not to let these conspirators infiltrate British lodges, too.

But Barruel's works went much further than Robison. Not only had the Illuminati wormed their way into control of Continental *Freemasonry,* he insisted, but they had also existed long before they surfaced under the name of Illuminati in Bavaria. In fact, they had existed for over a thousand years and had used the title *Knights Templar* when founded in the ninth century. The Inquisition had found the Templars guilty of devil worship and sodomy. (See *Christians Awake AIDs Theory*.) Abbe Barruel did not regard the Inquisition with any "secular humanist" skepticism. The devil-worshiping Templars, he decided, had lingered as an underground Satanic cult from their alleged dissolution in 1308 until their resurfacing as the Illuminati in Bavaria in 1776.

A thousand-year-old conspiracy really turns on the true Conspiracy Buff; and pretty quickly, Abbe Augustin Barruel heard from men of similarly active imaginations with even more epic-like conspiracy sagas. He changed his own theory several times, to incorporate the ideas that suited his uniquely off-kilter sense of how the world turns. The Templars, for instance, became the allies of the *Assassins,* the Islamic group that used hashish in its rituals and taught some weird variety of Sufism that sounds like the "Pantheistic Multi-Ego Solipsism" later invented by Robert Heinlein for a science-fiction story. "Nothing is true, all is permitted," an alleged Assassin slogan, gives you the flavor of their mystical nihilism.

Eventually the Abbe encountered a mysterious *Captain Simonini* who told him "the Jews" as a fungible group were behind everything; the jumbo conspiracy theory emphasized the international bankers, especially the *Rothschilds*. By 1808, more or less, Barruel had made a permanent contribution to the ideology of the Far Right by his unified Conspiracy Theory in which everything right-wingers don't like results from the machinations of Satanic/Sodomite Knights Templar, godless Freemasons, Arabian hashish fiends, and sinister Hebrew bankers. A large part of this Fu Manchu–style mythos quickly infested New England, and some Federalists, especially among the clergy, used it against Thomas

Jefferson, whom they claimed acted as the Illuminati's top man in the then-new U.S. government.

(*John Adams*, although titular head of the Federalist Party and personally at odds with Jefferson about the French Revolution— they had a reconciliation later—despised this labyrinthine horror story and tried to combat it. As a result, he—Adams himself— appears at the head of the U.S. Illuminati in the works of Matthew Josephson, a twentieth-century anti-Illuminati/anti-Rockefeller crusader.)

The whole Barruel Jewish-Masonic-Arab conspiracy appeared occasionally among the 1840s Anti-Masonic Party in this country, and has influenced all right-wing politics in Europe ever since, including Italian Fascism and German Nazism. A sanitized version, minus overt anti-semitism, currently circulates among that part of the Christian Right under the leadership of Rev. Pat Robertson. A very unsanitary version, including the anti-semitism, motivates a great deal of "militia" activity.

See also:

Gnomes of Zurich, Merovingians, Ezra Pound, *Protocols of the Elders of Zion*

References:

The Illuminoids, by Neal Wilgus, Sun Press, Albuquerque, N.Mex., 1977, passim

http://www.conspire.com/skeptic.html

A Short History of Anti-Semitism, by Vamberto Morais, WW Norton, New York, 1976, pp. 193–195

Beethoven as Illuminatus—and Virtual Rapist

Ludwig van Beethoven (1770-1827) may have been a member of the *Illuminati*, or at least a sympathizer—and we obtained this link not from a conspiracy buff but from a scholarly work on the great composer's life and ideas, by musicologist Maynard Solomon.

Solomon points out that Beethoven's first music teacher, and a major influence on the growing lad, was composer Christian Gotlob Neefe, who was a leader of the Order of the Illuminati. Beethoven wrote to Neefe on one occasion, "If I ever become a great man, you too will have a share in my success" (pp. 26–27).

Beethoven's first major work, the *Emperor Joseph Cantata,* 1790, was commissioned by the Illuminati themselves (p. 48); it celebrates Emperor Joseph von Hapsburg as a bringer of light and foe of superstition. (He closed the Catholic schools in Austria and replaced them with public schools.)

Solomon finds that Illuminati influence on Beethoven continued at least as late as the *Choral Fantasy* (1808) and that most of his friends were Freemasons and/or Illuminati (pp. 206–7).

These links are especially interesting in that Solomon is only interested in Beethoven's involvement with "Enlightenment" ideas and seems to have no awareness that he has incriminated Ludwig with a secret society that still arouses fear and suspicion in many quarters.

Another surprising view of Ludwig was penned by Feminist Susan McClary, who claims the Ninth Symphony, usually considered a hymn to universal love, is actually a rape fantasy. Ms. McClary finds most classical music just about as bad because of its "phallic violence" and "pelvic pounding."

See also:

Church of Mary Magdalene, Ewige Blumenkraft, Feminist Conspiracy Theories, Von Hapsburg Family

References:

Beethoven, by Maynard Solomon, Schirmer Books, New York, 1977

Ms. McClary, *Minnesota Composers' Forum,* January 1987

Albert Bender

In 1954, Albert Bender closed down his recently formed International Flying Saucer Bureau, saying he had been terrorized by three *men in black*. These sinister figures, always in black and often coming as a trio, have appeared repeatedly in later *UFO conspiracy* theories.

Bender described his experiences with the men in black in his book, *Flying Saucers and the Three Men;* Grey Barker added other cases and more frightening details in his *They Knew Too Much About Flying Saucers*. Both are summarized in the source below. Now the *Men in Black* are featured in a major film of that name.

Students of folklore and the occult may find here a haunting echo of the Three Ruffians who killed *The Widow's Son* in *Freemasonic* lore.

See also:

Mary Hyre, *Mothman Prophecies, Sirius Mystery,* UFO/Satanic Conspiracy

Reference:

UFO, 1947–1997: Fifty Years of Flying Saucers, ed. by Hilary Evans and Dennis Stacey, John Brown Publishing, London, 1997

Thomas Hart Benton

Just as England had two Winston Churchills (novelist and politician), America had two Thomas Hart Bentons (painter and politician). The latter, Senator Thomas Hart Benton, has become a favorite with anti-banker conspiriologists, because his speeches against the Bank of the United States rank among the most persuasive criticisms of our banking system ever uttered.

According to Benton, whose opinions on this matter were

shared by Presidents Jackson and van Buren, the Bank of the United States had usurped the powers of Congress by issuing its own paper money, and had used this paper to manipulate interest rates so as to favor the upper class and "rob" or at least disfavor the general public. Jackson vetoed the charter of the bank, and van Buren renewed the veto when pro-bank forces in Congress tried to reinstate it; Benton tells the details of this "bank war" (as it was called) in vivid and powerful prose. No institution like the Bank of the United States, issuing its own paper in place of government money, reappeared until Congress created the *Federal Reserve Bank* in 1913.

See also:

John Adams on Banking, Bank of England, R. Buckminster Fuller, Col. Edward House, Ezra Pound, Rosicrucianism

Reference:

Thirty Years View: The Working of Government for Thirty Years 1820–1850, by Thomas Hart Benton, New York, 1854

The Bermuda Triangle

The so-called Bermuda Triangle (also, more melodramatically styled the Devil's Triangle) has been the scene of over 200 more-or-less mysterious disappearances of ships and airplanes, and has become the subject of a variety of weird and/or supernatural theories. Partially, this results from the fact that the Triangle has no known boundaries, not being a scientific or political construct, and sensational writers have extended it to include as many strange vanishings as possible. Some have even stretched the "triangle" to include the Gulf of Mexico and part of the Pacific ocean.

The classic or original Bermuda Triangle, bounded by Bermuda,

Miami, and Puerto Rico, has its own share of oddities nonetheless. The first to record weirdity there was Christopher Columbus, who sailed through the area in 1492 and noted that his compass malfunctioned in a bizarre way and that the 15th-century equivalent of a UFO shot by his ship, described alternately as weird "lights" or a single "flame" that plunged into the sea.

The area became famous, however, chiefly due to the mysterious case of the *Mary Celeste*, a 103-foot brigantine that was found floating there in 1872, about 400 miles off its course, entirely abandoned. The lifeboat had been launched, but no trace of it or the crew was ever found, and no reason for them to flee to ship has been discovered. Several yarns about this, some published as fiction and some as fact, added even spookier details, including strange vortices dragging the crew to a underground world within the hollow Earth. (See **Dr. Raymond Bernard** and **Richard Shaver**.)

The case that really made the Bermuda Triangle a permanent part of folklore was the disappearance in 1945 of Flight 19—five Navy bombers on a routine training mission, which disappeared entirely after sending back an incoherent message that repeated the letters *FT* and then faded away. The search for them continued for weeks, but no trace of planes, crew, or even debris was ever found.

The official position of the U.S. Navy is that the mysteries of the Triangle result from three major factors:

1. *This part of the Atlantic is one of the two places on Earth where a magnetic compass does not point to true north and can vary by as much as 20 degrees. Most of the disappearances involve small craft and amateur sailors, who could easily have been baffled by these compass wobbles and gone seriously*

astray. The similar area in the Pacific is called "the Devil's Sea" by the Japanese, also has magnetic irregularities, and is known for many lost ships.

2. *The Bermuda Triangle lies in the most turbulent part of the Gulf Stream, where thunderstorms, waterspouts, and the weather in general can not only create disasters but also quickly drown all the evidence or cast it about like pebbles in a cyclone.*

3. *The topography of the area varies from extensive shoals to some of the deepest ocean trenches known to science. Strong currents, sudden storms, and many reefs combine to make accidents and sinkings highly probable.*

And those lights or that fire Columbus saw must have been part of a meteor shower. So there's nothing really eerie in our world after all and nothing to fear. Unless you start worrying morbidly about Flight 19 and what the devil they meant with their "FT FT FT FT" signals. . . .

See also:

Fortean Times, Mothman Prophecies, Noon Blue Apples

References:

http://www.history.navy.mil/faqs/faq8–1.htm

http://www.rpi.net.au/~ghostgum/castle/bermuda.html

Dr. Raymond Bernard

Dr. Raymond Bernard was a pen name of Walter Siegmeister (1901–1965), who also used the pen names Dr. Robert Raymond and Dr. Uriel Adriana. Under the Dr. Bernard pen name, he wrote *The Hollow Earth* (1963), which is still the most widely read book on that subject. Despite the hollow Earth idea and other off-beat notions discussed below, Siegmeister/Bernard/Adriana had a real Ph.D. from New York University (1932) and had earlier acquired a Master's from Columbia. His earliest interests were theosophy and anthroposophy.

An educated and seemingly sincere man (although occasionally guilty of financial mismanagement, to say the least of it) "Bernard" not only believed the Earth was hollow but also that it was inhabited by a race called Terras, who had survived the destruction of Atlantis, stood 12 to 14 feet tall, and ate the strict diet of uncooked vegetables that Bernard believed in. They also came out of a hole somewhere in Brazil, flew around in UFOs, and occasionally picked up a human, jokingly passing themselves off as Martians or Venusians.

This remarkable man also believed the prophecies of a Puerto Rican psychic who called herself Payita and predicted a nuclear war beginning in 1965 that would leave no living thing on the surface of the Earth by 2000. Those who ate the right diet, lived in the Utopian commune Bernard had founded in Ecuador, never used money, and abstained entirely from sex, however, would be rescued by the Terras and taken to Mars, just before the nuclear holocaust started.

The only reason these ideas did not become universally accepted, of course, was that an academic conspiracy to maintain geological and other orthodoxies either ignored or ridiculed Dr. Bernard.

Payita, the witch-woman, also convinced Bernard that she had regular visits from the Great Mother, goddess of the ancients, and that the Great Mother had revealed the true history of the world to her. Basically, the Great Mother had parthenogenetically (without sex) given birth to all the races in the solar system, starting with perfect superwomen on Uranus who also reproduced parthenogenetically, no males being needed. Accidentally, however, one gave birth to a "defective female," i.e., the first male. His name was Lucifer, and he has been making trouble ever since, by encouraging people to eat meat and use money. His offspring inhabited Saturn and were far, far from the perfection of their female ancestors. Eventually, even more degenerate offspring migrated to Earth and degenerated further, until now we (their most degenerate descendants) are sunk in habitual meat-eating and money-using. Worse yet, when we do eat vegetables, most of us cook them.

The present author once met a woman who had loaned Bernard $2,000 for his Utopian colony and never got it back. She remembered him as a sincere and intelligent truth-seeker. Another source, however, says Bernard, after moving to his Ecuadorian commune, became "filthy" and unsanitary, suggesting some kind of mental illness.

Bernard also wrote a book called *Menstruation: Its Causes and Cure,* in which he argued that menstruation is caused by eating meat, tight clothes, and having sex too often. Any woman who ate nothing but uncooked vegetables, wore loose robes, and had sex only once a year at the spring solstice, he said, would never have the Curse again.

When Bernard died in 1965 the predicted nuclear war was due to start. When it failed to happen, his disciples did not lose faith. Some, in fact, developed an even more intense belief and insisted that he wasn't dead at all but living in Shamballah or Agharti, two fabulous cities mentioned in theosophical lore. More recently, he has been reported alive in the little town of Houston, Missouri.

See also:

Abel, AYA, *MS. Magazine,* Richard Shaver, *Subterranean Worlds*

Reference:

Subterranean Worlds, by Walter Kafton-Minkel, Loompanics Unlimited, Port Townsend, Wash., 1989

Prince Bernhard

Prince Bernhard of the Netherlands appears in several popular conspiracy theories. He founded the *Bilderbergers*, the ultra-secretive group of rich white males who meet once a year and (according to those not personally rich enough, white enough, or male enough to get into the club) plot how to exploit the rest of us.

All of these suspicions about the Bilderbergers come from people who usually don't qualify as rich or male or even white themselves. This may have the same explanation as the oddity noted by philosopher George Carlin: You never see a SHIT HAPPENS bumper sticker on a Rolls Royce.

According to genealogical/conspiriological theorists Michael Baigent, Henry Lincoln, and Richard Leigh, Prince Bernhard was also a direct descendent of Jesus Christ and Mary Magdalene. This makes him part of the gene pool that, some occultists think, is divinely ordained to rule the world. Several other known Bilderbergers are also part of the same genealogy, related back to the *Merovingians*, who were allegedly part fish.

See also:

Church of Mary Magdalene, Gerard de Sede, Noon Blue Apples

Reference:

Holy Blood, Holy Grail, by Michael Baigent, Henry Lincoln, and Richard Leigh, Delacorte, New York, 1982

Best Evidence

Best Evidence, a video by JFK conspiriologist David Lifton, contains interviews with staff members of both Parkman Hospital in Dallas, where Kennedy was brought after the shooting, and Bethesda Hospital in Maryland, where the autopsy was performed hours later. The Parkman witnesses describe a small wound in the skull, but the Bethesda witnesses describe a much larger wound. Three different coffins are described, or two plain caskets and one of higher quality bronze. The body seems to have arrived at a back door of Bethesda and the casket at the front. The whole brain somehow disappeared between the two hospitals, a fact that has not yet been explained.

Many smaller contradictions support Lifton's argument that government agents (the only ones with access to the body between the two hospitals) significantly altered the body to fit the thesis of one assassin shooting from behind and undermine the rival theory of at least one shooter in front, on the Grassy Knoll. The only alternative is to assume that at least one of the hospitals was staffed by people who all had extreme memory lapses.

As Lifton points out, the wounds in the Bethesda corpse played a large role in the Warren Commission's "lone nut" verdict, even though nearly 75 percent of the witnesses thought all or some of the shots came from the Grassy Knoll. Also, the testimony on this video, if one accepts it, rules out all conspiracy theories exclusively blaming pro-Castro Cubans, anti-Castro Cubans, the *Mafia*, oil millionaires, etc. If the body was indeed altered as these witnesses indicate, it was done by agents of the government itself.

See also:

James Jesus Angleton, Albert Guy Bogard, John F. Kennedy Assassination, A.J. Weberman

Reference:

Best Evidence, Rhino Home Video, Santa Monica, Calif., 1990

Peter Beter

Peter Beter not only believed that the *Illuminati* run both the international communist conspiracy and the international banks— a common idea in right-wing literature—but that the KGB has also murdered dozens of American politicians and business leaders, replacing them with androids (humanoid robots). The "attempted assassination" of *Ronald Reagan* was a cover-up, while they killed the real president and replaced him with one of these androids. (Well, if your name was Peter Beter you'd be pretty weird by the time you got out of high school.)

Peter, alas, is dead, but his tapes are still available and will really shake up your conventional views of everything.

See also:

The Con, Philip K. Dick, Noon Blue Apples

Reference:

Peter Beter Audio Newsletter, P.O. Box 276, Savage, MD. 20763

Hakim Bey

Hakim Bey is the only writer in America today even more esoteric than Thomas Pynchon. (See *"The Crying of Lot 49."*) Not only does Bey refuse to be photographed, but he tells a variety of stories about his early life, sometimes claiming to have been court poet in an unnamed north Indian principality, sometimes the librarian to the Shah of Iran. When *Time* magazine tried to interview him, he spread a rumor that he was a Shiite terrorist and disappeared; when *High Times* tried they got no reply from his publisher, but the interviewer later found a note on his bed telling him to come to Mott Street at 9 P.M., where he was picked up by three men in black and taken to a cellar in

Chinatown. There he met Hakim Bey or somebody imitating Hakim Bey.

Writing in a style that combines the most outrageous elements of *Ambrose Bierce*, H.L. Mencken, Andre Breton, and Nietzsche, Bey is the source of dozens of weird, wonderful, and way-out ideas. Among his key concepts are ontological anarchy, *poetic terrorism,* the temporary autonomous zone, and the Millennium.

Ontological anarchy combines elements of traditional anarchism (see *Government as Criminal Conspiracy*) with *Discordianism*, mathematical chaos theory, surrealism, the Moorish Orthodox Science of *Noble Drew Ali,* and bits of several mystic traditions, especially the Sufi and Taoist. Basically, it consists of (a) the perpetual anarchist quest for maximum liberty of the individual and (b) a prose style of such post-modern density and Nietzschean fury that it continually "tricks" the reader into realizing just how very little liberty we ever experience, and how much bland tyranny we presently endure.

Poetic terrorism started out as a graffiti campaign, but Bey now defines it as "a strange mixture of clandestine action and lying (which is what art is all about)" and compares street theater with guerrilla theater. "If you call what you're doing a 'street performance,' you've already created a split between artist and audience. . . . But if you stage a hoax, make an incident, create a situation, it might be possible to draw people in as participants and to maximize their freedom."

The temporary autonomous zone (abbreviated TAZ, and known almost everywhere in the counterculture) derives from the ideas that the Elite will never give us any real freedom (see *The Con*) and the masses, or *Pinks*, are too hypnotized and robotized to demand it, so the best we can do is find temporary zones of freedom, keep them secret as long as possible, and then move elsewhere when the Authorities discover that somebody somewhere has been having a good time. Critics call this "a Club Med for hippies," but it actually contains a more radical idea than any summary can convey. As a Zen master said when asked what the Tao is, "Walk on!"

The Millennium as conceived by Bey is different from any previous ideas on that topic. The death of communism, first in the form of the fall of Soviet Union, then in its withering away as an idea intellectuals take seriously, means that the malcontents (anarchists, voodooists, and other people who think more or less like Bey) are the only opposition left to the current money-power Elite. Like it or not, the people of the fringe are in an apocalyptical struggle: either the Elite techniques of control will be perfected to the level where dissent can be abolished, or heretics will mutate to some level of consciousness where they can do holy and miraculous works to resurrect the old dream of freedom for all. This will not happen by 2001, necessarily; Bey merely means that we live in a millennialist emergency.

See also:

Bisociation, Association for Ontological Anarchy, "Bob", *F For Fake*, Noon Blue Apples, OM, Kerry Thornley

Reference:

http://www.hightimes.com/~hightimes/ht/mag/956/Bey.html

Ambrose Bierce

Ambrose Bierce (1842–?) fought in the Civil War, which left him with a profound contempt for humanity and for humanity's claim to "moral values." Migrating west, he became a muckraking journalist and developed a style of outrageous and often hilarious invective, which later influenced H.L. Mencken. He became famous, however, for his first collection of short stories, *In the*

Midst of Life (1891), which is notable for treating the horrors of war in the precise, emotionless, "objective" style later copied by and usually identified with Ernest Hemingway. He returned to the polemical style of his journalism in *The Devil's Dictionary* (1906), which may not be the funniest collection of cynical epigrams in the English language but has at least one vote.

Bierce's later writings deal increasingly with weird and uncanny subjects and often concern other worlds or other dimensions of being that sometimes impinge upon our ordinary reality: ***H.P. Lovecraft*** admitted that these stories powerfully influenced his own works.

In 1913, Bierce went to Mexico and simply vanished. No evidence of where or when or how he died has ever come to light, and many fantasy stories have depicted him as being dragged off into the alternative worlds he had described. ***Charles Fort***, more originally, noted that a Canadian businessman named Ambrose Small disappeared at about the same time and suggested that we should look for an Ambrose Collector.

See also:

Gods of Eden, Kenneth Grant, Robert Morning Sky, *Mothman Prophecies*

References:

Bierce's writings

Columbia Concise Encyclopedia

Webster's Family Encyclopedia

Bilderbergers

The Bilderbergers, originally convened in Bilderberg, Netherlands, by ***Prince Bernhard***, consists of males who are all very rich and almost all very white. Since they now meet in a different city every year, and only once a year, the name "Bilderbergers" is somewhat anachronistic—but nobody on the outside knows what they call themselves. . . . Although suspected of all manner of high crimes and treasons by those who believe rich white males never do anything but hatch evil plots, the Bilderbergers have never been convicted of any crime in any court. (That just shows the extent of their control, according to the more ardent conspiriologists.)

The most nefarious fact about the Bilderbergers—as distinct from nefarious accusations—is that they do have a marvelous capacity for avoiding publicity in the major media. For instance, Lawrence Wilmot, writing in *The Spotlight* on 10 May 1993, documents the almost total blackout of references to the Bilderbergers in standard publications. Wilmot points out that at least 50 journalists turn out for any U.N. announcement, but none even attempt to cover Bilderberger meetings; he says that when he mentioned this to some mainstream journalists, he was greeted with ironic laughter, and Anthony Holder of the *London Economist* said bluntly, "The Bilderbergers have been removed from our assignment list years ago by executive order."

Wilmot also quotes a somewhat less sinister theory of why we hear and read so little about the Bilderbergers:

We are barely aware of the [Bilderbergers'] existence, and we don't report on their activities," asserted William Glasgow, the senior writer responsible for covering international organizations at Business Week. *"Maybe it is a question of cost cutting. After all, we can't afford to cover everything, can we?*

Wilmot continues:

The reason why this imperious assembly should be granted the sort of secrecy for its deliberations the mass media would never accord to any government—not even to Europe's reigning royalty—was, in the consensus of UN correspondents, simple: "The Bilderbergers are too powerful and omnipresent to be exposed," as French broadcaster Thierry de Segonzac put it.

According to *The Spotlight*, both our current president, **Bill Clinton,** and our former president, **George Bush,** were members of the Bilderbergers. And so is **David Rockefeller. . .**

See also:

Hawthorne Abendsen, John Birch Society, Gnomes of Zurich, Insiders, Fletcher Prouty

Reference:

http://www.livelinks.com/sumeria/politics/bilders.html

John Birch

John Morrison Birch (1919–1945), a Christian missionary to China who became an intelligence officer for the U.S. Air Force, has achieved near-canonization by the *John Birch Society,* named in his honor.

Birch went to China against the warnings of his pastor, who told him that country was becoming unsafe for Christians. Birch allegedly replied, "I know the big enemy is communism, but the Lord has called me. My life is in his hands, and I am not turning back." During World War II, he adopted the garb of the country and dyed his hair black, working behind Japanese lines and gathering intelligence for the Air Force. He helped General Doolittle and his crew escape during the aftermath of their bombing of Tokyo and acquired a wide knowledge of Chinese language and culture.

On August 25, 1945, Birch was shot by communist guerrillas, and in 1958 Robert Welch named the John Birch Society after him as the first American killed in the Cold War.

Reference:

"John Birch: A Patriotic Exemplar," by William Norman Grigg, *The New American*, December 13, 1993

John Birch Society—The Capitalist-Communist Conspiracy

The John Birch Society holds to values and beliefs that are generally shared by both moderate conservatives and far-right extremists—the Judeo-Christian sexual code, the theory of free markets, the special glory of the U.S. Constitution, etc. What makes the Birch people unique is their very special conspiracy theory, which is rather like the mystic idea that all opposites are manifestations of a hidden unity (see *Sacred Chao* and *yin and yang*) but in a very concrete and sinister manner.

The Birch doctrine holds that communism and capitalism are both parts of a much larger conspiracy of financial *Insiders* who control both the capitalist states and the few remaining communist ones also. These Insiders sound a lot like the *Illuminati* in similar theories but only *copy* the Illuminati rather than being the Illuminati, according to leading Birch conspiriologist Gary Allen. They were organized by *Cecil Rhodes* and other European financiers in the last century, and they use fronts, such as the *Council on Foreign Relations,* to manipulate governments and public opinion.

Birch theory relies heavily on the testimony of Dr. Bella Dodd, once a member of the U.S. Communist Party and later a fierce enemy of communism. According to Dr. Dodd, on occasion top orders for the Party came not from Moscow but from three men at the Waldorf Towers in New York—all of them wealthy American capitalists. "I think the Communist conspiracy is merely a branch of a much bigger conspiracy," Dodd said. "I would certainly like to find out who is really running things."

The three mystery-millionaires may have a family resemblance to the three ruffians who killed *The Widow's Son* in *Freemasonic* legend, and maybe to the three *men in black* who haunt and vex UFO contactees (and maybe the three Soldiers—a Scotsman, an Englishman, and a Welshman—who torment the Irish dreamer all through Joyce's *Finnegans Wake*).

Another major source of Birch conspiracy theory, which has also influenced other right-wing conspiriologists, is a big fat book called *Tragedy and Hope,* by *Professor Carroll Quigley* of the Jesuit-run Georgetown University in Washington. Professor Quigley refers to "Round Table Groups" of intellectuals and politicians, financed and guided by the moneyed Elite, who control Western democracies behind the scenes. These Round Table Groups, the Birchers say, are the Insiders, and Cecil Rhodes was their founder. "This network," Quigley wrote, ". . . has no aversion to cooperating with the Communists, or any other groups, and frequently does so."

A rather different version of Professor Quigley's book and its meaning will be found in *A-Albionic Consulting and Research*.

See also:

Gnomes of Zurich, LAWCAP, MMAO, *None Dare Call It Conspiracy*

Reference:

http://www.jbs.org/

Bisociation

Bisociation is a term introduced into psychology and philosophy by novelist/philosopher Arthur Koestler (1905-1983). It signifies "the perceiving of a situation or idea...in two self-consistent but habitually incompatible frames of reference," a process which Koestler claims underlies the three most uniquely human of all our behaviors: the *joke*, the *scientific theory*, and the *work of art*.

The present author suggests that bisociation also underlies that other very human narrative: the conspiracy theory.

Frames of reference, which Koestler also calls matrices, are called glosses, grids, or reality-tunnels in various social sciences. A frame, matrice, reality-tunnel, etc. is a way of organizing experience: a code in our nervous system that tells the brain where to store each new bit of information. When bisociation occurs, we have two frames colliding or melding. This can be almost sexual in the joy it yields; and it is often fertile.

In humor, bisociation can be illustrated by Oscar Wilde's "Are the commentators on *Hamlet* really mad or only pretending to be mad?" Here, Hamlet as a character (who might be mad) merges with *Hamlet* the play, and the possible madness of one or both gets transferred to the commentators. (Underlying this double double-association is the paradox that we can identify with Hamlet even while remembering that he is really Laurence Olivier and we are only watching a play—a type of bisociation, or madness, or mystic oneness, which is socially acceptable because it is ritualized and localized in the theater. If you walked up to Lord Olivier on the street and treated him like Hamlet, that would be unacceptable madness.)

You can see the same collision of frames in Mae West's "Is that a pistol in your pocket or are you just glad to see me?" Or Groucho Marx's "I once shot an elephant in my pajamas. How he got into my pajamas I'll never know."

In scientific discovery, the same bisociation appears over and over. Newton looks at a falling apple, as many had before him, and suddenly bisociates it with the orbits of the planets: the classic theory of gravity is born. Nobody but a genius or a madman would try to relate a simple fruit falling from a simple tree to the movements of the heavens.

Similarly, although it may be hard for us to remember, electricity and magnetism were two different subjects before James C. Maxwell, whose bisociation into electromagnetism is as basic to modern physics as Einstein's bisociation of space and time into space-time.

In art, bisociation is everywhere; my favorite example is Yeats's "A terrible beauty is born." Terror and beauty never stood so close before. And the image of the pain and the glory of childbirth takes on another level, a bisociation of bisociation, when one remembers that this line describes the failed Irish rebellion of 1916, which led directly to the war for independence (1918-1921), in which a nation was born.

Or try Shakespeare's "Blood, thou art blood: Let's write 'good angel' on the devil's horn." Or, to jump to another art, look at that Picasso sculpture which seems to be a bull's head but is made up of parts of a bicycle.

Of course, as Koestler points out, many bisociations just yield false theories or banal nonsense. This may be the major thrill in the life of the humorist, the scientist, and the artist: you never know if you've just produced Genius or Bathos. You walk a tightrope, always.

Conspiracy theories have a strong element of bisociation, and one often does not know whether to classify them as (unintentional) humor, true social science, or merely dark art. Consider for instance:

The bisociation of three millionaires in the Waldorf Towers with the U.S. Communist Party (see *John Birch Society*.)

The bisociation of Queen Elizabeth II and a hippie crash pad in the Haight c. 1968 (see *Lyndon LaRouche*.)

The bisociation of *George Bush*'s oil wells and the aliens hidden by the CIA (see *William Cooper*.)

Some form of bisociation appears in every conspiracy theory, we suggest, and that explains why so many will laugh at a particular theory which others will embrace as a revelation of naked truth seen clearly as last.

See also:

F for Fake, Charles Fort, Priory of Sion

Reference:

The Act of Creation, by Arthur Koestler, Macmillan, New York, 1964, p. 35 ff.

Black People as Experimental Subjects

See:

CIA LSD Research, Haitian Experiment Claim, Tuskegee Syphilis Study

BOA: Bank of America Conspiracy

The initials of the Bank of America have aroused the suspicions of a writer using the pen name Wednesday N. Pointing out that BOA is the name of "a type of snake that constricts its victims to death," Wednesday suggests that the ever-increasing number of bank charges by BOA indicates their true motives and attitudes: "Boas are cold-blooded, unconscionable sneaks that will stop at nothing."

See also:

Banco Ambrosiano, Bank of England, First Interstate Bank, Gnomes of Zurich, Lucent Technologies

Reference:

http://www.hallucinet.com/asylem/asylem2/as_boa.html

"Bob"

The founder, savior, and martyr of the *Church of the Sub-Genius,* J.R. "Bob" Dobbs is called simply "Bob" by his disciples, and frenzied cries of "Praise 'Bob'!" frequently break the otherwise solemn tone of Sub-Genius devivals.

"Bob" had an unusual birth, his mother having been seduced by a milkman who was (perhaps) descended from Aztec gods. In early manhood, "Bob" became a champion aluminum-siding salesman and might have remained happy in that career if he had not gotten stuck in a stalled elevator with L. Ron Hubbard. Emerging from that ordeal, "Bob" soon started his own religion and quickly became as rich as Hubbard, Rajneesh, or even the Pope.

For some years "Bob" lived in Dobbstown, and even there it was very hard to meet him directly. Those seeking audience needed a special operation, by a medical rock group called Doctors for "Bob," to open the third nostril, but even after that the encounter with the semi-divine "Bob" left them with partial amnesia, eye strain, "sunburn," and morbid anxieties, often centered on the idea that *men in black,* disguised as Jehovah's Witnesses, would try to get into their homes and brainwash them.

"Bob" was shot dead in San Francisco in 1982 by a former disciple named Puzzling Evidence, or by six other people, depending on which conspiracy theory you believe.

See also:

The Con, Discordianism, Slack

References:

Rev. Ivan Stang, Church of the Sub-Genius, P.O. Box 140306, Dallas, TX 75214

Albert Guy Bogard

Albert Guy Bogard, a Dallas car salesman, claimed that shortly before the *John F. Kennedy assassination, Lee Harvey Oswald* test-drove a car of his, zooming along the freeways at 70 miles per hour. This seems strange because Oswald never learned to drive. Even stranger: Bogard claimed Oswald bragged of "coming into a lot of money" soon and dropped some pro-Soviet propaganda into their casual conversation. While some might think Bogard had a lively imagination and a desire to get his name into history, at least as a footnote, conspiriologists point out that the assistant sales manager, Frank Pizzo, and two other salesmen in the shop, Eugene M. Wilson and Oran Brown, each partially corroborated Bogard's story.

This case, conspiriologists say, proves the existence of a "second Oswald" who planted incriminating evidence here and there against the real Oswald, something only possible if there was a conspiracy and frame-up.

The matter became more obscure when Bogard's body turned up in a cemetery. Official verdict: suicide.

See also:

Hale Boggs, David Ferrie, Kennedy Death Links

References:

http://www.informatik.uni-rostock.de/Kennedy/WCR/wcr6.html

Big Book of Conspiracies, by Dough Moench, Paradox Press, New York, 1995, p. 13

Hale Boggs

Hale Boggs, a congressman from Louisiana, served as a member of the Warren Commission and expressed "strong doubts" about the "magic bullet" theory. He later received a package of "dirty" (seemingly incriminating) material about critics of the Warren Report, evidently sent by J. Edgar Hoover. Boggs then complained that "the FBI is using Gestapo tactics." Shortly thereafter he and the airplane that carried him disappeared somewhere above Alaska. Neither Boggs nor any debris of the plane was ever found.

See also:

James Jesus Angleton, Marina Oswald

References:

http://www.ratical.com/ratville/JFK/DW.html

The Big Book of Conspiracies, by Doug Moench, Paradox Press, New York, 1995, p. 12

The Book of the Law

See:

Liber Al

The Book of Lies

The Book of Lies is the most puzzling and deliberately perverse of all the magick-mystic manuals of the egregious *Aleister Crowley* and, for those who can decipher any of it, also one of his funniest books. He claims that one chapter reveals the inner secret of *Freemasonry* and the *Illuminati*, but refuses to tell which chapter it is. Basically, the text contains the same sort of paradoxes as the *Principia Discordia* or the koans (riddles) of Zen Buddhism, combined with lyrical passages that seem to concern various sexual acrobatics, if you read them that way or, on the other hand, describe the altered states of consciousness along the path to mystic Enlightenment, if you read them that way.

One chapter, for instance, begins:

Nothing is.
Nothing becomes.
Nothing is not.

This seems gibberish to most readers but describes, quite accurately, a mystic state called Shivadarshana among Hindus. The punch line will be found in our entry on the *Book of the Sub-Genius*.

See also:

Bisociation, Discordianism, Illuminati, Noon Blue Apples, Ordo Templi Orientis

Reference:

The Book of Lies, by Aleister Crowley, Samuel Weiser, Inc., New York, 1980

Book of the Sub-Genius

A chrestomathy of early Sub-Genius rants, the *Book of the Sub-Genius* includes such Zen flashes of brilliance as "Hell, it's even more relative than Einstein realized," "Act like a dumbshit and they'll treat you like an equal," "I pick the goddam terror of the Gods out of my nose," and "Don't just eat a hamburger—eat THE HELL out of it!"

The most enigmatic (but illuminating) text says:

"Bob" Is
"Bob" Becomes
"Bob" Is Not
Nothing Is. Nothing Becomes. Nothing Is Not.
Thus: Nothing Is Everything.
Therefore: Everything Is "Bob."

See also:

"Bob", The Con, Discordianism, OM

References:

The Book of the Sub-Genius, Sub-Genius Foundation, Simon and Schuster, New York, 1987

Born in Blood

John J. Robinson's *Born in Blood* argues that the *Freemasons* (and also, curiously, their most paranoid critics) are historically correct in claiming a direct descent of Masonry from the *Knights Templar*. Orthodox historians, who have always rejected this as a romantic fiction, simply overlooked a lot of evidence, Robinson says. Everybody admits that the suppression of the Templars by the Inquisition was never enforced in Scotland, but skeptical non-Masonic historians have never looked at the history of that country for evidence of the evolution from surviving Templars to Freemasons. Robinson looks and finds some fascinating data.

The major evidence he provides consists of previously unexplained tales of strange allies that assisted Scotch patriots at various times, old church and tomb inscriptions, re-examination of Masonic terms and legends, etc., all of which adds up to a persuasive (if not positive) case that the Templars of Scotland survived using new titles and eventually evolved into the Freemasons of the 18th century. Robinson also has some good arguments for Templar/Masonic influence behind the peasants' rebellion of 1381 in England, which may explain why the *Knights of Malta* were special targets of violence in that uprising. One of the firebrands, Wat Tyler, or Wat the Tyler, was a Masonic official, Robinson suggests. (One member of a Masonic lodge is still called a Tyler.)

The book documents Masonic influence on Sir Francis Bacon's

New Atlantis, and the influence of that Utopian novel on later radicals and secular humanists, but it never deals with the *Illuminati.*

See also:

A-Albionic, Christians Awake AIDs Theory

Reference:

Born in Blood: The Lost Secrets of Freemasonry, by John J. Robinson, Evans and Company, New York, 1989

Nicholas Bourbaki

For many years the status of Nicholas Bourbaki grew higher and higher among his fellow mathematicians, as he produced work in dozens of fields of pure analysis totally unrelated to one another. Some even compared him to Karl Friedrich Gauss, the 19th-century superbrain who invented more math than Euclid or Newton; everybody wanted to meet this towering intellect. Alas, Bourbaki never attended mathematics conferences: A shy, reticent man, it was said.

The truth finally came out: "Nicholas Bourbaki" never existed. His papers covered so many areas of math because they had been written by a whimsical committee of French mathematicians who all had different specialties.

See also:

Crop Circles, Elmyr, Ladder Conspiracies, OM, UMMO Letters

Reference:

The Counterfeiters, by Hugh Kenner, John Hopkins University Press, 1985

Lee Bowers Jr.

Lee Bowers Jr., a railroad employee, was stationed in a control tower behind the grassy knoll at the time of the *John F. Kennedy assassination.* He told the Warren Commission that he saw two men behind the stockade fence and saw a flash of light from there at the time of the shooting, but his testimony was disregarded.

Bowers died in a strange one-car accident on August 9, 1966, apparently crashing his auto into a bridge abutment. The pathologist said Bowers was in a "strange state of shock" at the time of the smashup.

See also:

Kennedy Death Links, Mary Pinchot Meyer, The Three Tramps, "The Whole Bay of Pigs Thing"

Reference:

The Big Book of Conspiracies, by Doug Moench, Paradox Press, New York, 1995, p. 15

Brainwashing

As a result of the recent group suicide of 39 members of the *Heaven's Gate* cult, renewed interest in brainwashing has permeated all mass media, including the Internet. Our researcher, Miriam Joan Hill, found several different definitions of this term on the net, typified by the following sources:

- *http://www.crashsite.com/SofTV/MindControl/ Brain-washing.html*

- *http://www.az.com/~bipolar/*

In most cases, writers seem to use "brainwashing" to mean *any form of teaching, indoctrination, training, etc. that imparts ideas that the writer does not like.* This appears wildly subjective. A more scientific and objective model has been offered by Dr. Timothy Leary and R.A.W., and we will summarize it briefly.

A brainwashing process begins with isolation of the subject, severing all ties with those persons (family, friends, lovers, etc.) who might interfere with the brainwashing process. The subject is then made to feel helpless and isolated, but is fed regularly. This re-activates infantile programs ("instincts"), which cause the frightened, disoriented subject to imprint the person who feeds them as a mothering or nurturing object, just as the newborn imprints the mother or the nearest mother substitute. This shocking arrival in a new environment and dependence on a mother-creature activates all the bio-survival circuitry of the brain, or the "consciousness" of the human or any living creature.

In the second stage, while still being isolated but fed regularly, the subject is humiliated, mocked, and made to feel "all wrong" about any ideas, habits, personal traits, etc., acquired before entering the brainwashing program. In the hierarchy of needs, right after food/nurture comes status—and the subject will soon try to behave in a manner more acceptable to the cult (or army boot camp, political prison, etc.) where this re-imprinting occurs. The same status programs cause the young child to imprint the roles, rules, and taboos of the tribe in which he or she is born. This activates the entire emotional-territorial circuitry of all human (and vertebrate) brains—the "ego" in ordinary language.

Third, the subject is taught to parrot the words and ideas of the group into which they are being initiated. Simultaneously, words and ideas from the past (pre-brainwash) are mocked and suppressed.

This follows as naturally as the schoolchild acquiring the semantic system and neurolinguistic reflexes of their culture, once they understand that food and status depend on cooperation. This activates/imprints the semantic-rational circuitry—the "mind" in ordinary language.

All of these steps must be accompanied by reward for compliance and some form of punishment or loss of status for "backsliding." The process is complete when the subject not only parrots the belief system of the captors but truly begins to believe it, as the child imprints the reality-tunnel of parents first and then of the school the parents chose.

Most government brainwashers go no further than this. Some cults move on (after the bio-survival, status, and semantic programs are re-imprinted) to re-imprint a new sex role and a whole new sex code, according to the whim of the cult leader.

Reference:

"How to Wash Brains," by Timothy Leary and Robert Anton Wilson, in *Neuropolitique*, by Leary, Wilson, and George Koopman, Falcon Press, 1988

Bring Back My Foreskin to Me

See:

Circumcision Conspiracy

Broederbond

Described by the Philadelphia *Inquirer* as a "shadow government," the Broederbond, a ritualistic secret society, allegedly controlled South Africa for more than four decades. Every South African head of state and virtually every cabinet minister were members of the esoteric group, which invented apartheid and enforced it ruthlessly for nearly 50 years. The Broederbond also decided when apartheid could no longer be upheld and supervised President F.W. de Klerk's negotiations with blacks for power sharing.

In a review of the new book *Anatomy of a Miracle: The End of Apartheid and the Birth of a New South Africa*, by Patti Walmeir, the *Christian Science Monitor* adds that the Broederbond also held secret talks with banned black groups in the last years of the 1980s when it was still enforcing white supremacy with extreme violence.

The head of the secret society was Prof. J.P. de Lange, who decided eventually that it was "impossible" to maintain white presence in the nation without sharing power with the blacks.

See also:

Bilderbergers, Council on Foreign Relations, Gnomes of Zurich, Octopus, P2 Conspiracy

References:

Philadelphia *Inquirer*, January 28, 1990

Christian Science Monitor, April 9, 1997

The Brotherhood

The Brotherhood: The Secret World of the Freemasons, by Stephen Knight, adds a few new charges to the usual anti-Masonic conspiracy story. Except for one section—proving yet again that the Freemasonic fraternity is open to men of all religions and is therefore anti-Christian, according to the logic of those who think that Christians who associate with heathens and infidels will inevitably be corrupted—Knight has his own axes to grind.

A large part of his book attempts to show that the KGB has infiltrated Masonry everywhere it could get a foothold, and that the Soviets therefore masterminded the *P2 conspiracy* in Italy. Knight also tries to prove that the KGB, through its control of freemasonry, has infiltrated the British government extensively, including the Intelligence services (MI5 and MI6), which is why England had more proven Soviet moles than any other NATO country.

Even the most vehement anti-Masonic conspiriologists would probably admit that this argument contains much more speculation and imagination than hard data, but Knight does better on the heavy Masonic presense in Scotland Yard and quotes former officers about the necessity of joining the Craft if you desired promotion. This lends some plausibility to his assertion that the Yard hurriedly arrived at a suicide verdict in the original investigation of the *Roberto Calvi* hanging because they recognized the Masonic symbolism in the details. (Calvi's pockets were stuffed with bricks and his body was hung where the rising tide covered it. Bricks are associated with the origins of Masonry and being hanged where the rising tide will cover your dead body is a threat that remained part of the first-degree initiation until after this case, when the Masons formally removed it.)

Most other investigators believe the P2 gang was taking money from both the KGB and the CIA (and double-crossing both of them).

See also:

Freemasonry, Illuminati, P2 Conspiracy

Reference:

The Brotherhood: The Secret World of the Freemasons, by Stephen Knight, Grenada, London, 1984

Gordon Brown

"Gordon Brown" was the pen name used in an early essay by anti-Vatican Irish writer James Joyce. It seems just an English transliteration of *Giordano Bruno*, also quoted in Joyce's pamphlet "The Day of the Rabblement" and *Portrait of the Artist as a Young Man*, in which the Dean tells Stephen (Joyce) that Bruno was a terrible heretic and Stephen replies that Bruno was terribly burned. Bruno is one of the major characters in Joyce's longest, most complex work, *Finnegans Wake*.

Reference:

FWread@lists.colorado.edu, by Terrence Ritchie, October 22, 1997

Susan Brownmiller

See:

The Rape Conspiracy

Giordano Bruno

Giordano Bruno (1548–1600), Italian philosopher/scientist and possible conspirator, was burned at the stake in Rome on February 16, 1600. Most historians merely mention that Bruno was charged with the heresy of teaching Copernican astronomy, but Frances Yates, a historian who specialized in the occult aspects of the early scientific revolution, points out that Bruno was charged with 18 heresies and crimes, including the practice of sorcery and organizing secret societies to oppose the Vatican. Yates thinks Bruno may have had a role in the invention of either *Rosicrucianism* or *Freemasonry* or both.

Bruno's teachings combined the new science of his time with traditional Cabalistic mysticism. He believed in a universe of infinite space with infinite inhabited planets, and in a kind of dualistic pantheism, in which the divine is incarnate in every part but always in conflicting forms that both oppose and support each other. Whatever his link with occult secret societies, he influenced Hegel, Marx, theosophy, James Joyce, *Timothy Leary, Discordianism,* and *Dr. Wilhelm Reich.*

See also:

Aeon of Horus, John Dee, Illuminati, Sacred Chao, Yin and Yang

Reference:

Giordano Bruno and the Hermetic Tradition, by Frances Yates, University of Chicago Press, 1964

Buckaroo Banzai: Across the Eighth Dimension

Buckaroo Banzai (or, to give it its full release title, *The Adventures of Buckaroo Banzai Across the Eighth Dimension*) is one of those films, like *Repo Man* and *The Magic Christian*, that has a small but dedicated cult following (who are all probably under surveillance by either the FBI or CSICOP). The hero, Dr. Banzai, is, very much like Doc Savage in the 1930s pulps, a great scientist, a brain surgeon, and a crime-fighting superhero all in one—but, more politically correct than Doc Savage, he is not a WASP stereotype but multi-ethnic (part Asiatic) and further adds to Doc's achievements by being also a Rock star and a New Age philosopher ("Wherever you go. . . *there you are!*").

The film contains a conspiracy theory, but you might skip this paragraph if the above blurb makes you want to rent the video: I'm about to spoil the major surprise in the story. You see, the Martian invasion of 1938 was *not* faked by *Orson Welles*—it really happened. Orson, and everybody else, just underwent brain programming after the invasion and forgot the real horror as false memories of a hoax were implanted in their memory circuits.

See also:

Area 51, Philip K. Dick, Charles Fort, *Gods of Eden,* Clifford Irving, Recovered Memory Therapy

Reference:

The Adventures of Buckaroo Banzai Across the Eighth Dimension, directed by W.D. Richter, LIVE Videos, 1984

President George Bush

According to the "novel" and/or "documentary" *American Hero,* George Bush, the greatest president between *Ronald Reagan* and *Bill Clinton,* was in the habit of taking his Halcyon (a heavy tranquilizer) with a shot of Scotch whiskey, against all medical advice. This may explain the oddest and most touching fact about Mr. Bush—his frequent inability to talk English. For example:

> *You can't be president of the United States if you don't have faith. Remember Lincoln, going to his knees in times of trial and the Civil War and all that stuff. You can't be. And we are blessed. So don't feel sorry for—don't cry for me, Argentina.*

> *I've got to run now and relax. The doctor told me to relax. The doctor told me to relax. The doctor told me. He was the one. He said, "Relax."*

> *You're not going to see me put as much—I mean un-put as much.*

See also:

Bilderbergers, William Cooper, Skull and Bones, Trilateral Commission, "The Whole Bay of Pigs Thing"

Reference:

Quotes from *Bushisms*, Workman Publishing, New York, 1992, pp. 7, 17, 47

The Second George Bush

According to an FBI memo, "George Bush of the CIA" had been briefed on November 23, 1963, about the reaction of Cuban exiles to the *John F. Kennedy assassination.*

Since George Bush denies that he ever had any connection with the CIA before President Gerald Ford appointed him director of the agency in 1976, either (a) Bush is a liar or (b) there is a second George Bush. Conspiriologists of both left and right prefer theory (a).

Paul Kangas, a conspiracy hunter who believes Bush was a longtime CIA agent, argues that the CIA would never allow anybody to be put in charge who wasn't a longtime "company man."

Reference:

"The Role of Richard Nixon and George Bush in the Assassination of President Kennedy," *The Realist*, No. 117, Summer 1991

Cara Calvi

Cara Calvi, widow of Roberto Calvi, testified at the second inquest on her husband's death, in London. Dissenting vehemently from the verdict of the first inquest, which had ruled the banker's death a suicide, Mrs. Calvi said he had been killed because he was about to turn state witness and "name names" of those higher in the *P2 conspiracy* than himself. Asked if Calvi intended to name persons in the Vatican, Mrs. Calvi said yes, and added that he would name some "at the top."

The second inquest reversed the ruling of the first and found the cause of Calvi's death was unknown.

See also:

Cardinal Jean Danielou, Licio Gelli, Paul "The Gorilla" Marcinkus, Naked Pope

Reference:

Irish Times, June 21, 1983

Roberto Calvi

See:

James Jesus Angleton, Cara Calvi, *Calvi Affair*, Gladio, Naked Pope, P2 Conspiracy, Michele "The Shark" Sindona

The Calvi Affair

The Calvi Affair, by Larry Gurwin of the *Institutional Investor* (London), attempts to make sense of the **P2 conspiracy** that shook up Italian finance, and European finance generally, for several years in the 1970s to 1980s. Gurwin concentrates chiefly on **Roberto Calvi,** president of **Banco Ambrosiano,** whose strange death—he was found hanging from a bridge in London, after disappearing abruptly from Italy—had especially shocked English investors.

Calvi had joined the P2 brotherhood, a secret society within the **Grand Orient Lodge of Egyptian Freemasonry,** because he believed that P2 held the keys to economic and political power in Italy. Through his P2 connections, his close links with Archbishop **Paul "The Gorilla" Marcinkus** of the Vatican Bank, and his fertile imagination—he created totally fictitious banks all over the world and used them to carry on illegal and clandestine activities—Calvi became indeed very rich, but also attracted unwelcome attention from bank examiners.

Through **Licio Gelli,** founder of the P2 group, Calvi became involved with the Mafia, the CIA, the KGB, and an assortment of criminal and terrorist organizations—but because of his ties to the Vatican, he was called "God's banker" and seemed immune to the hazards of his profession. Then the house of cards fell apart; Calvi found himself indicted for embezzlement and under suspicion for numerous other crimes, and fled Italy. The day he hung himself or was hung in London, his secretary threw herself or was thrown from a window of Banco Ambrosiano in Milan.

See also:

Gladio, *Godfather,* Potere Occulto, *Scandals of the Priory of Sion,* Michele "The Shark" Sindona

Reference:

The Calvi Affair: Death of a Banker, by Larry Gurwin, Pan Books, London, 1984

Campus Crusade for Cthulhu

"I found IT!"
—slogan of the Campus Crusade for Christ

"IT found me!"
—slogan of the Campus Crusade for Cthulhu

The Campus Crusade for Cthulhu claims to be the oldest college club in the world, claiming that before Ancient Greece or Atlantis, even "before the first *Illuminati* attempts at world conquest," they had "tentacles" gripping the whole world. Worshiping the Great Old Ones, interstellar giants from the *Necronomicon* of *Abdul Alhazred,* and/or the fiction of *H.P. Lovecraft,* the Cthulhu Cult has existed even before humanity appeared on earth, and created the Campus Crusade at Miskatonic University (in Arkham, Massachusetts) early in this century, gradually adding chapters at Yale, New York University, State University of New York, etc.

Cthulhu, usually pictured as a slimy green octopus of mountainous size, may not be an attractive deity, but the Campus Crusaders insist that he has no worse morals or habits than most of the other gods people have worshiped.

The Campus Crusade at Binghamton, New York, plans to build a Ziggurat of Doom using slave labor if students cannot pay for it. Other branches have proposed a racial program of "ethnic cleansing," based on the proposition that "if everyone takes a bath at least once a year—whether they need it or not—we believe relations between the races will be much improved." In 1996, the Crusaders ran Cthulhu for president with the slogan "Why accept the lesser evil?"

The Cthulhists, like their rivals in the Campus Crusade for Christ, put out a variety of proselytizing pamphlets, but they have livelier titles, e.g., "*Yog Sothoth* Neblod Zin," "Abdul Alhazred was NOT mad," "Cthulhu fthagn," etc.

See also:

Kenneth Grant, Holy Order of the Lemon, Robert Morning Sky

References:

http://www.emunix.emich.edu/~winterh/ccc/

http://www.primenet.com/~fedup/cthulhu/

William Casey

In 1981, Ronald Reagan appointed William Casey, a lawyer and stockbroker—who had also written prestigious books on law and history—as the new head of the CIA. Casey was a *Knight of Malta* with an urgent sense of morality: "Some things are right and some things are wrong, eternally right and eternally wrong," he once told an audience at a Saint Patrick's Day celebration. He had no doubt of his own ability to recognize the eternally right and the eternally wrong.

Since Congress had forbidden the CIA to engage in further illegal activities in Nicaragua, Casey, knowing that the government down there was eternally wrong, set about making war without Congress discovering what he was doing.

In 1982, Casey authorized "Black Eagle," a project to fund and supply the Contras who were trying to overturn the Nicaraguan government. Casey employed friends in various governments (Israel, Argentina, Saudi Arabia) who, in exchange for various favors, contributed arms and money to the Contras. Although this was illegal and Casey habitually lied to Congress about it, he had no guilt, since he was eternally right. Thus, he felt no qualms about making a deal with Juan Ramon Matta Ballesteros, usually called Matta, a major cocaine dealer in Honduras. According to *Newsweek*, by 1985, Matta's organization was supplying "perhaps one third of all the cocaine consumed in the United States." *George Bush* meanwhile quietly placed the Drug Enforcement Agency under the control of national security and then closed down their office in Honduras.

Major roles in the Black Eagle project were also played by General Richard Secord, a military logistics expert who is sometimes described as a CIA official, and Col. Oliver North, who later admitted to Congress that he "cleaned out the files, . . . shredded documents and altered others . . ." when some of the gun-and-drug deals began to leak to the press.

Casey died of a brain tumor while under investigation for a long series of crimes necessary to keep the war alive and invisible to Congress. The Christic Institute, a public interest law firm, tried to bring Secord and North to trial, but the courts dismissed their complaint. North, however, is still persona non grata in Costa Rica, and the Costa Rican government tried to extradite John Hull to stand trial for running the ranch where most of the guns and cocaine were exchanged.

See also:

"Ask About the Cocaine!", John Hull, P2 Conspiracy, *Veil,* World Finance Corporation

References:

General—

http://www.mcs.net/~rwor/rw_or/885/cia3.htm

Casey on right and wrong—

Veil: The Secret Wars of the CIA, by Bob Woodward, Pocket Books, New York, 1987, p. 119

Danny Casolaro

In 1990, Danny Casolaro, one of the owners of Computer Age Publications, sold his share of the company to have a nest egg as he launched a new career as freelance writer and investigative journalist. The first major story he discovered involved the *Inslaw* company, which alleged that certain persons in the Justice Department had stolen a new piece of software that Inslaw had invented called **PROMIS**. A federal court later rejected these claims. As Casolaro investigated the charges and coutercharges of the Inslaw-PROMIS story, he found evidence that seemed to reveal a truly gigantic (global) conspiracy, which he began to call the *Octopus*. As he discovered that more and more of the persons in this saga had died under mysterious circumstances, Casolaro told his brother never to believe he himself died of an accident.

On August 10, 1991, Danny Casolaro was found dead in a bathtub with his wrists slashed. Although many friends insist Danny was not the suicidal type, the official verdict was suicide.

Reference:

The Octopus: Secret Government and the Death of Danny Casolaro, by Kenn Thomas and Jim Keith, Feral House, Portland, Oreg., 1996

Castro as Super-Mole

The Soviets suspected for a long time, and certain elements in the KGB were especially firm in the belief, that Fidel Castro was not really a communist revolutionary but a CIA mole intended to penetrate the top ranks of Soviet intelligence just as a Soviet mole code-named *Sasha* had allegedly penetrated the CIA.

Shortly after Castro took power, a Russian settled in Havana, ostensibly as a correspondent for the news agency TASS. He was a senior KGB officer, evidently assigned to spy on Castro and learn whether he was a mole. The author of the website below notes that "a characteristic common to all intelligence officers, East and West, is that they have a special open-mindedness. For them nothing is impossible just because it is improbable" (words so wise we borrowed them to introduce this book) and also points out that *James Jesus Angleton* of CIA counterintelligence never abandoned his belief that Tito was a communist mole and that somebody at least as high in the CIA as himself was another communist mole code-named Sasha.

See also:

Franklin Delano Roosevelt Assassination, Fedora, Elmyr

Reference:

http://www.livelinks.com/sumeria/politics/supermol.html

Charlie Chaplin:
Will the Fake Charlie Chaplin Please Stand Up?

At a fancy-dress ball in Monte Carlo some years ago, there was a contest for the best imitation of Charlie Chaplin. The chaps who won first, second, and third prizes must have all been very talented, and certainly pleased the audiences—but none of them really equaled the art of the man who only won fourth. That loser was Charlie himself, who had heard about the contest and decided to see how well he could imitate himself.

See also:

F for Fake, Noon Blue Apples, Kerry Thornley

Reference:

The Act of Creation, by Arthur Koestler, Macmillan, New York, 1964, p. 402

Mona Charen

Mona Charen, a syndicated columnist, has recently suggested that the citizens of the United States have become too suspicious of their government and lack all faith. She blames this on Hollywood, saying of recent films:

> There are conspiracies everywhere. It isn't just Oliver Stone who peddles this stuff, though he is the worst offender—presenting falsified "historical" dramas. In film after film—even the essentially harmless "Independence Day"—the theme of a government that keeps secrets and engages in conspiracies is taken for granted.

Ms. Charen finds this notion of conspiratorial government (best typified by Stone's *JFK* and *Nixon*) "seriously demoralizing," "far-fetched," and downright "preposterous," and asks cuttingly, "Does everything have to be a conspiracy?"

We better keep an eye on this woman: She sounds like one of Them.

Reference:

San Jose Mercury News, March 30, 1997

Chicago Malaria Study

Nearly 400 convicts in the Chicago area were infected with malaria during World War II, as part of a crash program to develop new malaria drugs. Although the subjects were given general information that they were helping the war effort, they were not provided with full information about what was being done to them, as later demanded by the standards of the Nuremberg War Crimes Tribunal.

This case was actually cited by the defense in the case of the Nazi doctors at Nuremberg, as one of many precedents to defend their behavior in aiding their own war effort.

See also:

AIDS Conspiracy Theories, Cuban Germ War: Germ Warfare, Haitian Experiment Claim, El Salvador

Reference:

http://home.earthlink.net/~bkonop/GermIncidents2.html

Noam Chomsky

Noam Chomsky (1928–) has had two careers—one as a distinguished theorist in the field of linguistic science, and another as our most brilliant, incisive, hard-hitting, and extremist critic of American foreign policy. For some reason (see *Bilderbergers*), the major media has virtually never given any coverage to Professor Chomsky's work in his role as social critic; perhaps they do not think his ideas are worth discussing.

Like many critics of the left and some of the far right (pacifism and isolationism sometimes overlap) Chomsky has been opposed to all the wars our government has gotten us into in this century. His special emphasis has been on developing the theory of libertarian socialism (and/or anarchism) as an alternative to power politics of all sorts. (See *Lord Acton, Government as Criminal Conspiracy, Benjamin R. Tucker.*) Chomsky's most original and damaging critiques of the Establishment, however, deal with the role of the media, a running theme in all his social thought and the major topic of his *Necessary Illusions: Thought Control in Democratic Societies.*

As Chomsky sees it, and documents at length, the media does not serve a "watchdog" role but usually acts as Ministry of

Propaganda for the Establishment. This does not mean that he believes free speech and a free press do not exist; he merely argues that the spectrum of viewpoints presented to the public is increasingly narrow and many criticisms are marginalized to the extent that only those devoted to research can ever find them. (He has been marginalized in precisely that way for most of his career and to a large extent he still is.)

The major media are owned by a few billionaires, and those who occupy managerial positions also belong to lower rungs of the same privileged elite. Statistically, the same perceptions, viewpoints, and attitudes become more and more dominant. Those with deviant perspectives are "weeded out." The public thus gets to see a small part of the actual political spectrum—from far right to middle of the road—and virtually never learns of alternatives, a process Chomsky calls the "manufacture of consent," a phrase borrowed ironically from conservative intellectual Walter Lippman, who in 1921 said, in effect, that tyrannies control people by force but democracies "manufacture" the "consent" of the governed. Chomsky regards all forms of manufactured consent as Orwellian mind control.

Thus, in his criticisms of the Vietnam war, Chomsky emphasizes that the major media offered a choice he calls "Tweedledee and Tweedledum," i.e., the so-called hawks and the so-called doves. He put it in these words:

Both sides, the doves and the hawks, agreed on something: We have a right to carry out aggression against South Vietnam. In fact, they didn't even admit that aggression was taking place. They called the war the "defense" of South Vietnam, using "defense" for "aggression" in the standard Orwellian manner. We were in fact attacking South Vietnam just as much as the Russians are attacking Afghanistan.

Like the Russians in Afghanistan, we first had to establish a government in Vietnam that would invite us in, and until we found one we had to overturn government after government. Finally we got one that invited us in, after we'd been there attacking the countryside and the population for years. That's aggression. Nobody thought that was wrong, or rather, anyone who thought it was wrong was not admitted to the discussion.

Chomsky continues to apply this type of analysis to the official propaganda line of all recent U.S. foreign policy.

See also:

Mona Charen, Council on Foreign Relations, Media criticized, *Yankee and Cowboy War*

References:

Chomsky general—

http://wwwdsp.ucd.ie/~daragh/chomsky.html

Vietnam—

http://worldmedia.com/archive

Necessary Illusions: Thought Control in Democratic Societies, by Noam Chomsky, South End Press, Boston, 1989

Christians Awake AIDS Theory

A sincere group of God-fearing Americans, Christians Awake, has proposed one of the most original AIDS conspiracy theories: it is all the fault of the *Freemasons*.

According to Christians Awake, the Masons have run this country from the beginning, and they are a secret society because they are all Gay. Even George Washington was Gay, and the Washington monument is a phallic symbol. After almost 200 years of this Gay Freemasonic government, God vexed most irate and created AIDS to punish the culprits.

Ronald Reagan, according to this group, is another Freemason and shares the guilt not only for AIDS but for placing Jewish communists in government. And he secretly supported abortion, too.

See also:

GENISIS, Our Lady of the Roses, UFO/Satanic Conspiracy

Reference:

Christians Awake, PO Box 3513, Birmingham, AL 35211

Church of Mary Magdalene

The Church of Mary Magdalene plays a key role in what conspiriologists call the *Priory of Sion* mystery (or the Rennes-le-Chateau mystery.)

Béranger Saunière, the parish priest of Rennes-le-Chateau in southern France near the end of the last century, who built the church (and also built many other religious structures in the Rennes-le-Chateau area), had been so poor in 1885 that he relied on the generosity of parishioners to survive. Suddenly, within a few years, he became inexplicably rich and began the career of church-building that lasted until his death in 1917. He left the secret of where he got his wealth to his housekeeper, Marie Dernaud, who died of a stroke before revealing it to anyone else.

This small town mystery has attracted vast attention in Europe, and the various theories about it have even crossed the Atlantic in several popular books. Some claim that Father Saunière had found the lost treasure of the *Knights Templar;* others that he found even longer-buried Visigoth gold. A third theory claims he performed some service for, or simply blackmailed, the royal von Hapsburgs; and a fourth says he was blackmailing the Vatican itself. Another speculation claims Saunière had rediscovered the secret of alchemy.

The mystery grows more sinister when one learns that the priest who heard Father Saunière's final confession found it so shocking that he denied the last rites to the dying man and refused to grant absolution.

The Church of Mary Magdalene has mysteries of its own. For instance, the Stations of the Cross have distinctly odd features: One shows a Scotsman in kilts watching the crucifixion, and another seems to show conspirators carrying Jesus' (dead or unconscious?) body out of the tomb in the middle of the night (to fake the resurrection?). Worse yet, over the entrance to this eldritch edifice, Saunière carved the words, THIS PLACE IS ACCURSED.

See also:

Dagobert II, *GENISIS,* Noon Blue Apples, Von Hapsburg Family

Church of the Sub-Genius

See:

"Bob," The Con, Slack

CIA

See:

James Jesus Angleton, CIA LSD Research, Charles Colson, Gladio, John Hull, E. Howard Hunt, "The Whole Bay of Pigs Thing"

CIAC

Not a front for the CIA (we hope!), the CIAC (or Computer Incident Advisory Capability) functions as part of the U.S. Department of Energy and maintains a website (listed as reference below) that keeps computer users advised concerning real and imaginary viruses. In an update posted on April 7, 1997, CIAC noted that

> The Internet is constantly being flooded with information about computer viruses and Trojans. However, interspersed among real virus notices are computer virus hoaxes. While these hoaxes do not infect systems, they are still time consuming and costly to handle. *At CIAC,* we find that we are spending *much more time de-bunking hoaxes than handling real virus incidents.* [Italics added.]

In other words, a considerable minority among us are unusually malicious or have a very strange sense of humor.

See also:

Ladder Conspiracies

Reference:

http://ciac.llnl.gov/ciac/CIACHoaxes.html

CIA LSD Research

In 1953, the Central Intelligence Agency began a series of experiments with LSD (lysergic acid diethylamide), the most potent mind-altering drug known at the time (or now). The LSD research was part of a larger program called *MK-ULTRA,* which also included CIA-financed studies of hypnosis, electroshock, lobotomy, and sensory deprivation.

In one "experimental study" called Operation Midnight Climax, the Agency used a house of prostitution in San Francisco where the whores spiked clients' drinks with acid, while CIA spooks watched the results through one-way glass. At Lexington Narcotics Hospital, black patients (but not others) were given steadily increasing doses of the psychedelic for 75 days.

Congressional investigations in the 1970s discovered that between 1955 and 1958 thousands of U.S. citizens had been given LSD without their knowledge or consent; the government eventually paid millions of dollars in damages to incapacitated victims and the families of those who committed suicide.

See also:

AIDS Conspiracy Theories, MK-ULTRA, Tuskegee Syphilis Study

References:

The Big Book of Conspiracies, by Doug Moench, Paradox Press, New York, 1995, pp. 48–50

Circumcision Conspiracy

Although male circumcision is accepted by our society at large as a rational health measure, and only female circumcision (as practiced in other and, hence, less rational societies) is regarded as barbaric, some people have rather strongly held opposing views about this.

Dr. Paul Fleiss, generally best known as the father of the famous "Beverly Hills Madam" Heidi Fleiss—and the pediatrician for Madonna and Child—is also a vehement foe of circumcision. In his paper, *The Function of the Foreskin,* he argues that male circumcision has no more health justification than female circumcision. The real purpose of the ritual, he says, is the same as in the female version: to destroy the most sensitive sexual parts and thereby decrease sexual desire. "Those of us who have been circumcised were mutilated." He says the infant's cry during this rite "is not like any other cry you hear from a baby" and calls it a "cry of severe pain."

The National Organization of Restoring Men (NORM), with 21 chapters in the United States, attributes its inspiration to hippie mothers of the 1960s who realized that circumcision was "counterintuitive" and asked, "How could all males be born with a birth defect?"

Doctors Opposing Circumcision (DOC), headquartered in Seattle, says its educational programs have cut the male circumcision rate in this country from 90 percent when they began to 60 percent now.

Similar criticisms of other accepted medical theories will be found under *AIDS Conspiracy Theories* and *Dr. Wilhelm Reich*.

Reference:

"Bring Back My Foreskin to Me," by Paul Krassner, *The Realist*, Venice, Calif., Summer 1997

Cisalpine Bank

See:

Roberto Calvi, Paul "The Gorilla" Marcinkus

President Bill Clinton

See:

A-Albionic, Bilderbergers, Council on Foreign Relations, Princess Di's Death, Vince Foster

Cloned Out of Existence?

AIDS activist Larry Kramer noted a dark side to recent cloning experiments, remarking that "Gay people are always terrified we'll be genetically altered out of existence."

See also:

AIDS Conspiracy Theories

Reference:

New York Times, February 27, 1997

Jean Cocteau

Jean Cocteau (1889–1963) ranks as the most versatile artist of the 20th century, having worked in poetry, drama, graphic arts, painting, ballet, and cinema (his best-known works were in film: *Blood of a Poet* and *Beauty and the Beast*). He was also one of the founders of surrealism and, allegedly, the 23rd Grandmaster of the ultra-secret *Priory of Sion.*

Cocteau's involvement with the enigmatic Priory is documented by a charter of the Priory signed with his name. Michael Baigent, Henry Lincoln, and Richard Leigh had the signature checked by two experts who declared it Cocteau's handwriting and not a forgery—which settles the matter, except for those who remember *Elmyr* and *Clifford Irving.*

See also:

Church of Mary Magdalene, Gerard de Sede, Holy Order of the Lemon, Noon Blue Apples

Reference:

Holy Blood, Holy Grail, by Michael Baigent, Henry Lincoln, and Richard Leigh, Delacorte, New York, 1982

Collier Brothers

Kenneth and James Collier are brothers who both have long careers in journalism (Kenneth chiefly with the *New York Daily News,* and James with the *Miami News* and *Hialah Home News)* and they happen to believe that election frauds have become common since about 1970. They attribute this to the vulnerability of the computer system that tabulates early votes and projects expected final tallies, usually with astounding accuracy. This amazing precision, the Colliers believe, is not due to the marvels of technology but to the fact that only one computer system is used to provide projections for NBC, ABC, CBS, Associated Press, and United Press International. This system is vulnerable, the Colliers allege, to manipulation by sinister forces such as the *CIA*. The Colliers have written a book, *Votescam,* detailing their beliefs, and they have also filed lawsuits against persons and groups they consider parts of the "Votescam" conspiracy—including the Republican National Committee, the League of Women Voters, and Justice Scalia of the Supreme Court.

See also:

Bisociation, Noon Blue Apples, Veil

Reference:

Conspiracies, Cover-Ups and Crimes, by Jonathon Vankin, Paragon House, New York, 1992, pp. 19–32

Charles Colson

One of the many Nixon associates sent to prison as a result of the Watergate conspiracy, Charles Colson later became a born-again Christian; even more interestingly, he told *Time* magazine, "I don't say this to my people. They'd think I'm nuts. I think the CIA killed Dorothy Hunt."

See also:

Flight 553, E. Howard Hunt, "The Whole Bay of Pigs Thing"

Reference:

The Yankee and Cowboy War, by Carl Oglesby, Berkley Medallion Books, New York, 1977, p. 227, citing *Time* for July 8, 1974.

The Committee to Protect the Rights and Privileges of Low-Cost Housing

In 1973 in Switzerland, journalist Matthiew Paoli published *Les Dessous* (in English, *Undercurrents)*, a book about a monarchist conspiracy that he had uncovered in his own country and in France. This "conspiracy"—or this "affinity group," if you wish less paranoia and more charity of thought—originally came to Paoli's attention when, in the late 1960s, he found some copies of their internal newsletter, *Circuit,* in a chapter of the **Grand Loge Alpina,** the largest **Freemasonic** order in Switzerland.

The journal Paoli found seemed concerned only with vine cultivation, genealogy, and astrology but had many odd kinks and hermetic references, evidently intelligible only to initiates. Paoli found it listed its publisher as the Committee to Protect the Rights and Privileges of Low-Cost Housing—although it seldom discussed housing, low-cost or otherwise—but when he went to the address given, he found no such committee there.

With helpful hints from a few uncharacteristically communicative GLA members, Paoli finally found the true address of the **Priory of Sion,** the actual publishers of *Circuit.* The address turned out to lie within the de Gaulle government in Paris, at the Committee for Public Safety (once the engine of terrorism during the French Revolution, under the leadership of Robespierre, but now quite respectable). The managers of the committee appeared men of high culture and proven patriotism—André Malraux, Nobel laureate in literature, influential art critic, and Resistance fighter during the Nazi occupation; and *Pierre Plantard de Saint Clair,* scholar, occultist, and another former Resistance fighter (who had survived capture and torture by the Gestapo).

Both men had a long record of loyalty to de Gaulle. Nonetheless, Paoli felt that much of the mystical politics of *Circuit* either intended to restore the remnants of the Royal Family to the throne in France, or else it didn't mean anything at all—a shaggy dog story, or "mere" hoax (as distinguished from a purposeful or profitable hoax).

Most of Paoli's book tries to show, from the few issues of *Circuit* that he managed to get his hands on, that the group behind this magazine, the Priory of Sion (see also **Church of Mary Magdalene** and **Gerard de Sede**), wrote in a kind of code (wine making = a very specialized eugenics, because wine = human "blood," i.e., human genes in modern language) and that they seemed concerned with the special "blood" (genes) of the French Royal Family and of some related noble families in Spain, England, and elsewhere.

A great deal of Paoli's evidence does not quite lend itself to this theory or to any other rational explanation. For instance, the cover of the first issue of *Circuit* he saw—the one that originally aroused his curiosity—shows a map of France with the Star of David superimposed upon it, and something that looks much like a flying saucer hovering above.

Although the Star of David means something positive to Jews everywhere, it also means a great deal not-positive to anti-semitic Conspiracy Theorists. Superimposing a Star of David on a nation, in anti-semitic literature, generally implies that the nation has come under control of the alleged "International Jewish Conspiracy." Could a group named after Sion (an alternative title for Israel) also preach anti-semitism? Evidently not, in this case. *Circuit* strongly implies that the "wine"(genes) of the French aristocracy relates directly to the "wine" (genes) of the kings of Judea in Old Testament times, especially David and Solomon.

But what does this have to do with that flying saucer on the cover of *Circuit?* (See **UFO Conspiracies**.)

Oddly, after the publication of *Les Dessous,* Paoli took a journalistic assignment in Israel. The government there soon arrested him on suspicion of spying, found him guilty, and shot him.

See also:

Knights Templar, Merovingians, P2 Conspiracy, *Protocols of the Elders of Zion*

Reference:

Holy Blood, Holy Grail, by Michael Baigent, Henry Lincoln, and Richard Leigh, Delacorte, New York, 1982

The Con

The Con, short for *The* Conspiracy, controls all the other (and lesser) conspiracies you ever heard of, and some you never heard of or even imagined. The identity of the Con and all its members is known to J.R. *"Bob"* Dobbs, founder, Mahatma, Messiah, and CEO of the *Church of the Sub-Genius/*Sub-Genius Foundation. The Con includes the *Bilderbergers, Trilateral Commission Supporters,* the *Illuminati,* communist clones, *Nazi hell creatures,* interstellar bankers, and the leaders of all rival churches and cults. All *Pinks* (normal or "adjusted" humans) are indentured servants of the Con.

Many think the Con is just a joke or a parody of other conspiracy theories. To such doubters, the Church of the Sub-Genius says that this is "the *Time of Pee*—the time foretold, when people would be judged not by works, nor by family, nor even by looks, but by their urine.

"They listen to you through your telephone without its even being off the hook, and record you through satellites that can peer down any street, *anywhere.* . . .

"They kick your door in anytime they want to. All they have to yell is 'DRUGS!' and your spouse is in jail, your kids are farmed out to the state, your car and house are suddenly theirs. . . .

"Nobody up there is a friend of yours; nobody up there wants you to have what you would call freedom. The purpose of 'government' is to produce consumers and workers who will keep the cost of labor down, and the profits high for the owners. . . .

"For this has become so crooked and perverse a nation that your precious bodily fluids are no longer your own, and not even your bladder or bloodstream are private. *There is no place where they may not watch.*"

According to the "Book of Urinomics," an ancient sub-genius text recently published in *Revelation X*, "And the Beast said: 'By their pee shall ye judge them, and by thy pee shall ye be judged. And all will be divided by their pee. And in the snow shall their names be written.'"

See also:

"Bob", Mona Charen, Government as Criminal Conspiracy, Corey Hammond, S.O.B.

References:

http://www.subgenius.com

Revelation X, translated from the original tongues by the Sub-Genius Foundation, Simon and Schuster, New York, 1994

The Constitution: Fact, Fiction, or Fraud?

In *The Constitution: Fact or Fiction,* Eugene Schoder and Micki Nellis argue that the constitution was nullified on March 9, 1933 by President Franklin Roosevelt's declaration of national emergency. What has followed in the intervening 65 years, the authors describe in their subtitle: *The Nation's Descent from a Constitutional Republic through a Constitutional Dictatorship to an Unconstitutional Dictatorship.*

Senate Report 92549 written in 1973 says bluntly that since 1933 "the United States has been in a state of declared national emergency. . . . A majority of the people of the United States have lived all their lives under emergency rule. . . . (we now live in) a permanent state of national emergency."

The authors cite 470 Federal laws, since 1933, that have steadily increased the president's "emergency" powers. They claim this is why—although we haven't had a Declaration of War by Congress since 1941—American troops have been in battle continually in engagements great and small in one far-off place or another: our recent presidents have trod the world like Roman emperors rather than like the limited executives authorized by the constitution.

Under the 470 emergency power rules, the president may seize property, send military forces anywhere without public or congressional approval, institute martial law, restrict travel, seize and control all forms of communication, etc. And once the emergency had been declared by President Roosevelt, nobody could end the dictatorial situation except the president himself, by declaring the emergency over, or by a future president declaring the emergency over. Truman, Eisenhower, Kennedy, Johnson, Nixon, Ford, Carter, Reagan, Bush, and Clinton have all declined to do so. (See *Lord Acton*.)

That ultra-individualist, Lysander Spooner (1808–1887), not only thought the Constitution was dead but that it deserved to be dead. A lifelong abolitionist, Spooner hated slavery; but he hated the Civil War even more, and re-examining the Constitution skeptically, he wrote six pamphlets (*No Treason*, I-VI) arguing that the Constitution had no authority to bind later generations to remain subject to the federal government. Defining the Constitution as a contract, in the common law sense, Spooner, a superb lawyer, applies the rules of contract law to it and proves that, legally, it binds nobody but those who gave consent to it in 1789:

And it does not so much as even purport to be a contract between persons now existing. It purports, at most, to be only a contract between persons living eighty years ago. [Spooner wrote in 1869.] . . . Furthermore, we know, historically, that

only a small portion even of the people then existing were con-
sulted on the subject, or asked, or permitted to express either
their consent or dissent in any formal manner. [Blacks, women,
and unpropertied white males had no chance to give consent or
dissent.]

Those persons, if any, who did give their consent formally, are
all dead now. Most of them have been dead forty, fifty, sixty, or
seventy years, and the Constitution, so far as it was their con-
tract, died with them. They had no natural power or right to
make it obligatory upon their children.

Spooner, following common law, also insists that the Constitution can only bind those who voted for it, for a contract cannot
bind those who did not give written or oral assent. Thus, I can
make a contract with HarperCollins, which calls on me to write a
certain book and requires them to pay me a certain sum; but such
a contract does not bind Norman Mailer, Danielle Steele, or
Stephen King to write anything, nor does it bind HarperCollins to
pay them anything, nor does it bind any other publisher to pay me
moneys, except as specified in other contracts. Thus, if the
Constitution is a contract, it does not bind anybody now alive to
do anything whatsoever.

Spooner also examines the evolution of the American government and argues, like **R. Buckminster Fuller** and *Ezra Pound,*
that it is owned and controlled by international bankers. He
concludes:

. . . the writer thinks it proper to say that, in his opinion, the
Constitution is no such instrument as it has generally been
assumed to be; but that by false interpretations, and naked
usurpations, the government has been made in practice a very
widely, and almost wholly, different thing from what the

Constitution itself purports to authorize. He has heretofore written much, and could write much more, to prove that such is the truth. But whether the Constitution really be one thing, or another, this much is certain—that it has either authorized such a government as we have had, or has been powerless to prevent it. In either case, it is unfit to exist.

See also:

American Dynasty, Federal Reserve Bank, Noon Blue Apples, David Rockefeller

References:

Fact or fiction—

http://buffalo-creek-press.com/cffrev.htm

Spooner's critique—

http://www.creative.net/~star/notrsn6.htm

Conspiracy Nation

Conspiracy Nation appears as both a print magazine and a regular online feature of the World Wide Web, although the electronic version only contains highlights of the print version. It appears open to conspiracy theories of all sorts, right-wing and left-wing, plausible and outright kooky. Some recent highlights: an article on how "the U.S. National Security State" managed the murders of **Martin Luther King Jr.** and Malcolm X; how "selective perception" maintains the belief that all assassinations are the work of lone nuts; evidence that Mark Chapman was under "mind control" when he shot John Lennon; how banks arrange to loan customers' money at high interest and pay the customers low interest; why the independent counsel in the **Vince Foster** case, Robert Fisk, should have been disqualified for conflict of interest.

For a sample see also:

Princess Di's Death: Conspiracy Theories

Reference:

http://www.shout.net/~bigred/cn.html

Nadine Cool

See:

Demonic Duck, *MS. Magazine,* Dr. Kenneth Olson, Recovered Memory Therapy

William Cooper

William Cooper (or as he prefers, Bill Cooper) is a former naval intelligence officer who has been active on the *UFO conspiracy* lecture circuit for several years. He claims, among other things, that he personally saw papers about the alliance between our government and the alien invaders; that the treaty establishing this détente has repeatedly been broken by the aliens, but our government cannot stop them because the aliens have the superior weaponry; that alien scientists are behind both cattle mutilations and human abductions; that the notorious CIA/cocaine connection was begun as a method of obtaining funds (i.e., "drug money") unknown to either the president or Congress for certain CIA-alien conspiracies; that *George Bush* was in the CIA much longer than is openly admitted and that Bush's offshore oil rigs were actually a front for cocaine smuggling; and that the Secret Service itself assassinated John F. Kennedy when he tried to stop the CIA/alien conspiracy.

Cooper has classified the kinds of aliens haunting our planet:

1. *The ordinary* **Greys**, *whom we all know from abduction stories*
2. *Another type of Grey with a big nose*
3. *Tall blonde Nordic types*
4. *"Orange ones"*

Among their points of origin: Orion, the Pleiades, Betelgeuse, Barnard's star, and Zeta Reticuli.

In some speeches (e.g., one the present author heard at Phenomicon in Atlanta, Georgia, in 1991) Cooper says he is not sure any of the above is true, and that he might have been deceived. But in that case, he points out, the government is deliberately deceiving some of its own employees in the intelligence service and spreading the alien invasion idea to cover up and muddy the waters about something else—something (Cooper says) that must be *even more sinister* than selling us out to outer space monsters.

See also:

Aiwass, Philip J. Corso, Charles Fort, John F. Kennedy Assassination, Merovingians, James Oberg

References:

General—

Bill Cooper Exposes Top Secrets, Shining Star Productions, 7820 East Evans, Scottsdale, AZ 85260 (two-hour video)

Varieties of aliens—

Cooper quoted in *Revelations: Alien Contact and Human Deception*, Jacques Vallee, Ballantine, New York, 1991, p. 63

"Corruption" Index

Transparency International, a nongovernmental, nonprofit organization, in collaboration with Goettingen University, publishes a yearly index of relative corruption and bribery for the major nations of the world, as judged by business people who deal with many government officials regularly. Insofar as "corruption" and/or bribery represent the most blatant forms of conspiracy, this poll can also be considered a rough index of the perception of conspiracy.

Research on the index has been led by Dr. Johann Graf Lamsdorff with a research team of Goettingen University. Dr. Lamsdorff stated that "the Index is a poll of polls, putting together the subjective evaluations of business people." On a scale where 10 represents a total lack of clandestine/corrupt behavior and 0 represents the abyss of total corruption, the ten purest nations and ratings for 1996 were:

New Zealand	9.43
Denmark	9.33
Sweden	9.08
Finland	9.05
Canada	8.96
Norway	8.87
Singapore	8.80
Switzerland	8.76
Netherlands	8.71
Australia	8.60

And the ten most corrupt nations, in the evaluations of business persons, were:

Indonesia	2.65
India	2.63

Russia	2.58
Venezuela	2.50
Cameroons	2.46
China	2.43
Bangladesh	2.29
Kenya	2.21
Pakistan	1.00
Nigeria	0.69

Other nations in which readers may be interested ranked as follows: England, 8.44; Germany, 8.27; Israel, 7.71; United States, 7.66; Japan, 7.05.

Reference:

http://www.GWDG.DE/~uwvw/icr.htm

Philip J. Corso

Philip J. Corso, a retired Army Intelligence officer, has endorsed one of the most far-out of the theories about the *Roswell UFO crash* in 1947. According to Corso, real aliens crashed in Roswell and the U.S. military has been preparing for war with them ever since; the real purpose of *Ronald Reagan*'s SDI (Strategic Defense Initiative, widely known as "Star Wars" even before Corso gave forth) was not to block Soviet missiles but to prepare for war with what the military calls EBEs, or extraterrestrial biological entities.

Senator Strom Thurmond wrote the introduction to Corso's book *The Day After Roswell* but later repudiated it.

Corso's integrity has been harshly questioned by Kenn Thomas, who points out that Corso, 82, was a longtime CIA officer and implicated in several of the *John F. Kennedy assassination* theories. *James Oberg* has also charged that not only Corso but all the "former intelligence officers" who have supported the alien conspiracy theory are engaged in a massive disinformation campaign to hide actual U.S. government activities by a screen of confusing and conflicting UFO yarns.

See also:

Alien Autopsy, William Cooper, Robert Morning Sky, Planet X

References:

General—

Time, June 23, 1997, p. 66

James Oberg—

See entry for him

Kenn Thomas—

Fortean Times, No. 105, December 1997

Council on Foreign Relations

The Council on Foreign Relations, founded in 1921, grew out of the "round table groups" of *Cecil Rhodes* and the tireless energy of *Colonel Edward House.* As seen by themselves and their propagandists or friends, the round table groups in general aimed at securing "a new world order"[1] in which our previous chaos and international anarchy would give way to stability and peace.

According to its critics, the purpose of the CFR and other round tables (e.g., England's Royal Institute of International Affairs) is

---

[1]The origin of this controversial phrase remains debatable, but it was used as early as the July 17, 1926, issue of the *Saturday Evening Post,* to describe Col. House's goal in supporting the League of Nations and helping found the Council on Foreign Relations.

to ensure that a cabal of *Insiders* (rich Anglo-American families) rule more and more of the world forever and ever. According to the radical, rabid right, the whole thing is a front for the *Illuminati.*

According to Prof. *Carroll Quigley*, it was through the CFR that many liberal-left activists achieved high political positions in America—but "the power that these energetic Left-wingers exercised was never their own power or Communist power but was ultimately the power of the international financial coterie." All liberal-to-Marxist groups, if they become big enough to make a difference, Quigley says, ultimately derive their money from "Thomas Lamont and the Morgan Bank. . . (and) a whole network of interlocking tax-exempt foundations." Quigley expresses basic agreement with the goals of this financial elite, and the *John Birch Society* regards him as "accidentally" spilling the beans on them; but *A-Albionic* has a more subtle view of Quigley's role.

The *Washington Post* has acknowledged that the CFR is "the nearest thing we have to a ruling establishment in the United States." As of 1996 (see source below), CFR members in high places included President Bill Clinton, White House advisers George Stephanopoulos and John Gibbons, Associate Director of National Security Gordon Adams, Secretary of State Warren Christopher, Director of CIA John M. Deutsch, Chairman of the Joint Chiefs of Staff John Shalikashvili, Secretary of the Treasury Robert E. Rubin, Office of National Drug Control Policy Director Barry McCaffrey, Deputy Secretary of State Strobe Talbot, Arms Control and Disarmament Director John D. Holum, U.S. Information Agency Director Joseph Duffey, Supreme Court Justices Sandra Day O'Connor, Ruth Bader Ginsburg, and Stephen Breyer, Secretary of Housing and Urban Development Henry Cisneros, Secretary of the Interior Bruce Babbitt, Secretary of Labor Thomas Williamson Jr., 13 Senators, and 13 Representatives. Other CFR members in government include the ambassadors to

Australia, Chile, Czech Republic, Ethiopia, France, India, Italy, Japan, Kazakhstan, Korea, Mexico, Nepal, Nigeria, Philippines, Poland, Romania, Russia, Slovenia, South Africa, Spain, Syria, Ukraine, and the United Kingdom.

The major foundations are also stuffed with CFR people in top offices. The Carnegie Corporation has Newton Minow as Chairman of the Board and 18 other CFR folk in high positions; the Ford Foundation has seven, including their chairman of the board; the Heritage Foundation has five; the John D. and Catherine T. Mac-Arthur Foundation has nine, including their president; the Rockefeller Brothers Fund has nine, including the president and the vice president; the Rockefeller Family Fund has three; the Rockefeller Foundation has nine, including the chairman and the president; and the Twentieth Century Fund has 15, including the chairman, the president, and the vice president.

CFR members in the media include the president of ABC-TV, a vice president of Associated Press, two editors of *Atlantic Monthly,* two of *Business Week,* the president of CNN-TV, the chairman of *Forbes,* the editor in chief of *Entertainment Weekly,* two editors of the *Nation,* six of *National Review,* six of the *New Republic,* one at *Newsday,* one at the *New York Review of Books,* 16 at the *New York Times,* 10 at *Time,* 10 at *US News and World Report,* etc. (All these lists have been condensed to avoid boredom.)

If the CFR had millions of members like, say, the Presbyterian Church, this list might not mean much. But the CFR only has 3,200 members.

See also:

Gnomes of Zurich, Hughes vs. Rockefeller, Octopus, P2 Conspiracy, Fletcher Prouty

References:

New American, September 16,1996, pp. 13–19

Creation Science

Creation Science, also known to its believers as Good Science, contradicts all the Bad Science taught in most of our institutions of higher learning. Creation Science/Good Science has its own institutes and universities, its own Ph.D.'s, its own curriculum, and, like the Committee for Scientific Investigation of Claims of the Paranormal or the Vatican, its own methods of distinguishing between Good Science and Bad Science.

Basic tenets of Creationism/Good Science include: the physical universe has not always existed but was supernaturally created; the phenomenon of life did not develop by natural processes but was specially and supernaturally created by a personal Creator; each kind of plant and animal was created specially and none evolved from any other plant or animal; humans especially never evolved but were created with supernatural souls unlike any mere animals; etc. In short, Good Science is the science that agrees with the Judeo-Christian scriptures.

The Institute for Creation Research, typical of this movement, has a staff of seven Ph.D.'s, all with degrees from prestigious universities including Harvard and UCLA, one Ed.D. and one M.D. All have impressive credentials in their fields.

ICR has its own recommended reading list of Good Science. This includes, e.g., *What Is Creation Science?*, by Henry M. Morris and E. G. Parker, *Evolution: The Fossils Still Say No*, by Duane Gish, *Have You Been Brainwashed?*, by Duane Gish, etc., and a selection of books for "unsaved scientists." The fact that most of you have never heard of any of these works just shows the extent of the control that the evolutionist conspiracy has over the media.

See also:

AIDS Conspiracy Theories, Corrydon Hammond, Hemp Conspiracy, Hollow Earth, Dr. Wilhelm Reich, UFO/Satanic Conspiracy

References:

http://www.icr.org/abouticr/tenets.htm

http://www.icr.org/goodsci/faq-gs.htm

Crop Circles

The first reports of crop circles date from the 1950s in England, but the number began to increase rapidly in the 1980s and still continues to increase, in England and elsewhere. The circles always appear overnight and have been found in fields of corn, wheat, barley, oats, etc. The plants are all bent in the same direction with their stems, branches, and leaves interwoven in a symmetry that irresistibly suggests intelligent design or even artistry to most viewers. The crops are never damaged. In some cases, *orange lights* in the sky are allegedly seen just before the circles appear.

One farmer, Geoff Cooper, suggested that helicopters might be causing the mysterious circles and complained to the army. They said that a helicopter could only make the shapes found in Cooper's fields "if it was flying upside down and stationary." Cooper says another neighbor believed the circles were caused by hedgehogs rolling over and over in the fields, but Cooper calculated that it would take 40,000 of them to make all the circles in his field overnight.

Other theories devised in the '80s and still popular include:

1. *Violent atmospheric disturbances, or vortexes*
2. *Lung-mei, or earth energies believed in by most Chinese*
3. *UFO landing sites*
4. *Hoaxers*

The most elaborate theory, by a team of scientific investigators, suggested that some technicians working on the Strategic Defense Initiative (SDI, or "Star Wars") were playing an elaborate joke, using very high intensity lasers to generate and project beams of ultraviolet light. High intensity UV light cohered into lasers ionizes the air, which acts as a conductor for electrical energy that could form the circles and also occasionally create the orange lights (plasma.) One member of the group suggested that SDI technicians could not afford to get involved in such pranks and proposed that a hacker had found his way into their control system.

John Michell proposed that the circles were messages from the Earth itself, or Gaia (the Greek Earth goddess) as some prefer, and that we should learn to read them as art and prophecy.

All of this began to retreat into second place when the hoax theory seemed confirmed by no less than nine groups of hoaxers who demonstrated their techniques to the press. The hoax theory, however, had one outstanding flaw: New circles continued to appear and many of them had traits that none of the hoaxers could duplicate.

A new theory has been put forth by a person rejoicing in the wonderful name Buddha Maitreya. Mr. Maitreya says that such circles are known in Tibet as signals that an avatar (or prophet) is about to appear, and that we should look for somebody having the traits of Buddha, Jesus, and/or King Arthur. As for hoaxers, Mr. Maitreya says they, too, are part of the "Revelation" occurring:

> It doesn't matter if some of the crop circles are manmade. Man is made and moved by the Avatar. Even poems, books, songs— all forms of manmade communications are under the influence of the Holy Spirit.

See also:

Bisociation, *Secret Cipher of the UFOnauts,* Elmyr, UFO Conspiracy Theories, Orson Welles

References:

Cooper helicopter/hedgehog theories—
http://www.newphys.se/elektromagnum/physics/KeelyNet/ufo/england.asc
SDI theory—
http://www.newphys.se/elektromagnum/physics/KeelyNet/ufo/circles1.asc
Avatar theory—
http://www.bogo.co.uk/etheric/home.html

Aleister Crowley

Edward Alexander Crowley, born October 12, 1875 (in order to redeem the world from the disasters begun on that day in 1492, he claimed), led a life of mysticism, occultism, adventure, deception, and outrageous bohemianism. At the age of 23, in 1898, he joined the *Hermetic Order of the Golden Dawn,* an occult society dedicated to Gnostic and Cabalistic techniques of "spiritual advancement"—or what we nowadays call consciousness expansion. The Golden Dawn methods that Crowley mastered included attainment of those borderline states variously called "out of body experience," "guided visualization," or "ESP" and the assumption of god-forms—"becoming one" with various deities by techniques that occultists consider supernatural and skeptics would call enthusiastic method acting. Crowley himself habitually alternated between the occult and skeptical views.

Between 1900 and 1909 Crowley traveled widely and studied, sometimes at length and sometimes only briefly, in such non-European mystical systems as Buddhism, Taoism, a few varieties of Hinduism, and Sufism. In these years he became proficient in *dharana* (one-pointed concentration), *mantra* (the use of some repeated phrase to abolish wandering thought), yoga stretching/relaxing exercises, the Tantric technique of *sex magick* ("becoming one" with a deity by identifying that deity with a sexual partner during the sex act), and similar arts; he also developed his own system of eclectic mysticism by creating huge tables of "correspondences" to convert the terms of any mystical school into those of any other, e.g., the Greek god Pan, the Hindu god Shiva, the Tarot card called the Hanged Man, the color blue, the element water, the Hebrew letter mem, and the drug marijuana all refer to the "astral plane" Crowley numbers 23 (or to the 23rd level of human perception in another metaphor). To activate or re-activate that level, Crowley would invoke either Pan or Shiva in a ritual featuring marijuana, blue water, and wall decorations of the Hanged Man and the letter mem. And so on, through 32 levels.

In 1904, in Cairo, Crowley experienced a psychic revolution from which he emerged with *"Liber Al"* (also called *"The Book of the Law"*), a prophetic and perplexing document he always claimed he had "received," not written. At first, Crowley did not like the experience or the book, and managed to largely ignore them for nearly ten years. After 1914, however, he felt increasingly under their spell, and eventually he devoted the rest of his life to the "mission" the book imposed upon him. After 1919, he spoke of the Cairo experience as an encounter with a superhuman intelligence; one of his disciples, *Kenneth Grant,* has claimed the communicating entity emanated from the system of the double star, *Sirius,* while another student, *Israel Regardie,* prefers to say Crowley reached depths of the human evolutionary unconscious unknown to either Freud or Jung.

Whoever or whatever Crowley contacted, its major messages became the closest thing to dogmas in his largely agnostic mysticism: "Do what thou wilt shall be the whole of the law." "Love is the law, love under will." "Every man and every woman is a star." *Liber Al* also foretells wars and revolutions undreamed of by Crowley's conscious mind or by any other 1904 intellectual, but offers a promise of a new society rising from the universal wreckage somewhere in the future. Its last paragraph tells you that its message "is revealed and concealed." Revealed to those ready to receive it and concealed from others, perhaps?

During both World War I and World War II, Crowley appears to have worked for British Intelligence, although conflicting evidence suggests that he also worked for German Intelligence, at least in the first conflict. This mystery, and the unknown identity of the power or entity unleashed in Cairo, has made Crowley a central figure in most of the religious and demonological conspiracy theories of our time.

Early in his career, Crowley changed his first name to Aleister, so that the Cabalistic "number" of his name would add to *666*, identified with the *Antichrist* in the Revelation of St. John. He also delighted in frightening, baffling, and playing sadistic jokes on the orthodox and gullible. Thus, his reputation as a Satanist definitely does not result entirely from the paranoias of the religious right; he deliberately played the role at times, although always in an absurd and satirical manner.

In addition to "respectable" mystical practices from the traditions mentioned, Crowley also pioneered the study of shamanic/psychedelic states and used any and all mind-altering drugs with huge gusto, according to which of the 32 planes he wished to visit, ending his life as a heroin addict. He worked his way through the various degrees of several orthodox and unorthodox *Freemasonic* lodges, including the Scotch and York Rites, and the Order of Memphis and Mizraim, and the *Ordo Templi Orientis,* of which he became Outer Head. (The Inner Head presumably remains invisible to the un-Illuminated.) Since his death, Crowley has become accepted as the Magus of the New Aeon in some occult circles (a title roughly equivalent to the Master of the New Age) but still retains an even wider reputation (among rightwingers) as the major Satanist of our century.

Although he lived the second half of his life in acute poverty, Crowley also appears in many conspiracy theories as an ally of the international bankers, the *Illuminati,* or other world-movers; he presumably provided the demoniac energy behind their materialistic plots. His favorite Masonic symbol, the eye in the triangle, has also become mysteriously entangled with the *Great Seal of the United States,* the New Deal, the *Federal Reserve Bank,* and the *New World Order.*

Aleister Crowley died in 1947, at the age of 72, an amazing feat of longevity considering the shocks and strains he put on both his mind and body. He had written dozens of volumes of poetry, a few novels, scores of mystic essays, and had many achievements in the fields of chess, hunting, and mountain climbing, including the highest climb on the Himalayan peak K2 ever accomplished without oxygen tanks (1904; 23,000 feet).

See also:

Freemasonry, Golden Dawn, Illuminati, Merovingians, Ordo Templi Orientis, Rosicrucianism, 666

References:

http://www.crl.com/~thelema

The Eye in the Triangle, by Israel Regardie, New Falcon Press, Phoenix, Ariz., 1970

Portable Darkness, ed. by Scott Michaelson, Harmony Books, New York, 1989

The Crying of Lot 49

The Crying of Lot 49, by Thomas Pynchon, is often regarded as the ultimate post-modern novel; it is also the only novel, aside from the infamous and unspeakable *Illuminatus! Trilogy,* that deliberately attempts to maneuver the reader into and out of a paranoid framework *several times,* leaving each reader to decide after "the trip" which makes more sense—paranoia or consensus reality.

Basically, the plot concerns a lady named Oedipa Maas who is appointed executor of the estate of a fabulously rich former lover, who was also a compulsive practical joker. In attempting to handle the financial details of this estate, poor Oedipa stumbles again and again on evidence of an international conspiracy many centuries old; but in every case, she remembers, or tries to remember, that all this may be the last and most elaborate prank of her dead paramour.

Everything revolves around a mysterious corporation named Yoyodyne, and it did not help the present author's detachment to actually see a Yoyodyne factory in New Jersey one night (near Morristown). Was this proof that *Lot 49* is based on fact, or does it merely show that some young entrepreneur is a Pynchon fan and a prankster himself? Oedipa Maas faces that kind of challenge on virtually every page of the novel, as the links from Yoyodyne lead back to the Tristero postal system of the Middle Ages, a web spinning around the Bavarian *Illuminati* (which is never mentioned by name), and a strange clue taken from the dialogue of an old radio show, *The Shadow,* which starred *Orson Welles.*

Do the baskets on city streets saying WASTE really contain the acrostic *We Await Silent Tristero's Empire*? Does the horn, symbol of Tristero, contain hidden symbolism? Is a graffito saying:

D E A T H
Don't Ever Antagonize The Horn

part of the elaborate joke at Oedipa's expense, or sign of a real epoch-old plot against civilization?

Pynchon shows considerable knowledge of information theory and other scientific matters generally ignored by the literary intelligentsia. (In another book, *Gravity's Rainbow,* he uses calculus and quantum mechanics the way Joyce used Homer in *Ulysses.*) These are the only clues we have; he has never been interviewed and never allows himself to be photographed. They say he lives somewhere in California, but that may be a false lead; he might live anywhere, even next door to you.

It has even been suggested that Pynchon is a pen name for T.C. May (see ***Crypto-Anarchy***). In the same spirit, the present author suggests that he may be Dr. Jack Sarfatti, a quantum physicist with the most original cosmology in modern science. (See http://www.io.com/~hambone/web/sarfatti.html.) Why not? Two eerie fellows named Art Kleps and Jack Call have long insisted that "Robert Anton Wilson" is a pen name for Dr. Timothy Leary, and Dr. Leary has confessed to writing under pen names (in *Trajectories,* a magazine edited by Robert Anton Wilson, Summer 1989).

And both Charles Gimon and Dwight Eddins have found a religious element in Pynchon's black comedy: Like the Gnostics, Pynchon portrays humanity trapped in a universe manipulated by antihuman forces. Such a concept raises at once the possibility that some may know of tactics for fighting back. . . . (See ***Philip K. Dick*** and ***George I. Gurdjieff.***)

Selected references:

http://www.pomona.edu/pynchon/

http://www.hyperarts.com/

http://www.as.ua.edu/english/faculty/deddins.htm

Crypto-Anarchy

Crypto-space labels that part of cyberspace invisible to government snoopers—the high-tech equivalent of the survivalist communities of the far right. As Timothy May writes:

Strong cryptography, exemplified by RSA (a public key algorithm) and PGP (Pretty Good Privacy), provides encryption that essentially cannot be broken with all the computing power in the universe. . . . Digital mixes, or anonymous remailers, use crypto to create untraceable e-mail. . . . Digital cash, untraceable and anonymous (like real cash), is also coming.

J. Orlin Grabbe comments:

The government doesn't want you using cryptography, because they want to know where your money is, so they can get some of it. And they don't like you using drugs, unless the government is the dealer.

Virtual communities with virtual cash already exist in cryptospace. The first non-interest-bearing, non-taxable virtual money came into existence in Vancouver in 1983 and had spread as far south as San Diego by 1990. No visible trace of the idea moving further east has been found, but that doesn't mean that it isn't happening: They may be growing even more cryptic. . .

See also:

Desovereignization, Federal Reserve Bank, Internal Revenue Service, Ezra Pound

References:

General—

"Crypto-Anarchy and Virtual Communities," tcmay@netcom.com

Grabbe—

Quoted by T.C. May, above

Virtual cash already in existence—

Encyclopedia of Social Inventions, Institute of Social Inventions, London, 1990

CSETI

The Center for the Study of Extraterrestrial Intelligence (CSETI), founded by Steven M. Greer, M.D., holds that there is strong evidence for the existence of extraterrestrial civilizations and spacecraft; that extraterrestrials have been visiting Earth for a long time; and that this contact has intensified since 1947.

CSETI attempts to cultivate bilateral human/extraterrestrial contact with "peaceful, cooperative goals." The CE–5 initiative, sponsored by CSETI, aims to accelerate this contact; Project Starlight attempts to bring together persons from all fields to work on the project of revealing this contact to the rest of humanity in a non-harmful manner.

See also:

Aiwass, AYA, William Cooper, Charles Fort, Robert Morning Sky, *Sirius Mystery,* UMMO Letters

Reference:

http://www.cseti.org

Cuban Germ War?

In 1981, more than 300,000 Cubans were stricken with dengue hemorrhagic fever. *Covert Action Information Bulletin* claims this outbreak was the result of a release of mosquitoes by Cuban anti-Castroites aided by the CIA, but this has never been proven in court.

In the last 30 years Cuba has been subjected to an enormous number of human and crop diseases, which some sources attribute to the CIA.

See also:

Chicago Malaria Study, CIA LSD Research, esp. Mosquito Conspiracy

Reference:

http://home.earthlink.net/~bkonop/GermIncidents2.html

Dagobert II

One of the last kings of the *Merovingian* line, Dagobert II was long regarded as a purely mythic being, created by storytellers.

Even today, when his historicity is generally accepted, he remains semi-legendary and is intimately connected with the mysteries surrounding the *Church of Mary Magdalene* and *Priory of Sion.*

Dagobert II, for unknown reasons, spent most of his life in Ireland, according to legend and/or history, and when he did return to France he did not serve as king for long before he was murdered by persons unknown in the Ardennes Forest on December 23, 679.

According to *Gerard de Sede,* Dagobert was descended from matings between ancient Israelites and extraterrestrials from *Sirius.* According to Michael Baigent, Henry Lincoln, and Richard Leigh in *Holy Blood, Holy Grail,* Dagobert was descended from Jesus and Mary Magdalene.

See also:

Aiwass, George I. Gurdjieff, Noble Drew Ali, Bob Quinn, *Sirius Mystery*

References:

La Race fabuleuse, by Gerard de Sede, Editions J'ai Lui, Paris, 1973

Holy Blood, Holy Grail, by Michael Baigent, Henry Lincoln, and Richard Leigh, Delacorte, New York, 1982

Daimonic Reality

Daimonic Reality by Patrick Harpur examines UFOs and a wide variety of "paranormal" phenomena from a rather unique angle. Although Harpur never fully defines the *daimonic*—"the daimonic that can be defined is not the true daimonic," as Lao-Tse would say—it seems to exist both inside us and outside us. Like the Greek daemon and unlike the Christian demon, it takes both good/healing and bad/terrifying forms, depending on our commitment to rationalistic ego states.

In a sense, the daimonic is like the collective unconscious of Carl Jung, inside us as a part of our total self that the ego wishes to deny, outside us in all the other humans who ever existed and in the dreams, myths, and arts of all the world. But Harpur follows Irish poet (and *Golden Dawn* alumnus) W. B. Yeats as often as he follows Jung, and traces some of his ideas back to *Giordano Bruno* and the alchemical/hermetic mystics of the Renaissance. The daimonic is just a bit more personalized and individualized than Jung's species unconscious.

Harpur's major thesis is that unless we recognize the daimonic (make friends with it, Jung would say) it takes increasingly malignant and terrifying forms. For instance, the *Greys* of UFO abduction lore, he says, are deliberately mirroring our ego-centered and "scientistic" age—showing no emotions of the humans they experiment upon, just as the ideal science student feels no emotion and has no concern with the emotions of the animal being tortured in his laboratory.

Despite dealing with many subjects common to conspiracy theories, this book does not quite fit into that category. *We are the conspirators,* so to speak. We have repressed the most creative part of ourselves and now it is escaping in terrifying forms.

See also:

Abductees Anonymous, Aleister Crowley, Demonic Duck, *Mothman Prophecies,* Richard Shaver, UFO/Satanic Conspiracy

Reference:

Daimonic Reality: A Field Guide to the Otherworld, by Patrick Harpur, Penguin, London, 1995

John Daly

Journalist John Daly became most famous as host of a popular TV game show, "What's My Line?" Daly also married the daughter of the liberal Justice Earl Warren, an infamous villain to all John F. Kennedy assassination theorists (and to die-hard segregationists). Since one of the panelists on "What's My Line?", columnist Dorothy Kilgallen, died of an allegedly accidental drug overdose, many theorists have regarded her as one of the 100+ "post-JFK assassination victims." (She had interviewed Jack Ruby shortly before her death.)

The inevitable Kilgallen-Daly link finally found its way into conspiriology in the alt.conspiracy newsgroup in March 1996, where Eric Paddon wrote:

Frankly, I've always been amazed that some fool has never made something of the fact that John Daly, the moderator of "Line" happened to be Earl Warren's son-in-law, and that since Kilgallen died just hours after appearing on "Line" it might have been important to ask what Mr. Daly was doing after the show. It's a shame Oswald didn't get a chance to appear on What's My Line. *It would have cleared up everything.*

See also:

Kennedy Death Links, *Yankee and Cowboy War*

Reference:

ep993185@oak.cats.ohiou.edu in alt.conspiracy March 1996

Cardinal Jean Danielou

See:

Jean Cocteau, Paul "The Gorilla" Marcinkus, Naked Pope, *Scandals of the Priory of Sion*

Dr. John Dee

Dr. John Dee (1527–1608) was the greatest English mathematician of his time and also a devout student of astrology and ritual *magick*. Charged with sorcery against Queen Mary I, he was acquitted and later became a favorite of Queen Elizabeth I. According to his *Mysteriorum Libri Quinque*, Dee and Sir Edward Kelley successfully invoked a number of angels, or angel-like delusions, and accidentally summoned one demon, which they quickly put down; Dee also claimed they had discovered the hidden secret of alchemy.

H.P. Lovecraft quoted from Dr. Dee's translation of the "*Necronomicon*," adding further controversy to the debates about that text. Some even claimed that no translation of that book by Dr. Dee can be found; but one has been found and has scholarly introductions by Dr. Stanislaus Hinterstoisser and famed novelist/philosopher Colin Wilson. Lovecraft, according to Dr. Hinterstoisser, obtained his knowledge of this banned and forbidden text from an edition his father borrowed from the *Grand Orient Lodge of Egyptian Freemasonry* in Providence, Rhode Island

See also:

Campus Crusade for Cthulhu, Illuminati, P2 Conspiracy

References:

Concise Columbia Encyclopedia, Columbia University Press, New York, 1983, p. 224

Mysteriorum—

http://www.avesta.org/dee/sl3188.htm

Necronomicon—

The Necronomicon with Commentaries, Neville Spearman Co., Suffolk, England, 1978

Delano Family

See:

American Dynasty, Federal Reserve Bank, *Secret Societies and Their Role in the 20th Century*

Delilah

See:

Marilyn Walle

Eladio del Valle

A *David Ferrie* associate suspected by New Orleans D.A. Jim Garrison of being involved, with Ferrie and others, in the John F. Kennedy assassination, Eladio del Valle was found shot to death in Miami. His head was also split open with a machete. Whoever did it wanted to make damned sure del Valle was really dead.

The murder happened, oddly, the same day Ferrie died under mysterious circumstances in New Orleans, just before Garrison could indict him.

See also:

Mona Charen, John Daly, Kennedy Death Links

Reference:

The Big Book of Conspiracies, by Doug Moench, Paradox Press, New York, 1995, p. 16

George de Mohrenschildt

A man whose alleged links with the CIA appear often in conspiracy literature, George de Mohrenschildt seemingly became a close friend of *Lee Harvey Oswald* in the months before the *Kennedy assassination*—an odd friendship in that de Mohrenschildt held strong anti-Marxist views and Oswald allegedly held pro-Marxist opinions. De Mohrenschildt, after the assassination, said, "Lee is innocent." When called to testify before the House Select Committee on Assassinations, de Mohrenschildt seemingly shot himself with a .20-gauge shotgun.

His wife has always denied that de Mohrenschildt committed suicide and claims his death served "the cover-up."

See also:

Albert Guy Bogard, John Daly, Kennedy Death Links

References:

http://www.ratical.com/ratville/JFK/ToA/ToAchp10.html

The Big Book of Conspiracies, by Doug Moench, Paradox Press, New York, 1995, p. 12

Jacques de Molay

Jacques de Molay, the last Grandmaster of the *Knights Templar*, was burned at the stake in 1314. In the 32nd degree of Scotch Rite Freemasonry, it is revealed that it is the story of de Molay that is hidden behind the allegory of *Hiram Abiff*.

For further details, see also:

Born in Blood, Knights of Malta, The Widow's Son

Demonic Duck

See:

Corrydon Hammond, Dr. Kenneth Olson, Recovered Memory Therapy, *Satanic Panic*

The Demon Lover

"The terrorist is the logical incarnation of patriarchal politics in a technologist world," writes Robin Morgan, italics and all, in her book, *The Demon Lover: On the Sexuality of Terrorism*. Rejecting Establishment theories that terrorism is sponsored by some special group (communists, when she wrote; Arabs now), Morgan finds the real cause to lie in the male psyche: Men "dwell in a state of political savagery," and only women are peaceful.

Basically, Morgan sees the phenomenon of terrorism as "the son practicing what the father has practiced," a Freudian way of saying that what we call terrorism is the acts of the poor, the minorities, and the misfits fighting back against the power elite of the world, using the same tactics that the elite uses. When the rich do it, it is called war or at least "police action"; when the victims, or those who identify with the victims, use the same methods, we are trained to call it "terrorism." In another italicized passage, Morgan sums up: Terrorism is the *"democratization of violence."*

But settling differences violently has little to do with specific issues or specific quarrels; it results from the fact that men are trained to be "belligerent" by that monstrous entity, the Patriarchy. Violence is sexually exciting for males, she says, and one of her chapters takes its title from a Weather Underground slogan: "Wargasm."

See also:

Hawthorne Abendsen, Feminist Conspiracy Theories, *High IQ Bulletin, Irish Wisdom, MS. Magazine,* Protocols of the Elders of Zion, Recovered Memory Therapy

Reference:

The Demon Lover: On the Sexuality of Terrorism, by Robin Morgan, Norton and Co., New York, 1989, pp. 25, 27, 33 passim

Denial

In ordinary speech, denial simply means contradiction of something somebody else asserted, but in *recovered memory therapy* and some of the conspiracy theories derived from it, denial usually means a pathological condition in which fear of the truth makes you immune to the arguments of the therapists and their defenders; denial may also mean that you are part of the conspiracy devoted to covering up the evidence for the horror this type of therapy hopes to unmask: e.g., incest, Satanic rituals of human and animal sacrifice, extraterrestrial abduction, or whatever the particular hypnotist believes causes most of the patients' problems.

Under hypnosis, the patients eventually remember the right kind of trauma, i.e., the one the hypnotist was looking for. Those who go to therapists who believe in alien abduction, for instance, remember alien abductions; those who go to Christian therapists remember Satanic rituals; etc. Nobody seems to remember scenarios that would fit some other hypnotist's pet theory. Odd, that.

See also:

Creation Science, Demonic Duck, Hollow Earth, Corrydon Hammond

Deros

The deros are evil dwarfs who live inside the Earth and use superscientific mind machines to torture and torment the humans on the surface, according to the revelations of *Richard Shaver,* who claimed that everything awful that happened to people, especially the things that appear "supernatural" or "paranormal"—poltergeist disturbances, "demonic" possession, spontaneous human combustion, hauntings, and spooks in general—are due to the devilish science of the dero-monsters.

See also:

Dr. Raymond Bernard, The Con, Nazi Hell Creatures, UFO/Satanic
Conspiracy

Reference:

See Shaver entry

Gerard de Sede and Royal Families from the Stars

In 1973 in Paris, a mysterious fellow named Gerard de Sede published an odd tome called *La Race fabuleuse. La Race* deals with a dozen or more mysteries in French history, and only at the end does one realize that the author has explained, or pretended to explain, very few of them. In other words, much of the book deals with oddities that the author leaves dangling, for the reader to puzzle over—or perhaps to incite the reader to wild, original, or just plain goofy ideas.

The book begins, for instance, with the odd coat of arms of Stenay, a city near Paris. This coat of arms shows the head of Satan. (Neo-pagans might say "the head of a horned god," but it really looks much more like a conventional Christian image of the Devil than like any other horned god.) De Sede asks, reasonably, why would a Christian city in a Christian country want the Devil on their coat of arms? This leads to other oddities about Stenay, and about the *Merovingian* kings who had their capital there ca. 400–700 A.D. . . and only at the end do we realize that de Sede never did get back to that bizarre coat of arms and explain it.

Similarly, we learn that a familiar Fortean phenomenon—the fall of frogs from the sky, without any evidence of whirlwind to provide a rational explanation—occurs more often in the records of Stenay that in any other European city. This, also, never does get explained. It merely leads to a theory that the frog on the royal Merovingian coat of arms refers to these mysterious frogs that kept falling out of the sky onto the heads of the royal Merovingians.

We also read a great deal about Arduina, the early European bear goddess, and about her etymological/mythological link with the Greek Artemis, also a bear goddess originally, and about the *Ardennes Forest,* named after Adruina, but all this leads up to some shadowy speculations about why somebody murdered the last Merovingian king, Dagobert II, in the Ardennes Forest on December 23, 679.

De Sede also mentions, almost casually, that the principle church in Stenay faces south, so on summer mornings you can stand at the altar, look out the front door, and see *Sirius* rising behind the Sun.

One of the most interesting parts of *La Race* deals with Nostradamus, whom de Sede interprets in a novel fashion, suggesting that this strange physician's Jabberwockian poems have not remained in print continually because they "reveal the future" as New Agers believe, but because a secret society keeps them in print, and they do this because the verses *reveal the past*. The quatrains tell what really happened in past history, as distinguished from the lies of a certain sinister group that controls Europe.

The sinister group remains unnamed even at the end, but few will examine the text without suspecting that de Sede has arranged the evidence to point a strong finger of suspicion at the Vatican. The secret society opposing the Vatican also remains unnamed but sounds a lot like the Priory of Sion; see *The Committee to Protect the Rights and Privileges of Low-Cost Housing*.

A certain Marquis de B. (de Sede's abbreviation) reveals some of the hidden history. The Vatican murdered poor Dagobert II on December 23 in the Ardennes Forest for mystical reasons having to do with astrology and numerology. The Priory of Sion, or some similar but nameless group, serves to protect those who have carried the genes of Dagobert down to the present. These genes have special value, because the Merovingians descended from intermarriages between a few distinguished ancient Israelites and superhuman extraterrestrials from the Sirius system.

See also:

Bilderbergers, Dagobert II, *Fortean Times*, George I. Gurdjieff, Kenneth Grant, Priory of Sion, *Sirius Mystery*

Reference:

La Race fabuleuse, by Gerard de Sede, Editions J'ai Lui, Paris, 1973

Desovereignization

Never before in all history have the inequities and the momentums of unthinking money-power been more glaringly evident to so vastly large a number of now literate, competent, and constructively thinking all-around-the-world humans.

There's a soon-to-occur critical-mass moment when the intuition of the responsibly inspired majority of humanity, in contradistinction to the angered Luddites and avenging Robin Hoods, faced with comprehensive functional discontinuity of nationally contained techno-economic systems, will call for and accomplish a world-around reorientation of our planetary affairs.

—R. Buckminster Fuller, *Grunch of Giants*, p. 89

A term from the techno-sociological theories of **R. Buckminster Fuller**, *desovereignization* signifies the gradual decentralization of power that Fuller believed would inevitably follow the Internet revolution. In this model, the **Great Pirates** who seized control of Terra around the dawn of the Bronze Age are now finally losing control to the Internet itself and to the people who use the Internet—a group that Fuller believed would be the majority of humans soon and all of us eventually. This "desovereignization," Fuller believed, would lead to more feedback (system self-correction) in the world's political economy and thus more satisfaction for all and more rationality in decision making.

In other words, representative democracy having failed (in Fuller's view), direct electronic democracy must replace it, now that we have the technology to "advantage all without disadvantaging any."

In other words, the Great Pirates, the *Illuminati*, the *Insiders,* or whoever the various conspiriologists think rule the world, don't really rule it anymore. Power is migrating faster and faster into the decentralized human/electronic "brain" called the Internet.

See also:

Crypto-Anarchy, LAWCAP

References:

http://www.teleport.com/~pdx4d/grunch.html

Grunch of Giants, by R. Buckminster Fuller, St. Martin's, 1983

Philip K. Dick

Philip K. Dick, one of the most prolific science-fiction writers of our age and in the opinion of most critics one of the very best (two highly successful films, *Blade Runner* and *Total Recall*, were based on stories by him), entered an Altered State of Consciousness in his last years and became either a religious prophet, a major existentialist philosopher, or a raving nut, depending on how you want to look at it.

One of Dick's psychotherapists tried to convince him that his whole experience derived from sexual abuse suffered as an infant.

In a sense, it all began on November 17, 1971 when persons unknown broke into Dick's house while he was away, stole many of his files, and did enough pointless, malicious damage to suggest that some threat was intended. Since Dick had been active in both the civil rights movement and the anti-war movement, it is likely that the break-in was either part of the FBI's COINTELPRO operation—an attempt to terrorize dissidents—or one of the capers of Nixon's "plumbers" unit—later famous for the Watergate burglary. In any event, Dick felt that he had become a person of interest to powerful and unknown adversaries.

Three years later, in February 1974, Dick had a tooth extraction for which he was given sodium pentathol. He had previously used acid in the 1960s (who didn't?), frequently employed methamphetamine to finish books on deadline, and had more recently flooded his body with megadoses of vitamins in accord with 1970s' ideas of maximum health. He thought all of these might have played a role in what happened.

For over a month, February to March, Dick watched as his whole universe collapsed and was replaced not by a new universe but by a *series* of hypothetical or virtual universes. He was literally living in many of his own sci-fi plots and in the Gnostic theology that fascinated him. Sometimes, he thought that he was remembering a past life as a Gnostic Christian in Rome ca. 70 A.D.; sometimes, that his late friend, Bishop James Pike, had reincarnated within him; sometimes that three-eyed beings from *Sirius* controlled all life on Earth; sometimes that he was accidentally trapped in a telepathic transmission channel used between Russian parapsychologists and extraterrestrials; etc.

As he returned to comparative normalcy, Dick came more and more to think of the Experience as a revelation of the greatest *false memory case* in history, imposed on all humanity, from which he had partially awakened. That is, **The Empire Never Ended** (he always printed it in boldface, like that): most of the last 2,000 years of history never happened. We have been brainwashed by the Roman Empire to think he were are living in a totally false world (the Black Iron Prison, Dick called it), so we would not know we were actually living in the Messianic Age. Nixon is Nero, the assassinations we think we remember are distortions of the real memory of the Christians being thrown to the lions, and nothing inside the Black Iron Prison of ordinary perception is what it seems.

Being both a philosopher and a science-fiction poet, Dick came to doubt this theory also. In fact, the longest book he ever wrote, not yet published in full, is a 1,000 plus page *Exegesis* on his experience and some lingering aftermaths of altered perception, in which he tries one theory after another to understand what was happening to him and never does decide. At one point, he attributed his experiences to Zebra, a hypothetical giant intelligence that remains invisible because it looks like the environment, as some insects do—but Zebra looks like the *whole* environment. Often, he spoke instead of VALIS, a Vast Active Living Intelligence System, left here by the three-eyed Sirians to aid our evolution.

His last novel, *The Transmigration of Timothy Archer,* rejects all metaphysical interpretations of the hero's similar experiences and concludes that all we can learn from consciousness expansion is to be more tolerant, to love each other a hell of a lot more, and to do something concrete and practical about the suffering and injustice on this planet. He died of a stroke shortly thereafter; if he hadn't, his next book would undoubtedly have offered yet another exegesis of what was happening to Phil Dick and the world he lived in.

See also:

The Crying of Lot 49, Daimonic Reality, Candy Jones, Robert Morning Sky, *Sirius Mystery,* Kerry Thornley

References:

Divine Invasions: A Life of Philip K. Dick, by Lawrence Sutin, Underwood-Miller, Lancaster, Pa., 1989

The VALIS Trilogy, by Philip K. Dick, Quality Paperback Book Club, New York, 1990

In Search of VALIS: Selections from the Exegesis, by Philip K. Dick, Underwood-Miller, Lancaster, Pa., 1991

Discordianism

Discordianism claims to be the world's first *true* true religion and is based on worship of Eris, goddess of Chaos. One of its two founders has been accused of complicity in the *John F. Kennedy assassination.*

While some claim the Discordian movement is a complicated joke disguised as a new religion, Discordians counter that it is actually a new religion disguised as a complicated joke.

The Discordians are divided into two camps, according to the rule, "We Discordians must stick apart." On one side, the Erisian Liberation Front (ELF) led by Ho Chih Zen *(Kerry Thornley)* promotes anarchist/libertarian anti-authoritarianism, and on the other side, the Paratheo-Anametamystikhood of Eris Esoteric (POEE), led by Malaclypse the Younger (Gregory Hill), teaches a more mystic, passive doctrine, vaguely akin to *Charles Fort,* Pataphysics, and Deconstructionism. These two Discordianisms represent the material manifestation of the metaphysical hodge and podge (see *Sacred Chao*). Other high Discordian priests/priestesses include Lady L, Fucking Anarchist Bitch (a title given her by Eldridge Cleaver), Onrak the Backwards, Mordecai the Foul, Lola of Capitola, and Fang the Unwashed.

The founder of the Erisian Liberation Front, Kerry Thornley (Ho Chih Zen), was accused of complicity in the *John F. Kennedy assassination* by New Orleans D.A. Jim Garrison. At first,

Thornley believed Garrison was honestly mistaken, but later he decided that somebody had set him up to be the fall guy if the Oswald scenario collapsed. Although Garrison never found enough evidence to convict him, Thornley still sends out bulletins on the case, claiming he and Oswald were both brainwashed by Naval Intelligence, that his memory was erased, but he has deduced what must have happened, that the Discordian Society was neither a joke nor a new religion but a CIA assassination bureau, and other astounding claims.

Both the Discordians and the *Church of the Sub-Genius* eagerly distribute Thornley's accusations and denunciations.

See also:

Golden Apple Corps, Knights of the Five-Sided Castle, OM, Noon Blue Apples

References:

http://www.prairienet.org/~kkbuxton/discordia.html

Thornley—

Conspiracies, Cover-Ups and Crimes, by Jonathan Vankin, IllumiNet Press, Lilburn, Ga., 1996, p. 6

Princess Di's Death: Conspiracy Theories

The day after the death of Princess Diana (Spencer), the present author heard the first conspiracy theory at around 8 A.M. on a local radio station (KPIG, in Freedom, California). The Royal Family, a caller said, had ordered the "hit" out of fear that Diana's companion, Dodi Fayed, an *Arab*, might wield undue influence over the future king of England, Prince William. This scenario, with variations and additions, reappears in most of the conspiracy theories about Di's death.

According to the *Fortean Times,* the theory of an anti-Arab motive behind the "hit" has even been endorsed by President

Mummar al-Qaddafi of Libya, whom they quote as saying "Britain is the vilest of countries" for "executing an Arab citizen who wanted to marry an English princess." The same theory has appeared in the Egyptian newspapers, they say. But the Forteans also mention more imaginative theories circulating in England, including reports of "strange lights," so the *UFO conspiracy* and the Diana legend can be expected to merge in the near future. Among the alternative scenarios: Diana's opposition to land mines got her killed by arms dealers; an Arab Fundamentalist suicide bomber did it; the driver had been dosed with LSD by a "micro-injector"; the deaths were faked to allow Di and Dodi to escape from the damned tabloids.

The most intricately interesting scenario emerged from an online magazine called *"Conspiracy Nation,"* under the wonderful headline "Whoever Controls Princess Diana Controls the World." According to this version, the scene of the "accident" contains the real clue to what was afoot: the Pont de l'Alma tunnel, which "is ancient, dating back to the time of the *Merovingian* kings (ca. 500–751 A.D.), and before." "In pre-Christian times, the Pont de l'Alma was a pagan sacrificial site," *Conspiracy Nation* notes, going on to claim that the name combines *alma* (soul) and *pontis* (bridge), i.e., "bridge of the soul." All "true European royalty is descended from the Merovingians," the article continues, it then repeats the recent claims that the Merovingians were descended from Jesus.

Princess Diana, as a Spencer, was descended from the Stuarts who gave England four kings (James I, Charles I, Charles II, James II) and who are partially Merovingian in bloodline. By comparison, the article says, the current British royal family are "imposters."

Two factions vied for control of Diana: (1) the *New World Order* or *Bank of England* faction, founded by King William III of Orange, who allowed the founding of the (private) Bank of England, and (2) the "true nobility of Europe, i.e., those of the Merovingian blood-line," the article goes on. But it adds further complexity:

> *Within the New World Order faction, there are smaller, warring factions, exemplified by* **Rothschilds** *vs. Rockefellers. The plan of the New World Order faction was to marry Lady Diana to an American. Even though* **Bill Clinton** *has bastard roots in the Rockefeller clan, he is rejected by them and is aligned with the Rothschilds. Bill Clinton was the designated future husband for Lady Diana, with Hillary Clinton to be eliminated through divorce or even murder. The Rockefellers were furious; in no way would they allow a marriage between Bill Clinton and Lady Diana. In Great Britain, Prince William would be on the throne by age 25; if Prince Charles did not abdicate, he would be assassinated.*

But Lady Di refused to marry Bill Clinton and seemed inclined to marry Dodi, thus also marrying into the Saudi royal family; for this impropriety MI6 (British intelligence) decided to eliminate her. They picked the Pont de l'Alma to "send a signal" that would eventually lead to the creation of a Saint Diana, i.e., a new form of the triple moon goddess of the pagans, often called Diana.

Con Nation concludes: "It will be the start of 'the new religion.' Who controls the new religion controls the world."

Fortean Times, without endorsing any of the conspiracy theories, offers a similar view of the trajectory of the Dianic cult:

> *Reconciling most of the aspects of the Great Mother religion of antiquity, the new goddess Diana even borrows from the rival cults of Mother Teresa, Princess Grace, and Evita (Peron); perhaps in time, all will be rolled into one.*

They point out that healings have already been attributed to Diana and her apparition has been seen in a portrait of Charles I in St. James Palace.

Even cartoonist Jules Feiffer entered the Di Conspiracy World, or at least penetrated it, with his newspaper cartoon of September 21, 1997, in which an intense lady proclaims:

> *"The TRUE story is: Princess Di had fallen under the influence of these Egyptian fat-cat money guys—so once Prince William ascended, they would be the power behind the throne. The Royals were looking at a potential takeover of the crown by a nefarious bunch of Euro-Third World con artists. So they had MI5 set up Di for the 'accident,' which accounts for the attacks on the tabloids. . . to scare 'em off from printing the truth. I haven't yet worked out the connection to the Mother Teresa hit."*

See also:

A-Albionic, Bank of England, Dagobert II, Gerard de Sede, Grand Loge Alpina, Grand Orange Lodge of Ireland, Noon Blue Apples

References:

Jules Feiffer, *San Jose Mercury News*, September 21, 1997
Conspiracy Nation, Vol. 10, No. 95
Fortean Times, November 1997

Dr. Bella Dodd

See:

John Birch Society, Insiders

The Double-Cross System

The double-cross system, part of espionage since the first Elizabethan age, was perfected by the British during World War II and has left a heritage in which any intelligence agent who is not partly paranoid should be fired as a useless fool. Briefly, the 20 Bureau, so called in order that even MI5 and MI6 would not know exactly what they were up to, engaged in capturing and "turning" German agents. Turning (recruitment) is based on threat and bribery, since spies can be hanged and are also as mercenary as anybody else. The amusing thing about the 20 Bureau is that they succeeded beyond their wildest hopes and turned not many or most but literally *all* the German spies in England, an achievement so great that they dared not believe it themselves and only realized what they had done when they captured German records after the war.

The 20 Bureau was so called from the Roman numerals XX.

See also:

James Jesus Angleton, Fedora, Candy Jones

Reference:

The Double Cross System in the War of 1939–1945, by Sir John Masterman, Yale University Press, 1972

Peter Duesberg, M.D.

Dr. Peter H. Duesberg dissents from the popular view that AIDS is caused by HIV, and his supporters claim that the billions of federal dollars spent on AZT and other HIV-related therapies provide the hidden agenda behind the rejection of Duesberg's writings by the medical establishment.

Ever since the claim that AIDS is caused by HIV was announced at a 1984 National Institute of Health conference, Duesberg has charged that the medical community has "sacrificed academic freedom and self-correcting debate to conformism." The HIV theory was announced, he points out, without the standard scientific practice of peer review, and in his book *Inventing the AIDS Virus,* he gives numerous cases of persons who died of AIDS or AIDS-like symptoms without any trace of HIV. These deaths have been edited out of AIDS literature by redefining AIDS, so that anybody without HIV, even if originally diagnosed as having AIDS, is rediagnosed as not having AIDS. This, Duesberg says, plays a word game to avoid recognizing a widespread error. He also believes, like other critics, that AZT does not help its users; see *AZT/AIDS Conspiracy*.

Duesberg holds that AIDS is caused chiefly by stimulant drugs, especially amyl nitrate "poppers" and cocaine, and by malnutrition, both of which are found commonly among AIDS victims.

Although his writings on this subject have been bitterly contested, Duesberg continues to hold the post of professor of molecular biology at the University of California, Berkeley, and is a member of the National Academy of Sciences, whose associates are elected by the 1,600 fellow members. He also received a seven-year Outstanding Investigator Grant from the National Institute of Health.

See also:

AIDS Conspiracy Theories, Iatrogenic AIDS Theory, Jakob Segal

Reference:

Inventing the AIDS Virus, by Peter Duesberg, Regnery, 1996

Elders of Zion

See:

The Protocols of the Elders of Zion

Elmyr

Elmyr de Hory, also known as Baron Elmyr von Houry, Elmyr Herzog, Baron Elmyr Hoffman, Joseph Dory, and about a hundred other names, was convicted of forging paintings in France in 1968.

How many forgeries did this multinamed individual actually commit? That question has bothered quite a few art historians and students of criminal fraud, because after serving a short prison term Elmyr (or Baron Hoffman or whoever he was that day) glee-fully collaborated with a young American author, *Clifford Irving*, in writing the whole story of his criminal career in a book called *Fake!*—a title to ponder more than once. The book claims that Elmyr was responsible for more than a thousand of the classics of modern art now hanging in museums all over the world. This comprises a large part of our artistic canon, and the claim has, of course, been widely disputed.

Orson Welles later made a film about the Elmyr scandal, in which the baron or whatever we call him dashes off some very real-looking Picassos, Modiglianis, Van Dunkens, etc., right on camera before our eyes. As in the book, Elmyr in the film insists that he and other unnamed forgers can fool the so-called art experts easily, and that these experts keep their "authority" only through imposture and group conspiracy. Should we believe this old fraud, or should we believe the canonical Experts, who admit-tedly were fooled by him on at least some occasions?

The Experts say they can recognize a real style and distinguish it from a counterfeit, the way somebody sensitive to prose knows that "every galoot ahoof" was written by H.L. Mencken and not by a cunning counterfeiter.

The problem grows more thorny as the film reveals the fraudu-lent activities of Elmyr's collaborator, Mr. Irving, in the matter of a *Howard Hughes* biography. That bit of hokeypokey hinged for a while on whether the courts would believe *a voice* on a speaker phone that sounded like Hughes or *a signature* on a contract pro-duced by Irving, which three Experts *absolutely authenticated* as definitely by Hughes. Eerily enough, the courts eventually supported the mystery voice rather than the canonical Experts; Irving went to jail. (Later, conspiriologists would claim the voice as well as the signature were frauds.)

Things become even less easy on the simple-minded when Welles deliberately reveals that parts of this movie (a seeming documentary) are also fakes.

All this would be minor compared to some of the other shady dealings in this book, except that the Howard Hughes debate brushes very close to what look like major political conspiracies, and the canonicity of the art "experts" is now under renewed attack by post-modernists and multiculturalists in the universities, who claim, like Elmyr, that art experts operate largely on bluff, a claim proven, they say, by the fact that virtually all the "classics" recognized by them were created by white males like themselves.

See also:

Nicholas Bourbaki, *Buckaroo Banzai,* Castro as Super-Mole, Jean Cocteau, *Gemstone File,* Noon Blue Apples

References:

Fake!, by Clifford Irving, McGraw-Hill, New York, 1969

F for Fake, directed by Orson Welles, Sati Tehran Films, 1973

El Salvador: Germ Warfare?

In 1982, trade unionists in El Salvador claimed that epidemics of many previously unknown diseases had appeared immediately after U.S. aerial bombings. There is no hard evidence to support the accusation of germ warfare, but see also *Cuban Germ War?* and *Nicaragua: Germ Warfare?*.

In 1987, as a result of a lawsuit, the Department of Defense was forced to admit that the government still operates 127 chemical and biological warfare research programs in the United States, although this research was allegedly outlawed in 1972.

See also:

AIDS Conspiracy Theories

Reference:

http://home.earthlink.net/~bkonop/GermIncidents2.html

Every Knee Shall Bow

Every Knee Shall Bow, by Spokane journalist Jess Walter, is probably the most detailed and objective study of the Vicki and Randy Weaver case, in which all the hostilities, anxieties, and conspiracy theories of our time built to a bloody, crazy, and probably inevitable climax.

Vicki Jordison (b. 1949) grew up to fancy herself a combination Bible scholar and visionary, who could read hidden meanings in Bible texts. When in 1971 she married Randy Weaver (b. 1948), they became an average, only mildly right-wing Christian family—but soon Vicki's visions would change all that. After reading Hal Lindsay's *The Late Great Planet Earth*—a Fundamentalist interpretation of Bible prophecies, proving that we are living in the last days of this planet, after which the rest of the universe will become pointless—Vicki became increasingly apocalyptical, and read more and more conspiracy literature, especially which claimed the *Illuminati* and the *Freemasons* who control the *Council on Foreign Relations*. In Matthew 24, she found a "prophecy" that she interpreted to mean that the final battle between Christ and *Antichrist* would occur in 1987.

Randy, although more the follower than the leader, had equally visionary ideas of his own, and eventually the Weavers fled to Ruby Ridge, a mountain high in Idaho near the Canadian border, to arm themselves and prepare for the holocaust—the day in 1987 when the **ZOG** (Zionist Occupied Government) would begin slaughtering all the Christians.

Like all similar millennialist groups, the Weavers did not lose faith when 1987 passed without any Armageddon; they simply recalculated and waited, knowing that, although they as humans were fallible, the Bible was infallible. Then Randy made a cataclysmic mistake: Needing money, he sold a sawed-off shotgun to a government informant. The informant had previously done a good job in exposing The Order, a neo-Nazi terrorist group responsible for several bank robberies and at least one murder. He thought Randy was another of that ilk; actually, Randy had never belonged to any Nazi or neo-Nazi group. But when he realized he had been entrapped, Randy immediately decided the ZOG was planning to kill him and his family. The Weavers dug in and prepared to defend their little piece of mountain.

The 18-month siege and tragedy that followed were based on mutual paranoias: The government agents believed the Weavers were neo-Nazi terrorists (they were simply a little to the right of most rustic Christians), and the Weavers believed all the government agents who tried to persuade Randy to surrender and stand trial were the terrible Satanic ZOG, beginning the long-expected slaughter of the Christians at last.

In the climax Vicki was killed, shot dead while she held her newest baby in her arms. The Weavers' 14-year-old son and the family dog, Striker, were also killed in the general fury, and the government generally behaved as badly as the Great Beast the Weavers took it for. After prolonged self-investigation, the FBI and Bureau of Alcohol, Tobacco, and Firearms found themselves innocent of all misbehavior; but the man who fired the shot that killed Vicki took the Fifth Amendment, and another agent was suspended for shredding documents. In a civil trial, a jury awarded the surviving Weavers $3.1 million in damages.

See also:

Food and Drug Administration, War on Some Drugs

Reference:

Every Knee Shall Bow, by Jess Walter, HarperCollins, New York, 1995

Ewige Blumenkraft

The slogan of the *Illuminati*, *Ewige Blumenkraft* ("Eternal Flower Power") was first revealed by a magazine called *Teenset*. According to this expose, written for an adolescent audience, the Illuminati started out as the Ishmaeli sect of Islam and entered Europe several centuries before surfacing via *Adam Weishaupt* in 1776. The magazine describes the Ishmaeli as "dope fiends" and claimed Weishaupt "achieved illumination" by studying the teachings of Hassan i Sabbah and growing hemp in his backyard. The article also claims that Illuminism and "Flower Power" inspired all nine of Beethoven's symphonies.

Teenset also avers that Mayor Richard Daly of Chicago shouted "Ewige Blumenkraft!" during his off-microphone diatribe against Senator Abraham Ribicoff during the 1968 Democratic Party convention. (Ribicoff had angered Daly by criticizing the tactics of the Chicago police in dealing with anti-war demonstrators.)

See also:

"Bob," The Con, Discordianism

Reference:

"The Conspiracy," by Sandra Glass, *Teenset*, March 1969, pp. 34–40

Excluded Middle

The Excluded Middle is a magazine, edited/published by Gregory Bishop, devoted to exploring the vast alternatives that lie in between the two standardized UFO theories: "They're alien spaceships!" and "They're hoaxes and hallucinations!" While not dogmatically opposed to either of these responses in individual instances, *Excluded Middle* prefers to ponder those cases that look like neither aliens, jokers, nor psychos could have produced them, reports of things that suggest we need to enlarge our paradigm.

The title of the magazine seems to have come from one of the **UMMO Letters**, which says:

> *We deny the earth principle of the Third Excluded Term (The Excluded Middle Enunciated By Aristotle) According to which propositions can only be true or false. The whole ontology of terrestrial thinkers is saturated with expressions like "to be," "I am not," "I exist," without any option for other forms of different content. Unless you yourselves clarify your forms of informative communication, the process of seeking the truth will be very laborious and slow.)+(*

See also:

Charles Fort, *Fortean Times,* Language as Conspiracy, *Mothman Prophecies*

References:

The Excluded Middle, P.O. Box, 481077, Los Angeles, CA 90048
http://www.loop.com/~exclmid/

Extra-Dimensionals

See:

Area 51, Bermuda Triangle, *Necronomicon,* UFO/Satanic Conspiracy, Ultra-Terrestrials

The Eye on the Pyramid, or The Eye in the Triangle

See:

Great Seal of the United States, Ordo Templi Orientis, Israel Regardie

Face on Mars

See:

Fortean Times, UFO/Satanic Conspiracy

False Memory Syndrome Foundation

Founded in 1992, the False Memory Syndrome Foundation attempts to acquaint journalists (and the public at large) with the works of psychiatrists, psychologists, and others who have questioned the theory and practice of ***recovered memory therapy.***

Criticisms are based largely on the following facts: (1) that clinical research shows that false memories can be implanted easily, even without hypnosis, in small children especially, (2) that growing numbers of patients have themselves repudiated the alleged memories found in the hypnotic trance, and (3) that some of these angry ex-patients have successfully sued their hypnotists for malpractice.

See also:

Abductees Anonymous, Demonic Duck, Corrydon Hammond,
  MS. Magazine, Making Monsters, National Association for Consumer
  Protection in Mental Health Practices

Reference:

Making Monsters: False Memories, Psychotherapy, and Sexual Hysteria,
  by Richard Ofshe and Ethan Watters, University of California Press,
  Berkeley and Los Angeles, 1996

Fedora

In 1962, the FBI was contacted by an employee of the Soviet Mission to the United Nations in New York, who offered his service to the Americans because, he said, he was "seeking revenge against the KGB, which had treated him badly." Code-named "Fedora," this person supplied the FBI with a wide variety of what seemed valuable information, and J. Edgar Hoover was delighted to have his own Soviet informant, totally unknown to the CIA, against whom Hoover had a long and very bitter grudge. (All of Hoover's grudges were long and very bitter.)

The FBI kept Fedora as an asset for more than ten years and received a huge amount of "inside information" about the KGB. During the CIA's inner struggle over the two alleged defectors who contradicted each other, *Yuri Nosenko* and *Anatoli Golitsin*, Fedora's information supported Nosenko and undermined Golitsin.

In 1974 Fedora returned safely to Soviet Russia, and in 1982 it was agreed by both the CIA and the FBI that he had been a fake defector feeding Hoover a line of clever disinformation—the sort of high-level mole that *James Jesus Angleton* was always seeking.

See also:

Double-Cross System, Elmyr, Clifford Irving, Noon Blue Apples, Orson Welles

Reference:

http://www.jfkweb.simplenet.com/voice/nosenko.htm

Federal Reserve Bank

There are those who argue that the Federal Reserve was created in 1913 to function as nothing less than a tool of economic conquest aimed at making bankers and selected politicos rich while keeping the vast majority of the population poor, stupid, and easy to control. That may sound to you like typical conspiracy nut/survivalist crap, but think about it—most people ARE poor, stupid, and easily manipulated

–http://www.disinfo.com

The Federal Reserve System has been a target of much right-wing criticism, and some left-wing criticism, ever since it was founded. Basically, the Fed is a private corporation, under minimal government control, that creates the money we all carry in our wallets, and critics complain that the government does not control the Fed as it should, or that it is itself in hock to the Fed, or that in some manner the Fed has acquired more power than all our elected officials combined. (The same complaints were made by Andrew Jackson, Martin van Buren, and Senator **Thomas Hart Benton** against the first **Bank of the United States**.)

One critic from *Spotlight* magazine doesn't even like the fact that the Fed issues paper money. Quoting from historical records, he points out that the Constitution forbids the issuance of anything but gold and silver as money (Article One, Section 10) and says indignantly, "They really have a good deal. They can issue a piece of paper with the number one on it followed by as many zeroes as they feel necessary. Then it can be called money. They are also aware that gold and silver cannot be counterfeited. They prefer the paper method."

The same author tells an amusing, somewhat eerie story of finding a piece of "real" paper money in his attic—that is, a silver certificate, the old-fashioned paper dollar that could be redeemed for one dollar of silver. He tried to exchange the silver certificate for silver in various ways and was always sent somewhere else, until at last he discovered that banks stopped redeeming silver certificates for real silver in 1964 and this paper, like other Federal

Reserve paper, is now good only to exchange for other paper. Sounds like Kafka, doesn't it?

The first "money" or whatever it is issued by the Fed in 1914 stated clearly:

> *This Note Is Receivable By All National and Member Banks and Federal Reserve Banks and for All Taxes, Customs, and Other Public Dues. It Is Redeemable in Gold on Demand At the Treasury Department of the United States in the City of Washington, District of Columbia or in Gold or Lawful Money At Any Federal Reserve Bank.*

While many critics (e.g., **Ezra Pound**) doubt the legality or morality of the Fed issuing money, this money was worth something redeemable in gold or lawful money. (The Constitution, remember, demands that "lawful money" be made only of silver or gold). By 1950 this was revised to

> *This Note Is Legal Tender for All Debts, Public and Private, and Is Redeemable in Lawful Money At the United States Treasury, or At Any Federal Reserve Bank.*

While this was more ambiguous—how many citizens know the constitutional definition of lawful money?—it would still stand up in court as meaning that you could receive gold or silver on demand in exchange for the Fed's paper. But in 1963, this wording was replaced with the motto that still remains:

> *This Note Is Legal Tender for All Debts, Public and Private.*

This simply means that the money cannot be exchanged for any real metal, or even for cows (like ancient Roman money). It is money only because the Fed says so, and because nobody in government has challenged them effectively.

Such, in sum, is the right-wing view of the Fed—they see it, quite simply, as a gigantic counterfeiting ring that forces us to pay ever-growing interest on money the government could still issue by itself as it once did, without charging interest, if the people demanded that. As Thomas Edison once said, "If the government can print bonds, it can print currency."

After the Federal Reserve Act passed in 1913, Congressman Charles A. Lindbergh Sr. (whose son later became a famous aviator) told Congress:

> *This act establishes the most gigantic trust on earth. . . . When the President signs this act, the invisible government by the money power, proven to exist by the Money Trust Investigation, will be legalized. . . . The new law will create inflation whenever the trusts want inflation.*

Critics of banking rant so often against the *Rothschilds* and *David Rockefeller* because the Rothschild Bank of London and Chase Manhattan (Rockefeller's own) are said, we know not on what authority, to own most of the Fed. Matthew Josephson, a conspiriologist of the 1930s–1950s, whose works are currently unfindable, insisted the real power was held by the Warburg Bank of Amsterdam and was part of the "Orange" take-over of England and America, after the mildly illegal installation of the Dutchman William of Orange as King of England. (See *Princess Di's Death: Conspiracy Theories, Grand Orange Lodge of Ireland.*)

Congressman Wright Patman led a one-man crusade against the Fed for many years and only succeeded in becoming a hero to the anti-banking conspiriologists. Patman said:

> *In the U.S. today, we have, in effect, two governments. . . . We have the duly constituted government . . . then we have an independent, uncontrolled, and uncoordinated government in the Federal Reserve System, operating the money powers, which are reserved to the Congress by the Constitution.*

The Fed has never been audited. In recent years, Sen. Jack Metcalf, Congressman Henry Gonzales, Sen. Byron Dorgan, and Congressman Phil Crane have all led efforts to get the Fed audited, but have had no success thus far.

The AFL-CIO Executive Council issued a statement on February 21, 1996, condemning the Fed for "an unjustified assault on the Bureau of Labor Statistics" that will lead to false indexing of the consumer price index, depriving workers and retired persons in order to benefit the Fed itself and its member banks.

See also:

John Adams on Banking, GRUNCH, MMAO, Fletcher Prouty, Rosicrucianism

References:

Spotlight article—

http://www.webbindustries.com/spotlight/f_fr_art001.html

Most other Fed data—

http://www.empire.net/~danp/shadow.html

AFL-CIO statement—

http://www.aflcio.org/estatements/feb96/ecfed.html

Feminist Conspiracy Theories

See also:

Hawthorne Abendsen, Beethoven, Corrydon Hammond, Incest Survivors, *MS. Magazine*, Rape conspiracy

David Ferrie

A flamboyant New Orleans homosexual, talented amateur scientist, and general Man of Mystery, David Ferrie had strange links with both the *Mafia* and the CIA. New Orleans DA Jim Garrison also found enough links between Ferrie, *Clay Shaw,* and Lee Harvey Oswald that he planned to arrest him, but Ferrie died first, in New Orleans. Reports differ as to the cause of death, and although some claim Ferrie had succumbed to a karate chop in the back of the neck, this was never proven.

Ferrie associate *Eladio del Valle,* another Garrison suspect, died the same day as Ferrie, but in Miami. There is no doubt that he was murdered, no possible doubt whatsoever.

See also:

Kennedy Death Links, Kerry Thornley

Reference:

http://weberman.com

F for Fake

Perhaps the prime example of the post-modernist artwork, *F for Fake* is a somewhat faked film about the possibly fake biography of a truly great art faker—or a man who *claims* to be a truly great art faker. Allegedly directed by, certainly edited by, and starring *Orson Welles,* the film deals largely with the career of *Elmyr,* an art forger who may or may not have created a large share of the masterpieces of modern art now hanging in museums. Whether Elmyr was a real faker all the time or a fake faker part of the time (i.e., whether he faked as much as he gleefully claims) remains unresolved, but the film's evidence does tend to support Elmyr's basic claim that art "experts" cannot tell a real Picasso from a fake Picasso any more than you or I can and survive only through a conspiracy of brazen bluffing.

Interwoven with the Elmyr theme almost like a Bach fugue (the film uses extensive montage, flashback, flashforward, and deconstructs before our eyes) is the story of Elmyr's biographer, *Clifford Irving,* who later almost sold a seemingly faked biography of

Howard Hughes. A sort of climax arrives when the audience has to decide between the authenticity of opposing versions of the "truth" provided by (1) a seeming contract signed by Hughes (signature and notes authenticated by handwriting "experts") and (2) a voice on a phone claiming to be Hughes (after many conspiracy theories already asserted at least one Hughes impersonator, and maybe two, had replaced the dead-or-dying billionaire).

A third theme concerns Welles' own career as an "acting forger" (his own term) and a master of deception as both magician and stage/film director, but this gets confusingly intercut with the story of "fabulously rich" Oja Kodor, who swindled Picasso out of some of his own paintings, we are told, and who seems to have strange links with Clifford Irving and dark, sinister, never identified Swiss bankers. (See *Gnomes of Zurich.*) Welles adds darkly that "the lawyers" have warned him not to explore too far into that side of the story. But a Baroness is involved, and another art faker, and... at this point Welles reveals that some of the movie is itself fake and the audience is left to work out for themselves what to believe and what to doubt.

Parts of the film were directed by Francois Reichenbach, not Welles, and Reichenbach also once acted as a salesman for Elmyr's forged paintings, giving us further cause for suspicion. The story of Hughes walking around the desert with Kleenex boxes instead of shoes has many supporting witnesses; but the present author does not know what to think about the yarn concerning a ham sandwich hidden every night in a tree Hughes would pass. And Oja Kodor was not "fabulously rich" and did not swindle Picasso out of any paintings, but did become the last Mrs. Orson Welles...

See also:

Buckaroo Banzai, Jean Cocteau, Gemstone File, Hank Greenspun, Noon Blue Apples

Reference:

F for Fake, directed by Orson Welles, Sati Tehran Films, 1973

First Interstate Bank

Conspiriologist Wednesday N. has pointed out that the initials of First Interstate Bank give the word FIB, which suggests that they lie to their customers.

See also:

Bank of the United States, *In Banks We Trust,* Lucent Technologies

Reference:

http://www.hallucinet.com/asylem/asylem2/as_boa.html

Flight 553

On December 8, 1972, United Airlines Flight 553 from Washington to Chicago crashed a few miles short of Chicago's Midway Airport, killing two people on the ground and 43 of the 61 people on the plane. Among those killed was Dorothy Hunt, wife of *E. Howard Hunt,* and within days Chicago radical Sherman Skolnick began to claim that the evidence indicated that the plane had been sabotaged in order to kill Mrs. Hunt. While this matter remains in heated controversy, the basic case against conspiracy rests on the fact that the National Transportation Safety Board, the Federal Aviation Administration, and the FBI all conducted investigations and all concluded the crash was an accident.

To those with suspicious minds (especially about government agencies) that does not close the matter. Skolnick, for instance, points out that 50 FBI agents arrived at the scene of the crash almost immediately, although the nearest FBI office was a 40-minute drive away. Fifty FBI agents are seldom in one office; they are usually out in the field, unless they have gathered for a special project. This was what first led Skolnick to suspect foul play.

Other peculiarities noted by Skolnick, Professor Carl Oglesby, and others include:

- *Dorothy Hunt had allegedly received some of the $1 million Nixon had promised Howard Hunt to keep silent about "**The Whole Bay of Pigs Thing.**" Some say she received $350,000; some say $250,000—but after the crash only $10,000 was found on her.*

- *The pilot, eerily named Captain Whitehouse, had a significant amount of cyanide in his blood. The orthodox say he could have inhaled it from chemical reactions unleashed by the crash; heretics say this is absurd and the 3.9 micrograms per milliliter in the pilot could only result from deliberate poisoning.*

- *Acting quickly after the crash, President Nixon personally appointed two close associates to dominant positions in the investigation—Egil Krogh to the Department of Transportation, and Alexander Butterfield to the Federal Aviation Authority. Within a month, a third Nixon crony, Dwight Chapin, left the White House to take a position with United Airlines, which involved him in every phase of the investigation.*

- *After the crash the flight recorder disappeared and then reappeared mysteriously, allegedly returned by the Sanitation Department who had picked it up by mistake (at a crash site?).*

The major argument against believing that Nixon and/or his co-conspirators blew Flight 553 out of the sky is that our government wouldn't kill 44 innocent people just to get rid of one inconvenient woman. Historian Oglesby writes:

The act imputed is so monstrous that the imputation itself seems a monstrous act. Would this Sinister Force *of ours really kill so many innocent people to protect itself? Would it actually do that? In the time of My Lai? Secret wars? Allende? Dallas? Memphis? Los Angeles? Laurel? Fred Hampton's bedroom in Chicago? The Audobon Ballroom in Harlem? The road to Selma? Jackson State? Kent State? Watergate?"*

(My Lai: scene of proven American war crimes in Vietnam. Allende: democratically elected president of Chile, shot by the CIA, according to the Senate Intelligence Committee. Dallas, Memphis, Los Angeles: scenes of the John F. Kennedy, Martin Luther King Jr, and Robert F. Kennedy assassinations. Fred Hampton: Black Panther leader shot by Chicago cops in very questionable circumstances.)

See also:

James Jesus Angleton, Charles Colson

Reference:

The Yankee and Cowboy War, by Carl Oglesby, Berkley Medallion Books, New York, 1997, pp. 227–267

Flying Elephant Conspiracy

See:

Project Dumbo

Fogg Museum Experiment

In 1962, the Fogg Museum of Harvard Univeristy arranged an unusual art exhibit, in which some of the paintings were fakes and most were genuine: "experts" were invited to come and try to pick out the fakes. Among those who authenticated at least one fake were the chairman of the Art Department at Princeton and the secretary of the Fogg itself. Most of the guests kept their opinions private, just making notes, but when the truth was revealed they "quietly crumpled their papers."

See also:

Elmyr, *F for Fake*, OM, Ummo Letters, Orson Welles

Reference:

The Act of Creation, by Arthur Koestler, Macmillan, New York, 1964, p. 402

Food and Drug Administration

Over the past ten years, the Food and Drug Administration has engaged in raids on alternative health companies—companies operating openly and, they thought, legally—that more and more tend toward the violence of the DEA raids on suspected crack dealers. In every case, the companies were selling vitamins and herbs that a growing minority of the medical profession approves but which powerful interests and the FDA do not approve. As the Life Extension Foundation wrote:

> *The FDA's strong-arm tactics are used to intimidate and terrorize Americans into toeing their police-state party line on health care and medicine. The FDA's purpose is not just to destroy the business and lives of their targets but also to spread fear and terror throughout the land so that others who may be tempted to rebel against the agency will remain meek and submissive.*

See also:

Food of the Gods, Government as Criminal Conspiracy, Dr. Wilhelm Reich, War on Some Drugs

Reference:

http://www.livelinks.com/sumeria/health/raids.html

Food of the Gods

Food of the Gods, by Terrence McKenna, argues that, since every known society allows or even encourages some drugs and violently prohibits others, the drug choices of a culture tells us very significant facts about the worldview or reality-tunnel of that culture. Specifically, McKenna thinks the drugs considered okay-to-good in our society (sugar, caffeine, nicotine, alcohol, tranquilizers) help tailor us all to what he calls the Dominator style of patriarchy. That is, the sugar and caffeine and nicotine keep us all "wired" enough to maintain the competitive, mildly sociopathic personal ego necessary to survive in such a society and to perpetuate the values of that domination/submission system; the booze and tranks allow us the occasional numbing and escape without which we would all probably crack up or crumble under the stress.

Similarly, McKenna argues, the drugs subject to violent taboo in our society are incompatible with Dominator values and open us to shamanic, communal, and merging (mystic) experiences— e.g., marijuana and psychedelics. Cultures based on drugs of that sort, he tries to show, are mellower, kinder, and funnier than ours, and all tend to consider us a bit crazy.

This model, worked out with enormous erudition for 300 pages of closely reasoned text, may not be the whole truth or the only truth, but it has a lot of persuasiveness. For instance, it explains the oddity noted by Judge Robert Sweet: The government continually uses the very real dangers of crack cocaine in its propaganda, to keep us alarmed and enthusiastic about its drug wars, but it actually spends 85 percent of its anti-drug budget fighting the relatively harmless and often medicinal marijuana. If crack is so awful (and it is), why spend almost the entire budget fighting another drug? McKenna's thesis suggests that cocaine, in any form, is compatible with the ego trips of our society; but pot makes them seem silly.

Charles Fort

Charles Hoy Fort (1877–1932) set out to do to science what Voltaire had done to religion—undermine it with so much sarcastic wit that its dogmas would seem more uncertain and less absolute than its proponents wish us to believe. In four very funny, very well-documented, and (to the orthodox) very annoying books—*The Book of the Damned* (1919), *New Lands* (1923), *Lo!* (1931), and *Wild Talents* (1932)—he chronicled anomalies (now frequently called "Fortean events" in his honor), such as fish, frogs, bricks, hollow metal globes, and other oddities falling from the sky; evidence of giants and fairies; seeming violations of natural law; strange lights in outer space (he recorded the earliest UFO reports); people who allegedly possess superhuman powers; a dog that talked and then vanished in green smoke, etc.

Fort collected hundreds and hundreds of such reports, some admittedly from tabloids but the majority from scientific journals. He also developed his own philosophy of super-agnosticism (much like modern Deconstructionism), holding that nothing we think is absolutely true and every idea and perception exists in a probabilistic flux. Even if we could find an absolutely true statement at a date, Fort says, it would not remain true for very long.

Fort also conjectured, humorously, about things others would later take seriously, e.g., the possibility of alien invasions in the past, or of humans who currently have contact with aliens and aid them in some cosmic scheme unknown to the rest of us. "I think we're property," he wrote once. (See **Kenneth Grant.**) The notion of hostile aliens working in cahoots with some evil humans has now become entrenched in many conspiracy theories; see **UFO Conspiracies.**

Fort, as a consistent skeptic, always insisted he didn't believe his own theories any more than he believed anybody else's.

See also:

Daimonic Reality, H.P. Lovecraft, Robert Morning Sky

Reference:

http://www.forteantimes.com

Fort Detrick

See:

AIDS Conspiracy Theories, Jakob Segal, Umbrella Man and the John F. Kennedy Assassination

Fortean Times

The *Fortean Times,* published monthly, carries on the work of "thinking about the unthinkable" pioneered by **Charles Fort.** Issues run 66 pages and are crammed with current stories about falls of fish, spooks, unknown animals, spontaneous human combustion, etc., sent in by correspondents all over the world, together with thoughtful articles on subjects such as *crop circles,* UFOs, conspiracy theories, and just about anything regarded by the conservative as heretical or disreputable. In recent issues, for instance, one can read of:

- *A new book claiming the "face on Mars" is actually Elvis*

- *A seeming human-chimpanzee hybrid living in Texas, with 47 chromosomes (one more than a human)*

- *A growing list of Identified Flying Objects (IFOs) of the vegetable kind, thrown from speeding cars at evidently random pedestrians (cases include elderly people hit repeatedly by eggs in Middlesex; a man blinded in one eye by another flying egg in Yorkshire; a man of Leytonstone actually killed by a viciously hurled flying turnip; several people way across the globe in Australia hit by pumpkins)*

- *A strange jelly-like substance found after UFO sightings in Australia*

- *Crosses and angels seen in a Tennessee chapel, with a personal report by a* Fortean Times *writer*

- *A photo of a two-headed pig*

- *A sober analysis by Jurgen Heinzerling on alleged spirit communications received by radios and other electronic devices*

- *Accounts of hauntings that have scared motorists on Blue Bell Hill in Kent, England: Human figures that run in front of the car seemingly get hit and run over, but then disappear*

But that's only a small selection. The monthly column of "criminal croppers" shows that crime can be funny, too. For example, Daniel Bowden of Fort Belvoir, Virginia, robbed his own credit union. He came back 12 days later to deposit the loot—and was, of course, arrested. The "strange death" department is often amusing, if also tragic. In one story, editor Tim Nicholson of *Arena* threw himself off a cliff after some of his editorial decisions were overruled. He left behind a suicide note and a copy of the magazine with savage cross-outs. Another issue has some truly lovely crop circle photos with an article by John Michell arguing that, even if other such circles were hoaxes, these can't have been done by any known hoaxer techniques.

References:

http://www.forteantimes.com

Fortean Times, John Brown Publishing, The Boathouse, Crabtree Lane, Fulham, London SW6 6LU UK

Flying Vegetables

Fortean Times, No. 53, 1990

Vince Foster

Vince Foster, White House Deputy Counsel, *seemingly* committed suicide by shooting himself in Fort Marcy Park on July 20, 1993. Many people refuse to believe this and insist Foster was murdered by order of the President, Bill Clinton. The *New York Times* has documented that most of the money spent in spreading this particular conspiracy theory comes from far-right millionaires, but that alone does not mean it is necessarily false.

The Park police, the FBI, and an independent counsel, Robert B. Fiske Jr., all concluded that Foster did indeed kill himself. That just proves they were all in on the conspiracy, according to the opposition. Mike Wallace and *60 Minutes* (CBS News) investigated the case and also concluded Foster shot himself. That resulted in a full-page ad in the *New York Times*, showing the Clintons with a dog that had Mike Wallace's face, and the caption "The Clintons' Lapdog."

The independent counsel, the FBI, and *60 Minutes* all declare that the condition of Foster's body and clothing when found preclude the possibility of his having been shot elsewhere and moved to the park, an essential detail in the conspiracy theories. The conspiriologists reply that carpet fibers found on Foster's clothing contradict this. The fact that the keys to Foster's car were in his pocket is cited as proof that he drove to the park, but the conspiriologists say the keys were planted there. The gun in his hand? That was planted, too.

This debate has lasted five years and will undoubtedly last much longer. Meanwhile, the conspiriologists have added a long list of other victims to the Clinton Trail of Blood; some accuse him of as many as 56 murders.

Another aspect of the Foster case has been uncovered by *Forbes* magazine. Senior editor James R. Norman notes that Foster's job placed him in the ideal position to scan high-level political information and code/encryption secrets, and he also served on a secretive group that spied into banking transactions worldwide. These data suggest that he might have been a foreign agent, or under pressure to become one.

See also:

Bilderbergers, Council on Foreign Relations, Rosicrucianism

References:

60 Minutes and its critics—

http://www.ruddynews.com/ndjuly20.html

New York Times—

New York Times Sunday Magazine, February 23, 1997 (cover story)

Forbes—

http://fathers.zq.com/0G004.HTM

Franklin National Bank

See:

Michele "The Shark" Sindona

Freedom Is a Two-Edged Sword

Freedom Is a Two-Edged Sword, by John Whiteside Parsons, is the most eloquent statement of the philosophy of **Thelema** outside the works of **Aleister Crowley,** Parson's mentor.

Jack Parsons (as he is called everywhere except on the title page of his book) was an engineer who helped establish the Jet Propulsion Laboratory (JPL), which played a major role in the early days of America's space program; he also co-founded Aerojet General Corporation, now the manufacturer of the solid fuel booster rockets used in the space shuttle. For his many contributions to space science, Parsons has a crater on the moon named after him, located at 37° north, 171° west.

Parsons was also a member of the ***Ordo Templi Orientis*** and a fiercely libertarian philosopher. In *Freedom Is a Two-Edged Sword*, written in the 1940s and early 1950s, he denounces the favorite ideas of both liberals and conservatives, has some splendid invective against both communism and Sen. Joseph McCarthy's irresponsible witch-hunt against alleged communists who were very seldom allied with that ideology at all, and defends the most extreme individualist (nearly anarchist) political positions on all issues, personal, sexual, social, political, and economic. Like ***Dr. Wilhelm Reich's*** writings of that period, Parsons does not stop at rejecting all extensions of state power, but places the responsibility for such tendencies on the masses who tolerate oppression and even seem to welcome it. Referring to World War II and the Cold War that followed, he writes:

> *Another generation has gone down in blood and agony to make the world safe. But the evil things that make the world unsafe still go uncowed and undefeated, plotting new sacrifices and new blood. Nor is the blame entirely with the warmongers, plutocrats, and demagogues. If a people permit exploitation and regimentation in any name, they deserve their slavery. A tyrant does not make his tyranny possible. It is made possible by the people and not otherwise.*

Parsons, largely following Crowley but with odd additions of his own, sees the only hope for freedom in neo-Crowleyan *mag-*

ick—exercises and disciplines that train the individual for that "revolution in consciousness" that became a minor mass movement in the 1960s and still lingers as an underground resistance against which every government is still at war.

Jack Parsons died in a laboratory accident in 1952, at the age of 38. If he had lived he would certainly have become an even more important scientist and probably one of the great psychedelic/libertarian philosophers of our era.

See also:

Daimonic Reality, Food of the Gods, Government as Criminal Conspiracy, *Liber Al,* Minneapolis Massacre

Reference:

Freedom Is a Two-Edged Sword, by John Whiteside Parsons, Ordo Templi Orientis, New York, and Falcon Press, Las Vegas, 1989, quotation from pp. 18–19

Freemasonry

> *Freemasons* n, *An order with secret rites, grotesque ceremonies, and fantastic costumes, which, originating in the reign of Charles II among working artisans in London, has been joined successively by the dead of past centuries in unbroken retrogression until now it embraces all the generations of man on the hither side of Adam and is drumming up distinguished recruits among the pre-Creational inhabitants of Chaos and the Formless Void.*
> —Ambrose Bierce, *The Devil's Dictionary*

Many tribal peoples have both all-male and all-female secret societies, which help maintain the cultural values or reality-tunnel. Freemasonry is certainly the largest, probably the oldest, and still the most controversial of the all-male secret societies surviving in our world. No two scholars can even agree on how old it is, much less on how "good" or "evil" it is. (See *"Born in Blood"* for one book tracing it back to the Middle Ages; Masonic works of the last century traced it back much, much further, inspiring Bierce's sarcasm above.)

Although Masonry is often denounced as either a political or religious "conspiracy," Freemasons are forbidden to discuss either politics or religion within the lodge. Gary Dryfoos of the Massachusetts Institute of Technology, who maintains the best Masonic site on the web, always stresses these points and also offers personal testimony that after many years as a Mason, including high ranks, he has not yet been asked to engage in pagan or Satanic rituals or to plot for or against any political party. The only values taught in all Masonic lodges, Dryfoos and other Masons say, are charity, tolerance, and brotherhood. The more rabid anti-Masons, of course, dismiss such testimony as flat lies.

The enemies of Masonry, who are usually Roman Catholics or Fundamentalist Protestants, insist that the rites of the order contain "pagan" elements. This is probably true, but only to the extent that these religions themselves contain "pagan" elements, e.g., the Yule festival, the Spring Solstice festival, the dead-and-resurrected martyr (Jesus, allegedly historical, to Christians; Hiram, admittedly allegorical, to Masons). All these and many other elements in Christianity and Masonry have a long prehistory in paganism, as documented in the 12 volumes of Sir James George Frazer's *Golden Bough*.

The major offense of Masonry to orthodox churches is that it, like our First Amendment, encourages equal tolerance for all religions, and this tends, somewhat, to lessen dogmatic allegiance to any one religion. Those who insist you must accept their dogma fervently and renounce all others as devilish errors, correctly see this Masonic tendency as inimitable to their faith.

See also:

Grand Orange Lodge of Ireland, Grand Orient Lodge of Egyptian
    Freemasonry, Jack Harris, Illuminati, Jesus as a Freemason, P2
Conspiracy, Rosicrucianism

References:

http://thelonious.mit.edu/Masonry/Essays/ugl-whatis.html

Light on Freemasonry, by David Bernard, Vonnieda and Sowers, Washington, D.C., 1858

R. Buckminster Fuller

Richard Buckminster Fuller (1895–1983) has better claim to the title of polymath than any man since Leonardo. Fuller's contributions to architecture, mathematics, and design science generally are widely recognized as genius level; he was also a poet, a social scientist, and a global planner, and some of his geometry has proven useful in organic chemistry. One molecule, the buckminsterfullerene or "bucky ball" actually follows the synergetic geometry Fuller claimed would be found on all levels of nature once scientists began to look for it.

"Bucky" believed that modern design science makes it possible to provide a high living standard for every person on Earth—"advantaging all without disadvantaging any"—but the utilization of these sciences is hindered by "ignorance, fear, greed, and zoning laws." His theories about the role of various groups in maintaining this dystopia in spite of the possibility of utopia will be found under *Great Pirates, GRUNCH, LAWCAP,* and *MMAO.*

Reference:

http://www.teleport.com/~pdx4d/grunch.html

Fully Informed Jury Association

The Fully Informed Jury Association, or FIJA, attempts to block our devolution toward a totally regimented society by making the public aware of a fact that judges and lawyers would mostly prefer us to not know, namely, that a jury may acquit a defendant even if the evidence indicates that said defendant had broken the law. FIJA literature, which is quite well researched, demonstrates that this right of "jury nullification" has existed in both England and the United States at least since Magna Carta, both de facto (in fact) and de jure (in law.)

A few of the favorite quotations disseminated by FIJA include:

Every jury in the land is tampered with and falsely instructed by the judge when it is told that it must accept as the law that which has been given to them, or that they can decide only the facts in the case.

—Lord Denham, *O'Connell* v. *Rex* (1884)

The jury has the power to bring in a verdict in the teeth of both the law and the facts.

—Justice Holmes, *Homing* v. *District of Columbia*, 138 (1920)

If the jury feels the law is unjust, we recognize the undisputed power of the jury to acquit, even if its verdict is contrary to the law as given by the judge and contrary to the evidence.

—4th Circuit Court of Appeals, *U.S.* v. *Moylan* (1969)

When a jury acquits a defendant even though he or she clearly appears to be guilty, the acquittal conveys significant information about community attitudes and provides a guideline for future prosecutorial discretion. . . . Because of the high acquittal rate in prohibition cases in the 1920s and 1930s prohibition laws could not be enforced. The repeal of these laws is traceable to the refusal of juries to convict those accused of alcohol traffic.

—*Law and Contemporary Problems*, Vol. 43, No. 4 (1980)

FIJA also frequently points out that the two basic freedoms guaranteed in our First Amendment began with jury nullification:

- *In 1672, a jury refused to convict William Penn of preaching a religion not that of the Anglican Church, a serious crime in those days.*
- *In 1734, a New York jury refused to convict Peter Zenger of an equally odious crime, of which he was guilty—printing criticism of the government.*

Out of those jury nullifications grew our traditions of separation of church and state and freedom of the press.

See also:

Lord Acton, Government as Criminal Conspiracy, War on Some Drugs

Reference:

http://nowscape.com/fija/fija_us.htm

Gassing Citizens

According to the source below, the U.S. military released clouds of allegedly "harmless" gases over six U.S. and Canadian cities to observe the potential for similar releases under conditions of chemical warfare. A follow-up report noted that respiratory problems were widely experienced by the victims.

See also:

Chicago Malaria Study, Cuban Germ War?, El Salvador: Germ Warfare?

Reference:

http://home.earthlink.net/~bkonop/GermIncidents2.html

General Reinhard Gehlen

General Reinhard Gehlen served Hitler as chief of the Soviet Intelligence section, and performed so outstandingly that he has been called the "superspy" of World War II. Gehlen had succeeded at penetrating Soviet Intelligence because of his alliance with General Andrei Vlassov, a Red Army officer who secretly belonged to a pro-Czarist anti-communist underground. (See *Double-Cross System*.)

After the war, Gehlen had even more astonishing achievements—he not only avoided standing trial with the other top Nazis, but brokered a deal that got him out of his Nazi uniform and into an American General's uniform within a week. This deal also made him the most powerful U.S. spy in Europe, heading his own organization, the superspooky *Gehlenapparat* mentioned in many spy novels (it was made up mostly of ex-Nazis and White Russians). Gehlen had managed this "sweetheart contract" by burying 52 boxes of intelligence information about the Soviet Union and trading them for the best deal he could get from the U.S., and he soon became the major source of CIA ideas about what was going on in the Soviet Union.

As historian Carl Oglesby has noted, since the CIA's image of Soviet realities came mostly from die-hard Czarists by way of a Nazi general, it may not have matched perfectly with objective reality.

The *Gehlenapparat* acted entirely without U.S. supervision, under the terms of Gehlen's deal. The CIA told him what they wanted, and he got it for them, and they had no knowledge (and probably wanted no knowledge) of how he did it.

See also:

A-Albionic, Corrydon Hammond, Knights of Malta, Nazi Hell Creatures, *Yankee and Cowboy War*

Reference:

The Yankee and Cowboy War, by Carl Oglesby, Berkley Medallion Books, New York, 1977, pp. 15, 38–42

Licio Gelli

Licio Gelli (1919–) began his career as conspirator during World War II, in which he managed to act as an agent for both the Gestapo and the Communist Underground, persuading each that he was loyal to them and betraying the other side—no small feat with two groups for whom suspiciousness was almost as necessary as air and food. Gelli escaped prosecution as a war criminal, because members of the underground testified on his behalf.

After becoming involved in the CIA's *Gladio* project, Gelli repeated his previous feat and got himself on the payroll of the KGB also. After he formed the *P2 conspiracy* as an adjunct or outgrowth of Gladio, Gelli soon became one of the most powerful men in Italy, since the rules of P2 required a "confession" during the initiation and this provided mountains of future blackmail material.

When the whole P2 scheme collapsed and Gelli fled Italy (he had been tipped off that he was about to be arrested by another P2 member, in military intelligence) documents found in his house revealed that P2 members included 43 members of Parliament, three cabinet ministers, around 900 miscellaneous government officials, the heads of every branch of the armed services, the head of military intelligence, the head of civilian intelligence, the civilian coordinator of intelligence, top officials of the state-owned broadcasting company, and many top industrialists and financiers.

Gelli laid low in South America for a while, then returned to Europe with a false passport and tried to withdraw some money from a numbered Swiss bank account. He was recognized, arrested, and held for extradition to Italy; but the Swiss, who allegedly have the most incorruptible police in the world, were unable to hold him for more than 72 hours. Then he vanished from his cell—a miracle not yet explained—and returned to South America.

The Italians finally got him back, and he stood trial for one of the terrorist bombings P2 had performed. He was acquitted, and the government has not tried to bring him to trial on any of the numerous charges pending against him. Officials say this is because of his age and ill health, but skeptics think Gelli still owns heaps and heaps of blackmail material.

Many writers think P2 died with the 1980s scandals; others think it has regrouped under new names and is active in Italy, Latin America, and even the United States.

See also:

James Jesus Angleton, Roberto Calvi, *In God's Name, Scandals of the Priory of Sion*

References:

In God's Name, by David Yallop, Johnathan Cape, London, 1984

The Calvi Affair, by Larry Gurwin, Pan Books, London, 1984

The Gemstone File

Just as there are two Winston Churchills and two **Thomas Hart Bentons**, there are two *Gemstone Files.* The first or greater *Gemstone,* was written by somebody named Bruce Roberts, of whom little is known except that he died of some form of tumor on July 30, 1976—a tumor induced by the CIA, he claimed. His *Gemstone File* ran over 1,000 pages and so far nobody has been willing to publish it; but it had progeny—most of them bearing the title *Skeleton Key to the Gemstone File,* but otherwise differing in what they included and excluded. One version, with the original title, *Illuminati Research Report,* merges one of the Skeleton Keys with the *"Protocols of the Elders of Zion"* and the metaphysical time line from Neal Wilgus' *"The Illuminoids."* Various of the Skeleton Keys have appeared in such journals as *Shavertron, Conspiracy Digest, The Fanatic, Dharma Combat,* and Larry Flynt's *Hustler—*

just before Flynt was shot by an unknown assailant, leading some to theorize that it wasn't safe to move the *Gemstone* material out of the little press arena into Flynt's mass market.

The second *Gemstone File*, edited by conspiriologist Jim Keith, is a collection of essays by various "experts" (Mae Brussell, Jonathan Vankin, *Kerry Thornley*, the present author, etc.) attempting to evaluate the accuracy, or degree of accuracy, of the original epic.

The earliest *Skeleton Key* mailed out to many researchers while Roberts was dying was the work of a journalist named Stephanie Caruana, who believed every word of it; it begins:

> *1932: Onassis, a Greek drug pusher and ship owner who made his first million selling "Turkish tobacco" (opium) in Argentina, worked out a profitable deal with Joseph Kennedy, Eugene Meyer, and Meyer Lansky. Onassis was to ship booze directly into Boston for Joseph Kennedy. Also involved was a heroin deal with Franklin and Elliot Roosevelt.*

Anybody who gives up immediately, rejecting this as obvious paranoia, misses most of the excitement. Roberts/Caruana go on, year after year, from 1932 to 1975, linking every important figure in American finance, politics, and business with the *Mafia* in a whirling chaos of dope, murder, double-dealing, vendetta, and every type of felony.

We are told that Onassis, for instance, took over the Mafia itself, an organization all other authorities agree is all-Sicilian at the top. When *Howard Hughes* became a threat, due to his control of Nixon and other politicians, Onassis had him kidnapped, held prisoner on the island of Skorpios, and forcibly made him a heroin addict. A double named L.W. Rector thereafter impersonated Hughes. When Joe Kennedy had a stroke in 1961, John and Bobby rebelled against Onassis/Mafia control and had to be eliminated. Mary Jo Kopechne learned too much, reading files while working for the Kennedy organization, and was drowned to shut her up. Etc.

It sounds like Italy during the *P2 conspiracy* of the 1970s. Could it possibly be the real history of our own Sweet Land of Liberty during 40 years?

Mae Brussell, one-time Queen of Conspiracy Theory, thinks it's largely true, but objects to the amount of power attributed to Aristotle Onassis. She considers Onassis, like Nixon, a true villain, but not smart enough to outwit the supervillains, who are still unknown. (See *Potere Occulto* and *Fletcher Prouty*.) Jonathan Vankin is more dubious but is glad the book exists, since it challenges dominant paradigms and blows the reader's mind. Jim Keith thinks it contains both believable and unbelievable elements. Kerry Thornley insists that the work must be a hoax, because Roberts seems to know everything and those who really research this kind of material are more often confused and uncertain about parts of the picture (often, crucial parts).

Perhaps the most plausible part of the yarn: the story of how Howard Hughes set out to buy the U.S. government, a bit at a time, building up to virtually owning a president, Richard Nixon.

The most implausible part: the claim that Johnny Roselli personally shot John F. Kennedy in Dallas. The idea of a top Mafioso like Roselli doing his own shooting in a case like that belongs in a B movie. If Roselli was involved, as others have conjectured, you can be sure he would be in another town at the time and have no direct link to the gunman.

The best bit of classic myth: the explanation of how Onassis had to assassinate an associate of Hughes named Merryman for revealing some inside dirt to *Clifford Irving*.

Legends say the Bruce Roberts got his basic information hanging out in a bar where CIA agents met to relax. Some of these yarns sound like they could only come out of a bar full of drunken spooks.

See also:

A-Albionic, Hughes vs. Rockefeller, John F. Kennedy Assassination, *Yankee and Cowboy War*

Reference:

The Gemstone File, ed. by Jim Keith, IllumiNet Press, Lilburn, Ga., 1992

GENISIS

GENISIS: First Book of Revelations, by David Wood, takes a new slant on the *Priory of Sion* mystery, which has haunted the more metaphysical conspiriologists for over two decades now. Based on the English art, or science, or fad, of "ley hunting" (looking for hidden energy patterns in the landscape), Wood connects all the important sites in literature about the Priory—including the tomb in *Nicholas Poussin*'s *Shepherds of Arcadia*—and emerges with a pattern he calls The Vagina of Nuit. (See *"Liber Al."*)

From this design and various facts and legends about the buildings within the design, Wood deduces a whole revised history of France and of humanity in general, which reveals that we all came from Atlantis and that our creator was not the God of the Universe but a consortium of extraterrestrials from *Sirius* named the Elohim, who left us in a fairly botched and unfinished state.

("Elohim," the name for the creative power in Genesis, is a female plural, a fact that generations of learned rabbis and Christian theologians have all explained as merely a grammatical convention. The King James and most other Bibles translate it as "God," but if you take the grammar literally, it seems to mean "goddesses." Al Shaddai, god of battles, appears later, and YHVH, mispronounced Jehovah, later still.)

Wood also claims that members of the Priory amputate their penises, as a sacrifice to Isis. (See the opposing view of *Hawthorne Abendsen.*)

See also:

Gerard de Sede, Gnomes of Zurich, Kenneth Grant, Fletcher Prouty, *Sirius Mystery*

Reference:

GENISIS: First Book of Revelations, by David Wood, Baton Press, Tunbridge Wells, England, 1985

Sam Giancana

Sam "Mooney" Giancana (1905-1975) entered the *Mafia* as a hit man (contract killer) for Al Capone and eventually rose to crime boss of most of the western United States. It is estimated that he personally killed 20 men before he was out of his teens, and was involved in the assassinations of more than 200 in his lifetime.

Sam was called "Mooney" in the mob because of his reputation for bizarre and irrational episodes; the same pattern of borderline psychosis appeared in, and gave the nicknames to, George "Bugs" Moran and Benjamin "Bugsy" Siegel. Even among gangsters, some people are considered too far outside polite social norms, and Sam Giancana was one of them.

Sam bragged about having participated in the Saint Valentine's Day Massacre (February 14, 1929) in which seven members of the "Bugs" Moran gang were executed for impinging on Capone's territory; but from such uncouth beginnings he rose to control, or exert power within, most of the unions in Hollywood and the nationwide Teamsters as well. Giancana also played a large role in the election of John Kennedy as president, through his Chicago mob connections. Kennedy won by the smallest margin of any president in the 20th century, and most analysts agree he owed it to the Chicago vote, which netted him Illinois. Giancana had helped elect John F. Kennedy as a favor to Joe Kennedy, an old friend who had worked in the bootlegging business with Sam.

When the Kennedy brothers began their public war on the Mafia, Sam felt hurt and betrayed. According to testimony of his nephew, Sam Giancana Jr., Sam planned and supervised the *John*

F. Kennedy assassination. This claim is considered plausible by Professor Blakey of Notre Dame, former counsel to the House Select Committee on Assassinations, who has repeatedly said the Mafia managed the Dealy Plaza hit.

Sam's nephew also claims Sam arranged the *murder of Marilyn Monroe* in an attempt to put Robert Kennedy in a position where he could be blackmailed.

On the other hand, singer Phyllis Maguire, who had a long time affair with Sam, said of him, "He had a lot of charisma."

Sam died of gunshot wounds to the mouth while under investigation by the House Select Committee on Assassinations.

See also:

Gemstone File, Godfather, Kennedy Death Links, MMAO, Yankee and Cowboy War

Reference:

Arts and Entertainment TV, *Biography*, "Sam Giancana: The Gangster Who Dreamed," February 11, 1998

Glacier National Park MIB

Although *men in black* usually appear associated with UFOs, one of the strangest recorded in recent times concerns the two campers killed by a grizzly bear in Glacier National Park in August 1967. Among the persons who clustered around the mutilated victims was a man not dressed for the outdoors like the others but wearing instead a black suit, black tie, and black shoes. He disappeared as abruptly as he appeared and was never explained.

See also:

Mary Hyre, "Sarah," Satanic Abuse

Reference:

The UFO Silencers, by Timothy Green Beckley, Inner Light Publications, New Brunswick, N.J., 1990, p. 4

Gladio

Gladio was another of the amazing schemes to emerge from the fertile brain of *James Jesus Angleton.* In the closing days of World War II, Angleton, then an OSS officer, began forming a circle of common interests with various Italian fascists (or, rather, with Italy's surrender, newborn ex-fascists), who all shared his dread of the Italian Communist Party, the largest in Europe. To prevent the communists from winning control of the Parliament, or even seating enough members to be a large enough minority to make problems, Angleton and friends set about controlling the results of Italian elections by a variety of tactics.

When Angleton became chief of counter intelligence for the CIA, this scheme acquired an official name, Gladio, and enough budget to play havoc with Italian politics until the 1980s or maybe even to the present. Gladio forged secret alliances between the Mafia and certain Vatican officials; recruited former fascists to conduct terror attacks blamed on the left; paid millions to political parties, journalists, and others to tilt elections to the right and away from the left; and probably supervised the kidnapping and murder of Prime Minister Aldo Moro, who had included communists in his cabinet.

In May 1965, the master plan of Gladio was outlined in a paper called "The Strategy of Tension," which was a scenario to fake so much left-wing terrorism that the Italian people would want, and even demand, a more authoritarian or neo-fascist government. A copy of this was found in the home of *Licio Gelli* after he fled Italy, just as the police came to arrest him, in March 1981.

The *Knights of Malta* served as the backbone of Gladio, and Gelli, a Knight of Malta himself, when he formed his ultra-secret *P2* lodge within Freemasonry, gave major importance to two other Knights of Malta, *Roberto Calvi* and *Michele "The Shark" Sindona.*

See also:

Cisalpine Bank, John Hull, Paul "The Gorilla" Marcinkus, World Finance Corporation

References:

http://www.worldmedia.com/caq/articles/gladio.html

In God's Name, by David Yallop, Bantam, New York, 1984

Gnomes of Zurich

British Prime Minister Harold Wilson once denounced "the Gnomes of Zurich," saying that they had more power than any government in Europe. Most people have assumed that the Gnomes he referred to were the powerful banks centered in Zurich, but Steve Mizrach claims Wilson intended the *Grand Loge Alpina*, the largest Freemasonic society in Switzerland, which in fact has most of the major Swiss bankers as members, and almost everybody else of heft or weight in Switzerland.

The Grand Loge and/or the Gnomes have become matters of interest to conspiriologists due to Matthew Paoli, who documented their links with the *Priory of Sion* (see *Committee to Protect the Rights and Privileges of Low-Cost Housing*), and David Yallop, who claimed these Swiss Freemasons/bankers secretly backed the *P2 conspiracy* in Italy. If we believe these charges, the Gnomes plotted to restore monarchy in France and fascism in Italy. What plans they have for other countries remains unknown.

See also:

Gerard de Sede, Archbishop Lefebvre, Robert Morning Sky, Noon Blue Apples, Octopus, Fletcher Prouty

Reference:

http://www.clas.ufl.edu/anthro/fortpages/rennes-sion.html

The Godfather

Mario Puzo's popular novel of **Mafia** life, *The Godfather*, which gave birth to an immensely successful trilogy of films, had an extraordinary fascination for **Roberto Calvi**, president of **Banco Ambrosiano** and one of the key figures in the Italian **P2** scandal. He recommended it whenever books were discussed. "Read it," he would say. "Then you will understand the way the world really works."

Michele "The Shark" Sindona, president of Franklin National Bank and another member of the P2 conspiracy, purchased stock in Paramount for the Mafia, through one of his financial fronts.

See also:

Licio Gelli, Paul "The Gorilla" Marcinkus, Octopus, Shakespeare as Conspiriologist

References:

Calvi—

The Calvi Affair, by Larry Gurwin, Pan Books, London, 1984

Sindona—

In God's Name, by David Yallop, Jonathan Cape, London, 1984

The Gods of Eden

The Gods of Eden, a 535-page tome by a man who calls himself William Bramley (he admitted this was a pen name when interviewed by journalist Jonathan Vankin), puts forth an outstanding variation on the now-popular Cosmic Conspiracy Theories. In place of merely terrestrial villains like the **Illuminati** or the **Insiders**, Bramley posits a controlling group of extraterrestrials he calls the Custodians. In his own words:

> *Human beings appear to be a slave race, . . . once a source of labor for an extraterrestrial civilization and still. . . a possession*

today. To keep control over its possession and to maintain Earth as something of a prison, that other civilization has bred never-ending conflict among human beings, has promoted spiritual decay, and has erected on Earth conditions of unremitting physical hardship.

According to Vankin, Bramley uses a pseudonym because he is a successful lawyer and doesn't want to be laughed at. His book has a 15-page bibliography and scrupulously avoids the kind of hysterical language and dogmatism that appear in most conspiracy theories.

See also:

Area 51, AYA, Philip K. Dick, Charles Fort, Kenneth Grant, Robert Morning Sky, Fletcher Prouty

References:

The Gods of Eden, by William Bramley, Dahlin Family Press, San Jose, Calif., 1990

Conspiracies, Cover-Ups and Crimes, by Jonathan Vankin, Paragon House, New York, 1991

The Golden Apple Corps

The Golden Apple Corps is the central committee or "brain" of the Legion of Dynamic Discord, the activist branch of the Discordian Society. In official Discordian documents, members of the Golden Apple Corps affix the letters "K.S.C." after their names; this means "Keepers of the *Sacred Chao.*" Very little else is known about them, and it is perhaps wise not to inquire further.

There are only two Keepers of the Sacred Chao, and no others will ever be authorized. Mordecai the Foul, of the Santa Cruz cabal, has compensated by taking the title Keeper of the Notary Sojac.

See also:

Discordianism, Holy Order of the Lemon, Noon Blue Apples, OM

Reference:

http://www.prairienet.org/~kkbuxton/discordia.html

Golden Dawn, Hermetic Order of the

The Hermetic Order of the Golden Dawn possibly came into existence in 1881 due to some combination of mysterious events involving three Freemasons named S.L. Mathers, William Wynn Wescott, and William Woodman, and a mysterious Bavarian woman, *Anna Sprengel.* Either (1) Westcott found some ciphered papers in Freemason's Hall, London, which put him in touch with Fraulein Sprengel, or (2) he found the papers in a bookstall, or (3) he and Woodman and Mathers made up the whole story, or (4) Westcott made it all up alone and deceived Woodman and Mathers.

Those were the most accepted theories until very recently, when new evidence suggested that the Golden Dawn could have evolved out of (1) the *Loge zur augehenden Morgenrothe*, a Masonic lodge in Frankfurt, which established a branch in France called *Aurore naissante* (both titles mean "Rising Dawn") and a branch in London and/or (2) the *Chabrath Zerek Auor Bokher*, or Society of the Shining Light of Dawn, a Cabalistic college in London, founded by one Johannes Falk from Hamburg, Germany.

However created, the Golden Dawn became the most influential occult society of the turn of the century, numbering among its members such influential persons as Irish poet and Nobel laureate William Butler Yeats, fantasy writers Algernon Blackwood and Arthur Machen (who both influenced *H.P. Lovecraft*), famous actress Florence Farr, Arthur Waite, creator of the best-known modern Tarot cards, *Israel Regardie*, and the enigmatic jester *Aleister Crowley.*

Like ordinary Freemasonry, the Golden Dawn had a system of grades, each one marked by an initiatory ritual intended to make a lasting impression on the consciousness of the candidate—to bring him or her closer and closer to Illumination in the mystical sense. This was combined with profound study of Christian Cabala, a derivative of the original Jewish Cabala, a science or art that provides a religious language and numerology to discuss and clarify various altered states of consciousness.

The influence of the Golden Dawn extended far beyond conventional occultism. Much of modern literary culture owes its symbolism and themes to this group; not only Yeats' poetry, but even the works of James Joyce, *Ezra Pound,* and T.S. Eliot, show Golden Dawn elements, which were common currency in the London of 1900–1914, where all these writers met. Modern horror fiction is replete with themes *H. P. Lovecraft* acquired at secondhand from Blackwood and Machen. The Tarot deck, virtually forgotten by all but gypsy fortune-tellers, is now widely studied for both mystic and psychological meanings, due to the Waite and Crowley Tarot decks, both based on the Golden Dawn deck.

The Golden Dawn fell into dissension and acrimony in 1898 and has continued to remain disunited. In the late 1980s, when the present author lived in Los Angeles, that city alone rejoiced in three Outer Heads of three Golden Dawns, each claiming to have been appointed by Israel Regardie.

See also:

Gordon Browne, *Daimonic Reality,* Freemasonry, Ordo Templi Orientis, Rosicrucianism, Thelema

References:

http://www.unp.ac.za/UNPDepartments/Religious_Studies/golddawn.txt

The Eye in the Triangle, by Israel Regardie, Falcon Books, Las Vegas, 1988

Anatoli Golitsin

Anatoli Golitsin, a KGB officer, defected to the CIA in 1964 and became one of the most mysterious mysteries in spy history, largely because his yarns contradicted the testimony of a previous defector named *Yuri Nosenko*. One of the major issues on which Golitsin and Nosenko disagreed was the existence or non-existence of a Soviet mole (code-named *Sasha*) in the very top ranks of the CIA itself, Golitsin claiming that Sasha existed and Nosenko claiming that Sasha was only a notational agent, i.e., a manipulated myth intended to confuse and mislead the CIA.

This issue remains unclarified and highly debatable, because *James Jesus Angleton,* head of the CIA counterintelligence branch, endorsed Golitsin and discredited Nosenko. Angleton is believed to be the instigator of the *John F. Kennedy assassination* by many conspiriologists, and Nosenko's later testimony largely confirmed the Warren Commission and served to discredit most of the conspiracy theories about *Lee Harvey Oswald*'s CIA connections.

See also:

Fedora, E. Howard Hunt, "The Whole Bay of Pigs Thing"

References:

http://www.jfkweb.simplenet.com/voice/nosenko.htm

http://www.weberman.com/htdocs/

Good Times Virus–1

"Good Times" is the name of the most popular and also the most unpopular hoax virus on Internet—popular with malicious jokers and unpopular with novices who often believe it and are terrified.

The original "Good Times" message was posted in November 1994 and contained the warning:

> Here is some important information. . . . There is a virus on American
> Online being sent by E-Mail. If you get anything called "Good Times,"
> DON'T read it or download it. It is a virus that will erase your hard
> drive. Forward this to all your friends. It may help them a lot.

Although this was soon exposed as a hoax, it still continues to circulate and terrify novices. An improved version later appeared, saying among other things:

> The FCC released a warning last Wednesday concerning a matter of
> major importance to any regular user of the Internet. Apparently, a new
> computer virus has been engineered by a user of America Online that is
> unparalleled in its destructive capability. Other, more well-known viruses
> such as Stoned, Airwolf and Michelangelo pale in comparison to the
> prospects of this newest creation of a warped mentality. . . [etc.].

This, too, continues to circulate and cause alarm. Meanwhile, a parody has come into existence that seems quite amusing to the computer community but, considering human gullibility, may scare as many people as the original hoax (see below).

See also:

CIAC, Irina, Ladder Conspiracies, OM

Reference:

http://ciac.llnl.gov/ciac/CIACHoaxes.html

Good Times Virus–2

The "Good Times Virus" parody reads as follows (slightly condensed):

> Goodtimes will rewrite your hard drive. Not only that, but it will
> scramble any disks that are even close to your computer. . . . It will

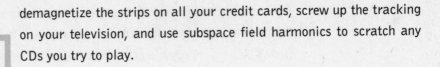

demagnetize the strips on all your credit cards, screw up the tracking on your television, and use subspace field harmonics to scratch any CDs you try to play.

It will give your ex-girlfriend your new phone number. It will mix Kool-Aid into your fishtank. . . . Goodtimes will make you fall in love with a penguin. It will give you nightmares about circus midgets. . . . It will seduce your grandmother. . . .

It moves your car randomly around parking lots, so you can't find it. It will kick your dog. It will leave libidinous messages on your boss' voice mail in your voice! It is insidious and subtle. . . .[It] will give you Dutch Elm disease.

Reference:
Same as **Good Times–1** above

Government as Criminal Conspiracy

The view that our government per se is nothing more nor less than one giant criminal conspiracy appears in both extreme right-wing and extreme left-wing forms.

Anarchists hold that government is not a "necessary evil" as conservatives think but an unnecessary evil. This viewpoint is expressed variously by Proudhon, Bakunin, Tolstoy, Kropotkin, Warren, Malatesta, and many others. It was probably stated most succinctly by Tom Paine, who wrote, "The trade of governing has always been monopolized by the most ignorant and most rascally individuals of mankind."

Tolstoy put it even more bluntly: "Government is an association of men who do violence to the rest of us."

Lysander Spooner, lawyer and libertarian, deflated the "democratic" claims of modern governments with succinct sarcasm:

The right of absolute and irresponsible dominion is the right of property, and the right of property is the right of absolute, irresponsible dominion. . . . But these men who claim and exercise absolute and irresponsible dominion over us dare not be consistent, and claim to be our masters or to own us as property. They say they are only our servants, agents, attorneys, and representatives. But this declaration involves an absurdity, a contradiction. No man can be my servant, agent, attorney, or representative, and be, at the same time, uncontrollable by me, and irresponsible to me for his acts.

Pierre Joseph Proudhon, the first writer to use "anarchism" as a positive word, put it even more brutally:

To be governed is to be watched over, inspected, spied on, directed, legislated at, regulated, docketed, indoctrinated, preached at, controlled, assessed, weighed, censored, ordered about. . . . To be governed means to be, at each transaction, at each movement, noted, registered, taxed, stamped, measured, evaluated, patented, licensed, authorized, endorsed, admonished, hampered, reformed, rebuked, arrested, . . . held to ransom, exploited, monopolized, extorted, squeezed, hoaxed, robbed, and then, at the least resistance, . . . to be repressed, fined, abused, annoyed, followed, bullied, beaten, disarmed, garroted, imprisoned, machine-gunned, judged, condemned, deported, flayed, sold, betrayed, and finally mocked, ridiculed, insulted, dishonored.

Machievelli had a similar view of government, but considered the condition incurable.

See also:

Lord Acton, The Con, *Every Knee Shall Bow, Godfather,* Internal Revenue Service, Minneapolis Massacre

Reference:

The Heretic's Handbook of Quotations, ed. by Charles Bufe, See Sharp
    Press, San Francisco, 1988, Paine, p. 33, Tolstoy p. 37, Spooner, p. 35,
    Proudhon, p. 33

Grand Loge Alpina

The Grand Loge Alpina is the largest Freemasonic lodge in
Switzerland and therefore attracts much attention from anti-Masonic
conspiriologists. European conspiracy buffs have long believed the
Grand Loge Alpina controls the finances of the Western world
through the banks they own in Zurich, Basel, and Geneva, and a per-
sonage as distinguished as former English Prime Minister Harold
Wilson denounced this group as "the *Gnomes of Zurich*" and said
they had more power than all the governments in Europe together.

In David Yallop's anti-Vatican blockbuster *"In God's Name,"*
he alleges several suspicious links between the *P2 conspiracy* in
Italy and the Grand Loge Alpina. He even claims some members
of the Council of Cardinals belonged to either the Grand Loge
Alpina or to P2 or to both, and that a few of them collaborated in
the murder of the last Pope, John Paul I, a theory hinted at also in
the film *Godfather III*.

Other writers on P2 agree that it took money from both the
KGB and the CIA, had over 900 agents in the Italian government,
used the Vatican Bank to launder Mafia and CIA drug money,
fomented fascism in Latin America, and was allegedly plotting a
fascist coup in Italy when, after the mysterious deaths of ringlead-
ers *Roberto Calvi* and *Michele "The Shark" Sindona*, the whole
house of cards came tumbling down.

See also:

Committee to Protect the Rights and Privileges of Low-Cost Housing,
    Freemasonry, Licio Gelli, Holy Order of Lemon, Noon Blue Apples,
    Rosicrucianism

References:

In God's Name, by David Yallop, Jonathan Cape, London, 1984

In Banks We Trust, by Penny Lernoux, Anchor Doubleday, New York, 1984

Grand Orange Lodge of Ireland

The Grand Orange Lodge of Ireland, founded in 1795 as another offshoot of *Freemasonry,* currently claims members throughout the world and has active branches in at least Scotland, England, Canada, and the United States. Named after the Protestant William III of Orange, who became king of England after defeating the Catholic James II at the Battle of the Boyne, the Orange Lodge—or "Orangemen," as they are called throughout Ireland—has maintained a steady animosity against what they call "tyranny and despotism," chiefly in the form of the dominant Catholic religion of the rest of Ireland.

Claiming no bias against any religion and asserting tolerance for all, the Orangemen nonetheless are considered bigots (and also often suspected of murderous conspiracies) by the Catholic majority. In reply to this canard, the Orange Lodge declares, "It should be remembered that the [Orange] Order has a worldwide membership and that wherever its Lodges exist there is to be found a brotherhood of men pledged to uphold the ancient concept of the Protestant faith and liberty under the law."

See also:

Gnomes of Zurich, Holy Order of the Lemon, Noon Blue Apples

References:

Orange view of itself—

http://www.gpl.net/customers/goli/

Catholic view of Orangemen—

Author's six years' residence in Ireland

Grand Orient Lodge of Egyptian Freemasonry

See:

Calvi Affair, Dr. John Dee, Grand Loge Alpina, *High IQ Bulletin,* H.P. Lovecraft, , Rosicrucianism, *World Revolution*

Kenneth Grant

In the 1970s and early 1980s, Kenneth Grant of London was one of the five claimants to the title of Outer Head of the *Ordo Templi Orientis.* Since ca. 1985, he has been reduced to one of the 1,005 claimants to the title, because a group of dissidents, in rebellion against him, sent out cards appointing one thousand other Outer Heads. (The present author proudly carries one of these cards in his wallet. It says, "The bearer of this card is a genuine and authorized Outer Head of the Ordo Templi Orientis, so *please* treat him right" and is signed by *Aleister Crowley* or a skillful forger.)

Grant's version of the OTO lays heavy emphasis on anal variations of *sex magick* and on dark hints about long-range political objectives known only to the inner circle, or perhaps known only to himself. He therefore seems deliberately to court the suspicions of professional conspiracy hunters—a trait he shares with his teacher, Mr. Crowley. Grant also seems to be the principle author of the interpretation, now widely shared in occult circles, that the superhuman being allegedly contacted by Aleister Crowley when he was Outer Head of the OTO was an extraterrestrial from *Sirius;* Crowley himself always spoke of the entity only as a "being of prætor-human intelligence." Grant informs us further that *Yog Sothoth* and the other interstellar beings or powers in the fiction of *H.P. Lovecraft* are allegories on the entities contacted by Crowleyan magick. He also traces the genealogy of the OTO back to the *Illuminati* of the 18th century, the *Knights Templar,* and certain Gnostic schools to a melding of Earthian adepts and entities from Sirius about 4,500 years ago in Sumeria.

More recently, Mr. Grant has added Outer Head of the A∴A∴ to his titles and claimed his rank in the OTO now stands as World Head.

See also:

Christians Awake AIDS Theory, Dr. John Dee, Freemasonry, Illuminati Copies or Revivals, *Necronomicon, Sirius Mystery*

References:

Aleister Crowley and the Hidden God, by Kenneth Grant, Samuel Weiser, New York, 1974

Cults of the Shadow, by Kenneth Grant, Samuel Weiser, New York, 1976

Great Pirates

In the sociological theory of **R. Buckminster Fuller**, the Great Pirates signify those men combining elements of what ethologists call the alpha male, historians call the despot, and sociologists call the sociopath. (Radical Feminists such as Susan Brownmiller and Robin Morgan believe that there are no other kinds of men.) Our primitive ancestors, Fuller says, were conquered by wave after wave of these despotic-sociopathic Great Pirates, until all humans became accustomed to being ruled by Great Pirates, since the only other choice was to be murdered by them.

The Great Pirates then discovered that other people were working at science, and hired the scientists to produce gadgets to suit their own needs. Therefore, Bucky says, science knows more about weaponry than about livingry. Fuller's experimental geometry and housing were attempts to contribute to the livingry he felt science had largely ignored.

The Great Pirates now make up a group Fuller called **MMAO** with a central steering committee called **LAWCAP**.

See also:

Federal Reserve Bank, Gnomes of Zurich, Government as Criminal Conspiracy, Insiders, *Yankee and Cowboy War*

Reference:

http://www.teleport.com/~pdx4d/grunch.html

"The Great Satanic Blasphemy"

"The Great Satanic Blasphemy" is an essay by *Philip K. Dick*, America's weirdest science-fiction writer. After 1973, Dick almost stopped writing science-fiction because he became too busy living in it, but he wrote thousands of pages of essays on his experiences in "orthogonal time" and other altered states, and "The Great Satanic Blasphemy" ranks high among them, and among Cosmic Conspiracy theories in general.

This essay holds that we (you and me, all of us) are "pluriforms" of God and thus gods ourselves: divine emanations "descended to this prison world, voluntarily losing our memory, identity and supernatural powers" but still capable of regaining them. This notion that "we shall be as gods," Dick acknowledges, is condemned as the Original Sin by orthodox Christian theology—the "sin of pride" for which we fell. Dick denies that we sinned or fell: We came here voluntarily to redeem this "prison world" and reunite it with the Divine.

The "prison world," also called the Black Iron Prison in some of Dick's fiction, represents all that we consider reality. It is not real at all, and doesn't exist in any sense; it is an enormous fake maintained by "the master magician, lord of the dark realm who poses as the creator."

This unreal world, or prison world, has no justice or sense or logic in it; hence, those who believe it is the only world either become atheists or embrace some kind of metaphysics that accepts the dark lord as the creator despite the horrors of the (alleged) creation. True religion begins when we begin to remember our starry heritage and the lord of light, of whom we are pluriforms, and then we can begin our true mission here, bringing light into the darkness, sanity into the irrational, justice into the chaotic, reality to the unreal.

Dick recognizes that something very similar to this model or narrative appears in Gnosticism and Taoism; it also appears in *Aleister Crowley;* and Christian critics of New Age ideas indeed consider it a Great Satanic Blasphemy. Basically, the question such models raise is: Can we worship the God of this world, or must we posit a better world somewhere to find a God worthy of worship?

See also:

Daimonic Reality, Corrydon Hammond, Recovered Memory Therapy, *Satanic Panic*

References:

http://deoxy.org/tcrime.htm

The VALIS Trilogy, by Philip K. Dick, Quality Paperback Books, New York, 1987

The Great Seal of the United States

The mysterious, seemingly Freemasonic design of eye-on-pyramid on the reverse of the Great Seal of the United States, and on the back of the dollar bill (since 1935), has become a symbol of conspiracy theories in general, largely because nobody really understands it. According to the Department of State, the pyramid merely represents strength and endurance. The pyramid is unfinished because the United States will always grow more perfect. The eye at the top represents divine guidance. In short, the government sees itself as strong, enduring, ever-improving, and divinely guided. (In individuals this is called megalomania.)

The inscription ANNUIT COEPTIS means "He has favored our undertakings," and NOVUS ORDO SECLORUM means "a new order of the ages."

Some conspiracy buffs on the far right doubt all this. The all-seeing eye is the eye of the ideally totalitarian government sought by the *Illuminati* and/or *Insiders* ("Big Brother Is Watching"). NOVUS ORDO SECLORUM means "New World Order." (See *Council on Foreign Relations*.) The repeated use of 13s in the design does not invoke the 13 original states of the Union but the 13 members of a Satanic coven. Etc.

Since there is some genuine mystery about how we got this Great Seal, legends have appeared to add more glamour to the mystery. For instance, UFOlogist Virginia Brassington gives an amusing occult legend: The Continental Congress, she says, appointed Benjamin Franklin, Thomas Jefferson, and *John Adams* to produce a design for the Great Seal. (That much is accepted by historians.) After many disagreements, Brassington says, Jefferson took a walk in the garden and returned with the Great Seal as we know it, the eagle on the obverse and the eye-on-the-pyramid on the reverse. Jefferson got the design, he said, from a man in black in the garden.

See also:

Freemasonry, Men in Black, UFO Conspiracies

References:

http://www.bep.treas.gov/newpub24.htm

Flying Saucers in the Bible, by Virgina Brassington, Saucerian Books, 1963, p. 43

The Great UFO Hoax

The Great UFO Hoax, by psychologist Gregory M. Kanon, claims to offer the final solution to the greatest scientific/cultural quarrel of our time, the identity of the unidentified. (Why psychologists are especially prone to thinking they've found the final solution to any and every mystery is itself a bit of a mystery, if you think about it.)

According to Kanon, the U.S. military has consciously and deliberately manufactured and manipulated the UFO "hoax" from the end of World War II. The **Roswell UFO crash,** for instance, was a deliberate bit of stage magic misdirection: First, the U.S. Air Force announced that a "flying disk" had crashed, allowed this astounding report to circulate across the nation, and then offered a lame and limping alternative story a few days later. Nobody believed their second story, and nobody believes it even now; defenders of orthodoxy have to invent more plausible versions of the air force yarns *for* them. In the atmosphere, every kind of paranoia flourishes, and that is the intent. The government needs fear of extraterrestrials to justify ever-higher military budgets, in case we ever run out of human enemies.

See also:

Mothman Prophecies, James Oberg, *Space-Time Transients*

Reference:

The Great UFO Hoax, by Gregory N. Kanon, Galde Press, Lakeville, Minn., 1997

Allen Greenfield

See:

Secret Cipher of the UFOnauts

Hank Greenspun

Hank Greenspun, editor of the *Las Vegas Sun,* was an associate of Robert Maheu, one of the top aides to **Howard Hughes.** Mahue has been connected with both the CIA and the **Mafia** by some conspiriologists. In 1972, for reasons never fully explained, the Nixon White House planned to send their top-secret "plumbers" unit to burglarize Greenspun's office and steal certain papers. Hughes, in turn, agreed to provide private airline service to get the burglars out of the country. For equally mysterious reasons, the burglary was never carried out, nor did the Senators who stumbled upon this inquire very far into it.

Watergate burglar James McCord allegedly said that:

Liddy said that Attorney General John Mitchell had told him that Greenspun had in his possession blackmail-type information involving a Democratic candidate for President, that Mitchell wanted that material, and Liddy said that this information was in some way racketeer-related, indicating that if this candidate became president, the racketeers or national crime syndicate could have a control or influence over him as president.

See also:

Gemstone File, Clifford Irving, MMAO, *Yankee and Cowboy War*

Reference:

The Yankee and Cowboy War, by Carl Oglesby, Berkley Medallion Books, New York, 1977, p. 173–74

Greys

The "Greys" are the most common type of alien life-form involved in close encounter UFO cases, especially in abductions. Grey in color, they stand two to five feet tall, have slits for mouths, no noses, and huge, buglike eyes. They first appeared in the Hill abduction case of 1961—a case typical of this field in that the data was all obtained by *recovered memory therapy* (hypnosis).

The Hills, Betty and Barney, remembered driving along a New Hampshire road, seeing a strange light, and then driving on home. Certain nervous symptoms eventually drove them to seek psychotherapy, and the fact that they were an interracial couple with plenty of reason to have nervous problems in this racist society was not considered at length, if at all. Under hypnosis they eventually remembered or imagined the UFO abduction experience that later cases all repeat endlessly—except that Barney Hill, the African-American in the couple, thought the Greys were wearing Nazi uniforms and Betty never did remember that.

No other abductee has reported the Nazi uniforms either.

Betty Hill remembered a star map on the spaceship and eventually, five years later, aided by an undergraduate astronomy student, identified the home planet of the Greys as part of the Zeta Reticuli system. Zeti Reticuli has remained a popular source of aliens in close encounters, although lately it has a lot of competition, including *Iumma*, Lanulos, *Sirius,* and huge constellations such as Orion and the Pleiades.

See also:

Abductees Anonymous, Philip J. Corso, *Daimonic Reality,* UFO Conspiracies

Reference:

http://www.profx.com/greyarea/guide.htm#Close-Encounter

GRUNCH

GRUNCH, an abbreviation devised by architect/sociologist *R. Buckminster Fuller,* means *Gross Universal Cash Heist,* Fuller's description of the overarching strategy of the *Great Pirates* who control this planet. According to Fuller, "sovereign nations" are actually sponsored entities, or puppets, of the Great Pirates and their behind-the-scenes financial networks (see *LAWCAP*). In this model, the Great Pirates keep governments afloat financially as a means of keeping them and their captive "subjects" in debt, and therefore, these governments, whatever they say in election years, will always raise taxes to pay ever-mounting interest on ever-growing national debts.

Fuller claims that it costs $100 million to run a campaign for president, $30 million to run for the Senate, and $10 million to run for the House (early 1980s estimates, not corrected for later inflation). Thus every politician is "sponsored" by one or more consortiums of Great Pirates. Fuller never believed any one gang of these Pirates ran the world, or even that there were two major factions, as in the *A-Albionic* theory. He believed there were many syndicates or gangs, and all of them were trying to steer Spaceship Earth in different directions, creating endless chaos and bad engineering.

See also:

Federal Reserve Bank, Gnomes of Zurich, Octopus, Ezra Pound, Fletcher Prouty, Benjamin R. Tucker

References:

http://www.teleport.com/~pdx4d/grunch.html

Grunch of Giants, by R. Buckminster Fuller, St. Martin's, 1983

Guardians of the Grail

Guardians of the Grail is the longest, most scholarly, and most intricate of the cosmic conspiracy books of *Robert Morning Sky*. It begins, like a lot of other great conspiracy books, with the destruction of the *Knights Templar*, a seemingly pious Christian order that was virtually wiped out when the Inquisition sentenced all its members to death or exile for a variety of sins, heresies, and crimes. Morning Sky argues that the real "crime" of the Templars was that they had discovered, during their years of investigating Solomon's Temple, that the original religion of the Jews was based on a goddess, not a god, and that Jesus married a priestess who carried on the goddess tradition, namely Mary Magdalene. The Templars were especially devoted to the *Merovingians*, as others indicate, but according to Morning Sky, this is because the Merovingians carried the sacred Magdelene genes, not because of her husband, Jesus, who was only a priest of the goddess religion.

All of this, however, is a small part of a much bigger picture, which involves interstellar war, the enslavement of humanity by certain extraterrestrials, and a hidden Order of Melchizedek, which is behind almost every other secret society you can think of.

See also:

John Birch Society, Church of Mary Magdalene, Dagobert II, *Gods of Eden,* Gnomes of Zurich, *Holy Blood, Holy Grail,* Noon Blue Apples, *Terra Papers*

References:

http://www.xroads.com/~rms/welcome.html

Guardians of the Grail, by Robert Morning Sky, Morning Sky Books, Phoenix, Ariz., n.d.

Gulf War Syndrome

Ever since the Gulf War, veterans have complained of a variety of related symptoms called Gulf War syndrome by the media, and the Pentagon steadfastly denied that the war had anything to do with the symptoms. In 1996, after *60 Minutes* (CBS News) did a segment on the suffering vets, pressure from the public forced Congress to demand some clarification from the Department of Defense. The Pentagon then admitted that 20,000 U.S. servicemen "may" have been exposed to chemical weapons during the war, due to the destruction of a weapons bunker.

Causes of similar symptoms in other soldiers, who were not in the area, remain unexplained, except for the vague notion of "post-traumatic stress syndrome." Veterans' groups continue to insist that some of the problems result from experimental vaccines given to the troops before sending them into battle.

See also:

American Hero, George Bush, Tampa Bay: Chemical Warfare

Reference:

http://home.earthlink.net/~bkonop/GermIncidents2.html

George I. Gurdjieff

George I. Gurdjieff must rank as the most mysterious of all the leaders of esoteric groups in the 20th century, since there is no agreement as to when or where he was born and a great deal of his life is wrapped in legends, some of which he invented himself. Basically, the Gurdjieff "school" (as he called it)[1] aims to teach the student:

1. *To become more* self-*aware, i.e., conscious of the role the self plays in creating impressions/perceptions (e.g., to change habitually from "that cheese smells awful" to "that cheese smells awful to me" and from "that music is terrible" to "that music seems terrible to me"), and*
2. *To break the habit of* identification, *Gurdjieff's name for the unconscious tendency to believe that ordinary human impressions/perceptions reveal objective reality. Learning to break down identification and begin to perceive true reality requires long, hard work, according to the Gurdjieff teaching; most people who haven't done "the work" (as the school exercises are called) simply live in a state of hypnosis or sleep-walking. (See* **Language as Conspiracy.***)*

Most mystics have said much the same, but Gurdjieff says it in the way most calculated to insult and humiliate ordinary people with ordinary opinions. (He called this "stepping on their corns.") His major work, *All and Everything*, is a history of humanity, full of jokes, allegories, and obvious put-ons; it is told by an extraterrestrial named Beelzebub (a name of Satan in some traditions) and portrays humans as backward, deluded, and generally the same sorry lot called Yahoos by Swift. The school teaches through such

[1]Other mystics have ashrams or lodges or orders, etc., but Gurdjieff had only "schools"; and where others had titles such as Guru or Master or Teacher, etc., Gurdjieff insisted on being called only Mr. Gurdjieff.

exercises as ritual movements, ritual nonmovements (freezes), ritual listening, etc.

The first aspect of hidden reality perceived in Gurdjieff's work is called "the horror of the situation," in which the student discovers that humans are enslaved robots. Who are our Masters? Gurdjieff always speaks allegorically or hermetically about that, but he says clearly that they herd us and butcher us like sheep.

According to philosopher-scientist J.G. Bennett, a sometime disciple of Gurdjieff, *All and Everything* was rewritten several times to make it harder for most readers to understand. Gurdjieff said this process was necessary "to bury the dog deeper." Bennett explains gnomically, "The dog is *Sirius*, the dog star, which stands for the spirit of wisdom in the Zoroastrian tradition."

Gurdjieff also taught about levels of consciousness above the human level, and surgeon Kenneth Walker, another sometime disciple, says these levels represent "angels and archangels" in some sense or "planets and stars" in another sense.

See also:

Aiwass, The Con, Philip K. Dick, Kenneth Grant, Great Pirates, *Sirius Mystery*

References:

Gurdjieff: Making a New World, by J.G. Bennett, Turnstone Books, London, 1973, p. 274

A Study of Gurdjieff's Teachings, by Kenneth Walker, Jonathan Cape, London, 1967, p. 167

Haitian Experiment Claim

In 1980–81, many male Haitian refugees held in detention centers in Miami and Puerto Rico developed gynecomastia, a condition in which males develop full female breasts. A number of the internees at Fort Allen (Puerto Rico) claimed that they were forced to undergo injections, which they believed to be female hormones.

See also:

AIDS Conspiracy Theories, Tuskegee Syphilis Study

Reference:

http://home.earthlink.net/~bkonop/GermIncidents2.html

Corrydon Hammond

Dr. Corrydon Hammond, a leading practitioner of *recovered memory therapy,* believes that his work proves the existence of an international Satanic cult of Nazis and CIA agents who have engaged in Satanic abuse of children for over 50 years. The purpose of the ritual abuse, Dr. Hammond says, is the creation of robotic humans, who are "programmed" to behave in specific ways when specific commands are given. In his own words, the Nazi-CIA group (which also includes NASA) hopes to create "tens of thousands of mental robots who will do pornography, prostitution, smuggle drugs, engage in international arms-smuggling. Eventually, those at the top of the Satanic cult want to create a Satanic order that will rule the world."

Dr. Hammond has even classified various types of "programs" that have been implanted in the victims of this cult: Alpha represents general obedience programming; Beta concerns performing oral sex and running child prostitution rings; Delta is the program that creates assassins; Omegas are self-destruct programs, which cause victims to kill themselves if a therapist almost recovers their other deep-buried Satanic programs; Zeta concerns the production of snuff films; etc.

Dr. Hammond is a licensed psychologist in Utah, founder and director of the Sex and Marital Therapy Clinic at the University of Utah, has served as both president and vice president of the

American Society of Clinical Hypnosis, and serves as abstracts editor of the *American Journal of Clinical Hypnosis*. He says he goes in fear of his life because of the revelations he has made. His theories have been accepted as literally true by countless Feminists and Fundamentalists.

See also:

Demonic Duck, Philip K. Dick, False Memory Syndrome Foundation, Making Monsters, Nazi Hell Creatures

Reference:

Making Monsters, by Richard Ofshe and Ethan Watters, University of California Press, Berkeley and Los Angeles, 1996, pp. 183–93

Jack Harris

Jack Harris is a gentleman who has been touring the country for several years claiming that the Freemasons are plotting to kill him. He also accuses them of Satanism, but he does not imply any human or animal sacrifices or the other medieval horror stories about the alleged Satanic underground spread by Feminists and Fundamentalists. Mr. Harris calls the Masons "Satanic" because they do not insist that all members accept Jesus as their Lord and Savior and allow heathens of all sorts to mingle with innocent Christians in their lodges. An ex-Mason himself, Harris quit the brotherhood when he discovered they had a rule against discussing religious differences in the lodge.

Two police forces have been involved in investigating Harris' charge of a Masonic plot to kill him, and both are extremely skeptical.

See also:

Hawthorne Abendsen, Freemasonry, *MS. Magazine*, Satanic Panic

Reference:

Arts and Entertainment TV, "The Unexplained: Secret Societies," January 8, 1998

Heaven's Gate

In 1978, in Houston, the present author was giving a lecture when a man and a woman in the audience got up and walked out. They were later identified as Bo and Peep, leaders of a typical UFO contact cult, and later we heard that they had changed their names to Him and Her. The female died of natural causes, the male changed his name again to Do, two decades passed, and then he and 38 disciples committed suicide with vodka and goofballs.

A year earlier another cult, the Solar Temple, had also committed suicide en masse in Switzerland.

Bo-Him-Do (real name: Marshall Applewhite) was terrorized by the 1993 FBI/ATF siege of the Branch Davidians in Waco and thought the FBI was stalking him. Similar paranoid fears about the CIA provoked Jim Jones of the People's Temple to lead his own cult in mass suicide back in the 1970s. Of course, the FBI and CIA never stalk anybody. (Well, hardly ever.) Yet, in a sense, the Heaven's Gate holocaust, like the Oklahoma City bombing, must rank as part of the psycho-social fallout of the Waco holocaust. A libertarian we know in Los Angeles stamps all of his mail: IS YOUR CHURCH ATF APPROVED?—more of the anxiety fallout.

If each of the 39 suicides had 5 close relationships (family, friends, lovers, etc.), that means that nearly 200 survivors suffered acute trauma from this "inexplicable" tragedy. And it is no longer wise to send these bewildered people to the Cult Awareness Network, which used to offer counseling and therapy in such cases. CAN was recently forced into bankruptcy by the Church of Scientology.

See also:

Brainwashing, George I. Gurdjieff, Language as Conspiracy

Reference:

http://www.trancenet.org/groups/faq/faqhg.shtml

The Hemp Conspiracy

According to marijuana crusader Jack Herer, pot *and all other forms of hemp* were made illegal in 1937 due to a plot by the Hearst and du Pont families, based on commercial motives. The Hearsts owned enormous woodlands and wanted the United States to use only wood-based paper, even though this wears out faster than hemp paper and produces massive pollution in its production; the du Ponts wanted us to wear clothes based on their new synthetics (nylon, Dacron, etc.) rather than the cheaper hemp. Together these two clans, and a few allies, launched a campaign to demonize the hemp plant; this continues to the present day.

Industrial hemp, as the non-intoxicating, non-medicinal variety is called, is one of the most versatile agricultural crops. In France, where 2 million pounds of industrial hemp are harvested annually, companies even use coated hemp to restore and build houses. Even in the United States, an estimated $25 million in sales of hemp products from abroad is a normal year's gross; that's $25 million lost to American farmers, forbidden to compete. Calvin Klein recently predicted that hemp would become the "fiber of choice" in the future, and many nutritionists urge legalization, because hemp has the highest concentration of amino acids in any food and is second only to soy in protein.

Hemp produces a much higher yield per acre than cotton and requires virtually no pesticides. Herer points out that if we returned to hemp paper (on which our Constitution was written) we could slow the destruction of forests almost to a standstill.

See also:

Fully Informed Jury Association, Government as Criminal Conspiracy, Holy Order of the Lemon, War on Some Drugs

References:

http://www.natlnorml.org/
http://www.drugtext.nl/lycaeum/

High Cabal

See:

Fletcher Prouty

High IQ Bulletin

High IQ Bulletin, written, edited, and published by Philip Campbell Argyle-Stuart, holds that all the conflicts in the world derive from an age-old conflict between Semitic peoples and Nordic peoples—a familiar idea to students of Nazism—but Argyle-Stuart adds that both groups are partly extraterrestrial.

This remarkable theory claims that the Khazars, a tribe converted to Judaism in the Middle Ages, were actually a "devilish" blend of humans and Vulcans; Vulcan not being the planet between Mercury and the Sun, as posited by 19th-century astronomers and rejected by those of the 20th century, nor even the home of Mr. Spock on *Star Trek,* but a planet that shares the same orbit as Earth, but always six months behind or ahead of us in circling the Sun and thus invisible to our telescopes. These Khazar/Vulcan hybrids, known as Jews to most of us, never cease plotting to conquer Earth. The Nordics, on the other hand, are Teutonic people intermarried with friendly folk from the planet Saturn.

The chief agencies of the Khazar/Vulcan plot, Argyle-Stuart avers, are the *Illuminati,* the *Grand Orient* Freemasons, the Zionists, the communists, the *Assassins* of Arabia, and the Thuggi from India.

See also:

A-Albionic, Gerard de Sede, *Gods of Eden,* Robert Morning Sky, Noon Blue Apples

Reference:

Philip Campbell Argyle-Stuart, *High IQ Bulletin,* Vol. 4, No. 1, Colorado Springs, Colo., 1970

History of Secret Societies

Since anti-Illuminism remains a major theme in most conspiracy theories, Akron Daraul's *History of Secret Societies* belongs in every conspiriologist's library.

Daraul, like **Abbe Barruel,** finds traces of Illuminist doctrine in the Ismaeli sect of Islam (also known as the *Assassins*), originated in 1092 by Hassan i Sabbah and currently led by the Aga Kahn (pp. 220–23). He also finds Illuminist ideas and symbolism in the *Roshinaya* (Illuminated Ones) active in Central Asia in the 16th century and also in the *Allumbrados* (Illuminated Ones) of Spain, in the same century. Thus, in Daraul's version, the Illuminati of Bavaria, founded by **Adam Weishaupt** in 1776, represents only a late manifestation of a much earlier tradition. "Documents still extant show several points of resemblance between the German and Central Asian Illuminists: points that are hard to account for on grounds of pure coincidence"(*History of Secret Societies*, p. 225).

Although Daraul mentions the revived Illuminati of Paris in the 1880s, he does not accept that the Illuminati still survive today.

See also:

Aleister Crowley, Illuminati Copies or Revivals, Merovingians, Noon Blue Apples, Ordo Templi Orientis

Reference:

History of Secret Societies, by Akron Daraul, Citadel Press, New York, 1961

Hoaxing the CIA

The CIA's very own website disappeared recently and was replaced with a new website proclaiming itself the Central Stupidity Agency. It contained parodies, denunciations, and various insults to the most feared organization on this planet, including a pungent greeting:

Power Through Resistance would like to say: FUCK YOU! to the Central Intelligence Agency World Wide Web site. ... But we already know you're all lame assholes. ... Never has so few brain cells done so little for no one.

This was signed by the Swedish Hackers Association, which may or may not provide the Agency with a clue as to where this gross indecency came from. The present author would suspect anywhere except Sweden.

The CIA got the website back under their own control in hours.

See also:

CIAC, Crypto-Anarchy, Desovereignization, OM, Poetic Terrorism

Ho Houses International

The author recently received an e-mail invitation to join Ho Houses International, allegedly a pyramid scheme intended to memorialize Ho Chih Minh. The basic pitch was that if I sent $20 in cash to Ho House at a certain address in Las Vegas, within three months I would get to the top of the list and receive $50,000 in cash from other members. "Send no checks," the letter said. "If everything is in cash, the IRS can't tax any member." This document concluded with the rousing slogan "Ho, Ho, Ho Chih Minh, Every member's got to win!"

Upon investigation, this differed very little (only a few words) from a more sober-looking document sent out by "Financial Friends" at the same address.

See also:

OM, S.O.B.

Hollow Earth

See:

Bermuda Triangle, Dr. Raymond Bernard, Nazi Hollow Earth Theory, Richard Shaver, *Subterranean Worlds*

Holmsburg Prison Conspiracy

In 1965, 70 volunteer prisoners at the Holmsburg State Prison in Philadelphia were given dioxin, the highly toxic chemical used in Agent Orange. Lesions that the men developed were not treated, and none of the subjects were informed that they were being studied for the development of cancer, thus violating the "informed consent" rule of the Nuremberg trials, under which Nazi doctors were condemned for similar research.

See also:

AIDS Conspiracy Theories, Mona Charen, Tuskegee Syphilis Study

Reference:

http://home.earthlink.net/~bkonop/GermIncidents2.html

Holocaust Deniers

Holocaust deniers claim that the planned extermination of 6 million Jews during the Nazi era never happened: Everybody who claims it did happen is either part of an international conspiracy to fake it, or a dupe of that conspiracy. All the journalists who saw the camps, all the eyewitnesses and "survivors," all the pedants who have screened the evidence, all the judges who passed sentences—every one of them got the facts wrong.

A typical Holocaust denier is Arthur R. Butz, an associate professor of electrical engineering at Northwestern University

(Evanston, Illinios), who presents the case against the Holocaust in a more academic and persuasive manner than most deniers. Butz admits that U.S. troops indeed found horrible piles of corpses in certain German concentration camps (e.g., Dachau and Belsen), but he claims they all died of typhus, carried by lice.

The fact that virtually every recognized historian believes the Holocaust happened does not faze Butz; historians once believed in the Donation of Constantine, he points out, and we now know that was a forgery. Besides, Butz carefully never refers to the Holocaust as anything else but "the legend": after pages of "the legend," "the legend," "the legend," repeated over and over, one may begin to feel that one is indeed reading about some fairy tale.

German documents referring to "the Final Solution" did not mean extermination, Butz asserts: They meant merely the transfer of Western European Jews to Eastern Europe. The confessions of major defendants at Nuremberg? Butz always puts quotes around the word "confessions"—and strongly suggests that they were obtained fraudulently.

And the death camps were not reserved exclusively for Jews. They also contained, Butz notes, political prisoners, ordinary criminals, homosexuals, and conscientious objectors.

Finally, the war destroyed so much that records of the death tolls in any part of the war are all largely guesswork. Maybe only 5 million Jews died and not 6. . . or maybe it was only one million. . . . And remember, they died of typhus.

"Surely any thoughtful person must be skeptical," Butz concludes one of his articles.

Despite criticism from professional historians, heated controversy, acrimony, and a lot of anger from the Jewish community, Prof. Butz continues to hold his post at Northwestern University, and gallantly battles on to restore the good name of Adolph Hitler.

See also:

American Hero, Creation Science, OM, World War II Deniers

Reference:

http://pubweb.acns.nwu.edu/~abutz

Holy Blood, Holy Grail

Holy Blood, Holy Grail is the only book about the ***Priory of Sion*** and the ***Church of Mary Magdalene*** mystery to have reached best-seller status, and it certainly does contain some of the most startling ideas of any of the literature on these subjects.

The authors—Michael Baigent, Henry Lincoln, and Richard Leigh—interviewed ***Gerard de Sede,*** the man who claims the Priory is made up of descendants of the Royal House of David who intermarried with extraterrestrials from ***Sirius***. De Sede also admitted, or certainly hinted strongly, that he did not write as an outsider studying the Priory but as an initiated member engaged in a process of gradual revelation, which the Priory has orchestrated for several decades.

For a true conspiriologist this raises the question: How about Baigent, Lincoln, and Leigh themselves? Shall we consider them outside the masque, studying it objectively, or inside feeding us the yarns the Priory wants us to believe?

Whatever or whomever we suspect, when Baigent, Lincoln, and Leigh met Mr. de Sede, they discussed mostly another of his books, *L'or de Rennes-le-Chateau (The Treasure of Rennes-le-Chateau),* which deals with the mysteries of the half-legendary ***Merovingian*** dynasty and with the strange Church of Mary Magdalene, in the town of Rennes-le-Chateau, built in the 1890s by the even stranger priest named ***Father Béranger Saunière,*** who allegedly found a treasure after deciphering some old parchments in another church there. (See ***Noon Blue Apples.***)

One of the stations of the cross inside the cathedral of Mary Magdalene shows conspirators smuggling Jesus' body out of the grave during the night, recalling the famous heresy that Jesus never died: Somebody slipped him a narcotic that simulated death, and after hiding out a while, he either faked a resurrection and/or went off to preach in India and/or ultimately died in Japan. Several versions of this yarn have circulated at various times, including the enigmatic verse in the *Koran,* where Jesus says, "They thought they crucified me, but I laughed at them." An even more remarkable passage in *some,* not all, early manuscripts of Tacitus says Jesus led riots in Rome 40 years after his alleged death.

Baigent, Lincoln, and Leigh eventually tracked down the Grand Master of the Priory of Sion—the same **Pierre Plantard de Saint Clair** whom Matthew Paoli discovered publishing *Circuit,* the journal of the seemingly non-existent **Committee to Protect the Rights and Privileges of Low-Cost Housing** out of the office of the Committee for Public Safety, which he shared with André Malraux. Plantard spoke at length but mostly in riddles, as befits the Grandmaster of a secret society. As to the treasure of Rennes-le-Chateau, Plantard described it as "spiritual" rather than "material," said it belonged to Israel, and promised it "would be returned to Israel at the proper time."

Holy Blood, Holy Grail also links the Priory—sometimes convincingly, sometimes weakly—with some interesting folks. Such as:

1. The **Knights Templar,** *the chivalric order that had 123 members burned by the Inquisition between 1307 and 1314. (Templar teachings got passed on to all later anti-Papist secret societies, according to many theorists.)*
2. *The rituals of Freemasonry and especially the archetype of the Widow's Son (all taken from the Knights Templar, according to Masonic historians).*
3. *The Rosicrucians and the Illuminati.*

4. *Such worthies as Isaac Newton, Claude Debussy, and* **Jean Cocteau,** *all of whom allegedly served as Grandmasters of the Priory before Plantard de Saint Claire.*

The authors also document that Father Saunière belonged to one or more occult orders in Paris. All of these influenced *Aleister Crowley* and, through Crowley (or through P.B. Randolph), further influenced all modern magick orders that have both a Masonic style of ritual and symbolism and a hidden Tantric (*sex magick*) teaching.

Ultimately, Baigent, Lincoln, and Leigh present their own theory of what the Priory intends to reveal in slow stages. This theory holds that (a) Jesus married Mary Magdalene, (b) they had a child, the really important Widow's Son of tradition, and (c) this child escaped to France after the crucifixion and became the progenitor of the Merovingian kings, and of various interesting people alive today who are related or allegedly related to the Merovingians.

In short, Baigent, Lincoln, and Leigh offer us the oldest of all millennial legends: The True King will return soon, very soon, and cast out the usurpers. They even claim that this archetypal myth occurs in all European countries *because the Priory planted it,* to prepare us for the day when the seed of Jesus sits in judgment on all nations.

See also:

GENISIS, Gnomes of Zurich, OM, Octopus

Reference:

Holy Blood, Holy Grail, by Michael Baigent, Henry Lincoln, and Richard Leigh, Delacorte, New York, 1982

The Holy Order of the Lemon

The Holy Order of the Lemon, another offshoot of *Freemasonry*, was either founded by Lord Glendale in 1798 or by a group of pranksters in 1996, who performed the first public Lemon Order event by dumping lemons—lots and lots of lemons—into the River Liffey in Dublin, Ireland. This mystic brotherhood declares itself frankly devoted to seeking large grants from corporations dealing in lemon products (such as Lemon Pledge) to sponsor rituals, primarily consisting of long, dour marches wearing drab suits and "lemon-colored derbies," through "places of no historical interest," holding aloft "rampant or couchant, fresh lemons in hands sinister." Patron saint of the order is 19th-century French socialist Charles Fourier, who believed in the overthrow of civilization and the founding of a "society of harmony" in which all passions and manias would be encouraged, after which the ocean would turn to lemonade.

According to another version, the actual founder of the Lemon Order was Elizabeth Adworth (1695–1775), the only woman ever initiated into Freemasonry (in Doneraile, County Cork) after being discovered asleep behind some curtains in the lodge. In her memory, the Lemon Order is bisexual, i.e., open to all genders.

The manifesto of the Holy Order of the Lemon begins, "Razorryn orderruin, XTCronny rocket, . . . John Lemon, lemon soda pop, Bellemon Laswellemon, Lemon flesh, Irish Spermanent lemonadelic, AC/DCitron, Vincent Van Gogh: Teller und citronen, The Lemonheadfucks, Babelllemon, Prince Lemon Crush, Better Lemonade. . . . Make Lemon not Orange, . . . " etc. (We don't have enough space to quote it all here.)

See also:

Golden Apple Corps, Grand Orange Lodge of Ireland, Noon Blue Apples

Reference:

http://www.fringeware.com/hell/lemon

Hono Intelligence Service 1901

In 1973, in Canuelus, Argentina, a man named Carlos Jerez opened a cancer center with a 1950s model "flying saucer" in the front yard and a plaque on the main building saying:

Hono Intelligence Service 1901
)+(

The strange)+(symbol, by then identified with the growing *UMMO Letters* cult in Europe, may or may not have attracted attention in Argentina, but Jerez soon had a reputation as a miracle healer and boasted of curing over 200 patients. He also let it be known that he came from another planet, and the government then became interested enough to conduct an investigation. It soon emerged that Jerez was medically incompetent (he failed to detect an advanced tumor in one patient, for instance). He then disappeared or went back to his home planet or at least was heard of no more.

See also:

"Bob," Elmyr, Madrid UMMO Sightings, Noon Blue Apples, OM, Voronezh, UMMO Visit

Reference:

Revelations: Alien Contact and Human Deception, by Jacques Vallee, Ballantine, New York, 1991, pp. 91–96

Dr. Leonard Horowitz

Dr. Leonard Horowitz of Harvard University has written two books that strongly support Gay conspiracy theories about the origin of AIDS. In *Emerging Viruses,* Dr. Horowitz presents evidence that HIV resulted from biological viral research and experiments that were hidden behind the title Special Virus Cancer Program (SVCP).

Dr. Gallo, on the other hand, still claims that HIV originated among monkeys and "spontaneously" mutated to attack humans, no friend to aid it in mutating.

See also:

AIDS Conspiracy Theories, Bisociation, MK-ULTRA, Tuskegee Syphilis Study, Umbrella Man

Reference:

http://www.trufax.org/research/horo.html

Colonel Edward House

Col. Edward Mandell House (1858–1938), a proponent of world government with close ties to the Morgan banking family, was an adviser and mentor to President Woodrow Wilson and later, to a lesser degree, President F.D. Roosevelt.

In 1912, House wrote a didactic novel entitled *Philip Dru: Administrator,* which has been reprinted several times by right-wing groups (latest edition: General Birch Service, Appleton, Wisconsin). In this book, Dru advocates and guides a "conspiracy" (the dread word is actually used) with three goals:

1. *the establishment of a central bank;*
2. *a progressive graduated income tax; and*
3. *control of both political parties in the United States*

President Wilson persuaded Congress to carry out the first two, by establishing the **Federal Reserve Bank** on December 23, 1913, and the **Internal Revenue Service** shortly thereafter. Many right-wingers (and also many left-wingers) believe the third goal has also been achieved.

House once described himself as a Marxian socialist, but he

might have been joking; he acted more like a Fabian socialist. In the 1920s, he went through a period of infatuation with Mussolini's fascist economy.

See also:

John Adams on Banking, Bank of the United States, Council on Foreign Relations, 23 Enigma

Reference:

http://www.empire.net/~danp/shadow.html

Howard Hughes Forgeries

In the celebrated *Clifford Irving/Howard Hughes* autobiography case, although two experts originally authenticated the "Hughes" signatures and notes, a 1972 Federal Grand Jury ultimately decided that the documents were forgeries and that Irving himself had penned them. According to *"The Gemstone File,"* Irving acquired the courage to attempt this swindle because he was intimate with the international jet set and knew that Hughes was dead and therefore could not contradict him: He had no idea that a double of Hughes existed and would denounce him over the phone.

After the death of Hughes (or the double) in 1976, leaving an estate of between two and three billion dollars, no apparent will was found at first. Then an alleged will, seemingly in Hughes' handwriting, was found on a desk in the office of the Church of Jesus Christ of Latter-Day Saints (Mormons). With the will was a note saying that the document had been found near the home of Joseph Smith (founder and martyr of Mormonism). This led to considerable excitement and legal action for a time, but eventually this, too, was judged a forgery.

See also:

CIAC, Elmyr, *F for Fake,* OM, Poetic Terrorism

Reference:

http://www.webmasters.net/qde/cases.htm

Hughes vs. Rockefeller

The fate of Trans World Airlines hung in the balance for over twelve years (ca. 1960–1973) while *Howard Hughes* and *David Rockefeller* battled through the U.S. court system, all the way to the top. Basically, Hughes, as the creator of TWA and an old-style entrepreneur, felt that Rockefeller was attempting to steal something Hughes himself had made, something that belonged to him. We know that Hughes thought that because he spoke about it openly and vehemently, even accusing the Rockefeller interests of *communism.* (See *John Birch Society.*) Rockefeller, typical of the stylistic difference between the two, did not have much to say. His lawyers, however, said that Hughes had mismanaged his own company, and poor old David Rockefeller and all the other stockholders were being deprived of the better profits they would have earned under saner management.

The first rumbles began back in the 1940s, when Hughes first found reason to believe the Rockefeller group was inciting the government to prosecute him on what seemed (to him) trivial technicalities. The real power struggle began in 1961. Hughes thought, as David Tinnin thought when he wrote *Just About Everybody vs. Howard Hughes,* that the problem began with an attempt to force Hughes to borrow money he did not wish to borrow. The proposal offered Hughes involved Dillon, Read, and Company, the Metropolitan, Equitable and Prudential Insurance Companies, the Bank of America, and Chase Manhattan, who wanted to jointly give TWA $260 million in exchange for the usual high interest—and two out of three voting members in a trust, with Hughes reduced to a permanent minority of one vote.

Hughes did not want the money, and he also did not want to become outvoted in control of the company he had built from almost nothing. He said no.

John Sonnett, a top Wall Street lawyer, then filed an antitrust action against Hughes on behalf of TWA. Now, an antitrust action against the owner of a company, allegedly *by* the company, is rather unique, and Hughes thought it had no chance of succeeding. Yet Sonnett and associates were hard workers; they produced ledgers claiming that Hughes' refusal to go into hock to Wall Street had cost his airline exactly $45,870,435.95. To Hughes and his lawyers, this seemed like Alice in Wonderland. They fought and they fought hard; and when the case arrived, finally, at the U.S. Supreme Court, Justice William O. Douglas, writing for the majority, found in Hughes' favor. But that didn't happen until 1973. In the 12 years of the battle, Hughes lost in every lower court, without exception: lost fighting a claim the Supreme Court found legally unsound. He also lost millions in legal expenses, and finally lost control of his airline.

Hughes became convinced that this long legal struggle proved the Rockefellers and their Wall Street cronies controlled almost all the courts in the United States and, after further struggles with the *Mafia* over who was running Las Vegas, grew morbidly preoccupied with conspiracies and bacteria.

See also:

Gemstone File, Hank Greenspun, Insiders, Clifford Irving, *Yankee and Cowboy War*

References:

Just About Everybody vs. Howard Hughes, by David Tinnin, Doubleday, New York, 1973

The Yankee and Cowboy War, by Carl Oglesby, Berkley Medallion Books, New York, 1977

John Hull

For several years John Hull, who has admitted he was a CIA employee but denies everything else, owned a large ranch in Costa Rica. According to sworn testimony, this ranch served as a center for a period in the 1970s–80s from which the Nicaraguan Contras received guns from the CIA and paid in cocaine, which the CIA then sold on the open market to finance this illegal operation. (Congress had forbidden the CIA to intervene further in the internal affairs of Nicaragua.)

The Costa Rican government believed this testimony and attempted to bring Hull to trial on these charges. He fled back to the United States, which has refused to extradite him. A public-interest law firm, the Christic Institute, then tried to bring Hull to trial in the United States, but their suit was dismissed.

The Christic suit, based on more evidence than the Costa Rican criminal charges against Hull, named as co-conspirators Col. Oliver North, General Richard Secord, and *George Bush*.

See also:

Cisalpine Bank, P2 conspiracy, Octopus, *Veil,* World Finance Corporation

Reference:

Cover Up: Behind the Iran-Contra Affair, 72-minute color video documentary, directed by Barbara Trent, Empowerment Project, 1988

E. Howard Hunt

A longtime CIA agent who helped overthrow the Arbenz government in Guatemala in the 1950s, E. Howard Hunt later participated in the Bay of Pigs invasion of Cuba. He also wrote spy novels and, according to fellow spook Frank Sturgis, participated in assassination operations.

Many conspiriologists believe that the oldest of the *Three*

Tramps photographed on the grassy knoll right after the *John F. Kennedy assassination* looks amazingly like Hunt—so much so that he must be Hunt. In their book, *Coup d'Etat in America*, which was endorsed by Congressman Henry Gonzalez, authors *A.J. Weberman* and Michael Canfield provide photographic overlays of Hunt and the alleged tramp to demonstrate the astounding similarities. In 1988, 3M Comtal Corporation analyzed photos of Hunt and the tramp and found strong resemblances.

Hunt has given conflicting accounts of where he was at the time of the shooting.

When *Spotlight* magazine published some of this in an article by Victor Marchetti, a former CIA officer who had turned against the Agency, Hunt sued for libel. Marchetti had said that Hunt and *James Jesus Angleton* were both involved in the John F. Kennedy hit. Hunt won in the first trail (the jury awarded him $650,000), but on appeal, the defense produced more and more damning evidence, including the testimony of Marita Lorenz, another former CIA agent, who said that on November 20, 1963 in Dallas she saw Hunt and Frank Sturgis (another of the "tramps" on the Grassy Knoll, according to some) seemingly preparing for an assassination, with some anti-Castro Cubans. Hunt also continued to contradict himself about his whereabouts on November 22. The jury found for the magazine, saying Hunt had not been libeled. The forewoman later told the press:

> *Mr. Lane [defense counsel] was asking us to do something very difficult. He was asking us to believe John Kennedy was killed by our own government. Yet, when we examined the evidence, we were compelled to conclude that the CIA had indeed killed President Kennedy.*

Hunt was later convicted of participation in the 1972 Watergate "burglary" (which was not a burglary at all, but an attempt to bug Democratic National Headquarters) and served three years in prison.

See also:

Mona Charen, Flight 553, Marina Oswald, "The Whole Bay of Pigs Thing," *Yankee and Cowboy War*

References:

http://ourworld.compuserve.com/homepages/MGriffith_2/suspects.htm

The photographic evidence—

http://www.netins.net/showcase/neuendorf/ehoward.htm

http://weberman.com

The libel trial—

Popular Alienation, ed. by Kenn Thomas, IllumiNet Press, Lilburn, Ga., 1995, pp. 48–51

Mary Hyre

Mary Hyre, a journalist on the *Point Pleasant* (West Virginia) *Messenger,* alleges an unusual encounter with the three **men in black** who haunt UFO witnesses. In 1967, that area of West Virginia had more than its share of weirdity—not only frequent UFO reports but, even more sinister, reports of "Mothman," a local monster with a humanoid body, blazing red eyes, and giant wings who appears in cycles, then goes into hiding for years or decades, then resurfaces, rather like Bigfoot in the West.

On December 22, 1967, Mrs. Hyre encountered her first two Men in Black, who seemed short and vaguely Oriental; they asked her about local UFO sightings and then inquired what she would do if ordered to stop writing about UFOs. She told them to go to hell and they left. Later that afternoon a third and taller Man in Black arrived, with a darker complexion and a pronounced stutter. He also tried to persuade her to stop writing about UFOs, and left when she got salty.

See also:

Daimonic Reality, 666, UFO Conspiracies

Reference:

The Mothman Prophecies, by John Keel, IllumiNet Press, Avondale Estates, Ga., 1991, pp. 11–14

Iatrogenic AIDS Theory

Some theorists hold that the practice of medicine itself creates some illnesses. This model, labeled iatrogenesis (from *iatro,* medicine, and *genesis,* beginning), claims that by overdosing the modern world, doctors have in fact created as many illnesses as they ever cure—or have created even more illnesses than they cure, in the opinion of the most hostile critics. Philosopher Ivan Illich even accuses modern medicine of what he calls *iatrogenocide,* a Joycean word that signifies iatrogenic destruction of whole populations.

Since AIDS patients are given astronomical amounts of medications, many AIDS conspiracy theorists think that AIDS itself may be an iatrogenic condition. Some even trace the problem back to the foundations of modern medicine and claim the "germ theory of disease" is badly flawed, citing cases of people who have the "germ" but not the disease, and arguing that hostile organisms alone cannot explain illness: The body must be weakened by other, environmental causes before it becomes unable to fight off disease.

This position is often expressed in the mosquito metaphor: Mosquitoes "cause" malaria, but killing off the mosquitoes does not solve the problem, since every generation new mosquitoes appear with resistance to the old pesticides. Draining the swamps where the mosquitoes breed *would* solve the problem, this viewpoint declares. In human terms, this means that we need less work on ever more powerful drugs to dose patients and more work on the environmental causes that make the patients weak and disease-prone in the first place.

This argument is usually accompanied by the further claim that modern medicine and pharmacology are multibillion dollar growth industries with little interest in alternative medical theories or new, more holistic approaches.

See also:

AIDS Conspiracy Theories, Dr. Wilhelm Reich

Reference:

http://www.livelinks.com/sumeria/health/fraud.html

The Illuminati

Although many conspiriologists want to trace it further back, the Illuminati known to most historians was founded on May 1, 1776, in Ingolstadt, Bavaria, by a *Freemason* (and former Jesuit) named *Adam Weishaupt*. According to the *Encyclopedia Britannica*, the Illuminati managed to influence many Masonic lodges and gained "a commanding position" in the movement of "republican free thought," i.e., anti-royalist and pro-democratic secularism. They attracted such literary men as Goethe and Herder, but the whole movement came to an end when the Illuminati were banned by the Bavarian government in 1785.

Many conspiracy hunters following *Abbe Barruel* believe the Illuminati merely regrouped under other front names after 1785 and still continues to the present, although they often disagree as to whether the Illuminati is promoting republicanism, communism, anarchism, Satanism, international banking, or some combination thereof. See the links at the end of this entry.

According to Masonic historian Albert G. Mackey, the Illuminati was very popular and had at least 2,000 members in Masonic lodges in France, Belgium, Holland, Denmark, Sweden, Poland, Hungary, and Italy. Mackey emphasizes that Baron Knigge, one of the most powerful and active members of the Illuminati, was a devout Christian and would not have worked so hard for the order if its aim had been, as Abbe Barruel and others claim, the abolition of Christianity. He concludes that it exercised no "favorable" or "unfavorable" effect on the history of Freemasonry.

On the other hand, Abbe Barruel linked the Illuminati positively to the Order of *Assassins,* the *Knights Templar* (condemned by the Inquisition for sorcery, sodomy, and heresy), and a worldwide Jewish plot.

See also:

Ewige Blumenkraft, *High IQ Bulletin, History of Secret Societies,* Nazi/Illuminati Theory, *None Dare Call It Conspiracy, Secret Societies and Their Role in the 20th Century, World Revolution*

References:

Encyclopedia Britannica, 1966 edition, Halicar to Impala, p. 1094

Encyclopedia of Freemasonry, by Albert G. Mackey, Macoy Publishing, Richmond, Va., 1966, p. 1099

Illuminati Copies or Revivals

Both Daraul's *"History of Secret Societies"* and Nesta Webster's *"World Revolution"* mention a revived *Illuminati* group in Paris in the 1880s; but Daraul regards it as a copy of Weishaupt's original order with no lasting influence, while Webster thinks it was the original order coming out in the open again and heavily influencing the modern labor and socialist movements.

More intriguing and complex was the Order of the Illuminati founded by Freemasonic druggist Theodor Reuss in Munich in 1880. This was joined by actor Leopold Engel, who founded his own World League of Illuminati in Berlin in 1893.

In 1896, Reuss, Engel, and occultist Franz Hartmann co-founded the Theosophical Society of Germany, and in 1901 Engel and Reuss produced or forged a charter giving them authority over the re-established Illuminati of Weishaupt. Also in 1901, Reuss, Hartmann, and metallurgist Karl Kellner founded the *Ordo Templi Orientis* and appointed William Wynn Westcott (of the *Hermetic Order of the Golden Dawn*) Regent of England.

In or about 1912, Reuss conferred the ninth degree of the Ordo Templi Orientis upon *Aleister Crowley*, claiming that Crowley already knew the occult secret of that degree. (See *"The Book of Lies."*) He later appointed Crowley his successor as Outer Head of the order.

In 1934 the Gestapo forcibly suppressed both the Order of the Illuminati and the Ordo Templi Orientis in Germany—along with all other Freemasonic orders and lodges, and schools of Esperanto to boot. The Ordo Templi Orientis survived elsewhere, but the Illuminati as an occult order only seems to exist in Switzerland at present.

Crowley includes *Adam Weishaupt*, the founder of the 18th-century Illuminati, among the Gnostic Saints in his Gnostic Catholic Mass, performed regularly in all Ordo Templi Orientis lodges. But that list also includes such odd birds as King Arthur, Parcifal, Pope Alexander Borgia, *John Dee*, Goethe, Wagner, King Ludwig ("the Mad King of Bavaria"), and painter Paul Gauguin. . .

See also:

Church of Mary Magdalene, *GENISIS,* Noon Blue Apples

References:

Paris Illuminati—

History of Secret Societies, by Akron Daraul, Citadel Press, New York, 1961

World Revolution: The Plot Against Civilization, by Nesta Webster, Constable and Company, London, 1921

German Illuminati and Ordo Templi Orientis links—

http://www.cyberlink.ch/~koenig/illumin.txt

Gnostic Catholic Mass—

Magick, by Aleister Crowley, Samuel Weiser, New York, 1973, pp. 423–36

The Illuminoids

The Illuminoids: Secret Societies and Political Paranoia, by Neal Wilgus, is a critical history of Illuminism and anti-Illuminism, written from a detached and mildly ironic view.

Wilgus grants that the original 18th-century Illuminati had more power than is generally accepted by academic historians. He quotes Robison's *Proofs of a Conspiracy*, which alleges 84 Illuminati lodges in Germany alone and claims that French aristocrats such as Mirabeau and Orleans were also members; the more skeptical Vernon Stauffer, who in *The Bavarian Illuminati in New England*, accepts that Metternich, Herder, Goethe, and Banfly were members; and J.M. Roberts' even more skeptical *Mythology of Secret Societies*, which accepts all of the above as members and includes Mozart also. Such a movement seems a lot more than a footnote to history.

Wilgus explores the various conspiriologists who have found Illuminati influence on 19th- and 20th-century politics/economics and finds them unconvincing. He tends to accept much of the recent and current conspiracy theories about the **Bilderbergers**, and a few other power groups, but judges all the evidence tracing them back to the Illuminati as weak and implausible.

The book includes a reading list featuring some excellent works and a few really funny crackpot books, too; and it has an outline of history as it appears if one accepts the idea that the Illuminati have always been around and always manipulating events behind the scenes.

See also:

Hawthorne Abendsen, American Dynasty, Beethoven, Council on Foreign
Relations, Federal Reserve Bank, Illuminati, Illuminatus Fletcher
Prouty, Cecil Rhodes as Illuminatus

Reference:

The Illuminoids: Secret Societies and Political Paranoia, by Neal Wilgus,
Sun Books, Albuquerque, N.Mex., 1978

In Banks We Trust

In Banks We Trust, by Penny Lernoux, examines the bank scandals and S&L monkey business of the 1980s and concludes that
drugs and drug money played a major role in most of the major
disasters. "The drug trail led all over the world, from the
Caribbean to Miami, Australia and eventually the Vatican," exposing a network of corruption involving "mobsters, right-wing terrorists, and CIA agents," she writes (page xix).

Lernoux is particularly good at explaining clearly the labyrinthine
system of drug deals involving the *World Finance Corporation* in
Miami, *Cisalpine Bank* in the Bahamas, and the *P2* group in Italy,
and the links of all of them with the CIA.

She also presents, more or less as asides, some evidence that
David Rockefeller is not the criminal mastermind painted by
many conspiriologists. The dreaded *Trilateral Commission,*
founded and funded by Rockefeller, accomplished none of his
goals, she says, and just shows that he could put a lot of money
and energy into projects that would never fly. She also mentions
that Rockefeller's Chase Manhattan Bank guaranteed the loans of
an eccentric little bank called Penn Square, which went bankrupt
after giving too many unsecured loans to dubious customers, cost-
ing Chase $46 million when the ax fell.

Penn Square's troubles were exacerbated by William Patterson, vice president in charge of loans, who was in the habit of wearing Mickey Mouse ears to the office and once appeared at a meeting with the Seattle First National Bank dressed as an Arab sheik. Lernoux offers no opinion about whether Penn's case is drug-related or not, but the *Wall Street Journal* noted that Patterson had hidden strings in his clothes, which made the Mickey Mouse ears wiggle while he discussed loans with clients.

See also:

Mona Charen, Federal Reserve Bank, John Hull, Noon Blue Apples, OM

References:

In Banks We Trust, by Penny Lernoux, Anchor/Doubleday, New York, 1984

The Mickey Mouse ear strings—

Wall Street Journal, July 27, 1982

Incest Survivors

"Incest survivors" appear as commonly among patients who have experienced *recovered memory therapy* as do victims of Satanic programming or extraterrestrial kidnapping. As with the other varieties of recovered memory therapy, anybody who does not remember this type of experience is suspected of "being in *denial*" or (among the victims of Satanists and extraterrestrials) of having memories artificially erased. In short, if you can't remember it, it probably happened to you.

Here are common signs of being an incest survivor without remembering it:

- *Fear of being alone in the dark*

- *Phobias*

- *Fear of being watched*

- *Feeling crazy*

- *Feeling oneself (or everything) is unreal*

- *Denial; repression of memories*

- *Avoidance of mirrors*

- *Desire to change one's name*

- *Fear of noise*

If you have more than one of these traits, you may well be another incest survivor. On the other hand, many of these traits are believed (by other recovered memory specialists) to indicate that you've been kidnapped and molested by aliens from outer space. Better look into **Abductees Anonymous**, in case that fits you better.

See also:

Philip K. Dick, Corey Hammond, *Making Monsters,* National Association for Consumer Protection in Mental Health Practices, OM

Reference:

Secret Survivors, by E. Sue Blume, Ballantine, New York, 1990

In God's Name

In God's Name, by David Yallop, was the most shocking best-seller of the mid-1980s, in both Europe and the United States, but the very sensational charges it makes were never brought to court and remain, like all-too-many conspiracy theories, in the area of speculation.

Yallop, who had two previous books that did result in legal actions that justified him, claims that the **P2 conspiracy** as revealed in court trials and other books was only part of the total corruption in which the Vatican Bank was involved under the presidency of **Paul "The Gorilla" Marcinkus**. As Yallop tells it, when **Licio Gelli** formed P2 as a secret society within the **Grand**

Orient Lodge of Egyptian Freemasonry, he immediately double-crossed his CIA employers and became a mole for the KGB, whom he also double-crossed.

The crimes of P2, Yallop says, not only involved laundering drug money for the CIA and Mafia, as charged by Italian authorities, but also gunrunning for various terrorist groups, plotting a fascist coup in Italy, assisting Nazi war criminals to get CIA employment in the death squads of various Latin American dictatorships, aiding fascist Juan Perón to regain the presidency of Argentina, and several murders, including those of Mino Pecorelli and Pope John Paul I.

Pecorelli, an angry former member of P2, had began publishing a muckraking journal revealing P2 activities. One issue actually included a list of 100 Freemasons in the Vatican, many of them members of the *Grand Loge Alpina.* Pecorelli sent every issue of his journal to Pope John Paul I, who, as a result, ordered an investigation of the Vatican Bank. The pope died almost immediately, on September 28, 1978, allegedly of natural causes. Pecorelli was shot through the mouth on March 20, 1979—the *sasso in bocca,* traditional *Mafia* punishment for informers. Yallop claims both deaths were plotted by Licio Gelli, *Roberto Calvi, Michele "The Shark" Sindona,* and Marcinkus.

As a sidelight, Yallop also tries to prove that various others, including Cardinal Cody of Chicago, might have been involved in the Pope's alleged murder because John Paul I, who had lived among the poor most of his life, was talking as if he might reverse the Church's long opposition to contraception.

See also:

James Jesus Angleton, Cara Calvi, Gladio, Knights of Malta, *Scandals of the Priory of Sion*

Reference:

In God's Name, by David Yallop, Jonathan Cape, London, 1984

The Insiders

See:

John Birch Society, The Con, Council on Foreign Relations, Gnomes of Zurich, Illuminati, Lyndon LaRouche, LAWCAP, *Yankee and Cowboy War*

Inslaw

The Inslaw case has a special fascination for conspiriologists because it seems linked to every other conspiracy, real and imaginary, that anybody ever heard of.

Inslaw, the Institute for Law and Social Research, owned by William and Nancy Hamilton, had sold the U.S. Justice Department a new software program called **PROMIS**. From all accounts, PROMIS appears the most sophisticated and versatile system for spying on people that has ever been devised. The Hamiltons expected to earn at least $5 billion from sales of PROMIS to law enforcement agencies, but instead, they found themselves paid nothing and engaged in a seemingly endless battle with the Justice Department, or persons within the Justice Department. There have been two court cases, both won by Inslaw and the Hamiltons, and one judge even said that the Justice Department had been guilty of "trickery, deceit, and fraud." The Nunn Committee also investigated and found that the Justice Department had victimized the Hamiltons and intimidated witnesses. Finally, in 1994, a federal court rejected the Hamilton's claims.

The whole Inslaw matter took on a new complexion when journalist **Danny Casolaro** began investigating it on his own and found a surprising number of mysterious deaths and unsolved murders among people involved in the feud. Casolaro also found links to the Iran/Contra scandal, **Area 51,** the crime-ridden Bank of Credit and Commerce International, the Nugan Hand Bank in Australia (which went bankrupt while under investigation for allegedly laundering CIA drug money) and dozens of other murky and seemingly criminal conspiracies.

Danny Casolaro himself died under mysterious circumstances, shortly after interviewing an unidentified Arab who promptly vanished.

Before his death, Casolaro had made notes for a projected book, in which he claimed all the interlinked conspiracies he had found were part of a cabal originated by *James Jesus Angleton.*

See also:

Mona Charen, *In Banks We Trust,* MMAO, Octopus, Fletcher Prouty

Reference:

The Octopus: Secret Government and the Death of Danny Casolaro, by Kenn Thomas and Jim Keith, Feral House, Portland, Oreg., 1996

Internal Revenue Service

The Internal Revenue Service (IRS) is the most widely feared and hated institution in this country and has attracted special, or one might almost say obsessive, attention by libertarian conspiriologists. A typical anti-IRS website informs us that the agency is not literally a part of the government: It is a private corporation, incorporated in Delaware in 1933; it does not collect taxes—it collects "tribute" (that is, the money IRS extracts from us goes straight to the *Federal Reserve Bank*, which holds it as "credit of the United States Treasury," i.e., interest on the National Debt). Nor is the Federal Reserve itself a government agency: It is private corporation owned by twelve families—one American and eleven foreign.

You don't even have to file a tax return, legally, according to many libertarian critics. The Income Tax laws never bothered to make compliance mandatory; if you want the heat and/or the risk, you can stand on your right of non-compliance and tell them to figure out your taxes for themselves. And you don't have to give them a scrap of paper to help them. Philip Marsh, author of *The Compleat Patriot*, could not find a law forcing cooperation with the IRS after eight years of searching.

(It is only fair to warn the impressionable, that although this appears true de jure, it is not true de facto: Those heresiarchs who have tried this non-cooperation have had long legal struggles ending always in fines, imprisonment, or both. Of course, many are still appealing their cases.)

The theory and practice of the IRS, according to the website below, causes 1,000 deaths per month in the United States, along with half the divorces and 75 percent of the bankruptcies.

The major fury against our tax system stems, actually, from the uncanny resemblance between the taxman and the bandit, as expressed over and over in libertarian literature but never more memorably than in the words of Massachusetts lawyer and individualist Lysander Spooner:

> *The fact is that the government, like a highwayman, says to a man: "Your money, or your life. . . ."*
>
> *[But] the highwayman takes solely upon himself the responsibility, danger and crime of his own act. He does not pretend that he intends to use [the money stolen] for your own benefit. He does not pretend to be anything but a robber. He has not acquired impudence to enable him to "protect" those infatuated travelers who feel perfectly able to protect themselves, or do not appreciate his peculiar system of protection. He is too sensible a man to make such professions as these. Furthermore, having taken your money*

he leaves you as you wish him to do. He does not persist in following you on the road, against your will, assuming to be your rightful "sovereign," on account of the "protection" he affords you. He does not keep "protecting" you, by commanding you to bow down and serve him, by requiring you to do this and forbidding you to do that, by robbing you of more money as often as he find it for his interest or pleasure to do so, and by branding you as a rebel, a traitor, and an enemy to your country, and shooting you down without mercy, if you dispute his authority or resist his demands. He is too much of a gentleman to be guilty of such impostures and insults and villainies as these. In short, he does not, in addition to robbing you, attempt to make you either his dupe or his slave.

See also:

Ezra Pound

References:

IRS in general—

http://www.livelinks.com/sumeria/politics/irs.html

Lysander Spooner—

The Heretic's Handbook of Quotations, ed. by Charles Bufe, See Sharp Press, San Francisco, 1988, p. 35

International Bankers

See:

Banco Ambrosiano, Cisalpine Bank, Federal Reserve Bank, Ezra Pound

Iran-Contra

See:

Cisalpine Bank, John Hull, *In Banks We Trust*, Inslaw, *Veil*, World Finance Corporation

Irina

Allegedly one of the most destructive computer viruses in the world, Irina has terrified countless Internet users. It is actually an inadvertent, or somewhat inadvertent, hoax, which was then picked up by various malign or whimsical imitators. It appears as an e-mail letter saying:

> FYI
> There is a computer virus that is being sent across the Internet. If you receive an e-mail message with the subject line "Irina," DO NOT read the message. DELETE it immediately. Some miscreant is sending people files under the title "Irina." If you receive this mail or file, do not download it. It has a virus that rewrites your hard drive, obliterating anything on it. Please be careful and forward this mail to anyone you care about.
> *(Information received from Professor Edward Prideaux, College of Slavonic Studies, London.)*

The former head of an electronic publishing company circulated the warning to create publicity for an interactive book of the same name, *Irina*. It created more fear than sensation, and the publishing company has apologized and recanted. Nonetheless, others have adopted "Irina," and it continues to plague "newbies" (as net novices are called) and may circulate for a long, long time to come.

Actually, according to the Department of Energy's research facility, there is no Professor Prideaux and no College of Slavonic Studies in London; but the School of Slavonic and East European Studies in London has received numerous anxious calls about this imaginary virus.

See also:
Good Times Virus—1 and 2, Ladder Conspiracies, OM

References:

http://ciac.llnl.gov/ciac/CIACHoaxes.html

http://www.telegraph.co.uk

Irish Wisdom

Irish Wisdom: Preserved in Bible and Pyramids, by Conor McDari, attempts to prove that the Irish not only wrote the Bible and designed the pyramids (an architectural code, as we will see) but were responsible for almost all the basic institutions of civilization as distinct from barbarism. It seems that Eire or Erin is the homeland of the Aryan or creative portion of humanity, but these facts were hidden since 1169 by a conspiracy between the British Royal Family and the Vatican, Ireland's two major oppressors and exploiters.

In the 12th century, the British first invaded Ireland, with the blessing of Pope Adrian IV, allegedly on a holy mission to Christianize the pagans. That much is accepted by all historians, although many find it hard to explain why the pope didn't know that St. Patrick had Christianized Eire over 700 years earlier, in 432. According to McDari, the St. Patrick story is a pure myth, invented later to make the Christianization of the Aryans/Erinians seem older and longer established than it was.

Both the pyramids and the Bible, when properly deciphered, reveal that the oldest and truest religion is sun worship. The decoding of the pyramids is complex, but the Bible is easier, once you realize that Hebrew is a degenerate form of Gaelic. Just look for the Gaelic root of every Hebrew word, and the meaning becomes clear. For instance, Jew, Jude, the slang Yid, etc., all come from the Irish Iudh, meaning light, i.e., the people who worship the sun. Hebrew, similarly, comes from Heber, Irish for the sun.

This book, first published in 1923, has many eerie resemblances to *Mein Kampf,* also written about that time, but is free of anti-semitism; it reserves all its venom for Rome and England.

See also:

A-Albionic (for contrast), Lyndon LaRouche, Noble Drew Ali, Bob Quinn

Reference:

Irish Wisdom: Preserved in Bible and Pyramids, by Conor McDari, Four
Seas, Boston, 1923; reprinted by Health Research, Mokelumne Hill,
Calif., 1967

Clifford Irving

See:

Elmyr, *F for Fake, Gemstone File,* Howard Hughes Forgeries

Iumma

Iumma is an alleged star, 14.6 light-years from Earth, which
remains invisible to us because of an area of "absorbing matter"
that lies between us and it. Some natives of the Iumma system,
known collectively as "UMMO" (not "the Ummo"), allegedly
live on Earth and send regular mail to various persons who can
profit by instruction in higher physics, higher ethics, and higher
civilization generally (see *UMMO Letters*). In the language of
UMMO, Iumma is written:

)+(

Remember that. It may be a clue.

See also:

Hono Intelligence Service 1901, Sirius

Reference:

Revelations: Alien Contact and Human Deception, by Jacques Vallee,
Ballantine, New York, 1991

Jack the Ripper

"Jack the Ripper," usually considered a lone maniac in the standard serial killer mode, was actually three men acting on behalf of a Freemasonic conspiracy, according to Stephen Knight. The six "ripper" murders had nothing random about them, Knight claims; all six women were at one time friends of an Irish Catholic girl who bore an out-of-wedlock child to the Duke of Clarence, Queen Victoria's grandson. The child, although a bastard, stood in line for the throne, and the Freemasons, unable to find either mother or babe, killed off all the witnesses to the affair and made the deaths look like the work of a sadistic maniac. Others Masons in Scotland Yard helped in the cover-up. This was all motivated by fear of a Catholic reaching the English throne, which, according to Knight, Masons are sworn to prevent even at the risk of their lives.

This thesis became the plot of a popular movie, *Murder by Decree,* starring Christopher Plummer as Sherlock Holmes. The film was unique not only in its portrait of a Masonic/royalist conspiracy reaching the top levels of British government, but in actually showing secret Masonic grips and signs on screen.

English author and criminologist Colin Wilson assured the present writer that this "solution" was defective in countless ways, and that one of the three alleged murderers had actually suffered a stroke and was bedridden at the time of his alleged participation in the plot.

See also:

A-Albionic, *Brotherhood*, Freemasonry, Grand Orange Lodge of Ireland, Lyndon LaRouche

Reference:

Jack the Ripper: The Final Solution, by Stephen Knight, Grenada, London, 1977

Michael Jackson: Alien?

In the writing of this work, the author and research associate Miriam Joan Hill maintained a website that invited browsers to send in any conspiracy theories we hadn't heard of. The best of all such contributions came from a chap who argued that "the government is trying to introduce aliens into our society, gradually. . . . I think they choose someone who is famous in the public eye and will not really alarm anyone when he reveals the truth. . . . Anyway, if you think about it, Michael Jackson is gradually turning into his alien form. His skin is lightening, his nose is shrinking, and his eyes will begin to get large soon."

Kind of makes you wonder, doesn't it?

See also:

Area 51, William Cooper, Inslaw, Merovingians

Reference:

http://www.cruzio.com/~blackops/register1.html

Jesus as a Freemason

Jesus was a Freemason, according to *The Crucifixion as Seen by an Eyewitness*. This remarkable document also says that baptism is part of Masonic ritual (it isn't) and that Jesus was initiated into the Craft while in Egypt, thus linking him more closely with the *Grand Orient Lodge of Egyptian Freemasonry* than with any other Masonic order.

See also:

Freemasonry, Grand Orange Lodge of Ireland, *Holy Blood, Holy Grail,*
Priory of Sion

Reference:

http://www.crocker.com/~acacia/text_tc.html

Joachim of Floris

The Italian mystic Joachim of Floris (1132–1202) is best known for his philosophy of spiritual history, which divided human development into three stages: the Age of the Father, based on authority, the Age of the Son, based on love, and the Age of the Holy Spirit, based on freedom, corresponding to the revelations of Moses, Jesus, and Joachim himself.

Conspiriologists find Joachim interesting because he founded an order called the Illuminated Ones or *Illuminati*, which after a few centuries of voluntary poverty and piety suddenly, under the influence of one Fra Dolcino, turned violent, plundered the homes of the rich, preached general revolution, and were wiped out by an army led by the bishop of Vercueil in 1507.

Joachim's historical ideas later reappeared, slightly altered each time, in Giambattista Vico's 18th-century theory of the Divine Age, based on poetic myth, the Heroic Age, based on militarism and conquest, and the Human Age, based on science and class warfare; and, later still, in *Aleister Crowley*'s three ages of Isis the Mother, corresponding to primitive matriarchy, Osiris the Father, corresponding to civilization as we know it, and Horus the Son, corresponding to the New Aeon, which began when Crowley received *"Liber Al"* from *Aiwass* in 1904. But the most influential variation on Joachim's historical cycle is the Hegelian-Marxist theory of thesis, antithesis, and synthesis, which has formed the ideological foundation of every communist regime.

References:

Webster's Family Encyclopedia, Vol. V, HAF-KLA, Archer Worldwide, Great Neck, N.Y., 1981

Violence, by Jacques Ellul, Seabury Press, New York, 1969, pp. 18–19

Candy Jones

Candy Jones was one of the most famous models of the late 1940s and early 1950s, married to radio talk-show legend Long John Nebel. By accident, she discovered or vividly imagined that she had been part of a CIA program in which alternate personalities had been created within her, and had acted as a CIA agent without remembering where she went or what she did. The purpose of the multiple-personality program was to create "sleeper agents" invisible not only to enemies but to themselves also; these mind-controlled "robots" were able to resist torture if captured because they didn't know anything of their espionage work.

See also:

Demonic Duck, MK-ULTRA, Recovered Memory Therapy, Kerry Thornley

Reference:

http://ourworld.compuserve.com/homepages/T_Porter/sec3.htm

John Keel

See:

Mothman Prophecies

John F. Kennedy Assassination

So many books have been written arguing that the John F. Kennedy hit was the result of a conspiracy that any attempt to review them all would fill this whole book and leave no room for any other material. If the reader will follow the links given in the following entry, *John F. Kennedy Death Links,* the general outline of several leading John F. Kennedy conspiracy theories will emerge.

The present author remains partial to the CIA theory (see *A.J. Weberman*), but admits there is also a strong case for the *Mafia* theory, as presented by scrupulous British journalist Anthony Summers and the website below. New Orleans Mafia boss Carlos Marcello, according to informants, bragged to other Mafia leaders that he had organized the hit. Two of the men he allegedly bragged to, Johnny Roselli, mob boss of Las Vegas, and Sam Giancana, mob boss of Chicago, died almost immediately after being subpoenaed by the House Select Committee on Assassinations: Roselli disappeared but then was found, dead, floating in a barrel in the Gulf of Mexico, and Giancana was simply shot through the mouth, traditional Mafia punishment for suspected informers. (See *Mino Pecorelli.*)

After the assassination, Marcello also sent a message, through a lawyer, to Jimmy Hoffa, who was a target of the Kennedy brothers' wrath: "You tell him he owes me." Hoffa subsequently disappeared utterly without a trace, and no clues have ever shed light on his vanishing.

Both *Lee Harvey Oswald* and *David Ferrie,* a leading suspect in the Garrison investigation, were part-time employees of Marcello, and Jack Ruby was "in the family."

The House Select Committee concluded only that there had been a conspiracy, but their chief counsel, Professor Howard Blakey, openly told the press, "The mob did it."

See also:

Martin Luther King Jr. Assassination, Mafia, MMAO, Murder of Marilyn Monroe

Reference:

http://www.clinton.net/~mewilley/jfk.html

John F. Kennedy Death Links

Various conspiriologists have produced lists of people who were connected in one way or another with the assassination of John Kennedy and who later died under questionable circumstances. (For instance, Sylvia Meagher produced a short but convincing list in her book, *Accessories After the Fact*; Mark Lane produced a very long but less convincing list in his book/film *Executive Action*.) Currently, the Assassination Investigation Bureau of Cambridge has a list of over 100 deaths that they regard as more probably due to foul play than to natural causes. It includes: *Robert Kennedy*, Mary Jo Kopechne, *Lee Harvey Oswald, David Ferrie*, Jack Ruby, *Clay Shaw, Buddy Walthers*, Roger Craig, *Eladio del Valle*, Rose Cherami, *Hale Boggs*, J. Edgar Hoover, *Louis Lomax, Lee Bowers Jr.*, Betty McDonald, Dorothy Kilgallen, *Marilyn Walle, Albert Guy Bogard*, Johnny Roselli, Sam Giancana, Jimmy Hoffa, *George de Mohrenschildt*, and quite a few others whose names are only known to full-time conspiracy researchers.

See also:

Flight 553, Potero Occulto, Fletcher Prouty, Three Tramps

Reference:

http://www.ratical.com/ratville/JFK/ToA/ToAchp10.html

Robert Kennedy Assassination

> *Once is happenstance, twice is coincidence, three times is enemy action.*
>
> —attributed to Ian Fleming

Coming in the wake of the assassinations of John Kennedy (November 22, 1963) and Martin Luther King Jr. (April 4, 1968), the assassination of Robert Kennedy (June 5, 1968) probably did as much to encourage conspiracy theory as all the films of Oliver Stone combined. Most Americans still find it hard to believe that the three most prominent "progressives" in America were all shot by deranged lone assassins within five years.

Conspiriologists emphasize that RFK was shot at a distance of no more than a few inches: Coroner Dr. Thomas Noguchi found powder burns around the wounds, only possible at "point blank" range. Sirhan Sirhan never got closer than about two feet from the senator.

Worse yet, Sirhan was in front of RFK, and the bullets entered from the back.

Many writers have tried to prove that Sirhan was in a trance at the time of the assassination. In this connection, it is well to recall the CIA's **MK-ULTRA** program, which, in addition to exploring other forms of mind control, investigated the feasibility of programming assassins who would not remember being programmed. The Artichoke project is described in a somewhat censored memo of 1954:

> *Can an individual. . . be made to perform an act of attempted assassination involuntarily under the influence of ARTICHOKE?*
>
> *As a "trigger mechanism" for a bigger project, it was proposed that an individual of (deleted) descent. . . be induced to perform an act, involuntarily, of attempted assassination against a prominent (deleted). . . . After the act of attempted assassination was performed, it was assumed that the SUBJECT would be taken into custody. . . and thereby "disposed of."*

Some conspiriologists claim the shots that killed Kennedy, fired from behind, were the work of Eugene Cesar, an alleged CIA asset. Cesar claimed he sold his gun prior to the assassination, but a receipt was later found showing that he sold it after the assassination. A hypnotized subject firing from in front would distract attention from such a possible real assassin in the rear.

See also:

CIA LSD Research, Candy Jones, John F. Kennedy Death Links, Kerry Thornley

Reference:

http://www.webcom.com/~lpease/assassins.html

Martin Luther King Jr. Assassination

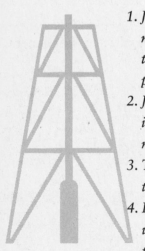

Attorney Mark Lane and comedian/activist Dick Gregory argue in their book, *Murder in Memphis,* that the FBI killed Martin Luther King Jr. The major arguments are:

1. *J. Edgar Hoover hated King violently and the FBI had made many previous attempts to destroy him (e.g., the famous tapes of King's extramarital affairs). The FBI are the last people to trust on the details of King's murder.*
2. *James Earl Ray, an ignorant petty criminal, was pressured into pleading guilty, but quickly repudiated that plea and has maintained his innocence for nearly 30 years.*
3. *There is no hard evidence connecting Ray to the assassination; even the rifle and bullet have not been matched.*
4. *Eyewitness Grace Stephens has always maintained that Ray was not the person she saw fleeing; the police turned her over to a mental institution under unconvincing circumstances.*
5. *Police protection was removed on the day of the shooting, and two black firemen were transferred out of the station across the street.*

In later developments a Memphis businessman, Loyd Jowers, confessed to involvement in the King murder and implicated both the FBI and Mafia. This matter is still before courts, and Jowers refuses to divulge more until granted immunity.

Members of the immediate family of Rev. King have declared they believe in a conspiracy and have joined in a court action to force a new trial of James Earl Ray and an examination of alternative suspects.

See also:

Flight 553, John F. Kennedy Assassination, John F. Kennedy Death Links

Reference:

http://ursula.blythe.org/NameBase/books.06

Henry Kissinger

The illegal we do immediately. The unconstitutional takes a bit longer.

—Henry Kissinger

Henry Kissinger is regarded as a major conspirator or villain by groups in every segment of the political arena. The wacko right (the ones further out than the "far right") regard him as virtually an Elder of Zion, or the brains of the *ZOG*, just because he's Jewish and powerful. Liberals and leftists detest him for his carpet bombings during the Indochina wars and the fact that he was born in Germany: Despite his Judaism, he seems like a neo-Nazi to them. And the John Birch Society, of course, has him high on their list of insidious *Insiders*: He is both a *Bilderberger* and a member of the *Council on Foreign Relations*. (And he has been a Director of the Rockefeller Brothers Fund. . .)

Kissinger, born in 1923 in Fuerth, Germany, was naturalized as a U.S. citizen in 1943, served with Army Intelligence between then and 1946, earned a Ph.D. from Harvard in 1954, and entered the world of Power in 1957 when he became the Study Director of Nuclear Weapons and Foreign Policy for the Council on Foreign Relations. Since then his life has been divided between high government posts and prestigious university positions.

As the most intellectual of the ruling Elite, Kissinger has expressed boldly and sometimes persuasively the philosophy that probably guides all of them. A fairly balanced judgment of that philosophy is provided by Patrick J. Garrity:

> *In his approach to diplomacy, Kissinger has sought to challenge and recast the traditional American approach to the world. He believes [in] a more realistic, sober tradition . . . often referred to as realpolitik. . . . This tradition can be summed up in two ideas. First,* raison d'etat, *where the interests of the state justify whatever means are necessary to pursue them. The national interest thus replaced the medieval notion of a universal morality that guided all men and nations. The second key concept is the balance of power, an international order in which no nation is dominant. Each nation maintains its independence by aligning itself [with], or opposing, other nations according to its calculation of the imperatives of power.*

This is much like the philosophy of Max Stirner (author of *The Ego and His Own*)—except that Stirner applied this amorality to the individual and Kissinger reserves it for the State. (See also *The Godfather.*) Because of this, pacifists and humanists tend to see Kissinger as a philosophical relative of Nazism, even though he fled Nazism in his youth; the mass bombings of civilian populations ordered by Kissinger certainly would rank as war crimes if his side lost. And this Machiavellian tradition reaches the dimensions of Dr. Strangelove (who was based on Kissinger, according to rumor) in Kissinger's 1957 book, *Nuclear Weapons and Foreign Policy*, in which he writes bluntly that "limited nuclear war is in fact a strategy which will utilize our special skills to best advantage" and that our "industrial potential" and "the broader range of our technology" almost guarantee an easy win if the U.S. government decides to drop nukes on people who vex it.

But nobody hates Kissinger more than *Lyndon LaRouche* does.

He not only regards Kissinger as a ringleader of the Anglo-American plot to destroy the Third World but as a "faggot" also (LaRouche prefers that word to Gay) and actually published a pamphlet titled "Kissinger: The Politics of Faggotry." (He later backtracked a bit, saying Kissinger had "the personality of a faggot.") LaRouche has also tied Dr. Kissinger to Satanism, by way of sinister links to Queen Elizabeth, Aldous Huxley, the drug culture, and "the Occult Bureau types in British Intelligence." He also believes Kissinger was behind the plot that put him, LaRouche, in prison for fraud and tax evasion.

See also:

Eugenics/AIDS Theory, Dr. Leonard Horowitz

References:

General—

http://nobel.sdsc.edu/laureates/peace-1973-1-bio.html

Kissinger quote about illegal and unconstitutional—

http://www.aphorismsgalore.com/author/Henry_Kissinger.html

Bilderberger link—

http://www.abbc.com/esa/sve/innehall/bb/bbig/kissinger.html

Analysis by Garrity—

http://www.ashland.edu/~ashbrook/publicat/onprin/v5n3/garrity.html

Kissinger/LaRouche issues—

Conspiracies, Cover-Ups and Crimes, by Jonathan Vankin, Paragon House, New York, 1991, pp. 37–43

Kissinger on nuclear war—

Ibid. p. 214

Knights of the Five-Sided Castle

The Knights of the Five-Sided Castle (also known as the Order of Quixote) is the title of a sacred order within the Discordian Society, made up exclusively of the current chiefs of staff of the U.S. Army and the top brass of the Pentagon generally. These intrepid warriors never asked for this honor, and may not even know that they possess it, but the Keepers of the *Sacred Chao* and the Keeper of the Notary Sojac have bestowed it upon them anyway, in recognition of their contributions to increasing the five degrees of stochasticism in the world (chaos, discord, confusion, bureaucracy, and international relations.)

See also:

Grand Orange Lodge of Ireland, Holy Order of the Lemon, Noon Blue Apples

Reference:

http://www.prairienet.org/~kkbuxton/discordia.html

Knights of Malta

Originally known as the Knights of the Hospital of St. John of Jerusalem during the Crusades (and later for a while called the Knights of Rhodes), the Knights of Malta were given that island in 1530 by Emperor Charles V but later lost it to Napoleon in 1798. They now occupy a small building in the Vatican, admit Dames as well as Knights, and are correctly called the Sovereign Military Order of Malta—but almost everybody still calls them the Knights of Malta.

According to *Covert Action Information Bulletin*, recent members of the Knights of Malta have included:

- *Franz von Papen, who persuaded President Paul von Hindenburg to resign and make Hitler the Chancellor of Germany;*

- **General Reinhard Gehlen,** *Hitler's chief of Intelligence, and later head of the CIA's Russian penetration bureau;*

- *General Alexander Haig, major architect of foreign policy in both the Nixon and Reagan regimes;*

- *Alexander de Marenches, former chief of French Intelligence;*

- **William Casey,** *head of the CIA during the* **Iran-Contra** *conspiracy;*

- *Otto von Hapsburg, also a member of the* **Bilderbergers** *and part of the* **Merovingian** *bloodline, according to Michael Baigent, Henry Lincoln, and Richard Leigh; and*

- **Licio Gelli, Roberto Calvi,** *and* **Michele "The Shark" Sindona,** *leaders of the* **P2 conspiracy** *in Italy in the 1970s–1980s.*

According to David Bernard, the 32nd degree in *Freemasonry* reveals to the initiate that Freemasonry is descended from the *Knights Templar* and devoted to fighting "tyranny and superstition" of which the main exemplar is the Knights of Malta.

See also:

In God's Name, Mafia, *Veil*

References:

Early history—

Concise Columbia Encyclopedia, Columbia University Press, New York, 1983, p. 454

Recent members—

Covert Action Information Bulletin, No. 25, Winter 1986

Gordon—

Quoted in *Irish Press* (Dublin), August 20, 1984

Light on Freemasonry, by David Bernard, Vonnieda and Sowers, Washington, D.C., 1858, pp. 287–304

Baigent, Lincoln, Leigh—

See *Holy Blood, Holy Grail*

Knights Templar

The Knights Templar, founded in 1118 by Hugh de Payens, were both knights and monks, an unusual combination for that time or any other. Originally, they inhabited the temple of Solomon in Jerusalem and followed an oath to protect pilgrims visiting the Holy Land.

Later, the Templars became money-lenders, and this led to their downfall, according to the most popular theory. Growing rich, they became objects of envy, and when they established castles in Europe, they became embroiled in politics as well as economics. In 1307, on Friday the 13th of October—a day regarded with superstition ever since—the Grandmaster of the Order, *Jacques de Molay,* was arrested by the Inquisition, along with 123 Knights. Under systematic and prolonged torture, they confessed to a series of charges that most historians regard as implausible—blasphemy, heresy, spitting on the crucifix, black magic, worship of a devil called Baphomet, and forcing all members into homosexual orgies.

In 1314, Jacques de Molay repudiated his confession, saying it had been obtained only to stop the endless torture. He also cursed the pope and the king of France, and oddly both died within the year, adding to the mystery and strange glamour of a Christian order condemned for Satanism.

Very few historians believe the Templars were guilty.

See also:

Abbe Barruel, Illuminati Copies or Revivals, Ordo Templi Orientis

Reference:

http://www.cnct.com/home/grantf/history.htm

Korea: Germ Warfare Charges

Some critics of American foreign policy claim that an array of germ warfare weapons were used by the U.S. Army in Korea

(1950–1953). The Eisenhower administration pressed sedition charges against the first three American servicemen to publish these charges, but none of the three were convicted.

According to the claims of these three and later critics, the Army released (1) feathers infected with anthrax, (2) fleas and mosquitoes dosed with bubonic plague and yellow fever, and (3) rodents carrying several diseases.

See also:

AIDS Conspiracy Theories, Chicago Malaria Study, Cuban Germ War?, Hughes vs. Rockefeller, Tuskegee Syphilis Study

Reference:

http://home.earthlink.net/~bkonop/GermIncidents2.html

Ladder Conspiracies

In this book, a ladder conspiracy signifies a hoax, prank, malicious trick, practical joke, or criminal activity that becomes widely imitated because of some intrinsic feature that makes it attractive to persons with antisocial tendencies or a peculiar sense of humor. A ladder conspiracy thus behaves much like a "real" conspiracy, even though the persons involved may not work together or even know each other.

The earliest ladder conspiracies encountered by the author, in his childhood and adolescence, involved hoax phone calls. The most popular was probably "Prince Albert in the can." In this game or nuisance, the victim is selected at random from the tobacco stores in a phone book. The "conspirator" calls the designated store and asks, "Do you have Prince Albert in the can?" (Prince Albert is a popular brand of pipe tobacco.) "Yes," says the victim. "Well, let him out!" the joker shouts, and hangs up. If enough children (of all ages) try this on the same store, the owner will begin to feel like the victim of a real conspiracy.

The most popular variation is to call somebody at random, in the wee hours of the morning, and pretend to be a representative of the local power company. Explain that you have been having power outages and ask him to go to the window and check if the street light is on. When he returns and reports that it is, tell him to blow it out.

Most chain letters, pyramid schemes, etc., however they begin, eventually become ladder conspiracies as imitators join in on the game.

See also:

CIAC, *Crying of Lot 49,* Good Times Virus—1 and 2, Ho Houses International, OM

Language as Conspiracy

Language as a mind-control device has been discussed by such philosophers as Vico (18th century), Stirner and Nietzsche (19th century), and Wittgenstein (20th century). The most radical scientific critics of language in our time include Count Alfred Korzybski and Dr. Richard Bandler.

Korzybski, who grew up in a house where four languages were spoken (Polish, Russian, French, German) and learned English much later, observed that the words we use influence our perceptions and conceptions of the world—e.g., even in the same language, a book may be called "realistic" by one reader and "pornographic" by another, and each will tend to perceive/conceive the book that way more and more automatically if they repeat their label ("realistic" or "pornographic") over and over. This underlies the mechanism of hypnosis, as Dr. Bandler discovered later. It also explains why you won't make much progress preaching radical equality to somebody who continually uses the word "nigger," or defending the first amendment to somebody who keeps saying "smut" (or "sexism").

But Korzybski made a more radical discovery, namely, that our perceptions/conceptions (reality-tunnels) are also shaped by the *structure* of the language we use. A Native American, an African, a Chinese, etc.—anyone using a non-Indo-European language structure—will live in a different universe than those who only know Indo-European. Considering mathematics a language, Korzybski also claimed that the mathematically literate live in a different semantic system than those who only know verbal structures.

From these starting points, Korzybski arrived at a devastating diagnosis of most of our culture's habitual linguistic structures (which he called neurolinguistic structures because they act as the software with which our nervous systems, including our brains, process data). Our worst habit, he thought, lay in the constant assumption of identity implied in most uses of the verb "is." Such sentences as "The photon is a wave," "The photon is a particle," "Beethoven is better than Mozart," "The thing I saw was a spaceship," would become, in Korzybski's system, "The photon behaved like a wave when measured with this experimental apparatus," "The photon behaved like a particle when measured with this different apparatus," "Beethoven seems better than Mozart to me," "The thing I saw seemed like a spaceship to me."

English including "is" and its cognates ("was," "be," "will be," etc.) appears as E in the writing of some of Korzybski's students, and English without "is" and its cognates appears as E' (pronounced E-prime.)

The present author has written two books in E-prime and finds it does tend to clarify, to de-dogmatize, and to make prose somewhat more scientific. Attempts to write the present book in E-prime quickly proved hopelessly baroque and created unreadable prose. *You need the "is of identity" to describe conspiracy theories.* Korzybski would say that proves that illusions, delusions, and "mental" illnesses require the "is" to perpetuate them. (He often said, "Isness is an illness.")

Korzybski also popularized the idea that most sentences, especially the sentences that people quarrel over or even go to war over, do not rank as propositions in the logical sense, but belong in the category that Bertrand Russell called propositional functions. They do not have one meaning, as a proposition in logic should have; they have several meanings, like an algebraic function. We do not notice this because Russell only discovered propositional functions in this century and the idea has not had wide publicity. According to Korzybski, many of our pet ideologies belong in the propositional function category ("This is an X," "This has too much Y in it," "Get away with that Z-ish Xism"), and we assume we can prove them or refute them, whereas neither we nor our opponents actually know what they mean. They don't mean anything, until the multivalued X, Y, Z, etc. become concretely or operationally related to specific space-time events perceived, touched, smelled, or otherwise encountered by observers making reports.

Propositional functions not recognized as such, or treated as propositions, Korzybski called "*noise*" (usually in italics). It seems odd to think that most human anger and violence derives from noise, but this also happens in other primate societies, does it not?

Novelist William S. Burroughs, who studied general semantics with Korzybski, has developed these notions into the surrealist theme of language as an invading virus, found in most of his novels. This virus, according to Burroughs, creates our thoughts, feelings, and sense impressions. Without the virus metaphor, Korzybski would agree, and so would Dr. Richard Bandler.

Dr. Bandler, out of the study of Korzybski and the verbal structures used by Dr. Milton Erickson (often considered the greatest hypnotist of his time), developed Neuro-Linguistic Programming (NLP), which shows how verbal structures create the world we think we live in; NLP also has some amazingly efficient gimmicks for changing our verbal habits and seeing/experiencing a much saner and more manageable world.

See also:

Book of Lies, George I. Gurdjieff, *Principia Discordia*

References:

Korzybski's system—

http://www.general-semantics.org/text/thome.html

Science and Sanity: An Introduction to Non-Aristotelian Systems and General Semantics, by Alfred Korzybski, Institute of General Semantics, Englewood, N.J., 5th ed., 1994

To Be or Not: An E-Prime Anthology, ed. by D. David Bourland Jr. and Paul Dennisthorne Johnson, International Society for General Semantics, San Francisco, 1991

Bandler and NLP—

http://www.purenlp.com/

Lyndon LaRouche

Lyndon LaRouche has made a long and kinky journey from the Far Left to the Far Right, with a stop off in federal prison for fraud and tax evasion. (All his disciples insist that he was framed, of course.) While his distinctive conspiracy theory has evolved somewhat over the years, it remains constant in finding the British Royal Family the most, or one of the most, sinister forces in the galaxy. Under Queen Elizabeth II and British Intelligence (MI5 and MI6), an "Anglo-American cabal" rules the world and presently is engaged in a genocidal program to de-industrialize and de-populate Third World nations. The International Monetary Fund, the World Bank, and *George Bush* are among the major co-conspirators in this fiendish scheme.

The Anglo-American cabal finances and reaps most of the profits of the illegal drug traffic, and also finances (as tools of genocide) the birth control and abortion movements; to further de-populate and deplete the planet, they also promote Feminism, homosexuality, Satanism, and "the sex-drugs-rock-and-roll counterculture." At one time LaRouche claimed that Queen Elizabeth II personally sent the philosophers Aldous Huxley and Alan Watts to America to corrupt us with drugs and Asian religions.

LaRouche is a high-tech advocate, with an agenda far different from others of that persuasion. He favors terraforming Venus to make it a second human habitation, but opposes space colonies in interplanetary space and has denounced the L5 Society (agitators for space colonization) as a Gnostic cult. ("Gnostic" is a very nasty word in his vocabulary, and he also hates Aristotle and modern painting.) He urges the use of atomic bombs to create huge irrigation canals in the Middle East and sees multiculturalism as a plot to destroy the benefits that Western science has brought to the world. And, like *Ezra Pound*, LaRouche believes that the major economic flaw in the present system is usury; enemies accuse him of anti-semitism often, but nobody has quite proven that charge totally.

It is only fair to note that LaRouche has charged in print that the present author is a member of the *Illuminati*.

See also:

A-Albionic, Insiders, LAWCAP, MMAO

Reference:

http://www.clas.ufl.edu/users/seeker1/activism/Larouche.html

LAWCAP

LAWCAP is *R. Buckminster Fuller*'s name for our current economic-political system: *law*yer-run *cap*italism. According to Fuller (a world-famous mathematician-designer), LAWCAP consists of people (some known, and some only traceable to numbered Swiss bank accounts) who manage world finance, deciding what governments will be loaned money for which projects, and what governments or projects will not be financed. "Governments propose, LAWCAP disposes" summarizes this part of Fuller's theory. But Fuller also holds that LAWCAP is based on a fundamental mathematical error, invented by Thomas Malthus (1766–1834), an economist employed by the British East India Company who allegedly "proved" that population increase will always exceed increase in known resources, thereby creating a struggle for life-support systems (food, shelter, etc.), which condemns the majority of people to misery and provides wealth and comfort only to the most cunning and predatory.

On the contrary, says Fuller, post–18th-century technology continually accomplishes greater and greater "ephemeralization" or "doing more with less," thereby increasing the energy yield of resources, and simultaneously discovering new resources, faster than Malthus thought possible. Thus, design science can not only feed the whole world with currently known resources, but it can actually give everybody an abundance. Furthermore, population does not increase steadily, as Malthus thought, but actually levels off when a society begins using comprehensive design science.

In short, LAWCAP, according to Fuller, governs the world at present and does so very ineptly and clumsily, because it is based on scientific errors 200 years old.

See also:

Great Pirates, GRUNCH, MMAO, Ezra Pound

Reference:

http://www.teleport.com/~pdx4d/grunch.html

John Lear

John Lear, son of the inventor of the Lear jet, holds many flying records and has an enviable reputation for coolheadedness and skill as a pilot. He claims that he has flown many missions for the CIA and through his contacts in the intelligence community has learned of a conspiracy involving aliens and the U.S. government. According to Lear, the first contact was made in 1964 and a formal treaty negotiated ca. 1969–71; the treaty involved an exchange of superior alien technology in return for our government's cooperation in covering up alien "research" on this planet—e.g., the famous cattle mutilations and human abductions. Lear also says the aliens and our government operate a joint research facility in *Area 51.*

See also:

Abductees Anonymous, William Cooper, Greys, James Oberg

Reference:

Revelations: Alien Contact and Human Deception, by Jacques Vallee, Ballantine, New York, 1991, pp. 56–57, passim

Timothy Leary

Dr. Timothy Leary has been denounced and demonized more than any American scientist since *Dr. Wilhelm Reich* and served over five years in prison for poor usage of the First Amendment—sentenced by a judge who condemned Dr. Leary's writings as a menace. (Technically, Leary was charged with possession of half a marijuana cigarette; he always claimed he was framed.)

Dr. Leary conducted extensive research on LSD and other psychedelics as a Harvard psychologist in the early 1960s, and always pointed out that among his subjects there were zero murders, zero suicides, and zero psychotic breaks. His convict rehabilitation project, using psychedelics, music, and mystic readings, rehabilitated more convicts than any similar experiment, almost exactly reversing the usual recidivism rate. Leary also claims that the CIA was behind his persecution, because they were trying to keep the brain-changing effects of LSD a secret (see *CIA LSD Research*).

When Dr. Leary got out of prison in 1974, he devoted himself to designing computer software and writing books on the trajectories of evolution, which he argued were leading us inevitably to more space, more intelligence, and more time—Space Migration, Intelligence Intensification, and Life Extension, or SMI²LE in his typical abbreviation. Most of these ideas seem more practical and less utopian 20 years later, but in the 1980s Leary decided they were further in the future than he had estimated and turned his attention more to the immediate possibilities of cyberspace and the cyberpunk philosophy of using computers to break down the authoritarian structure of our society.

When Dr. Leary learned he was dying of inoperable cancer in the 1990s, he hung a sign on his door saying THE MOTHER OF ALL PARTIES and invited friends from the sciences, arts, show biz, and especially the computer field to drop by and enjoy his celebration of the ecstatic possibilities of facing death without fear, a theme explored in his last book, *Design for Dying*. His last words were "Why? Why? Why?. . . Why not? Yeah!"

See also:

Food and Drug Administration, *Food of the Gods,* Terrence McKenna, Minneapolis Massacre, Newark Crash-In, War on Some Drugs

References:

http://www.deoxy.org/learyraw.htm
http://Leary.com/

Archbishop Lefebvre

Archbishop Lefebvre split with the Vatican during the reign of Pope John XXIII, mostly over matters of theological style. (Lefebvre wanted the mass spoken in Latin, as traditional, instead of in the language of the country where performed, as ordained by that rather progressive Pontiff.) Over the years, the quarrel between Lefebvre and the Vatican grew more heated, and the Archbishop's supporters frequently claim that the Vatican has been taken over by Freemasons and Satanists.

The highly secretive **Priory of Sion** was once described by a French magazine as a "front" for Lefebvre's crusade against the Vatican. This claim is rejected as baseless by Michael Baigent, Henry Lincoln, and Richard Leigh and indeed seems inconsistent with what is known of both the Archbishop and the Priory.

See also:

Church of Mary Magdalene, Freemasonry, Gerard de Sede, Noon Blue Apples, Our Lady of the Roses/Jesus-AIDS Theory

Reference:

Holy Blood, Holy Grail, by Michael Baigent, Henry Lincoln, Richard Leigh, Delacorte, New York, 1982

Liber Al

Liber Al, or *The Book of the Law*, represents a revelation to humanity by a superhuman being named *Aiwass*, as channeled by *Aleister Crowley*.

According to Crowley, he "received" this book in Cairo in 1904 while on a long honeymoon trip with his first wife, Rose. A set of strange omens—including Rose going into trance, something she had never done before, voices speaking "through" her, coincidences tying these events to exhibit *666* in the Cairo Museum, etc.—convinced Crowley that something important was occurring and he willingly allowed himself to channel Aiwass, who spoke in turn as first Nuit, the star goddess, then as Hadit, the "soul" or "self" of every atom in the body of Nuit, and finally as Ra-Hoor-Khuit, god of war and destruction.

Nuit represents the mother goddess of the ancients and/or the whole universe; Hadit represents the individual consciousness of each atom, cell, person, etc., and their erotic/mystic union—the part becoming one with the All—produces, in this case, a war god who predicts violent upheavals throughout the 20th century, ending with the dawning of the **Aeon of Horus**, the Crowned and Conquering Child, when every form of tyranny and oppression will be replaced by the law of **Thelema**, "Do What Thou Wilt."

Crowley left behind several magick lodges working in various ways to prepare for the Aeon of Horus. He also left three commentaries on *Liber Al*, the first of which reads in full:

THE COMMENT.

Do what thou wilt shall be the whole of the Law.

The study of this Book is forbidden. It is wise to destroy this copy after the first reading.

Whosoever disregards this does so at his own risk and peril. These are most dire.

Those who discuss the contents of this Book are to be shunned by all, as centers of pestilence.

All questions of the Law are to be decided only by appeal to my writings, each for himself.

There is no law beyond Do what thou wilt.

Love is the law, love under will.

See also:

Bisociation, Book of Lies, Joachim of Floris, Noon Blue Apples, Ordo Templi Orientis

Reference:

http://www.crl.com/~thelema/liber-al.html

Louis Lomax

Louis Lomax, a black author who was investigating the **Martin Luther King Jr. assassination,** was killed in Arizona when his car was forced off the road. The case is still unsolved.

See also:

Hale Boggs, Mona Charen, Inslaw, John F. Kennedy Death Links, Clay Shaw

Reference:

http://www.ratical.com/ratville/JFK/ToA/ToAchp10.html

H.P. Lovecraft

H(oward) P(hillips) Lovecraft (1890–1937) published mostly in pulp science-fiction and "horror" magazines in his lifetime and was almost unknown outside those circles when he died. His audience and his reputation has steadily grown since then, and he now ranks among the most widely read weird writers of any age; he has also inspired films, TV shows, and even computer games.

H.P.L. (as he liked to sign his letters) led a solitary life, seldom leaving his hometown of Providence, Rhode Island, with one brief marriage, which lasted only months. Erudite (he began reading classic literature at the age of four) and deliberately cranky, he even preferred to keep his friends at a distance but wrote all of them long, encyclopedic letters showing a keen sense of humor hidden in his stories or appearing there only as misanthropic irony.

Lovecraft's earliest works show the heavy influence of the moody tone of Edgar Allen Poe and the poetic whimsy of Lord Dunsany, but he later developed his own style, based on scientific literature, which, although often criticized as verbose, sets a mood of serious, almost pedantic scrupulosity, which leads the reader by very plausible steps to shockingly bizarre climaxes. His major stories, comprising what is called "the Cthulhu mythos," revolve around the concept that we humans are very petty and puny creatures, surrounded in infinite space-time by entities far stronger and stranger—and totally unsympathetic to us. This unique body of work reflects both Lovecraft's adult atheism and the "visions" of pagan gods he sometimes had as a bookish, lonely, and highly imaginative child. In the Cthulhu mythos, godlike entities do exist—godlike compared to us—but they are only parts of a mindless universe, and they are more likely to eat us than to do us any favors.

Much of the Cthulhu mythos is based on the *"Necronomicon,"* which some claim never existed until H.P.L. invented it. The Neville Spearman edition (see below) explains how Lovecraft came to read a copy of the *John Dee* translation, which Lovecraft's father had borrowed from the *Grand Orient Lodge of Egyptian Freemasonry* in Providence. *Kenneth Grant*, Outer Head of one branch of the *Ordo Templi Orientis*, claims that the Cthulhu "monsters" are allegorical figures representing the interstellar forces contacted by the "magick" (consciousness alteration) of *Aleister Crowley;* Lovecraft could only picture them in images of horror because of his conservative and anti-mystical bias; Crowley embraced them as a source of trans-human illumination.

References:

http://www.geocities.com/Area51/Dimension/4550/bio.html

The Necronomicon with Commentaries, Neville Spearman, Suffolk, England, 1978

Aleister Crowley and the Hidden God, by Kenneth Grant, Samuel Weiser, New York, 1974

Cults of the Shadow, by Kenneth Grant, Samuel Weiser, New York, 1976

Mrs. E. Loznaya

A female citizen of Kislovodsk in the then Soviet Union, identified only as Mrs. E. Loznaya, told of a rather singular UFO—or UFP (unidentified flying person)—to Dr. Vladimir Rubtsov. According to Mrs. Loznaya, one morning in 1936 (long before UFOs and *men in black* became famous) she saw a flying man in black.

She was 15 at the time and on her way to school when the flying man appeared in the sky. He seemed of medium height, and his black clothes "covered him completely, like overalls." Worse yet, in place of a face, he had only "an entirely black surface." The sighting lasted only about a minute, but Mrs. Loznaya remembered it until the 1970s when she met Dr. Rubtsov and reported it to him.

See also:

Charles Fort, *Mothman Prophecies*

Reference:

UFO, 1947–1997: Fifty Years of Flying Saucers, ed. by Hilary Evans and Dennis Stacey, John Brown Publishing, London, 1997, pp. 225–26

Lucent Technologies

Recently AT&T announced that their research subsidiary, Bell Laboratories, has been renamed Lucent Technologies. This did not escape the attention of ardent conspiriologist Texe Marrs, who asks with shrewd attention to detail: ". . . does AT&T's baby have horns? Does this name Lucent have any link to the name Lucifer? Could it be that, as one writer has suggested, Lucent stands for Lucifer's Enterprise?"

Mr. Marrs also finds dark significance in the fact that Lucent's network operating system is called "Inferno," and the company has an office at 666 Fifth Avenue in New York. However, he failed to note that Dell Publishing, which handles *Illuminatus*, also had that address for several years.

See also:

The Antichrist, Bisociation, Brainwashing, Language as Conspiracy, UFO/Satanic Conspiracy

Reference:

Project LUCID: The Beast 666 Universal Human Control System, by Texe Marrs, Living Truth Ministries, Austin, Tex., 1996

Madrid UMMO Sightings

In 1966 and 1967 three suburbs of Madrid—Aluche, San Jose de Valderas, and Santa Rosa—had some rather special UFO sightings. The first, on February 6, 1966, in Aluche, involved a whiteish disk seen by three independent witnesses, one of whom observed on the bottom of the disk the symbol:

)+(

The second incident, on June 1, 1967, in San Jose de Valderas, involved a disk 120 feet in diameter seen by several dozen witnesses. The third incident, a few hours later on the same day in Santa Monica, was observed by ten witnesses who saw a similar craft with the marking)+(land for a few moments and then take off again. Later, cylinders were found at the site, containing strips of Tedlar, a plastic recently invented by NASA, inscribed with indecipherable hieroglyphs—an extraterrestrial language or meaningless doodles, as you will. Each contained the symbol)+(.

Photos of the "spaceship" were later sent to a newspaper, rather mysteriously, and were soon proven to be fakes. But the symbol of UMMO, as it came to be known, would return in many forms to haunt and vex UFO investigators:)+(.

See also:

Abductees Anonymous, Philip K. Dick, *Gods of Eden,* Hono Intelligence Service 1901, Robert Morning Sky, UMMO Letters, Voronehz, UMMO Visit

Reference:

Revelations: Alien Contact and Human Deception, by Jacques Vallee, Ballantine, New York, 1991, pp. 91–96

Mafia

The Mafia is almost certainly the largest single criminal organization in the world and has had an unofficial relationship with the U.S. intelligence community since World War II, when convicted pimp Charles "Lucky" Luciano arranged to have the Sicilian Mafia aid the American invasion in return for a shortened prison sentence. Ever since then, the Mob and the Spooks have worked together on various projects, and it seems that each side sincerely believes it is using the other to its own advantage.

Nobody knows the origin of the Mafia. Some trace it back to as early as an alleged organization of that name that battled the Arab invasion of Sicily; others to a resistance movement against the French conquest of southern Italy, which supposedly had the slogan, "*Morte alla Francia Italia anelia!*" ("Death to the French, Italy shouts.") When Guiseppe Garibaldi (1807–1882) led the Young Italy movement, his peasant followers were called *squadri della maffia*, but that may not relate to the Mafia as we know it.

Undoubtedly, the Mafia has surpassed other criminal gangs in success and longevity because of its quasi-mystical, somewhat Freemasonic fraternal bonds and its spooky initiation ceremony, in which the candidate is cut on the hand and offers blood evidence of his serious intent. A picture of a saint is then burned in his hand, and he recites, "I want to enter this organization to protect my family and my friends. I swear not to divulge this secret and to obey with love and *omerta*. As burns this saint so will burn my soul. I enter alive into this organization and leave it dead."

Symbolic "death" is part of the initiation into most mystic and fraternal orders. *Omerta* means "silence" and "obedience," and has monkish overtones. Almost all members of the Mafia are pious Roman Catholics, and the others at least pretend to be.

The Mafia has been involved in extortion, murder, drug running (alcohol during Prohibition, others more recently), prostitution, gambling, terrorism, assassinations for government agencies, and, lately, more and more respectable businesses including hotels, restaurants, banking, and film producing.

See also:

Gladio, John F. Kennedy Assassination, MMAO, P2 Conspiracy, Michele "The Shark" Sindona, *Yankee and Cowboy War*

Reference:

http://home.earthlink.net/~donellio/Mafia101/facts.html

Magick

For definition and pronunciation see:

A∴A∴

Making Monsters

Making Monsters, by psychologist Richard Ofshe and journalist Ethan Watters, critiques **recovered memory therapy** and claims that it is not only scientifically invalid but often seriously harmful to patients and their families.

The major complaints of Ofshe and Watters are:

1. *Each recovered memory expert, using hypnosis, eventually persuades the patient that induced visions are real memories, but since each therapist finds the kind of memories he or she is seeking, this does not prove anything except that hypnotized subjects will eventually produce what the hypnotist demands. Thus, Christian therapists find Satanic rituals,*

Feminists find incest and other sexual abuse, and Budd Hopkins and his school find UFO abductions.

2. *The process of "finding" or creating these memories or pseudo-memories is often very long, sometime three to five years, sometimes even longer than that. This looks more like a process of joint imaginative creation than a process of remembering.*

3. *Many patients have been encouraged by these therapists to confront and denounce their alleged abusers, with great injury all around to every member of the afflicted family. With a procedure as uncertain as hypnotically induced belief, this borders on criminal irresponsibility.*

4. *Experimental studies of memory fail to support the doctrines underlying "recovered memory," and many famous studies (which every qualified psychologist should know) flatly contradict it.*

5. *Many of the most celebrated recovered memory cases are so absurd on the face of it that nobody would believe them if the recovered memory therapists did not have two support groups, the Radical Feminists and the Fundamentalist Christians, constantly assuring us that this therapy is "scientific."*

Despite these telling criticisms, and others published elsewhere, recovered memory therapy still has its devotees and patients continue to remember horrible incidents of sexual abuse, Satanic/cannibalistic rituals, and extraterrestrial abduction.

See also:

Daimonic Reality, Demonic Duck, Corrydon Hammond, *MS. Magazine, Satanic Panic,* UFO/Satanic Conspiracy

Reference:

Making Monsters: False Memories, Psychotherapy, and Sexual Hysteria, by Richard Ofshe and Ethan Watters, University of California Press, Berkeley and Los Angeles, 1996

Paul "The Gorilla" Marcinkus

Paul "The Gorilla" Marcinkus, a political priest so named because of his King Kong musculature, served as bodyguard to two Popes and eventually became Archbishop and was appointed president of the Vatican Bank (I.O.R.). He almost immediately plunged the Vatican into its first major financial scandal of the 1970s, when it was revealed that the *Mafia* had printed $1 billion in counterfeit stock, at least some of which got deposited in the Vatican Bank; according to many investigators, all of it was intended for deposit there, but what happened to most of it still remains unknown.

New York D.A. Frank Hogan, who prosecuted several local Mafiosi for this caper, attempted to extradite and prosecute Marcinkus also, but was blocked by White House intervention. (*Michele "The Shark" Sindona*, one of Marcinkus' colleagues in the *P2 conspiracy*, had contributed lavishly to Nixon's campaign, and P2 probably had high-level protection as part of the CIA's *Gladio* operation to control Italian politics.)

Later, still under Marcinkus, the Vatican Bank became intimately involved with some of the "ghost banks" (virtual banks) and drug laundromats in the Sindona-*Roberto Calvi* loop. Marcinkus was listed as co-owner with Calvi of the *Cisalpine Bank*, a center of drug traffic according to Italian investigating magistrates. When *Banco Ambrosiano* crashed and the whole P2 scandal made headlines day after day for more than two years, the Vatican stonewalled, but later they quietly removed Paul "The Gorilla" from their bank and made him mayor of Vatican City. Later still, they sent him away entirely, and he was last reported in semi-retirement in Cicero, Illinois.

See also:

In Banks We Trust, Knights of Malta, *Scandals of the Priory of Sion*

References:

The counterfeit stock deal—

The Vatican Connection, by Richard Hammer, Penguin Books, New York, 1982

Other P2 scandals—

In Banks We Trust, by Penny Lernoux, Anchor/Doubleday, New York, 1984

In God's Name, by David Yallop, Bantam, New York, 1985

The Mason Word

It was for refusal to reveal the Mason Word that the *Widow's Son* was murdered. That Word (and its associated telepathic powers) is admittedly lost, but Master Masons are given a substitute Mason Word by which they may test persons pretending to be Masons who perhaps are frauds. This modern, substitute Mason Word is, of course, a deep and darkly hidden secret, and it may take as long as two or three hours browsing in a library to find one of the "Secrets of Freemasonry Revealed" books that will tell you that it is Mah-hah-bone. Make of that what you will.

Reference:

Light on Freemasonry, by David Bernard, Vonnieda and Sowers, Washington, D.C., 1858

D.M. McArtor

Dr. D.M. McArtor has the unenviable position of appearing in almost all AIDS conspiracy theories, because on June 9, 1969, he appeared before the House Subcommittee on Appropriations to request funding for a project to produce a biological agent for which humans have no natural immunity. Dr. McArtor, then Deputy Director of Research and Technology for the Department of Defense, asked for $10 million to produce, over the next five to ten years, a germ agent that would be, in his words, "refractory to the immunological and therapeutic processes upon which we depend to maintain our relative freedom from infectious diseases." AIDS first appeared ten years later.

See also:

AIDS Conspiracy Theories, Tuskegee Syphilis Study

Reference:

http://www.earthlink.net/~bkonop/GermIncidents2.html

Terrence McKenna

Terrence McKenna has emerged, since the death of *Timothy Leary*, as the leading public proponent of psychedelics. He has also popularized the theory that human religion, language, and culture—all that differentiates us from other primates—resulted from the brain stimulation when early hominids stumbled upon psychedelic mushrooms.

Unlike Leary, who saw psychedelics as tools to prepare us for a sci-fi future of cyberspace, Outer Space, longevity, and higher intelligence, McKenna sees them as restoring the primitive in us—freeing us from the "Dominator Ego" characteristic of all civilized life. He has become probably the most effective propagandist for an "archaic revival" since Rousseau and is both influenced by and heavily influences Feminism, ecology, and neo-paganism.

See also:

Food and Drug Administration, *Food of the Gods,* Minneapolis Massacre, Robert Morning Sky, Newark Crash-In, War on Some Drugs

References:

http://www.cia.com.au/peril/texts/features/tmk-out.htm

http://www.levity.com/eschaton/index.html

http://deoxy.org/mckenna.htm

Media Criticized: AIDS

Many AIDS conspiracy theorists claim that journalists lack the scientific training to understand scientific criticisms of the accepted ideas about what causes AIDS and how it should be treated. (See *AIDS Conspiracy Theories.*) Thus, those who deny that HIV causes AIDS or that AZT is a safe and beneficial treatment often see their views ignored or distorted in the media, not because of a conscious conspiracy but because of sheer ignorance of science in the minds of those who decide what stories are newsworthy and how they should be reported.

Those who make this criticism often cite the case of Dr. Max Essex, who originally suggested that HIV had its origin in Africa. Although Dr. Essex has retracted and repudiated this hypothesis, it continues to be treated as proven fact by the major media and those who deny it are generally dismissed out of court.

Reference:

http://www.livelinks.com/sumeria/aids/john-l/epidemi.html

Media Criticized: Cultural

Mark Crispin Miller, who teaches media studies at Johns Hopkins University, regards television news as training in "how to be stupid." Writing of the "educational" Channel One specifically but generalizing to TV news on all networks, he observes:

> ... TV *news is loud, speedy filler, which—with minimal background and no context—leaves the mind with nothing but some evanescent numbers, a helpless sense of general disaster, a heavy mental echo of official reassurance, and (not too surprisingly) an overwhelming vague anxiety....*
>
> *Its real function is not journalistic but commercial.... It must constantly efface itself, must keep itself from saying any-*

thing too powerful or even interesting, . . . because it can never be allowed to detract in any way *from the commercials.*

Reference:

"How to Be Stupid," by Mark Crispin Miller, *Extra,* May–June 1997

Media Criticized: General

According to the Website below, "John Swinton," the former chief of staff of the *New York Times,* stated in a speech before the New York Press Club in 1953:

"If I allowed my honest opinions to appear in one issue of my paper, before twenty-four hours my occupation would be gone. The business of journalists is to destroy the truth; to pervert; to vilify; to fawn at the feet of mammon; and to sell this country and this race for their daily bread. We are the tools and vessels for rich men behind the scenes. We are the jumping jacks; they pull the strings and we dance. Our talents, our possibilities, and our lives are all the property of other men. We are intellectual prostitutes."

The New York Press Club denies that such a speech was ever given, and the *New York Times* never heard of John Swinton. In short, this quote is a fake.

See also:

American Dynasty, Insiders, MMAO, *Yankee and Cowboy War*

Reference:

http://www.astridmm.com/prouty/

Men in Black

"Men in black"—persons of sinister aspect, who evidently dress entirely in black (and often ride in black Cadillacs) solely to emphasize their spooky aura—have appeared in UFO lore since the 1940s. John Keel points out, in his introduction to Timothy Beckley's *The UFO Silencers,* that "men in black" also appear frequently in medieval legends, usually associated with Satan.

See also:

Daimonic Reality, Mary Hyre, *Mothman Prophecies,* "Sarah"

Reference:

The UFO Silencers, by Timothy Green Beckley, Inner Light Publications, New Brunswick, N.J., 1990

Merovingians

The Merovingians, a Frankish dynasty that reigned from the fifth century to 751 A.D., have become of great concern to conspiracy theorists because many of the "mysteries" connected with Rennes-le-Chateau, *Father Saunière,* the *Church of Mary Magdalene,* and the *Priory of Sion* have been linked back to them. *Gerard de Sede,* in a remarkable book called *La Race fabuleuse,* claims that the Merovingians were descended from matings between extraterrestrials from *Sirius* and the Tribe of Benjamin in ancient Israel, and other notions about them are equally remarkable. For instance, the semi-legendary founder of the dynasty, Merovech, allegedly sprang from a union of a woman with a sea-creature. Elizabeth van Buren, like de Sede, also claims an extraterrestrial origin for the Merovingians and sees them as the "good" force in the cosmos perpetually at war with an "evil" force that seems centered in the Vatican.

In their *"Holy Blood, Holy Grail,"* Michael Baigent, Henry Lincoln, and Richard Leigh produce elaborate bloodlines relating the Merovingians to many important persons in the modern world, including *Prince Bernhard* of the Netherlands, founder of the *Bilderbergers*, and Otto von Hapsburg, member of both the Bilderbergers and the *Knights of Malta.*

See also:

Kenneth Grant, Robert Morning Sky, Sirius Mystery

Reference:

Concise Columbia Encyclopedia, Columbia University Press, 1983

Mary Pinchot Meyer

Mary Pinchot Meyer was another of John F. Kennedy's mistresses who, like *Marilyn Monroe*, died under ambiguous circumstances. Curiously, she had also been, at times, the lover of Dr. *Timothy Leary*.

Mary Pinchot came of a socialite Washington family (she was the sister-in-law of Ben Bradlee of the *Washington Post*) and was known as an exceptional beauty and a talented painter. She also seems to have dabbled in espionage, doing small jobs for the CIA, but they never trusted her, due to her habit of becoming involved in sudden passionate love affairs that interfered with her judgment. She eventually married Cord Meyer, a top CIA officer, and devoted herself mostly to her art.

In 1962, after becoming another Kennedy mistress—his major mistress, according to one source who claims he even thought of divorcing Jackie to marry her—Mary Pinchot Meyer invented her own plan to save the world from atomic war and told Dr. Leary about it. He appears to have encouraged her.

According to Deborah Davis, there was a group of society-type women in Washington who thought that if they could get men in power involved in mind-altering drugs they could see the world in a different way and this would end the Cold War and end all warfare. It was a very ambitious plan and a lot of them got LSD from Timothy Leary, who at that time was a professor of psychology at Harvard and had access to this drug.

Mary and her psychedelic sisterhood tried to turn on as many high officials as possible, and nobody knows to what extent they succeeded. One report claims that Mary and JFK had sex sessions together around 30 times and she usually brought pot or acid with her.

Mary Pinchot Meyer was murdered on October 12, 1964— shot twice in the head. A black laborer was arrested, tried, and acquitted. The murder officially remains unsolved. *James Jesus Angleton* acquired Mary's diary and allegedly burned it, although some say he held it for some time before the burning.

In 1979, Deborah Davis published *Katherine the Great,* a book about the *Washington Post,* which included some details on Mary Pinchot Meyer. The publisher printed 25,000 copies but within a few days withdrew them from the bookstores and pulped them.

See also:

CIA LSD Research, John F. Kennedy Death Links, War on Some Drugs

References:

Angleton—

http://www.weberman.com

General, and JFK's thought of marrying Mary—

http://www.umsl.edu/~skthoma/hpage.htm

30 sex sessions—

http://www.clinton.net/~mewilley/jfk.html

Popular Alienation, ed. by Kenn Thomas, Illuminet Press, 1995, pp. 79–85

Minneapolis Massacre

In January 1989, the Minneapolis police smashed down the door of the home of an elderly black couple, using "flash bang" grenades, which accidentally set the house on fire and killed both old people.

The cops were looking for drugs, but never found any. The chief of police justified the murders of two innocent citizens by saying, "This is war."

See also:

"Every Knee Shall Bow," Food and Drug Administration, Government as Criminal Conspiracy, Haitian Experiment Claim, Newark Crash-In, Tuskegee Syphilis Study, War on Some Drugs

Reference:

Pissing Away the American Dream, ed. by David Ross, Digit Press, Norcross, Ga.

MK-ULTRA

The origins of MK-ULTRA go back to World War II, when the U.S. Army began researching barbiturates and marijuana as aids to interrogation. George Eastbrooks was a leading proponent of hypnosis as the key to interrogation and general mind manipulation of all sorts, and in 1971 he said he had used hypnosis to create multiple personalities for military intelligence purposes. (See *Candy Jones*.)

After the Korean War, the CIA began MK-ULTRA as a top secret effort to discover the best techniques, or combinations of techniques, to alter minds in any way desired. Hypnosis, drugs newer and more complex than barbs and pot, psycho-surgery, and various attempts at a "truth serum" were all extensively investigated. One aim was to extract information from captured enemies; another, equally important, was to create agents with so many levels of mental control that they could not have information tortured out of them or even, in some cases, be aware that they were carrying secret information.

Research moved on to include LSD, ketamine, psilocybin, and the implanting of electrodes in the brain. Lobotomy was tested, along with electroconvulsive shock. One CIA researcher believed total mind control could be achieved by combining electroshock, LSD, and having the subject's own voice played back through headphones. That sure sounds like it might fry your brain, doesn't it?

After the Church Committee of the U.S. Senate exposed these facts, with their echoes of Frankenstein and Dr. Mengele, the CIA solemnly promised to discontinue such horrors. Many conspiriologists believe they merely changed the names of various projects and moved them to different departments.

See also:

Abductees Anonymous, CIA LSD Research, Corey Hammond, Mary Pinchot Meyer, James Oberg, Frank Olsen, Kerry Thornley

Reference:

http://ourworld.compuserve.com/homepages/T-Porter/secs3.htm

MMAO

This is an abbreviation coined by philosopher-scientist *R. Buckminster Fuller* to describe the group currently in control of this planet. Unfortunately, Fuller sometimes defined MMAO as "Machiavelli, Machiavelli, Atoms and Oil" (bankers, more bankers, and the atomic and oil magnates) and sometimes as "Machiavelli, Mafia, Atoms and Oil" (bankers, racketeers, and atomic and oil magnates). This ambiguity derives from Fuller's failure to track ownership of many corporate entities further than numbered Swiss bank accounts.

See also:

Gnomes of Zurich, Federal Reserve Bank, Mafia, P2 Conspiracy

References:

Critical Path, by R. Buckminster Fuller, St. Martin's Press, 1981

Grunch of Giants, by R. Buckminster Fuller, St. Martin's Press, 1983

Marilyn Monroe, Murder of

Rumors and legends about the murder of Marilyn Monroe have circulated ever since Marilyn's tragic death and have even been endorsed by Hank Messick, an award-winning journalist and former consultant to the New York Joint Legislative Committee on Crime, who says informants in the *Mafia* told him the mob killed Marilyn to entrap and frame Robert Kennedy.

According to a very scrupulous British journalist, Anthony Summers, the evidence does not support a murder verdict but does support a conspiracy. That is, Marilyn died either of an accidental or deliberate overdose of barbiturates, but her death was covered up for hours, and her body driven around in an ambulance, which eventually returned the body to her home, so that federal agents could go through her house, removing all evidence of her affair with Kennedy.

Summers also produces evidence that the Mafia, probably by authority of Sam Giancana (a suspect in many *John F. Kennedy assassination* theories, oddly), had planted a bug in the cottage where Marilyn and Bobby met to enjoy sweet dalliance. The cottage belonged to actor Peter Lawford, who appears to have acted as a virtual pimp for both Kennedy brothers, setting them up with many beautiful actresses. Ironically, Bobby learned of the bug because of another bug that the Justice Department had placed on Sam Giancana, so he broke off his affair with Marilyn before the mob had enough tape to blackmail him.

This part of the story is particularly well documented, and should give pause to anyone who says that no conspiracies ever exist. Imagine: The Attorney General is bugged by a criminal he is simultaneously bugging; it is as if we are living in a John le Carré novel.

Another version of Marilyn's death reveals that she was indeed murdered, and Marilyn gives all the details herself, as channeled by psychics.

See also:

Sam Giancana, Kennedy Death Links, Mary Pinchot Meyer

References:

Hank Messick—

Goddess, by Anthony Summers, Gollancz Ltd., London, 1988

Marilyn's own story—

The Murder of Marilyn Monroe, by Leonore Canevari, Carroll and Graf, 1992

Robert Morning Sky

Half-Apache and half-Hopi, Robert Morning Sky is leader or non-leader of a group calling themselves Renegade Warriors. Morning Sky emphatically and repeatedly denies that he is a shaman, a guru, an Elder, a Messiah, or any kind of expert and says his ideas should be judged on the evidence and not any claim to "authority" of any sort. His only religious role, he says, is dancing at powwows.

Morning Sky, who studied linguistics at the University of Arizona, claims that the reason Native American, Egyptian, Hindu, and various other deities look half-human and half-animal is that they are based on extraterrestrial visitors to and conquerors of Earth. In this scenario, intelligent life evolved in many forms throughout the universe, but each has something partially humanoid about it. The groups that played the largest role in Earth history were a wolf-human type from *Sirius* and a snake-human type from somewhere in Orion.

Robert Morning Sky's works dissent openly and rather pugnaciously from the views of both traditional white historians and New Age mystics. He also says he is proud to be a primitive rather than a sophisticate, tracing "primitive" back to roots meaning not derived from anything else, original, primary, etc. and "sophisticate" back to roots signifying deception, falsification, and corruption.

See also:

AYA, Charles Fort, *Guardians of the Grail,* Merovingians, Noon Blue Apples

Reference:

http://www.xroads.com/~rms/welcome.html

Mosquito Conspiracy

In 1956–58, the U.S. Army conducted field experiments in Savannah, Georgia, and Avon Park, Florida, in which mosquitoes were released into residential areas. Many people were "swarmed" by the mosquitoes and later fell ill; some even died. U.S. Army personnel posed as public health officials to photograph and test the victims. Although details of these experiments on unwitting citizens remain classified, some conspiracy buffs think that the mosquitoes were infected with yellow fever.

See also:

AIDS Conspiracy Theories, Mona Charen, Chicago Malaria Study, Tuskegee Syphilis Study

Reference:

http://home.earthlink.net/~bkonop/GermIncidents2.html

The Mothman Prophecies

In 1968, West Virginia, especially in the area bordering on Ohio, became the scene of an outbreak of weirdity that crisscrosses several categories of controversy. As documented in John Keel's *The Mothman Prophecies*, the phenomena included:

- *the first in the series of mysterious "cattle mutilations" that have recurred regularly in many other states, usually further west;*

- *over 100 sightings of strange lights (or UFOs) in the sky;*

- *three classic "close encounter" cases, in which people saw, or thought they saw, extraterrestrials, or critters they considered extraterrestrial;*

- *about 70 sightings of Mothman, a traditional "monster" of the area who, like Bigfoot and Nessie, keeps coming back to shock or terrorize a few witnesses, but never lingers long enough to be scientifically confirmed; and*

- *a long parade of* **men in black**, *most of them driving black Cadillacs and looking vaguely "Oriental."*

Mothman is, or appears as, or is hallucinated as, a humanoid figure with giant mothlike wings and glaring red eyes.

Another spook visiting the area called himself Indrid Cold and said he came from a planet named Lanulos. He appeared twice to a salesman named Woodrow Derenberger, with whom he seemed to communicate by telepathy. Derenberger was thereafter vexed by strange phone calls combining threats, electronic hums, and code-like beeps. (See *"Secret Cipher of the UFOnauts."*)

While trying to investigate this combination of real weirdity (the cattle mutilations, the UFO sightings confirmed on radar) and growing mob hysteria, Keel himself became the target of the weirdness. A maelstrom of electronic and mechanical accidents haunted him, and strange people contacted him by strange means to prophesy future events. The major repeated prophecies were (1) the Pope would be stabbed while visiting the Middle East, (2) Robert Kennedy was in danger, and the threat waited for him in a hotel kitchen, (3) there would be a nationwide power failure on December 24 at noon.

The Pope was not stabbed in the Middle East; he was stabbed the next year in Manila. Robert Kennedy was shot dead in a hotel kitchen by Sirhan Sirhan and/or persons unknown. There was no power failure on December 24 at noon, but at that exact hour a bridge collapsed in West Virginia, right in the center of the UFO/Mothman activities, killing over 100 people.

Keel claims that most major UFO flaps have this penumbra of magick and surrealism about them, usually ignored by both skeptics and the ardent believers in the ETH (extraterrestrial theory.) He prefers to call the entities involved *ultra-terrestrials*, existing on the borderland between matter and energy, or reality and dream, and regards them as mischievous, deceptive, often dangerous, and likely to produce mental illness in those who insistently try to communicate with them.

See also:

Abdul Alhazred, *Daimonic Reality,* Charles Fort, *Gods of Eden, Guardians of the Grail, Necronomicon,* UFO/Satanic Conspiracy

Reference:

The Mothman Prophecies, by John Keel, IllumiNet Press, Avondale Estates, Ga., 1991

MS. Magazine

In 1993, *MS. Magazine* printed an article entitled (their own capitals) "RITUAL ABUSE EXISTS: BELIEVE IT." Although the *Satanic abuse* hysteria had largely been promoted by two Feminists named Ellen Bass and Laura Davis, it had become increasingly unbelievable to most of the public; this article gave the new witch-hunt an official seal of approval by the official journal of Feminism and helped perpetuate the reign of panic.

See also:

Hawthorne Abendsen, Dr. Raymond Bernard, Demonic Duck, *Making Monsters,* Recovered Memory Therapy, *Satanic Panic*

Reference:

MS. Magazine, January 1993

The Naked Pope

Vanni Nistico, press officer of the Socialist Party of Italy, says that *Licio Gelli* once showed him some photos of Pope John Paul II standing naked next to his swimming pool. Gelli commented, "If it's possible to take these pictures of the Pope, imagine how easy it is to shoot him." Vanni says he has no idea what use Gelli intended to make of the photos, but David Yallop, in his book on the *P2 conspiracy,* has evidence that Gelli was blackmailing some of the most important people in Italy.

See also:

A-Albionic, *Godfather,* Pope John Paul I, *Scandals of the Priory of Sion*

References:

The Calvi Affair, by Larry Gurwin, Pan Books, London, 1984, p. 51

In God's Name, by David Yallop, Jonathan Cape, London, 1984

Nameless Virus

Among all the computer viruses, virus hoaxes, and parodies of virus hoaxes, something absolutely unique appeared in 1988: the creation of one Robert Morris III. His name is the only accurate part of the message he sent out on the web:

Date: 11–31–88 (24:60) Number: 32769

To: ALL Refer#: NONE

From: ROBERT MORRIS III Read: (N/A)

Subj: VIRUS ALERT Status: PUBLIC MESSAGE

Warning: There's a new virus on the loose that's worse than anything I've seen before! It gets in through the power line, riding on the power line 60 Hz subcarrier. It works by changing the serial port pinouts, and by reversing the direction one's disks spin. Over 300,000 systems have been hit by it here in Murphy, West Dakota alone! And that's just in the last 12 minutes.

It attacks DOS, Unix, TOPS–20, Apple-II, VMS, MVS, Multics, Mac, RSX–11, ITS, TRS–80, and VHS systems.

To prevent the spread of the worm:

1) Don't use the power line.
2) Don't use batteries either, since there are rumors that this virus has invaded most major battery plants and is infecting the positive poles of the batteries. (You might try hooking up just the negative pole.)
3) Don't upload or download files.
4) Don't store files on floppy disks or hard disks.
5) Don't read messages. Not even this one!
6) Don't use serial ports, modems, or phone lines.

7) Don't use keyboards, screens, or printers.

8) Don't use switches, CPUs, memories, microprocessors, or mainframes.

9) Don't use electric lights, electric or gas heat or air-conditioning, running water, writing, fire, clothing or the wheel.

The ninth rule, the most amusing one, exposes neatly the ignorance of technology that other virus hoaxes exploit.

See also:

CIAC, Good Times Virus—1 and 2, Ladder Conspiracies, OM

Reference:

http://ciac.llnl.gov/ciac/CIACHoaxes.html

NASA, Nazis and JFK

NASA, Nazis and JFK is a reprint, with new introductory material, of a work originally published by "William Torbitt" (an admitted pen name) as *Nomenclature of an Assassination Cabal.* Its thesis is that the *John F. Kennedy assassination* was supervised by a conspiracy including Werner von Braun, J. Edgar Hoover, Lyndon Johnson, Roy Cohn, and Ferenc Nagy, former Prime Minister of Hungary, who was also the *Umbrella Man.*

The assassination was under the direction of Division Five of the FBI, Torbitt claims; this department, organized in the 1920s to spy on internal subversives, had become an assassination bureau. D-5 worked closely with the Security Division of NASA and the Defense Industrial Security Command, headed by von Braun. William Sullivan, the head of D-5, actually did spend the day after the assassination in a very private conference with *James Jesus Angleton* of the CIA, allegedly rehearsing their cover stories.

This most curious of all JFK assassination books traces an intricate set of links between Nazis, Hungarian politics, NASA, Roy Cohn, *Clay Shaw,* and *David Ferrie*—e.g., when von Braun surrendered to the U. S. Army in 1945, he surrendered to Major Clay Shaw—but never does clarify what motive drew all these groups and persons into one giant conspiracy to kill a president. There are dark hints, however, about faked moon landings, undisclosed Mars landings, *Area 51,* and "genetically created 'aliens',"suggestive of an unstated thesis that NASA is engaged in a different business than we have been told.

As for "William Torbitt," he claims to be a conservative lawyer who didn't even write this book alone, but paid two professionals to do the research and write most of it for him. He identifies them only as agents for the Customs Bureau and the Narcotics Bureau.

See also:

Bisociation, Sam Giancana, Marina Oswald, OM, Noon Blue Apples, UFO Conspiracies

Reference:

NASA, Nazis and JFK, by "William Torbitt" and Kenn Thomas, Adventures Unlimited Press, Kempton, Ill., 1996

National Association for Consumer Protection in Mental Health Practices

The National Association for Consumer Protection in Mental Health Practices, founded by Christopher Barden, is engaged in a state-by-state drive to enact laws that would require mental health practitioners to provide scientific evidence that their methods are safe and effective, before they can receive state insurance money. Largely inspired by the dismal record of the *recovered memory therapy* movement, this organization wants every therapist to show that the methods used have been proven "safe and effective by rigorous, valid, and reliable scientific investigations and accepted as safe and effective by a substantial majority of the relevant scientific community."

The model law written by Barden, who is both a lawyer and a Ph.D. in psychology, says that patients "have a legal and moral right to be fully and fairly informed of the risks and hazards and relative benefits of all proposed mental health treatments."

In 1995 the American Psychological Association set aside nearly a million dollars to fight this proposed legislation.

See also:

Abductees Anonymous, Demonic Duck, Corrydon Hammond, Incest Survivors, *Making Monsters, Satanic Panic*

Reference:

Making Monsters: False Memories, Psychotherapy, and Sexual Hysteria, by Richard Ofshe and Ethan Watters, University of California Press, Berkeley and Los Angeles, 1996, pp. 318–319

NaughtyRobot

A classic *ladder conspiracy* or hoax that got out of hand, NaughtyRobot has freaked out many a net-surfer. It seems to originate from the user's own website manager, but these headers are forged to hide the real sender, and it says:

Subject: Security breached by NaughtyRobot

This message was sent to you by NaughtyRobot, an Internet spider that crawls into your server through a tiny hole in the World Wide Web.

NaughtyRobot exploits a security bug in HTTP and has visited your host system to collect personal, private, and sensitive information.

It has captured your Email and physical addresses, as well as your phone and credit card numbers. To protect yourself against the misuse of this information, do the following:

1. Alert your server SysOp,
2. Contact your local police,
3. Disconnect your telephone, and
4. Report your credit cards as lost.

Act at once. Remember: Only YOU can prevent DATA fires.

See also:

Inslaw, OM, PROMIS

Reference:

http://ciac.llnl.gov/ciac/CIACHoaxes.html

Nazi Hell Creatures

See:

The Con, Corey Hammond, Satanic Abuse

Nazi Hollow Earth Theory

Some of the Nazis had a *hollow Earth* theory, but it was even weirder than those of **Dr. Raymond Bernard** and **Richard Shaver.** They held that the Earth was not only hollow but that we are living on the inside of it.

This model derived from an American prophet of the last century named Cyrus Teed, who had a vision of the Great Goddess and was told by her that he would convert all the world because she would reveal to him the truth unknown to both Christian Fundamentalists and heathen scientists. The truth was that the universe consists of solid rock, we live inside its only cavity, and the lights we think of as stars and planets are the lights of other cities, also inside. Teed changed his name to Koresh (Hebrew for Cyrus), and his doctrine became known as Koreshanity. Furthermore, he and a disciple proved the theory with a strange instrument called the rectilineator, which they employed to show that the Earth was not flat (as Fundamentalists then claimed) nor convex (as science claimed) but concave (as the Goddess revealed).

Koreshanity had a brief success in America, then withered away to a small cult in Florida. But in Germany in the 1920s, a World War I veteran named Peter Bender became a convert and, as a pilot, was able to attract the attention of Hermann Göring, an old comrade from the Luftwaffe. Bender made the Koresh theory more appealing to Nazis by writing, "An infinite universe is a Jewish abstraction. A finite, rounded universe is a thoroughly Aryan conception."

The first attempt to prove the finite, rounded universe theory occurred in the city of Magdeburg, where engineers attempted to fire a rocket that would hit the other side of the hollow Earth. The rocket never got off the ground, but some of the technicians later worked on the V-2 program, which did manage to fire rockets but not at the other side of the Earth.

A second experiment at Rigen Island in 1942 involved many naval officers and some scientists, who attempted to locate the British Navy by looking across the hollow Earth with powerful telescopes. All they saw was sky, and the Reich was furious at Bender for misleading them. He and his family perished in one of the death camps.

See also:

Creation Science, Holocaust Deniers, OM

References:

Subterranean Worlds, by Walter Kafton-Minkel, Loompanics Unlimited, Port Townsend, Wash., 1989, pp. 217–221

Koreshanity

Ibid., pp. 90–107

Eccentric Lives and Peculiar Notions, by John Michell, Citadel Press, Secaucus, N.J., 1984, pp. 41–50

Nazi/Illuminati Theory

In a very intriguing article entitled "The Nazi Religion: Views on Religious Statism in Germany and America," J.F.C. Moore argues that Nazism and American conservatism are both deeply rooted in the *Illuminati* conspiracy. According to Moore, (1) Nazism emerged from the Thule Society, a right-wing occult lodge in 1920s Germany, which was influenced by the Illuminati, and (2) Nazism has too many resemblances of right-wing movements in America for the parallels to be coincidental.

Basically Moore's theory holds that ever since the American and French revolutions, certain rightist groups have seen anarchy as the ultimate result of too much democracy and have tried to prevent this by forming secret societies devoted to State-worship and/or Christian Socialism, combined with a Gnostic mystique of receiving guidance from heavenly or otherworldly beings. This guidance produces the state called "Illumination" and causes the initiate to feel a deep need to fight for Good and against Evil; the problem is that Good and Evil are both defined in terms of the ideology of Authoritarianism, with all rebels against "proper authority" defined as devils incarnate. J. Edgar Hoover and Congressman Otto Passman are named as members of such occult lodges.

Although Moore's style is scrupulously academic and impersonal, the data of his study is arranged to indicate that most right-wing groups in America, especially those with anti-Illuminati conspiracy theories, are themselves unknowing dupes of the Illuminati.

See also:

A-Albionic, James Jesus Angleton, The Con, P2 Conspiracy

Reference:

"The Nazi Religion: Views on Religious Statism in Germany and America," by J.F.C. Moore, *Libertarian American,* Vol. III, No. 3, August 1969

Necronomicon

Necronomicon, or "Book of Dead Names," is the title of most European translations of the "forbidden" book, *"Al Azif,"* written by "The Mad Arab," **Abdul Alhazred**. A matter of heated and sometimes fetid controversy, the *Necronomicon* is so feared and ill-reputed that some even deny that such a terrible work could exist.

In the latest translation, adapted from coded papers found in the archives of **Dr. John Dee**, Robert Turner writes, "In the myths of every race and clime we see the hallmarks of those extra-cosmic denizens that populate the pages of the *Necronomicon*. . . . In the Himalayas, . . . the Abominable Snowman, . . . Sightings of the West Virginia Mothman, . . . sea serpents and monsters fill the oceans and lakes; UFO encounters have become an almost daily occurrence."

See also:

Diamonic Reality, Gods of Eden, Kenneth Grant, Robert Morning Sky, *Mothman Prophecies*

Reference:

The Necronomicon with Commentaries, Neville Spearman, Suffolk, England, 1978

New World Order

The New World Order—an expression originally used in the 1920s to describe the views of **Col. Edward House**—became a hot issue again when **George Bush** used it in a speech. A typical view is expressed by the *Pennsylvania Crier,* which describes the NWO as the joint product of the ideas of **Cecil Rhodes**, Andrew Carnegie, and the Fabian Socialists (e.g., H.G. Wells)—an attempt to extend the British Empire to the whole Earth and thus prevent future wars. This gradually evolved into the idea of world governance by an English-speaking union, and should be resisted, the *Crier* says, because it would eliminate "freedom, self-determination, liberty, limited government, free enterprise, the U.S. Constitution and the Bill of Rights."

See also:

A-Albionic, Council on Foreign Relations, Insiders, *NASA, Nazis and JFK, None Dare Call It Conspiracy,* Noon Blue Apples, Trilateral Commission

Reference:

http://nwo.syninfo.com/Crier/pcabtnwo.html

New York Subway Experiment

In 1966, the U.S. Army released a bacillus throughout the New York City subway system. The name of the bacillus is unknown, and no harmful effects have been proven, partially because all details of the experiment are still classified.

The Army's justification for this experiment was that there are many subways in the former Soviet Union.

See also:

AIDS Conspiracy Theories, Chicago Malaria Study, Eugenics/AIDS Theory, Tuskegee Syphilis Study

Reference:

http://home.earthlink.net/~bkonop/GermIncidents2.html

Nicaragua: Germ Warfare?

In 1985 Nicaragua suffered an outbreak of dengue fever shortly after an increase of U.S. aerial reconnaissance missions. Many died, and many others, perhaps half the population of Managua, were badly stricken. Some critics suspect germ warfare, because Nicaragua had never had such an epidemic before and the outbreak was nearly identical with the incident in Cuba four years before (see **Cuban Germ War?**).

Dengue fever variations were studied experimentally at the Army's Biological Warfare test facility in **Fort Detrick**, Maryland, before the alleged "ban" on such research in 1972.

See also:

AIDS Conspiracy Theories, Chicago Malaria Study

Reference:

http://home.earthlink.net/~bkonop/GermIncidents2.html

Noble Drew Ali

Noble Drew Ali was possibly born Timothy Drew probably in 1886 among the Cherokee Indians. Nothing about him is certain, but the Cherokees did often adopt runaway slaves, and some say his parents were slaves. Others say his father was Moorish, his mother Cherokee. He may have left the Cherokees to join a gypsy band, and he possibly worked as a seaman and/or a carnival magician.

He seems to have visited Egypt and possibly was initiated into High Magick in a Masonic-like ceremony in the Great Pyramid.

After about 1912 things become a bit more specific. Now known as Noble Drew Ali, he founded a Temple of Moorish Science in Newark, based on a book called *The Holy Koran of the Moorish Science Temple of America,* which has very little in common with the orthodox *Koran.* Noble Drew's doctrines included the belief that so-called Negroes or Blacks (now called African-Americans) are actually Asiatics, descended from the prophetess Ruth in the Old Testament, and that the Moors of North Africa and the Irish shared a common ancestry. (See **Bob Quinn.**) He also claimed that Moors reached this continent long before any Europeans, an idea currently revived by novelist/poet Ishmael Reed.

Noble Drew also taught that most American Blacks were Moors but had forgotten their true identity; his favorite symbols, incidentally, were the Masonic square-and-compass and the quasi-Masonic Eye in the Triangle (see *Great Seal of the United States*). Some of his other teachings: "Aught is Allah" (see *Book of Lies*) and "Be yourself and not somebody else."

The Moorish Science Temple gained converts, and eventually Noble Drew moved on to Chicago. A poster from May 16, 1927, announces that the prophet Noble Drew Ali will reveal "events in the last days" and then be bound with several yards of rope and escape before the eyes of the audience. The movement grew even faster, but Noble Drew Ali died under mysterious circumstances the next year, perhaps as the result of a police beating. Some of his ideas live on in surviving Moorish Temples and, adapted slightly, in the Nation of Islam (Black Muslims).

Recently, the *"Fortean Times"* examined the strange case of the Melungeons, a group of unknown racial stock in our southern states, who have been the subject of controversy for centuries because of their European features and dark skin. Local Indians never regarded them as "white" and said they came here before any white people. The *FT* finds the most plausible theory is that the Melungeons were of mixed Moorish, Turkish, and Portuguese ancestry. Perhaps they were also part of the gene pool of Noble Drew Ali, and family lore gave him some of his ideas.

The *FT* also suggests that Abraham Lincoln may have had some Melungeon ancestry.

See also:

Assassins, *Irish Wisdom*

References:

Sacred Drift: Essays on the Margins of Islam, by Peter Lamborn Wilson, City Lights Books, San Francisco, 1993, pp. 14–50

"Meet the Melungeons," by Ian Morphitt, *Fortean Times*, No. 106, January 1998

None Dare Call It Conspiracy

None Dare Call It Conspiracy, by Gary Allen, is the best-known and most influential book on the *John Birch Society*'s version of the One Big Conspiracy That Controls Everything.

According to Allen (some Birchers disagree with him here), *Adam Weishaupt* and his *Illuminati* do not directly influence the current form of the One Big Conspiracy. Rather, the One Big Conspiracy—consisting of *Insiders,* not of Illuminati—was founded by statesman-financier-philosopher *Cecil Rhodes* (1853–1902) but based on the same tactics Weishaupt's group had used a century earlier. Rhodes, an Englishman who made his fortune in South Africa, endowed 170 Rhodes scholarships at Oxford, but this was not disinterested charity according to Allen: The scholarships serve as recruiting "hooks" to find the personnel to manage an Anglo-American financial/political cabal that Rhodes devised with the intent of taking over the world. The chief agencies of the Rhodes conspiracy are identified as the *Council on Foreign Relations* in the U.S. and the Royal Institute of International Affairs in England; both groups seemingly have played a large role in guiding and advising the two major parties in both countries. Many Birchers feel that the Rhodes "Insiders" now have fairly well taken over, and the more extreme secessionists and survivalists of the Far Right largely believe this: It explains why, although fiercely patriotic in their own way, they hate and fear the U.S. government.

See also:

A-Albionic, LAWCAP, Lyndon LaRouche, Ezra Pound, Carroll Quigley

References:

Webster's Family Encyclopedia, Vol. 8, Pha-Sch, "Rhodes"

Conspiracies, Cover-Ups and Crimes, by Jonathan Vankin, Paragon House, New York, 1992

Noon Blue Apples

The most tantalizing part of the the **Church of Mary Magdalene/ Priory of Sion** mystery concerns the coded parchments found by **Father Béranger Saunière** in 1891. These parchments, on the surface, were mere transcriptions from the Latin Gospels, but certain letters were highlighted so as to yield another set of messages in French. These messages contained references that, evidently, only somebody already initiated into the mystery could understand. They contain such memorable lines as:

> *This treasure belongs to Dagobert II King and to Sion and he is there dead.*

And in the second parchment:

> *Shepherdess no temptation that Poussin Teniers hold the key peace 681 by the cross and this horse of God I complete this daemon guardian at noon blue apples.*

See also:

Jean Cocteau, Committee to Protect the Rights and Privileges of Low-Cost Housing, Dagobert II, Gerard de Sede, Gnomes of Zurich, Grand Orange Order of Ireland, Holy Order of the Lemon, Nicholas Poussin

Reference:

Holy Blood, Holy Grail, by Michael Baigent, Henry Lincoln, and Richard Leigh, Delacorte, New York, 1982

Yuri Nosenko

In January of 1964, Yuri Nosenko of the KGB, who had been a CIA asset since June 1962, asked the CIA for help in defecting to the West. At first, the CIA refused to cooperate and insisted on keeping Nosenko "in place" within the KGB Moscow headquarters, but eventually accepted him with grave reservations.

James Jesus Angleton, head of counterintelligence for the CIA, distrusted (or claimed to distrust) Nosenko from the first and at one point even tried to arrange the would-be defector's assassination. Some evidence indicates that after Nosenko was accepted in Washington, Angleton had him interrogated and/or brainwashed with various drugs as part of the *MK-ULTRA* program. Those who believe Angleton played a pivotal role in the *John F. Kennedy assassination* find it significant that after this alleged brainwashing, Nosenko's testimony before the House Select Committee on Assassinations tended strongly to support the Warren Commission and discredit conspiracy theories.

One of the major unresolved issues in the Nosenko case revolves around the matter of *Sasha,* a possible Soviet mole said to be high in the upper ranks of the CIA. An earlier Soviet defector, *Anatoli Golitsin,* had claimed that Sasha really existed, but Nosenko denied this. Since Golitsin also claimed that the Soviet Union was planning to flood the CIA with fake defectors carrying disinformation, this conflict between Nosenko and Golitsin created much difference of opinion within the Agency and among conspiracy theorists ever since. The matter is made more murky by the proven KGB infiltration of the highest ranks of the British intelligence community, as indicated by the Hollis case.

See also:

Castro as Super-Mole, Double Cross System, Fedora

Reference:

http://www.jfkweb.simplenet.com/voice/nosenko.htm

Novus Ordo Seclorum

See:

Great Seal of the United States

James Oberg

James Oberg, a longtime skeptic of the extraterrestrial interpretation of the UFO phenomenon, has more than once suggested a rather conspiratorial countertheory.

In June 1980, Moscow had a major UFO flap. People saw a giant light and some claimed that aliens were chasing cars and drilling holes through house windows. Tens of thousands of citizens allegedly saw some or all of this weirdity. In *Omni* magazine, Oberg proposed that the KGB was behind it: "The KGB, eager to muddy the waters and cover up public recognition of the military space center at Pietsk, is only too happy to promote scintillating stories about aliens chasing cars and boring nasty holes in windows."

More recently, Oberg has pointed an accusing finger at agencies of the U.S. government:

. . . Government representatives—officials, military officers, etc.— used "UFO" as a convenient camouflage for other official classified activities (such as retrieval of crashed aircraft or nuclear weapons or other objects); or used artificial "UFO stories" (in oral, written, photographic, film, etc. form) as "tracers" in studying the function of security safeguards and personnel psychological responses; or used "UFO" as an excuse (either intended or accidental) to cover up improper, forbidden, or diplomatically delicate activities. . . or any other activity that the government— or any part of it—wanted to keep hidden.

Oberg made these charges in an open letter to Dr. Stephen Greer of the *CSETI* organization, who is trying to force the government to release UFO secrets. Oberg supports Greer in wanting the secrets given to the public, even though Greer expects the hidden data will support the extraterrestrial hypothesis and Oberg believes it will just show that the government lies to us a lot of the time.

Most conspiriologists would certainly like to see the release of any alleged "UFO secrets" dealing with lost nuclear weapons and "improper, forbidden, or diplomatically delicate" activities.

See also:

William Cooper, Crop Circles, *NASA, Nazis and JFK,* UMMO Letters

References:

KGB lies—

Omni, September 1982

U.S. government lies—

Saucer Smear, Vol. 44, No. 6, June 1997 (P.O. Box 1709, Key West, FL 33041)

Octopus

When journalist *Danny Casolaro* began investigating the *Inslaw* scandal, he found links to so many other conspiracies that he could barely believe his own research. The more Casolaro dug into the Inslaw/*PROMIS* story, the more it led him to a world of tangled treachery that tied into almost anything you can find in the present book, even the alleged extraterrestrials at *Area 51* (Danny became convinced that the real secret of Area 51 concerned spy planes), the death of *Vince Foster,* and a series of murders connected with an Indian reservation in California.

Casolaro became convinced that no single conspiracy could explain the Inslaw links; he created the metaphor of "the Octopus," a hypothetical network of local conspiracies and/or affinity groups that could act together as a single entity at certain times (when they had a motive to act together) and then at other times would go back to working on their own goals unrelated to each other.

See also:

A-Albionic, John Birch Society, The Con, *Gods of Eden,* Great Pirates, Irish Wisdom, Lyndon LaRouche, MMAO, Priority of Sion, Fletcher Prouty, *Yankee and Cowboy War*

References:

http://www.federal.com/6298.html

http://www.amphibiouszone.com/inslaw.html

The Octopus: Secret Government and the Death of Danny Casolaro, by Kenn Thomas and Jim Keith, Feral House, Portland, Oreg., 1996

Frank Olson

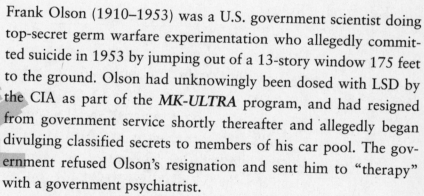

Frank Olson (1910–1953) was a U.S. government scientist doing top-secret germ warfare experimentation who allegedly committed suicide in 1953 by jumping out of a 13-story window 175 feet to the ground. Olson had unknowingly been dosed with LSD by the CIA as part of the **MK-ULTRA** program, and had resigned from government service shortly thereafter and allegedly began divulging classified secrets to members of his car pool. The government refused Olson's resignation and sent him to "therapy" with a government psychiatrist.

In 1965, Olson's son Eric read a story that the CIA had experimented with LSD as a truth serum, testing it on their own scientists without their knowledge in the 1950s. The CIA confirmed that Frank Olson had been one of the scientists given LSD. In 1975, Gerald Ford awarded the Olsons $750,000 and an apology.

In 1994, Eric was granted legal permission to exhume his father's body. It was surprisingly well preserved, and forensic scientists immediately x-rayed it and then examined all fractures.

What they found was inconsistent with either an accidental fall or a suicide—e.g., there was an unexplainable bruise on the side of Olson's forehead that did not hit the ground. They decided that Olson had probably been hit with a blunt object and was thrown out the window. The forensic evidence is strong enough that the case has been reopened by the district attorney of New York City to determine whether Olson was murdered by the CIA.

See also:

AIDS Conspiracy Theories, Mona Charen, Chicago Malaria Study, New York Subway Experiment

Reference:

Discovery Magazine, June 1997 (TV Discovery channel)

Dr. Kenneth Olson

Dr. Kenneth Olson, in treating a patient named Nadean Cool, persuaded her to disclose some 126 previously repressed alternative personalities. These included Satan, many angels who brought messages from God, a cannibal, and even a demonic duck.

Cool's father dropped dead of a heart attack after she confronted him with her "memories" of Satanic rituals and infant sacrifices. She eventually sued Dr. Olson for malpractice and collected $2.4 million in damages.

One other woman has sued Dr. Olson successfully for false multiple-personality diagnosis.

See also:

Corrydon Hammond, *Making Monsters*, Recovered Memory Therapy

References:

Fortean Times, No. 99, June 1997

CBS *60 Minutes,* November 30, 1997

OM

OM, or Operation Mindfuck, is a long-range *Discordian* project that some consider to belong in the category of concept art and others regard as anarchist pranks. Due to the basic Discordian catma—"We Discordians must stick apart"—nobody, not even Discordians, know what real or alleged phenomena belong to OM and what does not. All we can say for sure is that OM intends to enlarge our concept of the possible.

In a sense, OM predates the Discordian revelation and might include the Dada movement, ca. 1914, which featured poetry readings at which the poet was drowned out by other Dadaists with noisemakers. Certainly, a classic mindfuck occurred at the first surrealist art show in 1923 in which the audience first passed through a garden that contained a taxicab tampered with by Salvador Dali, in which it was raining inside but not outside, and then entered a gallery where the first thing they saw was a sign saying

dada is not dead
watch your overcoats

Nobody knows for sure how much of the oeuvre of Andy Warhol or how many UFO reports are part of OM. Might the *Priory of Sion* be an OM project, or that odd film *"F for Fake"*? The present author would include *Ho Houses International,* but that is just a guess.

See also:

CIAC, *Crying of Lot 49,* Hoaxing the CIA, Irina, News Election Service, Kerry Thornley, UMMO Letters

Reference:

http://www.prairienet.org/~kkbuxton/discordia.html

Order of Memphis and Mizraim

The Order of Memphis and Mizraim seems to have had a relatively short existence, but is intimately connected with many other orders of *Freemasonry,* Illuminism, and *Rosicrucianism.*

The Grandmaster of the Order of Memphis and Mizraim, John Yarker (1833–1913), claimed his was the oldest of all Masonic lodges and had the magick secrets lost by the others. Memphis and Mizraim also had more degrees of initiation than any other lodge—97 of them, as compared to the 33 degrees of Scotch Rite Masonry and the 11 of the *Ordo Templi Orientis.*

In 1895, two German Freemasons, Karl Kellner and Theodor Reuss, attempted to found an Academia Masonica, which eventually evolved into the Ordo Templi Orientis. The higher orders they borrowed from the rite of Memphis and Mizraim, other details from the (Rosicrucian) Hermetic Brotherhood of Light, and they decided that both men and women would be admitted.

This last point proved a hard one for most Masons, wedded to the tradition of an all-male secret society, so eventually the OTO became unacceptable to most other Masonic orders. It was absolutely necessary, however, because of Reuss' conviction that sex magick is the lost secret of Masonry and the Rose Cross symbol. Meanwhile, Reuss and another Mason, Leopold Engel, formed the revived Order of the *Illuminati.*

Reuss also became the Grand Master of the Swedenborgian Rite of Freemasonry in Germany (1901) and Magus of the Societas Rosicruciana in Anglia (1902)—the latter under the rule of W. Wynn Wescott of the *Hermetic Order of the Golden Dawn.* Reuss then formed three distinct but similar lodges in Germany, the Ancient and Primitive Rite of Memphis with 97 degrees, the Ancient Oriental Rite of Mizraim with 90 degrees, and the Ancient and Accepted Scotch Rite with 33 degrees.

Aleister Crowley obtained all 97 degrees of Memphis and Mizraim from Yarker, the 9th and later 10th degree of the OTO from Reuss (the 10th made him Outer Head), and all 33 degrees of the Scotch Rite from a Mexican Mason he met while mountain climbing in that country.

See also:

Illuminati Copies or Revivals, Noble Drew Ali, Priory of Sion, *Secret Cipher of the UFOnauts*

Reference:

http://otohq.org/oto/history.html#amas

Ordo Templi Orientis

The Ordo Templi Orientis is a *Freemasonic*-style ritualistic occult order that traces itself back to the *Knights Templar.* Although several groups have claimed to be the real OTO, and there were 1,005 competing Outer Heads at one time, the federal courts have ruled that the order represented on the World Wide Web (see references) is the "true" OTO of *Aleister Crowley* and have granted it tax-exempt status as a charitable corporation and religious entity.

The OTO has eleven degrees, the first nine and the eleventh involving Freemasonic-style "initiations" in which the candidate is tested and, hopefully, illuminated by deeper insight into the world and himself/herself. The 10th degree represents the Outer Head of the Order, a post currently held by one Hymeneus Beta, according to the claims of U.S. courts, and by 1,004 others according to their own claims.

Aleister Crowley became an initiate of the OTO in 1912 after publishing *"The Book of Lies."* The Outer Head at that time, Theodore Reuss, came to Crowley and said that, since he knew the secret of the 9th degree, he had to accept that rank in the OTO and its attendant obligations. Crowley protested that he knew no such secret, but Reuss showed him a copy of *The Book of Lies* and pointed to a chapter that revealed the secret clearly. Crowley looked at his own words, and "It instantly flashed upon me. The entire symbolism not only of Free Masonry but of many other traditions blazed upon my spiritual vision. . . . I understood that I held in my hands the key to the future progress of humanity." Crowley, of course, does not tell us which chapter contains the secret. (The present author nominates chapter 69.)

Crowley succeeded Reuss as Outer Head and was succeeded by one Karl Germer who died without appointing a successor, leading to the long struggle between various factions. Charlie Manson once belonged to an alleged Ordo Templi Orientis, but not to the one currently recognized by U.S. courts as a legitimate charitable and religious organization.

See also:

Aiwass, Kenneth Grant, *Liber Al,* Thelema

References:

http://www.crl.com/~thelema/oto.html

The Book of Lies, by Aleister Crowley, Samuel Weiser, New York, 1988, p. 7

The Magical World of Aleister Crowley, by Francis King, McCann and Geoghegan, New York, 1978

The Eye in the Triangle, by Israel Regardie, Falcon Press, Las Vegas, 1989

Organ Vampires

Many people believe that "organ vampires" are at large in major American cities, especially New Orleans. These medical monsters are allegedly "harvesting" kidneys from unsuspecting travelers and reselling them to be used as kidney transplants for the rich.

This belief falls midway between a conspiracy theory in the classic sense and "urban folklore"—stories that get repeated endlessly but fall more in the area of scary anecdotes than parts of a consistent system of suspicion/accusation aimed at a specific group. In urban folklore, as in this tale, the story usually takes the form of an experience that supposedly happened to "a friend of a friend" (abbreviated FOAF by scholars who study this field). Investigations never do succeed in finding the FOAF who started any of these yarns.

The National Business Travel Association reports that the New Orleans police have no records of any such kidney snatchings reported to them by travelers.

References:

Travel Security Information, "Special Report: Urban Myths," *Kroll Travel Watch,* January 29, 1997

Playboy, August 1996

Lee Harvey Oswald

Lee Harvey Oswald either shot John Kennedy all alone, or in collaboration with other shooters, or was a patsy set up by the real assassins. These issues have been debated for 35 years and will continue to be debated for a long time to come.

We do know some disturbing facts: The majority of witnesses thought the shots came from the grassy knoll, not from Oswald's window in the Texas School Book Depository. Kennedy's head jerks back as if shot from the front (Grassy Knoll) in the *Zapruder film.* Oswald was a mediocre marksman, and yet, to fit the official theory, he had to fire three almost perfect shots in only seconds. The last government inquiry, that of the House Select Committee on Assassinations, did not support the Warren Commission but concluded that there were at least two shooters in Dealy Plaza that day.

And yet, just because Oswald himself was shot before he could stand trial, the case never underwent the challenge of our legal adversary system, and New Orleans D.A. Jim Garrison's attempt to prove conspiracy collapsed for lack of evidence. The case remains painfully open.

See also:

James Jesus Angleton, *Best Evidence,* Hale Boggs, E. Howard Hunt, Kennedy Death Links, *NASA, Nazis and JFK,* Three Tramps, A.J. Weberman, "The Whole Bay of Pigs Thing", and the further links therefrom

Reference:

http://gate.cruzio.com/~tdbooks/library/lhowords.html

Oswald to Hunt: An Unsolved Mystery

There is a letter in Lee Harvey Oswald's handwriting, dated November 10, 1963, addressed to a "Mr. Hunt" and asking for a job with Hunt's organization. Conspiriologists differ as to what "Mr. Hunt" Oswald wrote to, some guessing it was oil millionaire H.L Hunt, a bitter foe of John Kennedy, and others claiming it was CIA mystery man *E. Howard Hunt,* who later requested money from Richard Nixon and looks a lot like one of the *Three Tramps* on the grassy knoll on November 22, 1963.

See also:

Flight 553, "The Whole Bay of Pigs Thing"

Reference:

"Interview With A.J. Weberman," *Popular Alienation: A Steamshovel Press Reader*, IllumiNet Press, Lilburn, Ga., 1995, p. 174

Marina Oswald

Although Marina Oswald has given a variety of stories about her ex-husband and his involvement or non-involvement in a *John F. Kennedy assassination* conspiracy, her latest version, given to A.J. Weberman in 1994, is especially interesting and unexpected:

> *"The answer to the Kennedy assassination is with the **Federal Reserve Bank**. Don't underestimate that. It's wrong to blame it on **Angleton** and the CIA per se only. This is only one finger of the same hand. The people who supply the money are above the CIA."*

See also:

Albert Guy Bogard, Fedora, Ezra Pound, David Rockefeller, Sasha

Reference:

http://www.weberman.com/htdocs/

Our Lady of the Roses/Jesus-AIDS Theory

Our Lady of the Roses Shrine in Bayside, a suburb of New York, has been called "the Lourdes of America" because the proprietor, housewife Veronica Lueken, sees the Virgin Mary regularly, and even channels her. Along with a lot of support for *Archbishop Lefebvre* and right-wing Catholicism in general, the Virgin reveals many shocking bits of news, such as the UFO phenomenon being produced by demons who sexually molest children. Her most startling revelation, however, is that the creator of AIDS was her own son, Jesus, who was so vexed by the Gay community that he decided to kill them off en masse.

Because HIV was designed by Jesus himself, the Blessed Mother says, scientists will never find a cure for it.

See also:

Antichrist, Christians Awake AIDS Theory, UFO/Satanic Conspiracy

Reference:

Our Lady of the Roses Shrine, Box 52, Bayside, NY 11361

P2 Conspiracy

P2, or *Propaganda Due,* was a secret society within a secret society, just like the original *Illuminati* of Bavaria. Probably founded by *Licio Gelli* sometime in the 1970s, as part of the CIA's *Gladio* operation, P2 originally recruited exclusively among third-degree members of the *Grand Orient Lodge of Egyptian Freemasonry,* but eventually had 950 members in the Italian government and the higher reaches of banking and finance. Accused of plotting a fascist coup, masterminding the 1980 Bologna railway bombing, drug running, massive financial frauds, and sundry misdemeanors, the group was either crushed by criminal convictions and press exposés or regrouped under a newer name, depending on which sources you believe. Archbishop *Paul "The Gorilla" Marcinkus* was removed from the presidency of the Vatican Bank because of his associations with P2 and eventually was ejected from the Vatican and sent home to Chicago in disgrace.

So many charges and wild tales surround P2 that it seems wise to treat the various parts of the puzzle in separate entries.

See also:

A-Albionic, James Jesus Angleton, Banco Ambrosiano, Roberto Calvi, *In Banks We Trust, In God's Name,* Knights of Malta, Merovingians, Michele "The Shark" Sindona, *Scandals of the Priory of Sion*

Reference:

The Mysterious Death of God's Banker, Foot and della Torre, Orbis, London, 1984

Ray Palmer

Ray Palmer (1910–1977) was run over by a butcher truck at the age of six and permanently disabled. Hunchbacked and standing only four feet eight inches, he had a tremendous drive to compensate for his physical handicaps; he wrote 99 science-fiction stories before selling one, but very quickly he became editor of a series of increasingly sensational sci-fi and fringe science pulps (*Amazing Stories, Fate, Other Worlds, Flying Saucers,* etc.) and influenced his times more than most of the better-known literary figures of our age.

As Walter Kafton-Minkel very accurately wrote:

[Palmer] almost single-handedly created the myth of UFOs as extraterrestrial visitors; he promoted many of the earlier "flying saucer" sightings, and he started the stories of a government "cover-up" of UFO reports. Palmer was the P.T. Barnum of alternative-reality promotion. . .

In short, *The X Files,* and all the mass fears and conspiracy theories that fed into it, largely owe their existence to Pay Palmer, who reached millions with his pulps, even though the mythos he created never became as universally known in his lifetime as it has since his death.

In the words of F.W. Fairman:

A Palmer promotion has the touch of genius. It has zing, sparkle, and true showmanship. It can be spotted a mile away by the bright lights. The thing to do is sit back and enjoy it.

Palmer also launched "the Shaver Mystery" (see **Richard Shaver**) and either invented or first publicized the **men in black**.

In sum, many millions of people are living in the world of Ray Palmer, even though most of them have never heard his name.

See also:

The Con, Crop Circles, Elmyr, Holy Order of the Lemon, Clifford Irving, Orson Welles

Reference:

Subterranean Worlds, by Walter Kafton-Minkel, Loompanics Unlimited, Port Townsend, Wash., 1989, p. 134

Fairman—

Same source, same page

Passive Conspiracy

An interesting theory placed on the World Wide Web by a New York University student holds that *passive* conspiracy is much more common and powerful than *active* conspiracy. Following a Darwinian metaphor, this model holds that "things which can't successfully compete and reproduce themselves die out." This applies to social systems as well as to individual organisms, the author holds, and even drugs and diseases only survive as long as no powerful force truly wishes to eliminate them. For instance, the author claims that heroin would not have survived as a social "problem" if the government had a true motive for wishing to eliminate it; as long as it remains largely a Black inner city problem, the government passively allows it to continue while only pretending to "war" on it.

Dr. Wilhelm Reich had a more disturbing model of passive conspiracy, holding that the masses neurotically yearn to surrender to some fascist leader and will throw away their liberties as soon as a leader of that sort appears.

Reference:

http://www.itp.tsoa.nyu.edu/~student/jamie/philo/conspiracy.html

Pearl Harbor

Everything that the Japanese were planning to do was known to the United States.
    —Army Board, 1944

This is the touchiest "conspiracy" in this whole book. Professors Charles Beard and Harry Elmer Barnes, for instance, once ranked among the most prestigious historians in the U.S. (ca. 1920–40); but when they rejected our government's official version of Pearl Harbor, they became known as nuts, cranks, dingbats, etc. and were eventually removed from curricula. Most young readers have probably never even heard of these once famous scholars.

The case for conspiracy, which we present here but dare not endorse, runs as follows:

Pearl Harbor was especially vulnerable. In 1932, in a Joint Army-Navy Exercise, Admiral Yarnell "attacked" Pearl Harbor with 152 planes and caught the defenders completely by surprise. In 1938, Admiral Ernest J. King led a carrier-based attack on Pearl Harbor with equal success. When President Franklin D. Roosevelt ordered the fleet transferred from the West Coast to Pearl Harbor, Admiral James O. Richardon protested vigorously and repeatedly. He eventually refused orders and was replaced by Admiral Husband E. Kimmel, who also protested but obeyed orders.

In March 1941, when Roosevelt began the Lend-Lease program—providing weapons to one side in a war in which the U.S. was allegedly neutral—he violated international law and virtually invited the other side to retaliate.

On July 22 that year, Admiral Richmond K. Turner advised Roosevelt that cutting off the supply of American petroleum to Japan would invite an attack on the Philippines and "immediately involve us in a Pacific war." On July 25 Roosevelt cut off the oil, and Intelligence about Japanese activities was withheld from Army and Navy officials in Hawaii from this point forward, giving Admiral Kimmel no warning of what was coming.

The Army and Navy Intelligence services had cracked the following Japanese codes:

- *Purple—the top diplomatic code*

- *J–19—another, lesser diplomatic code*

- *PA-K2—another diplomatic code*

- *JN–25—the Japanese Naval code*

A Naval report of 1946 concluded that 188 of the messages in these codes, deciphered by U.S. Intelligence, clearly concerned an impending attack on Pearl Harbor. In addition, Dutch, British, and Russian Intelligence all reported Japanese war plans to the U.S. government.

On November 25, Secretary of War Henry Stimson wrote in his diary about a conversation with President Roosevelt: "The question was how we should maneuver them into the position of firing the first shot without too much danger to ourselves. . . . It was desirable to make sure that the Japanese be the ones to do this (the first shot) so that there should remain no doubt in anyone's mind as to who were the aggressors."

A Navy Court of Inquiry from July 24 to September 27 examined the possible negligence of Admiral Kimmel at Pearl Harbor. They exonerated him when they learned that he had been deprived of all intelligence information obtained from the decoded Japanese messages. An Army report of October 1944 concluded that, with the decoded messages, it was possible to indicate precisely the intentions of the Japanese, "including the probable exact hour and date of the attack."

See also:

Colonel Edward House, Fletcher Prouty

Reference:

http://www.clinton.net/~mewilley/pearl.html

Mino Pecorelli

Mino Pecorelli was an early member of the *P2 conspiracy* in Italy, but had a falling-out with the leadership and began publishing a tabloid called *OP* exposing his former associates. He was shot dead in Rome on March 20, 1979.

See also:

In God's Name, Scandals of the Priory of Sion

Reference:

In God's Name, by David Yallop, Bantam, New York, 1985, pp. 308–10

Albert Pike

See:

Hiram Abiff

Pinks

"Pinks" in the terminology of the *Church of the Sub-Genius* are sub-sub-sub-geniuses, i.e., normal or average humans. They can be recognized by the following stigmata: They believe what they are told by those above them in the power structure (family, school, corporation, etc.); they obey orders; they pay their taxes; if drafted, they will kill whomever they are told to kill; they actually enjoy most of what's on TV; they never have an original or rebellious thought; they are the persons you meet most often and have to deal with, especially in business and government.

The Church of the Sub-Genius has no ban on admitting Pinks (as "Bob" said, "They may be Pink, but their money is green") and actively encourages trying to pass unnoticed among them— "Act like a dumbshit and they'll treat you like an equal."

The Pinks serve *The Con* without even knowing it and will all be destroyed on "X Day."

See also:

"Bob", Planet X, S.O.B.

Reference:

Rev. Ivan Stang, Church of the Sub-Genius, P.O. Box 140306, Dallas, TX 75214

Lt. William Pitzer

Lt. William Pitzer of the Dallas police took the original autopsy photos of John F. Kennedy's body after the November 22, 1963, assassination. These photos show an exit wound at the back of the head, although the later examination at Bethesda Hospital in Maryland shows a much smaller wound, looking like an entrance wound. This seems crucial to many conspiracy buffs, since Pitzer's photos fit the "assassin on the grassy knoll" theory and the later Bethesda evidence fits the "assassin from behind" (Texas School Book Depository) theory.

Pitzer later told friends he underwent "horrifying" debriefings by government agents. He was found dead of a wound that the coroner ruled had been self-inflicted. Oddly, Pitzer's body was found holding the gun in his right hand. He was left-handed.

See also:

Kennedy Death Links, Octopus, Fletcher Prouty

Reference:

Big Book of Conspiracies, by Doug Moench, Paradox Press, New York, 1995, p. 15

Planet X

Planet X is the home planet of the Xists (not to be confused with sexists), godlike beings of superhuman intelligence allied with the *Church of the Sub-Genius*. According to J.R. "Bob" Dobbs, the Short Term Interim Savior of this group, the Xists will invade Earth on July 5, 1998, at 7:30 in the morning and destroy the *Pinks* ("normal humans") with death rays. Those who are tithing 10 percent of their salary to "Bob" will be spared, however, and taken up in the Pleasure Ships of the Love Goddess to live forever on the planet of immortality.

See also:

Anti-"Bob", "Bob," The Con, Discordianism, Terrence McKenna, S.O.B.

Reference:

http://sunsite.unc.edu/subgenius/

Revelation X: The "Bob" Apocryphon, trans. out of the original tongues by the Sub-Genius Foundation, Simon and Schuster, New York, 1994

Poetic Terrorism

Poetic terrorism is the name given by *Hakim Bey* to the type of graffiti that causes consternation or confusion or in some way might provoke the onlooker to think in new categories. Some examples:

For scrawling or rubber-stamping on advertisements:

THIS IS YOUR TRUE DESIRE

For scrawling or rubber-stamping anywhere:

THE CHAINS OF LAW HAVE BEEN BROKEN

TANTRIK PORNOGRAPHY

IMAGINARY SHIITE FANATICS

GAY ZIONISM (SODOM FOR THE SODOMITES)

CHAOS NEVER DIED

See also:

Association for Ontological Anarchy, Discordianism, Ladder Conspiracies

Reference:

http://www.0.or.at/hakimbey/conspire.htm

Pope John Paul 1

See:

In God's Name

Potere Occulto

In Italian, *potere occulto* means "hidden power," or the clandestine group behind the visible rulers. Roberto Calvi, murdered president of **Banco Ambrosiano**, was a fervent believer in *potere occulto*, and before the **P2** scandal erupted, many ridiculed him for his fascination with this melodramatic view of the world. Calvi believed that the secret of success was to find which hidden group held the most power and then join it. Since he ended up hanging from a bridge in London, he perhaps did not find the strongest group after all.

After the P2 revelations and indictments, many seemed to see realism in Calvi's view of power. A radical member of the Italian government, Massino Teodori, said that the P2 revelations showed an interpenetration of "financial criminality and common criminality"; former Prime Minister Giovanni Spaldolini described the Calvi-**Licio-Gelli** network as "a new Mafia. . . a multinational (corporation) of crime"; another member of Parliament, Guiseppe D'Alema, described the P2 crew as part of "a political-military-business complex. . . in which fascist and other forces co-exist." Larry Gurwin, of the staid *Institutional Investor*, concluded his study of the conspiracy with the blunt statements that "the U.S. government and the Vatican. . . have, in their war against communism, allied themselves with. . . gangsters, drug pushers, and terrorists" and "Roberto Calvi's world view may have been far more accurate than anyone realized."

See also:

Cara Calvi, *Godfather,* Government as Criminal Conspiracy, Paul "The Gorilla" Marcinkus, Octopus, Fletcher Prouty

Reference:

The Calvi Affair, by Larry Gurwin, Pan Books, London, 1984, pp. 179–80, 195–96

Ezra Pound

Considered by his peers one of the greatest poets of the twentieth century, Ezra Loomis Pound (1885–1972) also considered himself a major political and economic philosopher and filled his later poetry (and prose) with theories that range from the analytically plausible to the weirdly conspiratorial.

Pound's *Cantos*, the longest (824 pages) and most ambitious of all modern poems, sees history as a perpetual battle between individual rights and the schemes of those possessed by avarice and power lust. The battle is seen as *political* in its early stages (thus, Mons of Jutland, a little-known figure, is praised highly for refusing to get involved in a religious war, saying other people's opinions were not his concern), and the major heroes of the poem are Confucius, Lord Coke (who set permanent limits on the British monarchy), and Thomas Jefferson/*John Adams* as the dialectical twins out of whom the best American traditions emerged.

In its later stages, the battle becomes *economic*, as the greedy and power-mad erect "governments" outside government through *international banking,* which Pound calls the Age of Usury. Here the heroes are Adams again, Sen. ***Thomas Hart Benton***, Andrew Jackson, an odd collection of Utopian money reformers, and, alas, Benito Mussolini.

Certainly, no other poet ever attempted to write history on so large a scale or carried off most of it with such brilliant detail of imagery and sound. This poem, despite its conspiratorial weirdness, has influenced almost all subsequent poetry, and at the end Pound repudiates the anti-semitism that disfigures the middle sections. His only defense, he realizes, is no defense:

> *Let the Gods forgive what I*
> *have made*

Let those I love try to forgive
what I have made

See also:

Bank of the United States, Federal Reserve Bank, *Protocols of the Elders of Zion*

Reference:

The Cantos of Ezra Pound, New Directions, New York, 1995

Nicholas Poussin

Nicholas Poussin (1594–1665), a French painter of the academic style, has become hopelessly entangled in the *Priory of Sion* mystery because of the research and speculations of *Gerard de Sede* and the authors of *"Holy Blood, Holy Grail."* A believer in the theory that painting should include philosophical lessons, Poussin left many works that lend themselves to endless interpretation, but none more so than his *Shepherds of Arcadia.*

The painting shows four shepherds and a tomb; the shepherds are not looking at the tomb but out of the painting, toward the viewer and gesturing toward the inscription on the tomb, which unhelpfully says, ET IN ARCADIA EGO ("And in Arcadia, I. . . ").

The books cited suggest that the tomb actually exists (photos are shown in the latter). It is near Rennes-le-Chateau, home of the mysterious *Church of Mary Magdalene*, where the priest Father Saunière found some treasure or some secret that made him rich in the 1890s. We are invited to believe that if we can deduce who is actually buried in that tomb, we would know what the Priory of Sion is all about.

Holy Blood suggests that if we permute the letters of *Et in Arcadia ego*, we can obtain "I TEGO ARCANA DEI" ("I conceal the secrets of God").

See also:

Noon Blue Apples, *Scandals of the Priory of Sion*

References:

La Race fabuleuse, by Gerard de Sede, Editions J'ai Lui, Paris, 1973

Holy Blood, Holy Grail, by Michael Baigent, Henry Lincoln, and Richard Leigh, Delacorte, New York, 1982

Power on Earth

Between his conviction for fraud in New York and his death in prison in Italy, **Michele "The Shark" Sindona,** one of the major figures in the **P2 conspiracy,** gave a series of interviews to a journalist named Nick Tosches, and *Power on Earth* presents Sindona's view of the events that led to his downfall.

Sindona was not very forthcoming about drug deals, gun-running, CIA involvement, terrorist bombings, or any of the more serious charges against the P2 cabal. The P2 people were not working to restore fascism, Sindona says, but to establish democracy. **Licio Gelli** did not have all the power he claimed, and just invented stories about being on the CIA payroll. In general, the "conspiracy" was just an overenthusiastic bunch of businessmen in love with democracy and fearful of communist tyranny.

Tosches does give us Sindona's last words, as he keeled over after breakfast in his cell in Milan (after being convicted of murdering the bank examiner, Giorgio Ambrosoli): "*Mi hanno avvelenato!*" ("They have poisoned me!").

See also:

Cara Calvi, Gladio, *Scandals of the Priory of Sion*

Reference:

Power on Earth, by Nick Tosches, Arbor House, New York, 1986

Principia Discordia

The *Principia Discordia, or How I Found Goddess and What I Did to Her After I Found Her* is the official Holy Book of the Discordian Society. It explains how humanity fell due to the Original Snub (the gods had a party on Olympus but deliberately did not invite Eris, who as goddess of chaos, vengefully created the Apple of Discord and unleashed the Trojan War and all subsequent International Relations) and all the other Discordian mysteries, including the Law of Fives (all events in the universe are related, directly or indirectly, to the number five, given enough ingenuity on the part of the interpreter).

The most original of all Discordian teachings probably is their rejection of dogma and its replacement by catma. A dogma is a proposition and thus either true or false, but a catma is a propositional function and thus has many meanings, some true, some false, and some in the Excluded Middle. (See **Language as Conspiracy**.)

The greatest Discordian catma of all is the Syadastan Affirmation, which says "All affirmations are true in some sense, false in some sense, meaningless in some sense, true and false in some sense, true and meaningless in some sense, false and meaningless in some sense, and true and false and meaningless in some sense." Some claim that if you repeat this 666 times, you will achieve Total Enlightenment, in some sense.

See also:

Golden Apple Corps, Illuminati, Knights of the Five-Sided Castle, Slack

Reference:

http://www.cs.cmu.edu/~tilt/principia

The Priory of Sion

The Priory of Sion is one of the most enigmatic of all secret societies, and can seriously be suspected of being a serious conspiracy and also of being nothing but an elaborate hoax by some witty French aristocrats.

See also:

Church of Mary Magdalene, Committee to Protect the Rights and Privileges of Low-Cost Housing, Gerard de Sede, Noon Blue Apples, Nicholas Poussin, *Scandals of the Priory of Sion*

Project Dumbo

Project Dumbo, the U.S. secret project to breed flying elephants, originally grew out of Project DNA, a more far-reaching investigation of genetic engineering. Allegedly, the first success of Project DNA, a half-bird–half-lizard, was created in April 1981, and this inspired the search for something that could fly and carry a large cargo. The underground scientists then combined the DNA of bats and elephants, producing the first flying elephants in 1983.

Some of the elephants showed a tendency to come down too fast and crash; one allegedly smashed into a research building and killed two scientists. Others had to be shot when they flew outside of the secure zone and it was feared civilians might see them.

This yarn has all the signs of a hoax, but. . .

See also:

OM, Our Lady of the Roses, UFO Conspiracies

Reference:

http://haven.ios.com/~masson12/elephants.html

PROMIS

PROMIS (Prosecutor's Management Information System) was a software program created by the *Inslaw* company and allegedly stolen by the Justice Department or persons within the Justice Department. It has allegedly been sold to more than 80 governments, who can use it to spy on their citizens to an extent undreamed of even in the satires of Orwell and Kafka.

According to several investigators of the Inslaw/PROMIS controversy, the CIA secretly installed a backdoor code in PROMIS so that they can spy on everybody who uses PROMIS and everybody that these users are spying on.

Danny Casolaro believed he had evidence that PROMIS was originally stolen from Inslaw to obtain the unrecorded money used by the Reagan campaign as a bribe for the Iranians to hold the American hostages until after Reagan won the 1980 election. Casolaro died under mysterious circumstances before he could publish his research.

According to reports, the PROMIS program allows anybody who owns it to spy on you whether you're online or not, e.g., they can monitor your bank account, water consumption, electricity use, etc., and get a rather clear picture of what you have been doing and even if you have somebody living with you.

See also:

James Jesus Angleton, Octopus, P2 Conspiracy

References:

http://www.federal.com/6298.html

http://www.amphibiouszone.com/inslaw.html

The Octopus: Secret Government and the Death of Danny Casolaro, by Kenn Thomas and Jim Keith, Feral House, Portland, Oreg., 1996

Proofs of a Conspiracy

Proofs of a Conspiracy, by John Robison, originally published in 1801, is one of the two primary sources, along with *Abbe Barruel,* on the theory of the *Illuminati* conspiracy. Robison probably has more credibility for more readers than the French royalist Barruel, because he does not denounce *Freemasonry* in general (he was a Freemason himself), does not engage in anti-semitism, and generally avoids most of the excesses of right-wing anti-Illuminati theorizing.

Robison's thesis is simply that the Illuminati had infiltrated the **Grand Orient Lodge of Egyptian Freemasonry** and were trying to infiltrate other lodges as well; he wrote chiefly to warn other Freemasons of this plot. He claims that the Illuminati controlled 84 lodges in Germany, 8 in England, and lesser numbers throughout Europe and in the United States (*Proofs of a Conspiracy,* p. 116). Their goal, he says, is to abolish all government and organized religion, establishing a world based on a kind of anarcho-communism or anarcho-syndicalism; other anti-Illuminati books would later have more colorful theories about them.

Robison's observation about secret societies of the Illuminati type is worth quoting:

Nothing is as dangerous as a mystic Association. The object remaining a secret in the hands of the management, the rest simply put a ring in their own noses, by which they may be led about at pleasure; and still panting after the secret they are the more pleased the less they see (Proofs of a Conspiracy, p. 269)

See also:

Noon Blue Apples, P2 Conspiracy, Priory of Sion

Reference:

Proofs of a Conspiracy, by John Robison, Christian Book Club of America, Hawthorn, Calif., 1961

The Protocols of the Elders of Zion

The Protocols of the Elders of Zion, although proven to be a forgery to the satisfaction of academic historians, still enjoys a wide popularity. The present author, in fact, has received three copies of it free, from people who think it is real and that every writer on conspiracy theory should know about it. When meeting people who believe in the *Protocols* and trying to tell them it has been proven a forgery, I have always heard the same counterargument: "Well, if it's a forgery, how come so much of it has already come true?"

Historians find three sources of the Protocols: (1) the anti-semitic legends of the Middle Ages, in which "The Jews" were accused of sacrificing Christian infants in their religious rituals, poisoning wells, and other barbarisms, (2) the revised conspiracy theory of **Abbe Barruel,** who originally found **Freemasons** behind the French revolution and later found "The Jews" behind the Freemasons, and (3) a satire called "Dialogues in Hell Between Machiavelli and Montesquieu," by Maurice Joly, which portrayed Napoleon III and the French aristocracy in general as cold-blooded sociopaths intending nothing but harm to the masses. Although Joly's targets were gentiles and he never mentioned the Jewish people, the "fiendish" (or hilarious) motives he attributes to the French government were picked up virtually verbatim in a novel called *Biarritz* by a German anti-semite, Hermann Goedsche, and transferred to a council of 12 rabbis who meet secretly—at *midnight* in a *cemetery*—to plot the destruction of Christianity. In 1893–95, agents of the Russian secret police rewrote Joly and Goedsche into the *Protocols of the Elders of Zion* in the form we now know it.

In 1905, under the direction of a mystic priest named Sergius Nilus, the work was widely published in Russia to blame "the

Jews" for the Russian army's failure to win the war against Japan that year. In the civil war following the Bolshevik Revolution of 1917, the "Whites" made extensive use of the *Protocols* to blame "the Jews" for that disaster also. Although several proofs of the forgery were published in several countries during the 1920s, the book was again widely distributed in the 1930s, by Adolph Hitler in Germany and Henry Ford in the United States. After World War II, the book had less and less circulation until various Islamic groups, opposed to the new state of Israel, began reissuing it; it still forms part of the ideology of the Islamic Resistance Movement (Hamas).

See also:

Language as Conspiracy, The Rape Conspiracy

References:

http://www.nizkor.org/ftp.cgi?documents/protocols/protocols.zion
http://www.nizkor.org/ftp.cgi?documents/protocols/protocols.001

Fletcher Prouty

Col. L. Fletcher Prouty (U.S. Air Force, retired) was the model for the Pentagon officer "X" in Oliver Stone's film *JFK*—the man who tells Jim Garrison about the extent of "black ops" (criminal activities) in the modern Intelligence services. Col. Prouty also acted as an adviser and consultant on the movie script.

Prouty graduated from the University of Massachusetts and the Graduate School of Banking at the University of Wisconsin before entering the Air Force. He became Military Manager at Tokyo International Airport, and later became a member of the office of the Secretary of Defense and the Joint Chiefs of Staff, and has been a special officer on assignments dating back to the Cairo and

Tehran conferences of 1943. Prouty retired from the military in 1964 and has worked as vice president of two banks. Unlike most other conspiriologists, he does not work from deduction but from personal experience and observation of those in high places.

In his book, *The Secret Team*, he describes how this personal inside view led him to conclude that those seemingly in control of the world are taking orders from unknown and clandestine forces, which he calls the High Cabal. He insists the Cabal is *not* the **Council on Foreign Relations**, the **Trilateral Commission,** or any similar group with a front name, a hind name, and an address. The Cabal avoids any publicity, and nobody knows who they are except for those near the very top, who take orders from them.

He often cites **R. Buckminster Fuller** as a writer who understood the Cabal fairly well; see *Great Pirates, LAWCAP.*

Prouty believes that the **John F. Kennedy assassination** was plotted within the U.S. government and that the media cover-up of that was only part of a much larger cover-up of why the Cold War was provoked and what commercial motives it served.

See also:

A-Albionic, The Con, Octopus, Priory of Sion, *Yankee and Cowboy War*

Reference:

http://www.astridmm.com/prouty/

The Secret Team, by Fletcher Prouty, Prentice-Hall, 1973.

Queen Elizabeth II

See:

A-Albionic, Princess Di's Death: Conspiracy Theories, Lyndon LaRouche, *Secret Societies and Their Role in the 20th Century*

Carroll Quigley

A historian trained at Harvard, Carroll Quigley wrote a book that has become a favorite with conspiriologists—*Tragedy and Hope* (1966). In this 1,348-page history of our century, Quigley makes several damaging admissions that have become central to the conspiracy theories of most of the Far Right and part of the Far Left.

The most significant and widely quoted passage says bluntly:

There does exist, and has existed for a generation, an international Anglophile network which operates, to some extent, the way the radical Right believes the communists act. In fact, this network, which we may identify as the Round Table Groups, has no aversion to cooperating with the Communists, or any other groups, and frequently does so.

Quigley identifies the founder of this network as **Cecil Rhodes** and describes the **Council on Foreign Relations** as the American affiliate of the Anglo network.

See also:

A-Albionic, John Birch Society, LAWCAP, *None Dare Call It Conspiracy*, Ezra Pound, Father Edmund Walsh, *Yankee and Cowboy War*

Reference:

The New American, Vol. 12, No. 19, September 1996, p. 13

Bob Quinn

Bob Quinn has presented his ideas in three television programs on Irish TV and in a book (see below). He holds that Ireland has a strong cultural and genetic link with North Africa, going back to the dawn of civilization. In this view, "Atlantis" was not a continent in the middle of the Atlantic, but a culture extending over the areas now known as Morocco, the Gaelic-speaking Atlantic coast of Spain, Breton France, and Ireland, especially West Ireland. In sum, just as modern Ireland has a Celtic bedrock overlaid with English language and genes, the original Celtic bedrock was overlaid on a Moorish foundation. Some of his evidence seems quite impressive, e.g.:

- *Type O blood is common in North Africa and West Ireland but rare on the European mainland.*

- *Roman authors describe the Celts as tall and blonde, but most of the Irish are short and dark-haired.*

- *West Irish music is unlike any other European music. When Quinn played some samples for European musicologists and asked where they thought it came from, all but one guessed Africa. The one who guessed otherwise said Asia.*

- Issa *means "Jesus" in both Arabic and Irish Gaelic.*

- *A Celtic cross found in County Kerry and carbon-dated at ca. 900 A.D. has the Arabic word* Bism'illah *(In the name of Allah) on it.*

- *A type of dancing in which the body remains rigid and the feet move rapidly is common to North Africa, Celtic Spain, Breton France, and West Ireland.*

Quinn has reams of similar evidence and makes a persuasive, if not incontrovertible, case. He believes the Irish/Moorish connection was hidden by the Roman Catholic Church as part of a scheme to cover up the fact that St. Patrick never existed, and the earliest Irish Christians were Gnostics from North Africa.

See also:

Dagobert II, *Irish Wisdom,* Noble Drew Ali

Reference:

Atlantean: Ireland's North African and Maritime Heritage, by Bob Quinn, Quartet Books, London and New York, 1986

Ra-Hoor-Khuit

See:

Hawthorne Abendsen, Aeon of Horus, *Liber Al*

The Rape Conspiracy

According to Susan Brownmiller, rape is not a crime committed by a minority of disturbed males but rather "nothing more or less than a conscious process by which *all men* keep *all women* in a state of fear." (Italics in original; this is one of the fungible conspiracy theories. Compare *Captain Simonini.*)

See also:

Hawthorne Abendsen, Dr. Raymond Bernard, Demonic Duck, *Demon Lover, MS. Magazine,* Nazi Hell Creatures

Reference:

Against Our Will, by Susan Brownmiller, Penguin, New York, 1988, p. 1

Jon Rappoport

Jon Rappoport, in his book *AIDS Inc.: Scandal of the Century,* examines several heretical AIDS theories and finds merit in some of them. He thinks there is much to support Dr. *Peter Duesberg*'s model of American AIDS being caused by stimulant drugs and suggests that syphilis plays a role, too. He also finds evidence to support the *iatrogenic theory* that AIDS, and probably other diseases, result partially from overdosing of the population by the medical establishment.

Rappoport chiefly deals with how AIDS became "big business" and how pharmaceutical interests have manipulated the media to publicize the HIV hypothesis and ignore or downplay rival theories.

See also:

AIDS Conspiracy Theories, links from Chicago Malaria Study

Reference:

http://www.newagenet.com/LightParty/Health/JonRappoport.html

Ray Ravenhott

In 1977, Ray Ravenhott, director of the population program for the U.S. Agency for International Development, announced the agency's intent to sterilize a quarter (25 percent) of the world's women.

See also:

AIDS Conspiracy Theories, Eugenics/AIDS Theory

Reference:

http://home.earthlink.net/~bkonop/GermIncidents2.html

Ronald Reagan—Alien Fighter

See:

Philip J. Corso

Ronald Reagan—Man or Robot?

See:

Peter Beter

Ronald Reagan—Gay Conspiracy

See:

Christians Awake AIDS Theory

Recovered Memory Therapy

Recovered memory therapy is based on the assumption that a great many people suffer various forms of sexual abuse and other horrors in childhood (e.g., incest, Satanic cult abuse) or have been abducted and experimented upon by extraterrestrials. According to this model, such highly traumatic experiences produce "robust repression," i.e., total amnesia. This means literally that if it happened to you, you will have absolutely no memory of it, until or unless you enter this type of treatment.

Recovered memory therapists help you remember by hypnotizing you and telling you to visualize and feel the type of trauma you probably experienced, over and over. Within three years usually, or five years in hard cases, you will begin to believe that what you are visualizing and feeling is a real memory. The cure is only complete, however, when you confront your abusers, denounce them, and then break off all relations with them. More often than not, this type of therapy will also uncover "multiple personalities" hidden deep in the psyche, allegedly caused by the original traumatic experience. (Skeptics say the multiple personalities, like the alleged memories, are created, not discovered, by the hypnosis.)

This type of therapy was popularized by two Santa Cruz Feminists, Ellen Bass and Laura Davis, endorsed by *"MS. Magazine,"* and has been under vigorous attack by dubious psychologists in recent years, who say that using this method you can be made to "remember" or think that you "remember" virtually *anything.* Bass and Davis reply that saying this is *denial,* a terrible state to be in, and shows that you yourself are either an abuser or a victim of abuse.

See also:

Abductees Anonymous, Demonic Duck, False Memory Syndrome Foundation, Corey Hammond, *Making Monsters, Satanic Panic,* UFO Conspiracies

References:

The Courage to Heal, by Ellen Bass and Laura Davis, Harper & Row, New York, 1988

Backfiles of *Good Times* magazine, Santa Cruz, Calif. ca. 1990–95, in which skeptics repeatedly attack this theory and Bass and Davis reply to them

The Red Serpent

See:

Abel, Illuminati, Priory of Sion, *Le Serpent Rouge*

Israel Regardie

Dr. Israel Regardie (1907–1985) was both a psychotherapist (under the name Dr. Francis Regardie) and a Cabalistic magician in the tradition of the **Hermetic Order of the Golden Dawn.** As a youth Regardie read extensively in theosophy and yoga, and in his very early 20s he secured a position as secretary to the notorious *Aleister Crowley*, who aided and encouraged his further studies in Cabala and ritual magic. An emotional split between Crowley and Regardie eventually drove them apart, but Regardie retained an affection for the old man, dedicated his first book to him, and eventually wrote the first objective or non-hostile biography of the controversial "Uncle Al," whom the tabloids had called "the wickedest man in the world."

In 1937 Regardie performed the most shocking act of his life, publishing all the previously secret rituals and teachings of the Golden Dawn in four large volumes, because he had lost faith in the leaders of that society and believed the tradition might die out completely without such an "outrage" as his public disclosure. Although widely denounced at the time, this publication has won more praise than censure in recent decades. Occult historians Francis King and Isabel Sutherland typically attribute "the rebirth of occult magic" to Regardie's policy of open disclosure.

Francis Israel Regardie returned to the United States in 1937, where he continued writing on occult subjects under the name Israel Regardie and studied and later practiced psychotherapy under the name Francis Regardie. His major psychotherapeutic teachers were Drs. E. Clegg, J.L. Bendt, and Nandor Fodor, but he gradually developed his own system based chiefly on Carl Jung and *Dr. Wilhelm Reich,* two "opposite poles" of the neo-Freudian world, whom nobody else had ever tried to combine. One of Regardie's pupils, Dr. Christopher Hyatt, also practices Jungian-Reichian therapy and publishes books on both the Golden Dawn and Crowleyan schools of magick.

Dr. Regardie, by combining psychological and occult theories, created some of the most unusual, and perhaps most fruitful, books in those fields.

See also:

Kenneth Grant, Ordo Templi Orientis

References:

http://www.hermeticgoldendawn.org/page6.htm

The Eye in the Triangle, by Israel Regardie, New Falcon Press, Phoenix, Ariz. 1989

Dr. Wilhelm Reich

Dr. Wilhelm Reich was condemned for unscientific claims by the *Food and Drug Administration* in 1956 because of his theories about sexual freedom and his discovery of an alleged "orgone" energy. He quickly became the most world-famous victim of the FDA's quest to impose One True Faith on medical practice in the United States, because the Feds not only destroyed all the equipment in Dr. Reich's experimental laboratory but burned all his books, too, in an incinerator, and then they put him in jail where he died of a heart attack.

Since many disapprove of this unconstitutional way of silencing heresy, Dr. Reich has remained a center of controversy. Dr. James De Meo, who earned his own master's for experiments that confirmed certain of Reich's weather experiments, has a list of over 400 scientific papers, mostly by persons with M.D.'s or Ph.D.'s also confirming other Reich experiments (available from Orgone Biophysical Research Laboratory, P.O. Box 1395, El Cerrito, CA 94530).

Dr. De Meo was prevented from doing further Reichian research for his own Ph.D., so he wrote his dissertation on the history of desert formation, which also confirmed Dr. Reich without mentioning him.

Marburg University in Germany granted a Ph.D. a few years ago for a dissertation on Dr. Reich's orgone accumulator, which validated most of Reich's claims. (This is also available, in German, from Dr. De Meo at the above address.)

In addition to his bio-physical heresies, Dr. Reich vastly offended many people by his sociological theory, which holds that fascism is just an exaggerated form of the basic structure of sex-negative societies and has existed under other names in every civilization based on sexual repression. In this theory, the character and muscular armor of the average citizen—a submissive and frightened attitude anchored in body reflexes—causes the average person to want a strong authority figure above them. Tyranny, in this model, is not created by tyrants alone but by neurotic masses who *want* tyrants.

See also:

Minneapolis Massacre, Passive Conspiracy, War on Some Drugs

References:

Reichian research online—

http://www.doit.de/orgon/e_index.htm

Dr. James De Meo—

Address above

Fury on Earth: A Biography of Wilhelm Reich, by Myron Sharaf, St. Martin's, New York, 1983

Cecil Rhodes

Cecil Rhodes (1853–1902) is described by an admirer as having a philosophy of "mystical imperialism." Having started as a small farmer, he went into diamond mining and became hugely wealthy, owning 90 percent of the world's known diamond mines by 1891. Eventually he had his own country, named after himself—Rhodesia.

Before his death, he established the system of "round table groups" to impress his mystical imperialism on the 20th century; these grew into the Royal Institute of International Affairs in

London and the *Council on Foreign Relations* in New York. His will established the Rhodes scholarships at Oxford, which have drawn some of the best and brightest of every subsequent generation into the round table groups and the philosophy of Cecil Rhodes.

See also:

A-Albionic, *None Dare Call It Conspiracy, Yankee and Cowboy War*

Reference:

http://www.omnipotent.com/addvalue/cecil_rhodes.html

David Rockefeller

David Rockefeller, as honorary chairman of both the *Council on Foreign Relations* and the *Trilateral Commission*, owner of Chase Manhattan Bank, and, through Chase, a top stockholder in the *Federal Reserve Bank*, appears in more conspiracy theories than anybody since Adam Weishaupt.

The Rockefellers, even at a cursory glance, are major players in the power game. As early as 1890, the family was refining about 90 percent of all crude oil in the country; their fortunes have prospered since then. One Rockefeller, Nelson, was governor of New York and vice president of the United States, as a Republican; another was governor of Arkansas, as a Democrat. By 1916, the Rockefellers were worth $500 million, an astronomical sum for those days; by 1930, they owned a substantial portion of the assets of many of the 40,000 registered corporations in the United States. The Rockefellers currently have major holdings in Exxon, Rockefeller Center, Standard Oil of California, IBM, and Chase Manhattan Bank, adding to a net worth of over $2 billion, and they also have significant stock in about 50 other companies. They also have controlling stock in City National Bank and own parts of 50,000 affiliated banks in over 100 countries.

Sounds good? The Rockefellers also have major interests in some of our four largest insurance companies (Metropolitan, Equitable, and New York Life) with assets over $100 billion. And they have enough stock to influence or control 37 of the top 100 manufacturers, 9 of the top 20 transportation firms, and scores of smaller companies.

Of our 122 top moneymaking corporations, David and other Rockefellers are among the top five vote holders in 93.

See also:

Hank Greenspun, Hughes vs. Rockefeller, *Yankee and Cowboy War*

Reference:

http://www.empire.net/~danp/shadow.html

Franklin Delano Roosevelt, Assassination of

According to *Fletcher Prouty,* Stalin believed that President Roosevelt had been poisoned and that Eleanor Roosevelt was part of the conspiracy, or aided in the cover-up.

Prouty says he learned of this from Lt. Colonel Elliott Roosevelt, the President's son, whom he had met earlier, in Tehran in 1943, and who later interviewed Stalin for *Look* magazine in 1946. During the *Look* interview, Stalin said he had stopped trusting Eleanor Roosevelt when she refused to allow Soviet ambassador Andrey Gromyko to examine the dead president's body to check that FDR had indeed died of cerebral hemorrhage as claimed. When this request was denied, Stalin decided Eleanor was part of the cover-up.

Prouty does not inform us of what Elliott Roosevelt thought of this, but he does go on to say that Elliott bluntly asked Stalin what Gromyko hoped to learn from the corpse. Stalin shouted, almost in a rage, "They poisoned your father, of course, just as they have tried repeatedly to poison me."

"They, who are they?" Elliott asked.

"The Churchill gang," Stalin shouted. "They poisoned your father, and they continue to try to poison me. . . the Churchill gang!"

Earlier conspiracy theories about Roosevelt's death appeared in right-wing magazines decades ago, but we can find no record of them currently. Usually, they claimed either Eleanor or Stalin had killed him. One out-of-print novel, *The Rat Race*, by Jay Franklin, claimed French intelligence did the job, using the same poison they had given President Woodrow Wilson after World War I.

See also:

A-Albionic, Bank of England, Princess Diana's Death: Conspiracy Theories, Robert Morning Sky, Ezra Pound

Reference:

http://www.astridmm.com/prouty

Rosicrucianism

The Rosicrucians, or Order of the Rose Cross, began either in ancient Egypt or about 1313 or 1490 or 1616, depending on which source you believe. The founders were Egyptian sages, friends of Martin Luther (whose coat of arms had a rose and cross on it), *Giordano Bruno*, or persons unknown. Whatever the truth of these murky matters, the Rosicrucians definitely influenced *Freemasonry*, which still has a rank of Knight of the Rose Cross among its higher degrees. The eye-in-triangle design, often called Masonic, only vaguely resembles Masonic symbols but has a long history of usage by the Rosicrucians.

The first public notice of the Rosicrucians occurred ca. 1614–20 when books titled *Fama Fratenitatis, Confessio fraternitatis Rosseae Crucis,* and *The Alchemical Marriage of Christian Rosecross* appeared from unknown sources in major European centers of learning. These books announced the existence of the Order, proclaimed its possession of all advanced scientific and mystical knowledge, and invited the worthy to join it—if they could find it. Nobody ever did admit to finding the secret Order, and most historians regard the matter as an inscrutable or pointless hoax.

According to one Rosicrucian manifesto now online, the Rosicrucians "hide in the open" by creating "as many false orders as possible" to confuse their enemies, identified only as the Technomancers. The Rosicrucians, this manifesto says, are "the secret masters of several Masonic groups and a lot of different secret societies." The Technomancers, meanwhile, secretly attempt to infiltrate and subvert these groups. (See *A-Albionic, Sacred Chao, "Yankee and Cowboy War," Yin and Yang*.) As a result:

This secret war have [sic] been raging among the secret societies for several centuries, and there are no indications of an end. Everyone is tangled up in a web of intrigue, and paranoia is rampant among all involved.

The *Hermetic Order of the Golden Dawn* was a genuine Rosicrucian order, this source says, but was destroyed by Technomancer infiltration, internal strife, and *Aleister Crowley*, who mixed it up with "the Cult of Ecstasy," a veiled reference to *sex magick*. In a cheerful (or sinister) mood, the manifesto concludes happily:

The Rosicrucians have amassed more mundane power and wealth than any other group in the Order of Hermes. Through the charity trusts they control through different Masonic groups, they can put pressure on banks and invest money as they wish.

Another source informs us that the Rosicrucian Order was formed by Christian Rosenkreus in 1313 to prepare for a new phase of the Christian religion: "The great spiritual entities in charge of evolution change the religions of the world in harmony with the passage of the marching orbs in the heavens." Specifically, the Rose Cross intends to teach us a form of "sixth sense" by which we may transcend both faith and reason and know directly the meaning of rose, cross, and other mystic symbols and what evolutionary message they carry.

The late *Philip K. Dick* has conjectured that the Rosicrucian order began as an anti-Vatican conspiracy, created within the Vatican by advanced adepts who knew the Church needed to be shaken and reformed.

See also:

Gnomes of Zurich, GRUNCH, OM, Order of Memphis and Mizraim

References:

Current Rosicrucian manifesto no. 1—

http://www.student.nada.kth.se/~nv91-asa/Mage

Current manifesto no. 2—

http://www.primenet.com/~fedup/pagan_101/chapt-13.txt

Influence of Bruno—

Giordano Bruno and the Hermetic Tradition, by Frances Yates, University of Chicago Press, 1964

Philip K. Dick theory—

Personal correspondence, Philip K. Dick to Robert Anton Wilson

Roswell UFO Crash

In either late June or early July 1947, something crashed in the desert near Roswell, New Mexico—or maybe two things crashed on different days. One or both of them may have been a Japanese FUJI balloon that had been drifting around since World War II, or a secret American spy balloon, or an extraterrestrial spaceship. The proponents of these theories have been arguing ever since, and the argument has gotten more fervent, not less, as the decades have passed. Roswell, otherwise known only as the birthplace of actress Demi Moore, has become the name of the biggest and still fastest-growing *UFO conspiracy* debate this side of *The X Files*, much of which it inspired. ("I don't like this," said Bill Pope of the Roswell Chamber of Commerce. "I don't want to be known as the kook capital.") The fury nonetheless grows: Almost every major Roswell investigator has been accused of being either a CIA agent or a damned liar or both by another Roswell investigator.

Most of the really heated debate has appeared in *Saucer Smear,* a small, irregular journal published by Jim Moseley, some issues of which are now online. Alternately using the subheads "SHOCKINGLY CLOSE TO THE TRUTH!" and "A boil on the ass of UFOlogy—John Keel," *Smear* prints all sides of every argument and treats them all with equally cool skepticism.

The ET theorists seem to be winning, at least in the court of public opinion: according to a *Time*-Yankelovich poll, 65 percent of our citizens believe in the crashed alien spaceship version of the Roswell incident(s).

Since no one file can do justice to this tangled web of claims, counterclaims, accusations, and counteraccusations, we refer the curious to *"Alien Autopsy," Philip J. Corso,* and *Robert Morning Sky.*

References:

Time, June 23, 1997, pp. 62–71

http://www.mcs.com/~kvg/smear/v42/ss950901.htm

Rothschilds

See:

Princess Di's Death, Federal Reserve Bank, *Secret Societies and Their Role in the 20th Century*

Round Table Groups

See:

Council on Foreign Relations, Cecil Rhodes

Ruby Ridge

See:

Every Knee Shall Bow, Government as Criminal Conspiracy, Minneapolis Massacre, Newark Crash-In, James Oberg, War on Some Drugs

The Sacred Chao

The Sacred Chao is the Holy Symbol of the Discordian Society in general and the *Golden Apple Corps* in particular. Like the Taoist yin and yang, it is made of two interlocked "commas," one up and the other down. The two sides of the Sacred Chao, however, are not yin and yang but hodge and podge. The hodge, symbolized by the Pentagon, represents the oppressive, authoritarian, and destructive forces in the world, especially the *Knights of the Five-Sided Castle* and the *Illuminati*. The podge, symbolized by the Golden Apple of Discord, represents satire, anarchy, merrymaking, and free thought in general. According to Discordian teaching, any increase in either side of the Sacred Chao leads to an immediate increase in the other side, so authoritarian bureaucracy leads to rebellion and chaos, and rebellion and chaos provoke more authoritarian bureaucracy, in a dance that never ends, unless the funding runs out.

See also:

"Bob," Discordianism, OM, Slack

Reference:

http://www.prairienet.org/~kkbuxton/discordia.html

Pierre Plantard de Saint Clair

Pierre Plantard de Saint Clair, an enormously learned occultist, a very rich man, a proven hero of the Resistance during World War II, an associate of Charles de Gaulle with some of de Gaulle's aura clinging to him, was the last publicly acknowledged Grandmaster of the mysterious *Priory of Sion*.

According to the genealogies in the speculative *Holy Blood, Holy Grail*, Plantard de Saint Clair is directly descended from Jesus and Mary Magdalene. Of course, if we glance back at *Gerard de Sede*, the same genealogies can be used to show that Saint Clair is descended from extraterrestrials who came here from *Sirius*.

In December 1983, a strange new event cast the whole P2/Priory mystery in a weird new light. First, on December 16, Pierre Plantard de Saint Clair resigned as Grandmaster of the Priory of Sion, after a cryptic interview with Michael Baigent, Henry Lincoln, and Richard Leigh (the *Holy Blood* theorists) in which he said the *Knights of Malta* had infiltrated the Priory to an extent he found worrisome. He also refused to name his successor as Grandmaster.

Then a book called *"Scandals of the Priory of Sion"* linked the Priority to the P2 conspiracy in Italy.

See also:

Grand Loge Alpina, Kenneth Grant, Noon Blue Apples, P2 Conspiracy

Reference:

Holy Blood, Holy Grail, by Michael Baigent, Henry Lincoln, and Richard Leigh, Delacorte, New York, 1982

The Messianic Legacy, by Henry Lincoln, Michael Baigent, and Richard Leigh, Henry Holt, New York, 1987

Salk Vaccine and AIDS

CNN reported on March 3, 1992, that Dr. Robert Bohannon, who has done AIDS research at Baylor University, requested samples of the original Salk vaccine so that he could test them for HIV. Rumors that the original Salk vaccine trials in Africa were accidentally contaminated continue to circulate, but we have failed to find anybody who believes them.

See also:

AIDS Conspiracy Theories, San Francisco Experiment, Tuskegee Syphilis Study

Reference:

http://radio.cbc.ca/programs/ideas/Aids/vienna.html

San Francisco Experiment

In 1950 the U.S. Navy deliberately sprayed a cloud of bacteria over San Francisco, to see how fast a real use of germ warfare would spread through an urban population. When this story leaked, the navy insisted that the bacteria was a "harmless" variety, but quite a few Bay Area residents remain skeptical. However "harmless" a given bacteria may be, this one produced many pneumonia-like systems among the victims, and one San Franciscan died.

See also:

AIDS Conspiracy Theories, Mona Charen, Chicago Malaria Study, Holmsburg Prison Conspiracy, Tuskegee Syphilis Study

Reference:

http://home.earthlink.net/~bkonop/GermIncidents2.htm

"Sarah"

"Sarah" is the pseudonym of a Canadian teenage girl who, under recovered memory hypnosis, told of being abducted by extraterrestrials, taken aboard a UFO full of computers and houseplants, and subjected to tests "to see what humans are made of." Some days thereafter, Sarah alleges, she was in the school cafeteria when a man in black approached. She described him as six feet tall, with gray skin, looking "like a dead man." He questioned her about all events aboard the UFO and also, oddly, wanted a list of all her friends, which she refused to provide.

The reality of Sarah and her belief in her memories of these incidents are asserted by Lawrence J. Fenwick, a director of the Canadian UFO Research Network (CUFORN).

See also:

Corrydon Hammond, Mary Hyre, Men in Black, Recovered Memory Therapy

Reference:

The UFO Silencers, by Timothy Green Beckley, Inner Light Publications, New Brunswick, N.J., 1990, pp. 70–81

Sasha

Controversy surrounds "Sasha," an alleged KGB mole who may have penetrated the highest ranks of the CIA.

A Soviet defector named *Anatoli Golitsin* said definitely that Sasha existed and that the KGB intended to flood the CIA with false defectors in an attempt to confuse everybody and divert attention from Sasha. A later defector, *Yuri Nosenko*, denied the existence of Sasha and was, accordingly, called a false defector by Golitsin. *James Jesus Angleton*, head of counterintelligence for the CIA, supported Golitsin and violently denounced Nosenko, but the controversy was never resolved within the CIA and now occupies conspiriologists outside the Agency, because Nosenko also supported Angleton's version of the *John F. Kennedy assassination*.

As Bill MacDowall writes about the Golitsin-Nosenko conflict, "Such is the intrigue inherent in espionage, Golitsin could easily have been a false defector himself. He could easily have invented the story of the mole known as Sasha and the plan to protect Sasha by the use of false defectors. The upshot of such a strategy would be to make future genuine defectors who had no knowledge of this fictitious mole appear false defectors. . . the perfect example of a self-fulfilling prophecy."

See also:

Castro as Super-Mole, Double-Cross System, Fedora

Reference:

http://www.jfkweb.simplenet.com/voice/nosenko.htm

Sasso in Bocca

See:

Sam Giancana, Mino Pecorelli

Satan Claus

While most of us accept Santa Claus as either a genuine Christian saint or a old Norse elf who innocently adds to the merriment of the Yule season, some Fundamentalists have darker ideas about him. The Truth Tabernacle Church in Burlington, North Carolina, held a mock trial of Mr. Claus in 1990 and found him guilty of paganism, perjury (for pretending to be St. Nicholas), encouraging child abuse (by appearing in whiskey ads), and seven other counts. They then took an eight-foot dummy of "Satan Claus," as they dubbed him, and hanged him in effigy.

Mr. Claus was also removed from the official list of Roman Catholic saints in 1969 and adopted by the Discordian Society.

Reference:

Fortean Times, Winter 1990–91

Satanic Panic

Satanic Panic, by sociologist Jeffrey S. Victor, studies over 60 episodes of "Satanic panic" in the United States between 1982 and 1992. Victor documents that the whole structure of the medieval Satanism hysteria has returned—allegations of large (national or international) Satanic cults, massive orgies involving human sacrifice, cannibalism—and attributes this to the growing economic anxiety and uncertainty of our times. Nervous people seek scapegoats to blame, his theory says, and we have a lot of nervous people in America since downsizing has broken up the home and sent both parents out into the workforce.

The stimuli that trigger Satanic panic and wild rumors of human sacrifice, etc., can be almost anything, but major sources of the new mythos are school textbooks, which may contain ideas the parents never heard of before, rock, which doesn't sound like music at all to many older persons, and role-playing games such as Dungeons and Dragons, which encourage those intellectual/creative functions the parents had to suppress in themselves to adjust to the hierarchical social structure.

The importance of these panics is indicated by the fact that the FBI's Behavioral Science Unit has had to investigate dozens and dozens of alleged "mass graves" for victims of Satanic sacrifice, a great waste of time and tax money, since they never found a single body, or even a toe.

The chief sources of the panic, Victor says, are sensational tabloids and Fundamentalist preachers, but radical Feminists have increasingly joined the hysteria.

Kenneth Lamming of the FBI's Behavioral Science Unit has been denounced as an ally of the Satanists for saying he has not found any evidence to support the existence of a Satanic cult performing human sacrifice, and he has been investigating the horror stories since 1983. (The same thing happened in medieval Europe and in Salem, Massachusetts, to those who expressed similar skepticism: Doubt and you are the next suspect.)

See also:

Hawthorne Abendsen, Corey Hammond, Rape Conspiracy, Recovered Memory Therapy

Reference:

Satanic Panic: The Creation of a Contemporary Legend, by Jeffrey S. Victor, Open Court, Chicago, 1993

Father Béranger Saunière

See:

Church of Mary Magdalene, Gnomes of Zurich, Noon Blue Apples, Priory of Sion

Scandals of the Priory of Sion

On May 20, 1974, Cardinal Jean Danielou died in the apartment of a young striptease dancer named Mimi Santini. Because high Catholic officials do not normally die in the apartments of young ladies who take off their clothes in public, and because the Cardinal had a "large sum of money" on him, the case attracted a certain amount of curiosity. Nothing, alas, ever emerged with any great clarity, except that Cardinals sometimes visit strippers and sometimes carry hefty wads of the long green.

Medical examiners pronounced that the old man had died of a heart attack.

Cardinal Danielou had served on the Academie Française, which almost certainly means he had known André Malraux and *Jean Cocteau,* two prime suspects in the *Priory of Sion* caper. It certainly doesn't mean that the Cardinal must have co-conspired with them in that group artwork—or hoax, or conspiracy, or whatever we identify the Priory as.

Second, a pseudonymous *Scandals of the Priory of Sion* came to leading Priory investigators in ordinary mail, just like a new bulletin from UMMO, an alleged extraterrestrial correspondence school.

Scandals, signed by "Cornelius" (an unhelpful name), claimed that Cardinal Danielou had been involved with the Priory of Sion since he met Cocteau in the 1930s. (The Cardinal, at that time, did compose a Latin translation of Cocteau's *Orpheus.*) The Cardinal had also acted a middleman in many shady financial transactions involving the Priory and *Michele "The Shark" Sindona,* this pamphlet further asserted.

Scandals also claims that Sindona did *not* kill the bank examiner, Giorgia Ambrosoli, for whose murder he had been convicted in Rome. That murder, the pamphlet claims, intended to cover up the links between the *P2 conspiracy* in Italy, the Priory of Sion conspiracy in France, and the *Grand Loge Alpina* in Switzerland. The Priory of Sion itself ordered the hit on Ambrosoli, *Scandals* says.

In *Scandals,* Cornelius also claims the *Mafia* has long worked in cahoots with both the Priory of Sion and the P2 lodge.

See also:

Dagobert II, MMAO, Naked Pope, Noon Blue Apples, Potere Occulto

References:

The Messianic Legacy, by Michael Baigent, Henry Lincoln, and Richard Leigh, Henry Holt, New York, 1987

New York Times, June 25, 1974

Secret Cipher of the UFOnauts

A very strange book, even for the field of UFOlogy, *The Secret Cipher of the UFOnauts,* by Allen Greenfield, attempts to show that the same cipher appears in the strange words used in UFO contact cases, in some "channeling," in certain Freemasonic rituals, and in the enigmatic *"Liberal Al"* received by *Aleister Crowley* in 1904. When deciphered as a form of English Cabala they reveal that "the Fully Illuminated" have interacted with the UFO phenomenon throughout history.

The UFO phenomenon itself is defined in Jungian terms:

". . . The phenomena themselves are inherently intangible, but are able to impinge on our reality in a phenomenological way because they are archetypal."

That is, in the sense of Jungian psychology, "myths," if archetypal (rooted in the depths of the mass unconscious), have the power to shape events and change history. The word "myth" is used here not as a synonym for lie or falsity but as a different order of communication from daily language, as poetry and allegory are also different. Jung himself expressed much the same view in a 1952 book called *Flying Saucers: A Modern Myth of Things Seen in the Sky.*

Greenfield goes further than Jung (who didn't know about the Illuminati): "The Fully Illuminated are in control of reality to the extent that the mythos itself is in control. They also, in a very real sense, acquire its intangibility" (p. 13). Or, as Don Juan told Carlos, they create a fog about themselves so that nothing about them is for sure or certain. They can be discussed better in the language of poetic myth than in that of grocers and tax auditors.

Although Greenfield links some of the cipher to *Sirius* and Orion, he never unambiguously identifies the "entities" as extraterrestrial, preferring *John Keel*'s word, ***ultra-terrestrial***. He does, however, point out (p. 32) that Crowley's 1920s sketch of an "Enochian" (angelic/demonic) entity, LAM, looks surprisingly like the *Greys* in modern abduction stories.

See also:

Robert Morning Sky, *Mothman Prophecies*

Reference:

The Secret Cipher of the UFOnauts, by Allen Greenfield, IllumiNet Press, Lilburn, Ga., 1994

Secret Societies and Their Role in the 20th Century

Secret Societies and Their Role in the 20th Century, by Jan van Helsing, attempts to prove that all the other conspiracies anybody has ever claimed to have uncovered serve as fronts for the original *Illuminati*, which is itself a front for the *Rothschild* family. The purpose of this supposed conspiracy is to create endless wars, forcing nations to borrow money and get into debt to international banks owned directly or indirectly by the Rothschilds.

Van Helsing provides a handy list of the major culprits in the Illuminati plot: This includes occult novelist and British statesman Lord Edward Bulwar-Lytton, McGeorge Bundy, *George Bush*, the Delano family (including Frederic Delano of the *Federal Reserve Bank* and Franklin Delano Roosevelt), the du Pont family, Lloyd George, *Colonel Edward House, Henry Kissinger*, J.P. Morgan, *Queen Elizabeth II, Cecil Rhodes, David Rockefeller*, Earl Warren, and many other household names in conspiracy-hunting circles. He also believes that the *Roswell UFO crash* really happened and another spaceship crashed soon after in Laredo, Texas, and that the Illuminati killed John F. Kennedy. The actual assassins were CIA agents Orlando Bosch, *E. Howard Hunt*, Frank Sturgis, and Jack Ruby. (Compare *A.J. Weberman*.)

Despite the anti-Rothschild emphasis and some passages about rich rabbis in the conspiracy (the "Elders of Zion"), the book avoids denouncing Jews in general and depicts the Nazis as mad hate-mongers. Although much of its thesis sounds like what Hitler was saying in the 1930s, it ends with a plea for love and open-mindedness.

See also:

The Con, *History of Secret Societies, World Revolution*

Reference:

Secret Societies and Their Role in the 20th Century, by Jan van Helsing, Erwalt Verlag, Gran Canaria, Spain, 1995

Jakob Segal

Dr. Jakob Segal, a biologist at Humboldt University in Berlin, was the first to declare the theory that AIDS was created at Fort Detrick, a biological warfare laboratory near Washington, D.C., as part of U.S. Army biological warfare research. Although Segal assumed the virus escaped accidentally, his theories have often been cited by others who think AIDS was intended as a "eugenics" measure to reduce world population by eliminating Gay men and Africans—the two groups most afflicted by this plague.

Dr. Segal argues that HIV was formed by visna (a sheep virus) and HTLV-I (human T-cell leukemia virus). His critics repeatedly point out that this part of his theory at least seems unlikely since the "monkey virus" (SIV—simian immunodeficiency virus) has since been discovered and seems a more likely precursor of HIV than the sheep virus.

See also:

AIDS Conspiracy Theories, El Salvador: Germ Warfare?, Tuskegee Syphilis Study

Reference:

http://cerebus.iscs.nus.sg/hypermail/cypherpunks-970127/0437.html

Le Serpent Rouge

An especially provocative work, privately printed and then deposited in the Bibliotheque Nationale in Paris, *Le Serpent Rouge* concerns the **Merovingians**, the murder of **Dagobert II**, a hidden race of kings, **Rosicrucian** symbolism, astrology, and Mary Magdalene. The authors' names appear on the title page as Louis Saint-Maxent, Gaston de Koker, and Pierre Feugere.

In the two days after this hermetic little book appeared, the Paris police investigated three cases of men found hanged in conditions where suicide and murder both seemed possible. The victims, of course, had the names Louis Saint-Maxent, Gaston de Koker, and Pierre Feugere.

Le Serpent Rouge means "the red serpent". This symbolizes male sexual energy in many occult traditions and relates to the Hindu kundalini theory of induced brain change by sexual/yogic stress. The book seems to hint obscurely at some sort of astrological sexual mysticism, but it also insists, again and again, that only Mary Magdalene fully received the Divine Transmission that came through Jesus. Michael Baigent, Henry Lincoln, and Richard Leigh interpret it to suggest that Mary Magdalene was married to Jesus. They also point out that most of the privately printed books about the Magdalene/**Priory of Sion** mystery have false names for the authors, but whether this was the case with the unfortunate Saint-Maxent, de Koker, and Feugere remains uncertain.

See also:

Church of Mary Magdalene, Noon Blue Apples, Ordo Templi Orientis, Priory of Sion, Rosicrucianism, Sex Magick

References:

Holy Blood, Holy Grail, by Michael Baigent, Henry Lincoln, and Richard Leigh, Delacorte, New York, 1982

Sex Magick

Sex magick (pronounced mage-ick) is the occult and hidden secret behind many mystic orders, including some known as *Illuminati*, hermeticists, alchemists, and, in the East, some schools of Buddhism and Taoism. Although a jealously guarded secret for many centuries, allegedly because the powers unleashed are too dangerous to be revealed to all, the technique is simple enough to be revealed in a single sentence: Orgasm should be avoided for as long as possible, by always slowing down or altering position when it seems imminent, and each partner should visualize/idealize the other as some specially meaningful divinity—e.g., in Thelemic magick the male usually identifies the female with Nuit, the sky goddess, and the female usually identifies the male with Pan.

The only problem with this simple description is that you need considerable training in very advanced yoga before you can begin to even approximate the desired result. If you don't see the "astral" light or some sort of blue-white energy fields, you need more practice.

See also:

Book of Lies, Aleister Crowley, Illuminati Copies or Revivals, Order of Memphis and Mizraim

References:

http://www.crl.com/~thelema

Portable Darkness, ed. by Scott Michaelson, Harmony Books, New York, 1989

Shakespeare as Conspiriologist

William Shakespeare, as the most widely read and most frequently performed dramatist in the world, has probably contributed more to the conspiratorial view of politics than even

Oliver Stone. In fact, since more people know Shakespeare's dramatized histories than any purely factual historical works, he may be the fountainhead of conspiriology. Some have proposed that the Bard's view of power and the men who wield it derives mostly from Machiavelli.

In *Julius Caesar,* Brutus and Cassius (with fellow miscreants) plot and carry out the assassination of Caesar and attempt a coup d'etat, which is prevented by the demagoguery of Mark Antony, who forms an opposing conspiracy. In another Roman play, *Titus Andronicus,* all the characters are involved in conspiracies and counterconspiracies; lies, murders, rape, mutilation, and cannibalism are among the tactics in this struggle.

In the chronological English histories, we have several generations of conspiracy and double-dealing. *King John* depicts a lying and conniving king who inspires several conspiracies to unseat him and is finally poisoned by a monk who comes pretending friendship. In *Richard II*, Richard exiles Bolingbroke, who immediately hatches a conspiracy to return and seize power, with the help of other nobles who dislike Richard. At the climax, Bolingbroke pays for the murder of Richard and makes himself Henry IV. In *Henry IV, Parts I and II*, a series of conspiracies, angered by the "indirect crooked ways" Bolingbroke acquired the throne, unsuccessfully attempt to overthrow him. In *Henry V*, the heir of Bolingbroke conspires to justify a war against France, to "busy giddy minds with foreign quarrels" and prevent further internal dissent—a technique still widely used and even more widely suspected. (See *"American Hero"*.) In *Henry VI, Parts I, II, and III*, every noble in England seems to get drawn into one conspiracy after another against Henry VI ("holy Harry"), who shows more talent for religious piety than for hardball politics, and the Yorks and Lancasters murder each other in a rising crescendo of horror. In *Richard III,* after the Yorks have won out over the Lancasters and all other conspiracies, young Richard York sets about conspiring against his own family to win the crown for himself; his victims include, but are not limited to, one brother and two nephews. All of this derives from the best historical records Shakespeare had available to him; but have you read worse than this record of murder and deceit in the present volume?

In the other histories, Macbeth conspires to murder his way to the throne of Scotland, and Macduff conspires to unseat the tyrant; *Hamlet* is a labyrinth of deceit and illusion ("Seeming, seeming!" the baffled hero cries at one point), and the sensitive reader is as unsure as Hamlet is about who is most guilty; and in *King Lear*, both the aged Celtic king and, in the subplot, the Duke of Gloucester are both betrayed by members of their own families.

In *Othello*, Iago of Venice weaves a web of slander that deceives almost everybody on stage at one point or another, and Othello murders his wife because of this network of lies.

Even in the comedies this theme appears frequently. In *The Tempest*, Prospero and his daughter Miranda are on their desert island because of a conspiracy that deprived him of his dukedom, and in *Measure for Measure*, the puritan Angelo, entranced by one woman, loses all his morality and sets in motion a conspiracy to force her to his bed, but another conspiracy, untypically benevolent, is watching from above and intervenes to set matters right.

The famous sonnets also, in the second half, deal with betrayal and the suspicion of betrayal.

See also:

Lord Acton, Government as Criminal Conspiracy

References:

The Complete Works of William Shakespeare, Vols. 1-6, Bantam, New York, 1980

Richard Shaver

In September 1943, *Ray Palmer* received a barely literate letter from a man named Richard Shaver, who had discovered or invented an "ancient alphabet" that explained the occult meaning of all the letters of later alphabets. For instance, "A" always signifies animals, and thus appears in animal itself, animate, avian, aardvark, etc.; "T" means integration and hence appears in Christian art as the cross, and in words like totality, tonality, triumph, etc. "D" always signifies death, decay, and destruction; hence its prominent position in those words (but what is it doing in deity, divinity, delightful, etc.?).

The author of the letter, Richard Shaver (1908–1975), encouraged by Palmer, soon turned out a "novel" or a channeled communication from one of Shaver's past lives. Rewritten by Palmer, this epic, entitled "I Remember Lemuria!" appeared in the March 1945 issue of *Amazing Stories* and immediately sold out. The "Shaver Mystery," as Shaver's revelations came to be called, quickly became the hottest property in the pulp magazine world and had around a million believers by the mid–1950s.

The Shaver stories or revelations were based on Shaver's "racial memories" of a time 12,000 years ago when Titans living thousands of years and standing 300 feet tall lived on Earth, having come from a distant planet. A solar disaster forced them to move inside the hollow Earth, where some of them still remain. Others returned to the surface prematurely and became the stunted, short-lived humanity we know. Those who stayed in the caves evolved into deros (bad dwarfs) and teros (good dwarfs).

The deros, who take up more space in Shaver's writings than the teros, are not only evil but have superscientific machines that cause people to hallucinate, go mad, kill, or just burst into flames inexplicably (the "spontaneous human combustion" documented by *Charles Fort*). Dero mind machines controlled Hitler and the Nazi Party (see *Nazi Hell Creatures*), burst the blood vessel that killed Franklin Delano Roosevelt, hypnotized *Lee Harvey Oswald* into shooting John F. Kennedy, and even supervised the crucifixion of Jesus. When not engaged in such devilish anti-human activities, the deros enjoy themselves with "stim machines" that allow them endless sexual debauchery "that actually deforms their bodies in horrible ways almost beyond mentioning."

Shaver's stories are full of scenes of sexual horror and torture, performed by the deros upon women who all look, in the illustrations provided by Palmer's artists, as sensually lovely as the later Playmates of the Month, but are screaming in pain rather than flirting with the reader. Between new revelations about dero deviltry and these sado-porn illustrations, the Shaver Mystery probably gave sexual nightmares to as many people in the 1950s as *recovered memory therapy* has in the 1980s–90s.

Shaver said he "heard voices" most of his life, usually a symptom of schizophrenia, but he believed his voices were the ancient Titans using him as a medium to awaken humanity to the dero peril beneath our feet.

Some critics of the Shaver saga deny that he or Palmer believed any of their yarns or that Shaver even heard voices from the giants of the Dawn Age. The Shaver Mystery, in many histories of science-fiction, is called the Shaver Hoax.

The deros would want it that way, wouldn't they?

See also:

Dr. Raymond Bernard, Men in Black

Reference:

Subterranean Worlds, by Walter Kafton-Minkel, Loompanics Unlimited, Port Townsend, Wash., 1989, p. 136–53

Clay Shaw

New Orleans businessman Clay Shaw was accused of complicity in the *John F. Kennedy assassination* by D.A. Jim Garrison, brought to trial, and quickly acquitted. That would seem to close the matter, except:

- *In 1974, former CIA agent Victor Marchetti produced evidence that Shaw was a CIA contract employee. Shaw died shortly thereafter, and was embalmed and buried without any investigation or autopsy.*

- *Shaw was behaving nervously before his death.*

- True Magazine *found many aspects of Shaw's death suspicious.*

- *The Assassination Information Bureau of Cambridge, Massachusetts, considers Shaw's death one of over 100 deaths among key figures in the Kennedy case where foul play seems more probable than natural causes.*

- *Richard Helms, when CIA director, admitted that Shaw had been a CIA employee.*

See also:

James Jesus Angleton, Albert Guy Bogard, David Ferrie, Kennedy Death Links

References:

http://www.ratical.com/ratville/JFK/ToA/ToAchp10.html

"The Mysterious Death of Clay Shaw," by Richard Russell, *True Magazine,* cited in the above

Assassination Information Bureau (AIB), Cambridge, Mass., also cited in the above

Helms—

Cited in *JFK* (film), directed by Oliver Stone

Captain Simonini

In 1806 the *Abbe Barruel* had the most complicated conspiracy theory of his time, finding Freemasons behind the French Revolution, the *Knights Templar* behind the Freemasons, and Moslem Satanists behind the Knights Templar; then he met, or invented, a certain Captain Simonini, who persuaded him that "the Jews" as a fungible group were actually behind all conspiracies. The captain, in fact, said that he himself had pretended to be Jewish to enter the inner cabal of the conspiracy, and that the evil masterminds of Judaism were easily deceived by him and told him all their secrets.

According to Simonini, the Jews had infiltrated the Catholic Church by pretending to be Catholics; in Italy alone, he said, there were over 800 Jewish priests, including bishops and cardinals. They planned to take over the whole world within a hundred years (i.e., by around 1906), and then they would turn all Christian churches into synagogues and reduce the remaining Christians "to a state of absolute slavery."

After these shocking revelations, Barruel's conspiracy theory always featured the Jewish conspiracy as the center or puppetmaster of all the secret societies he feared. In fact, most of the ideas later found in the *"Protocols of the Elders of Zion"* first appeared in the abbe's five volumes of Judeo-Masonic-Islamic horror stories.

See also:

Illuminati, Ezra Pound, Rape Conspiracy

Reference:

Short History of Anti-Semitism, by Vamberto Morais, W.W. Norton, New York, 1976, p. 194

Michele "The Shark" Sindona

Michele "The Shark" Sindona started his career as a *Mafia* lawyer, got inducted into *P2*, and soon collaborated with *Roberto Calvi* and *Archbishop Paul "The Gorilla" Marcinkus* in major drug money laundering operations. Moving to the United States Sindona founded his own Franklin National Bank in New York, was a guest at Richard Nixon's second presidential inauguration, and acquired a reputation as a financial wizard for his shrewd investments of Vatican funds in the World Trade Center, Procter and Gamble, and other big moneymakers. Then suddenly, it all fell apart. Franklin National went bankrupt; Sindona got convicted of 65 counts of stock and currency fraud in New York, was extradited to Italy after a prolonged legal struggle, and once returned to his homeland, was convicted of murdering a bank examiner in Rome. Sindona died in a cell while awaiting trial on charges that he and Calvi and the P2 crowd in general had conspired toward a fascist coup in Italy. Like the deaths of Calvi and several others in the P2 shadow world, Sindona's death remains in the murky area where nobody has quite proven either suicide or murder.

See also:

Cisalpine Bank, Knights of Malta, Octopus, World Finance Corporation

References:

In God's Name, by David Yallop, Jonathan Cape, London, 1984

In Banks We Trust, by Penny Lernoux, Doubleday, New York, 1984

Sirius

Sirius, named the Dog Star because it is in the constellation of the Great Dog, has played a major role in occultism since ancient

Egypt, when its annual feat of rising behind the sun on July 23 was first noticed and, with what seemed like a mystical connection, the flooding of the Nile always followed. The days around mid-July to late-August, featuring many feasts to the Dog Star became known as "dog days," a label that still clings to that torrid part of summer.

The five-pointed star in every Freemasonic lodge represents Sirius, according to *Albert Pike*.

See also:

A∴A∴, Aiwass, Kenneth Grant, George I. Gurdjieff, Iumma, Robert Morning Sky, *Sirius Mystery*, UFO Conspiracies

References:

Morals and Dogma of the Ancient and Accepted Scottish Rite of Freemasonry, by Albert Pike, Supreme Council of the Southern Jurisdiction, Washington, D.C., 1871

Aleister Crowley and the Hidden God, by Kenneth Grant, Samuel Weiser, New York 1975

The Sirius Mystery

The Sirius Mystery, by Robert K.G. Temple, is an attempt to prove that visitors from Sirius landed in the Middle East about 4,500 years ago and left a living occult tradition in that region and in parts of Africa and Europe. Temple uses two major sources of evidence: Egyptian-Sumerian mythology, which he interprets in a novel way, and the traditions of an African tribe named the Dogon, who still claim memories of the Sirians, who looked like fish-people and preferred to spend most of their time in the water.

Mr. Temple demonstrates, from an anthropological study by two French scholars, Griaule and Dieterlen, that the Dogon have actual knowledge of the Sirius system, which is hard to explain, e.g., the Dogon know that Sirius has a dark companion, Sirius B, which was not suspected by European astronomers until this century and not photographed until 1970. The Dogon also know the exact period of rotation of Sirius B (50 years) and know that it is one of the heaviest stars in the universe.

Temple finds evidence of similar knowledge in the mythos of the ancient Near East and Egypt, and tries to document a tradition that includes Dante, the **Knights Templar, Giordano Bruno,** Sir Philip Sydney, and **Dr. John Dee.**

The Sirius Mystery does not belong in the nut category; the London *Times* praised Temple's "caution" and "integrity," and the *Manchester Guardian* called this book "a work of respectable scholarship."

See also:

Gerard de Sede, Robert Morning Sky, *Necronomicon*

Reference:

The Sirius Mystery, by Robert K.G. Temple, St. Martin's, New York, 1976

666

According to Revelation 13:18, the Beast who shall appear in the last days (before the Apocalypse) shall have the number 666. Most attempts to interpret this invoke Cabala, the Jewish system in which every letter has a number value (e.g., "A" or *aleph* = 1, "B" or *beth* = 2, etc.). Fortunately for those who like to play games, many Hebrew letters have more than one numerical value, depending on where they appear in a word, and letters in other languages do not all correspond to Hebrew letters (e.g., "V," "W," and even "O" have all been interpreted as corresponding to the Hebrew *vauf*). Thus, many interpretations are possible, and almost every controversial person in the last 2,000 years has been shown to have a name that, by one system of correspondence or another, adds up to 666. Nero, Luther, Napoleon, and Hitler have all had this dubious honor, and *Aleister Crowley* deliberately changed his name to make it equal 666.

Since by Greek Cabala (the New Testament was written in Greek) IESUS CHRIST = 777, the most traditional interpretation is that 666 means 777 – 111, or the Perfect Man (777) deprived of unity (111) becomes his own opposite, *666, the Antichrist.*

The *Catholic Encyclopedia* says bluntly: "This is a condemned form of numerology that has no place in the Christian understanding of the message of Christ."

See also:

Antichrist, Lucent Technologies

Reference:

http://www.aloha.net/~mikesch/cath.htm

Skull and Bones

If the Freemasons are the world's largest secret society, Skull and Bones may be the smallest. Limited to a select group of Yale students who remain members for life, Skull and Bones has never had its secrecy broken. Legends about it—i.e., the candidate has to lie in a coffin, naked, and recite his/her whole sexual history—remain only legends. The story about the lodge owning the skull of Pancho Villa is another legend—that is, maybe true, maybe false. Nobody but the bonesmen know for sure what goes on in their clubhouse, cheerfully called the Tomb.

Many have suspected that Skull and Bones is a recruiting agency for the intelligence community. In World War II, the Whiffenpoof Song became the unofficial song of the OSS, which was full of Bonesmen and members of other Yale clubs. Gaddis Smith, a history professor at Yale, has said, "Yale has influenced the Central Intelligence Agency more than any other university, giving the CIA the atmosphere of a class reunion."

Prominent Bonesmen associated with the CIA include *George Bush* and William F. Buckley Jr.

See also:

Council on Foreign Relations

Reference:

http://www.parascope.com/articles/0997/skullbones.htm

Slack

> *Give me some Slack!*
> —Clint Eastwood in *The Eiger Sanction*

Slack is the goal of the *Church of the Sub-Genius*, as Salvation is in Christianity, Enlightenment in Buddhism, Virtue in Confucianism, etc. But Slack is ineffable, unspeakable, indefinable—"The Slack that can be spoken is not true Slack."

It is known, however, that at one time we all had Slack, but then *The Con* stole it from us. How The Con stole our Slack, and how we can get it back, are the major studies of the Sub-Genius Foundation, and the major theory is that The Con wants to turn us all into *Pinks* ("slaves"), and this can only be accomplished when nobody anywhere has any Slack anymore. But we can get our Slack back by tithing 10 percent of our earnings to the Church, which puts us on the list of those who will not be destroyed on X Day but taken to the planet of immortality, which is somewhere between Plan 9 and Publishers Clearinghouse.

See also:

Discordianism, OM; Planet X; Yin and Yang

Reference:

http://www.subgenius.com/

S.O.B.

"Stamp Out 'Bob,'" or S.O.B., is an organization devoted to combating the *Church of the Sub-Genius,* which it denounces as a mind-control cult and not a real religion at all. For $20, they will send you a bundle of Sub-Genius books and pamphlets, so you can see for yourself how dangerous, obscene, blasphemous, and degrading the Sub-Genius cult is.

See also:

"Bob," Discordianism, OM, Slack

Reference:

S.O.B., P.O. Box 140306, Dallas, TX 75214

Soviet AIDS Theory

According to Reuters for September 30, 1993, the CIA has announced that the first AIDS conspiracy theory was created by the former Soviet Union as deliberate disinformation. The "disinformation," alleging that AIDS emerged from U.S. biological warfare research, according to the CIA story, was created in 1983 and was circulated in 25 different languages in 80 countries.

The Reuters story quotes the CIA quite soberly, as if that agency never lied, and does not mention the alternative interpretation that AIDS conspiracy theories emerged spontaneously in the minds of many skeptical scientists without the Soviets to help them think subversive thoughts.

See also:

AIDS Conspiracy Theories, Tuskegee Syphilis Study

Reference:

http://www.aids.wustl.edu/aids/consp.html

Space-Time Transients

Probably the only book on the UFO mystery without a conspiracy theory, *Space-Time Transients and Unusual Events* is worthy of inclusion here, not just for a change of pace, but for its inadvertent support of those who believe UFOs are linked more closely to the occult than to the extraterrestrial.

Persinger and Lafreniere, behavioral scientists, did a computer analysis of 1,242 UFO cases and 4,818 other "fringe science" reports (poltergeists, anomalies, Fortean data, etc.)—6,060 instances of things that scientific orthodoxy says could not have happened. The computers, scanning for patterns, found a few: Such reports tend to cluster around earthquake fault lines; there is some peaking before earthquakes; and a certain topology appears in the wider and better documented cases. For instance, those at a distance report only strange lights, or light moving strangely; those closer in report poltergeist effects (as in Steven Spielberg's *Close Encounters of the Third Kind*): electrical and electronic malfunctions, machinery turning itself on and off, jumping furniture, etc.; those who blunder into the center of the phenomenon come back with strange yarns full of Freudian and/or Jungian dream symbolism (sexual assaults, abductions, encounters with Jesus or "beings of light," rebirth experiences, etc.).

Persinger and Lafreniere suggest that the strange lights and poltergeist effects represent real energy anomalies triggered by Earth's occasional magnetic and gravitational fluctuations, and that the mythic elements—Persephone abducted by Hades, rebirth, resurrection, etc.—come up from the back brain when these abnormal energies alter the brain's normal wave patterns.

This theory has a certain appeal to some occultists, who have a long tradition about psychic "windows"—times and places when the "other world" impinges upon this one.

See also:

Daimonic Reality, Fortean Times, The Mothman Prophecies, Ultra-Terrestrials

Reference:

Space-Time Transients and Unusual Events, by Persinger and Lafreniere, Nelson-Hall, 1977

Spontaneous Conspiracies (Ladder Conspiracies)

Some weird, inexplicable or seemingly (and/or actually) criminal actions, which look like conspiracies, often appear later as pranks, hoaxes, or malicious jokes, which became widely imitated after the original "artist" had set an example for similar minds to imitate. In fact, some of these projects might, as hinted, qualify more as group artworks than as either hoaxes or conspiracies. We therefore refer to them as spontaneous or ladder conspiracies.

See also:

Campus Crusade for Cthulhu, Church of the Sub-Genius, CIAC, Crop Circles, Discordianism, Elmyr, Clifford Irving, H.P. Lovecraft, UMMO Letters, Orson Welles, and (perhaps) Priory of Sion

Lysander Spooner

See:

Constitution, Government as Criminal Conspiracy, Internal Revenue Service, Benjamin R. Tucker

Anna Sprengel

In 1881 an English Freemason named William Wynn Westcott allegedly contacted a mysterious Anna Sprengel, a high initiate of the true Rosicrucian order in Bavaria. Fräulein Sprengel provided

Westcott with the knowledge and authority to revive *Rosicru-cianism* in England under the title of the *Hermetic Order of the Golden Dawn.*

The existence of Anna Sprengel has been disputed by some who claim that Westcott invented her to justify his own pretensions; but she came from Bavaria, home of the most infamous of *Illuminati* orders, so. . . ? Let us pass that up and just note that her magic motto (all Rosicrucians have magic mottoes) was SAPIENS DOMINABITUR ASTRIS, or "The wise are ruled by the stars."

See also:

Aiwass, Aleister Crowley, Merovingians, Robert Morning Sky, Sirius

References:

http://www.unp.ac.za/UNPDepartments/Religious_Studies/golddawn.txt

The Eye in the Triangle, by Israel Regardie, Falcon Press, Las Vegas, 1988, pp. 59–77

John Steinbacher

See:

Abel

Subterranean Worlds

Subterranean Worlds, by Walter Kafton-Minkel, is probably the most exhaustive study of hollow Earth theories in English, from a skeptical point of view.

Kafton-Minkel (or his publisher) provides a subtitle that very adequately conveys the scope of the book: "100,000 years of dragons, dwarfs, the dead, lost races, and UFOs from inside the Earth." Beginning with tribal legends and "classic" (Greek-Roman) myths, the book shows that almost everybody, before the rise of modern science, believed in a hollow Earth—an idea closely related to the familiar theme of the Earth Mother whose womb gave birth to all living things. Later, the hollow Earth became the home of the dead, and, in Christianity, it became Hell, the home only of dead sinners, where they were punished sadistically for all eternity.

After the foundations of geology and related sciences developed, the hollow Earth gave way to a solid Earth, at least among the majority of the educated, but a colorful minority continues to devise ingenious new variations on the old hollow Earth model. Captain John Cleves Symmes, a military hero in the War of 1812, created such cunning arguments for this theory that Congress was actually persuaded to send an expedition to the South Pole to find the hole that must exist there (according to Symmes' calculations) and then sail inward to find the new lands for colonization that he theorized. Due to malnutrition and mutiny, the expedition fell apart halfway, and no later government was willing to finance more research on Symmes' idea, which scientists continually ridiculed.

Many 19th-century occultists, however, took up the idea, and Madame H.P. Blavatsky made the hollow Earth a central part of her revelations (written under the influence of hashish), which became the basis of the Theosophical Society, still a large organization and much admired by Gandhi (who did not, however, say anything pro or con about the hollow Earth theory). William Butler Yeats, probably Ireland's greatest poet and a Nobel laureate, believed all of Blavatsky's visions, including the hollow Earth. *Aleister Crowley,* who disliked Theosophists in general, excepted Blavatsky from his sarcasm and considered her a major guru, but he also did not mention her hollow Earth theory.

In the 20th century, the hollow Earth theory has been revived several times.

See also:

Dr. Raymond Bernard, Nazi Hollow Earth Theory, Richard Shaver

Reference:

Subterranean Worlds, by Walter Kafton-Minkel, Loompanics Unlimited, Port Townsend, Wash., 1989

Tampa Bay: Chemical Warfare

In 1955, the Tampa Bay area of Florida experienced a sharp rise in whooping cough cases, including 12 deaths. Later this was revealed as a CIA study of bacteria released into the environment, but details of the test are still classified.

See also:

AIDS Conspiracy Theories, Chicago Malaria Study

Reference:

http://home.earthlink.net/~bkonop/GermIncidents2.html

The Terra Papers

The Terra Papers, by **Robert Morning Sky,** claims to be the true story of the conspiracies, planetary and extraplanetary, that have governed Earth since early times. This volume is based largely on the stories Morning Sky heard from his grandfather, who found one of the extraterrestrials who survived the 1947 *Roswell UFO crash,* although in other works by the same author, the interstellar scenario is backed up by scholarly studies in comparative mythology and linguistics.

According to *The Terra Papers,* many humanoid races have arisen in the course of cosmic history—mammal-people, bird-people, insect-people, etc. All of these became models for the deities of various religions; but especially important were the wolf-people of *Sirius* and the snake-people of Orion, the latter of whom conquered Earth and made us their property.

Human servitors of the snake-people founded the *Bank of England* and the *Grand Orange Lodge* to control the world by financial hocus-pocus. Freemasons who served as fronts for this conspiracy in the United States include George Washington, James Madison, James Monroe, Andrew Jackson, James Polk, James Buchanan, Andrew Johnson, William McKinley, Theodore Roosevelt, William Howard Taft, Warren Harding, Franklin D. Roosevelt, Harry S. Truman, and J. Edgar Hoover. The Vietnam War was a front for a CIA drug-smuggling operation, and when John F. Kennedy attempted to disband the CIA and other snake-people conspiracies, they assassinated him.

See also:

John Birch Society, The Con, *Guardians of the Grail,* Merovingians, Ezra Pound

References:

http://www.xroads.com/~rms/welcome.html

The Terra Papers, by Robert Morning Sky, Morning Sky Books, Phoenix, Ariz. n.d.

Thelema

We entered the *Aeon of Horus* in 1904, according to *Aleister Crowley*, and in this new Aeon "the word of the law is Thelema." This Greek word means "will," but its etymology is from earlier roots meaning magical power or sorcery.

Because Crowley abhorred religions and was careful not to establish one of his own, those heavily influenced by him—who might even be called disciples, if he didn't hate disciples—never call themselves Crowleyans or Crowleyites or anything like that. They call themselves Thelemites.

See also:

Aiwass, *Liber AI,* Sirius

Reference:

http://www.crl.com/~thelema

Kerry Thornley

Kerry Thornley, one of the founders of the Discordian Society and (briefly) a suspect in the Jim Garrison investigation of the *John F. Kennedy assassination,* believes that he was a victim of the *MK-ULTRA* program, like *Candy Jones*.

Thornley claims that although he cannot remember all the details even yet, he is sure that both he and *Lee Harvey Oswald* were part of an experiment in mind control (they served in the same marine regiment). He thinks that, thereafter, he was manipulated by Naval Intelligence or the CIA in many subtle ways; for instance, as Garrison discovered, Thornley and Oswald lived within blocks of each other in New Orleans for several months before the assassination, but Thornley does not remember meeting Oswald again. He does remember meeting *David Ferrie,* another of Garrison's suspects, but only recalls a brief, meaningless conversation; even more sinister, and weird, Thornley remembers meeting somebody calling himself Gary Kirstein, who said he was writing a book called *Hitler Was a Good Guy*. In memory, Thornley thinks "Kirstein" was *E. Howard Hunt,* one of his CIA controllers. In sum, Thornley believes he was programmed as a substitute fall guy if the Oswald scenario collapsed and that Garrison almost swallowed the bait.

More recently, Thornley has remembered or imagined even more. He now believes his parents were not Irish, as they claimed, but German, and that he himself was the product of a neo-Nazi breeding program that failed; instead of becoming a Nazi racist, he became an anarchist/satirist.

Some people believe Thornley is joking about all this. Others think he is clinically paranoid. Maybe he is at least partially remembering some very real fallout of MK-ULTRA?

As Jonathan Vankin writes:

Nonetheless, I still wonder if it's all a put-on. Is Thornley's intricately conspiratorial autobiography an elaborate mind-game he plays with himself and anyone who'll join in? Or is he really an intelligence agent, with a macabre cover story for his role in the John F. Kennedy conspiracy? Or could the story be true? Is Kerry Thornley a helpless pawn in a game beyond anyone's comprehension, who somehow figured out what has been happening to him?

See also:

The Con, OM, Sacred Chao, "The Whole Bay of Pigs Thing"

Reference:

Conspiracies, Cover-Ups and Crimes, by Jonathan Vankin, IllumiNet Press, Lilburn, Ga., 1996, pp. 3–21

The Three Tramps

A lot of the controversy around the **John F. Kennedy assassination** involves the three tramps apprehended on the infamous grassy knoll. Some defenders of the Warren Commission say they were held four days, positively identified, and released because there was no evidence against them. Critics say they were released as soon as the cops picked them up and were not identified in police records. This mystery has been somewhat clarified and somewhat muddied over the years.

Just as there were six people who at various times made up the

Three Stooges, there were six men who collectively became known as the Three Tramps. First there were John Gedney, Harold Doyle, and Gus Abrahms, who were picked up immediately after the assassination and released after four days. These are not the notorious Three Tramps in the famous photos, who were released almost immediately and never recorded in police records. In fact, the police never would have stumbled upon the famous Three Tramps if not alerted by *Lee Bowers Jr.,* who saw them hiding on a freight train.

The photo of the latter Three Tramps is the source of the continuing dispute, because one of them looks a good deal like *E. Howard Hunt* of the CIA. In fact, many people who have studied the photos extensively swear it is E. Howard Hunt.

See also:

Hiram Abiff, John Birch Society, Flight 553, Men in Black, "The Whole Bay of Pigs Thing"

References:

http://ourworld.compuserve.com/homepages/MGriffith_2/suspects.htm

Popular Alienation, ed. by Kenn Thomas, IllumiNet Press, Lilburn, Ga., 1995, pp. 173–174

Tobacco Wars: Genetically Engineered Tobacco

Food and Drug Administration officials charged in late May 1997 that not only have some tobacco companies increased the nicotine content of cigarettes to make it harder for addicts to quit—a charge the FDA and others have made repeatedly—but that Brown and Williamson specifically arranged for the production of genetically engineered tobacco with double the normal nicotine content. This new, human-made tobacco, or tobacco+, was grown in Brazil and smuggled into the United States in a clandestine manner to blend with the normal tobacco in Brown and Williamson's cigarettes.

See also:

AIDS Conspiracy Theories, Chicago Malaria Study

Reference:

CBS News, *60 Minutes,* May 25, 1997

Trilateral Commission

Founded by *David Rockefeller* in 1973, the Trilateral Commission has the declared goal of becoming "a high-level consultative council for global cooperation." It has roughly 100 members, all rich, powerful, and influential. It has been denounced by Irish pacifist and Nobel laureate Sean MacBride as "funded by certain large U.S. banks and serving the financial interests of those banks."

The John Birch Society has an even lower opinion of it, as do many radicals of the left and the right.

Prominent Trilateralists have included three U.S. presidents (Jimmy Carter, *George Bush,* and *Bill Clinton*).

See also:

Bilderbergers, The Con, Council on Foreign Relations, Insiders

References:

Sean MacBride's view—

Interview with MacBride in *Coincidance*, by Robert Anton Wilson, New Falcon Publications, Tempe, Ariz. 1996, p. 185

Birch Society view—

New American, September 16, 1996, p. 14

Benjamin R. Tucker

Benjamin R. Tucker (1854–1939) is generally considered the most plausible expositor of individualist-anarchism and continues to influence both the anarchist and libertarian movements.

Born of Abner Tucker, a Quaker and owner of whaling ships, and Caroline Cummings, a Unitarian admirer of Tom Paine, Benjamin grew up amid lively intellectual conversation. After attending Massachusetts Institute of Technology (which he entered at 16), he decided to devote his life, not to engineering, but to publishing and political agitation. Major influences were Josiah Warren, America's earliest anarchist, *Lysander Spooner,* P.J. Proundon, founder of mutualist-anarchism, and Max Stirner, atheist and egotist. Tucker's brand of individualism is thus based on rational appeals to the intellect (long-range pragmatism: also called enlightened self-interest) and rejects all supernatural morality.

Benjamin Tucker's basic analysis of modern capitalism hovers somewhere between scientific objectivity and conspiracy theory—just like the analysis of Karl Marx, Tucker's opposite in almost everything else. Beginning, like Marx, from Adam Smith, Tucker agrees with Smith's axiom that labor is the source of all value; like Marx, he then asks why the worker does not receive all the value he or she creates. Unlike Marx, however, Tucker does not attribute this to the private ownership of the means of production but to four mechanisms that he calls four types of usury.

The first and most nefarious variety of usury, Tucker says, consists of a monopoly on the issue of currency held by certain banks; in the United States today that monopoly is held by the *Federal Reserve Bank.* This dominance of currency allows the major bank of issue, and all banks subordinate to it, to charge interest on every dollar that goes into circulation (and accounts for our staggering $6 trillion national debt, modern Tuckerists say).

The second form of usury, Tucker has it, lies in monopoly of the land, by lords-of-the-land (the king's relatives) and, nowadays, by landlords (not necessarily related to the king). This underlies rent and mortgages.

The third and fourth forms of usury are tariffs, which prevent free competition on a worldwide basis, and patents, which allow inventors (or often those who employ the inventors) to prevent others from producing a cheaper form of a monopolized product.

All four of these practices, Tucker claimed, interfere with the free market and thus are inconsistent with capitalist theory. In other words, he charges that capitalists do not, in fact, practice capitalism.

Thus, Tucker believed that all economic misery derives from monopolies that block competition and that when the four kinds of usury are removed from our current system, free enterprise will produce all the good effects expected by Adam Smith. The fact that these special privileges enrich a minority at the expense of the majority is never explicitly attributed to conspiracy by Tucker (he more often blames ignorance), but his followers, like Marx's, often write as if the rich consciously plot to exploit the rest of us. In either case, Tucker opposed violent revolution and believed in the achievement of his goals by education: When all are rational egotists, none will submit to exploitation, and by passive resistance they will starve out the State and the monopolists.

See also:

John Adams, Thomas Hart Benton, Ezra Pound

Reference:

http://www.dis.org/daver/anarchism/tucker/tucker.html

Tuskegee Syphilis Study

In 1932, the U.S. government began the Tuskegee Syphilis Study, in which 200 poor black men with syphilis were studied over a long period of time, without being given any treatment or even being told of their illness. As many as 100 of the original 200 died, and the wives and children of the men also routinely acquired the disease.

The government office supervising this experiment still survives and is now called the Center for Disease Control (CDC).

See also:

Chicago Malaria Study

Reference:

http://home.earthlink.net/~bkonop/GermIncidents2.html

The 23 Enigma

Ever since the *The Illuminatus! Trilogy* pointed out the absurd (or sinister) linkage between the number 23 and all sorts of conspiratorial and/or "paranormal" (Fortean) phenomena, others have tracked the mystic 23 across time and space, and it even has its own website now. This data provides an ideal measurement of how much weirdity you can happily attribute to "coincidence" before that starts to sound hollow and you begin sliding down the slippery solipsistic slope to seeing a Dark Design in almost everything. Here are some hot examples:

2/3 = .666, the number of the Beast. . .

AOL chat rooms only allow 23 people at a time.

In the film *Airport,* the mad bomber has seat 23. . .

In the film *Airplane II*, the name of the spaceship is XR–2300. . .

230 people died in the conspiracy-haunted TWA Flight 800 disaster.

The letter W is 23rd in the alphabet and has two points down and three points up.

The first Apollo landing on the moon was at 23.63 degrees east; the second landing was 23.42 degrees west.

April 19th is the date of the battle of Lexington, the holocaust at Waco, and the Oklahoma City bombing. Americans write this date as 4/19; Europeans as 19/4;. Either way, it adds to 23. . .

William Shakespeare was born on April 23, 1556, and died on April 23, 1616.

Area 51, site of unknown government research (and CIA/alien headquarters, according to UFO conspiriologists) breaks down to 23 + 23 + (2+3) = 51.

August 23, 1305, William Wallace executed for treason.

August 23, 1970, River Phoenix born.

The original *Star Trek* was set in the 23rd century; so is *Babylon Five*.

The human biorhythm cycle is 23 days.

It takes 23 seconds for blood to circulate through the human body.

Julius Caesar was stabbed 23 times by the assassins.

Sydney Carton was the 23rd man beheaded in the climax of Dickens' *Tale of Two Cities*.

According to **Noam Chomsky,** over half of the national media is owned by 23 corporations.

In the act of conception, male and female each contribute 23 chromosomes.

The average cigarette smokers inhales 23 butts a day.

There are 23 chapters of the Cult Awareness Network.

Joseph Smith, founder of the Church of Jesus Christ of Latter-Day Saints, was born on December 23, 1805.

On December 23, 1913, the conspiriologist's arch-demon was created: The Federal Reserve Act passed Congress.

On December 23, 2012, the world will end, according to ancient Mayan prophecy.

In both ancient Sumeria and Egypt, July 23, when Sirius rises behind the sun, was the beginning of the new year.

The Nissan car takes its name from "ni," which means 2 in Japanese, and "san," which means 3. Nissan = 23.

The Articles of Impeachment for Richard Nixon were under Article 2, Section 3, of the Constitution.

The United States set off 23 atomic bombs at Bikini Atoll in the Pacific.

Lines 22–23 of Book I of Milton's *Paradise Lost*: ". . . What in me is dark / Illumine, what is low raise and support. . ."

In a recent film of *Alice in Wonderland,* a stuffed rabbit comes alive and runs away. He leaps out of a case numbered 23.

The first prime number in which both digits are primes and add up to another prime is 23.

On one *Seinfeld* show, Kramer hides an air-conditioner of Level Purple 23 in a parking garage.

Shakespeare was 46 (2 x 23) years old when the King James Bible was published. Psalm 46 (2 x 23) has as its 46th word "shake," and the 46th word back from the end is "spear." To quote the webmaster, "Go ahead, explain that one. I dare ya."

In *Star Wars*, Princes Leia was held in cell AA–23.

The address of the Freemasons lodge in Stafford, England, is 23 Jaol Road. In New York City, it's on 23rd Street.

The Unabomber killed or wounded 23 people.

Every 23rd wave crashing on a beach averages twice as large as normal.

There are exactly 23 characters (numbers and letters) on the face of all U.S. coins.

The uranium isotope used in nuclear bombs is U235.

The New York Yankees have won the World Series 23 times.

That's only a sample. I could add that Morgan Guarantee Trust—a hotbed of Illuminati international banking according to some of our sources—is at 23 Wall Street; that Ireland was freed of foreign domination when Brian Boru drove out the Vikings at the battle of Contaft, April 23, 1014, and was re-conquered by foreign invaders on August 23, 1169, an event known as the Anglo-Norman invasion. And on August 23, 1921, James Joyce saw a giant black rat which scared the blue Jesus out of him, by Christ.

See also:

Ardennes Forest, Second George Bush, Jean Cocteau, Philip J. Corso, Aleister Crowley, Gerard de Sede, Col. Edward House, War on Some Drugs, "The Whole Bay of Pigs Thing"

UFO Conspiracies

See:

William Cooper, Philip J. Corso, *Daimonic Reality,* Philip K. Dick, *Gods of Eden,* Kenneth Grant, Men in Black, Madrid UMMO Sightings, Robert Morning Sky, *Mothman Prophecies,* Roswell UFO Crash, *Sirius Mystery, UFO Crash at Roswell,* UMMO Letters

UFO Crash at Roswell

A one-hour CD, *UFO Crash at Roswell*, presents a good documentary introduction to the most controversial mystery of our time. Beginning with the July 7, 1947, ABC news bulletin announcing that a "flying disk" had crashed near Roswell, the CD then introduces Bill Brazel, son of Mack Brazel, the rancher who found the major debris. Bill says it was strange material—it felt like balsa wood but couldn't be cut, and was unlike anything that he had seen. Neighbor Loretta Procter next tells of being shown some odd debris by Mack Brazel and suggesting that he take it to Sheriff Wilcox. Reporter Frank Joyce tells of seeing the debris, too.

Major Jesse Marcel tells of going to the site and seeing debris, without any comments on its oddity. Jesse Marcel Jr., the major's son, says his father showed it to the whole family, and they all agreed it was unlike anything they'd ever seen. Employees of a local radio station tell of trying to file a story on the debris and being stopped by the FBI. Reporter Frank Joyce returns to tell how Mack Brazel—the rancher who first found the debris, remember?—changed his story after being held by the air force for several days. Several air force men, retired, tell of crating material and sending it to various places—Dayton, Fort Worth, Denver—a most confusing part of the story. Then the most challenging story of all: Col. Thomas Dubose confesses to removing some of the debris, under orders, and replacing it with balloon debris.

Other air force personnel talk of seeing odd debris, as does a local mortician, who was asked to supply two small coffins. The wife and daughter of a pilot named Henderson say he told them of seeing "small people" with "slanted eyes." Major Marcel and his son reappear to assure us the debris was not part of a balloon and they don't know what it was. The CD ends with the air force's latest story: It was a balloon, part of a spy program called Project Mogul.

In recent issues of *Saucer Smear,* several critics of the extraterrestrial theory argue that the air force has engaged in a campaign of confusion and disinformation to keep us from discovering other things they don't want us to know; UFOs may serve to distract us from projects that might cause as much protest as nuclear waste disposal. But that gives the conspiriologist even more to worry about.

References:

UFO Crash at Roswell, Baraka Foundation, P.O. Box 12933, Berkeley, CA

Saucer Smear, P.O. Box 1709, Key West, FL, issues of 1997, passim

UFO/Satanic Conspiracy

According to one school of Christian eschatology, the UFO phenomenon is produced by the fallen angels who followed Satan—"Prince of the Powers of the Air, Lord of Those That Fly, Intelligence Behind UFO Manifestations and Alien Encounters."

This theory, in one form, states that the angels built civilizations on every planet in this solar system; the face on Mars is an angelic construction depicting the symbols of Virgo and Leo, representing the first and second advent of Christ on Earth. Although that face survives, another whole planet was destroyed in the battle between God and Satan; its remains make up the asteroid belt, which is the model for all the *crop circles*.

Supporting opinions are quoted from one Dr. Pierre Guerrin ("UFO behavior is more akin to magic than to physics as we know it") and offbeat UFOlogist John Keel ("The UFO manifestations seem to be, by and large, merely minor variations of the age-old demonological phenomenon"). The Bible, therefore, should be consulted to explain what is happening, and it clearly reveals that we are living in "the tribulation, or End Times," which will lead on directly to the Apocalypse after Israel signs a treaty with the head of government of a unified Europe to establish a Jewish temple in Jerusalem and resume the "ancient sacrificial system of worship."

See also:

Hawthorne Abendsen, Antichrist, *Daimonic Reality, Holy Blood, Holy Grail, Satanic Panic*

Reference:

http://www.MT.net/~watcher

Ultra-Terrestrials

The ultra-terrestrials are journalist John Keel's suggested name for the entities in UFO cases and in other, even weirder tales of the paranormal. He conceives them as not quite material and not quite real, but on a fringe between energy, dream, and mythos. (Compare *extra-dimensionals*.)

See also:

Mothman Prophecies, Secret Cipher of the UFOnauts

The Umbrella Man and the John F. Kennedy Assassination

Two seconds before the first shot was fired in Dealy Plaza, a man in the crowd opened an umbrella. Since it was a sunny day with no sign of rain, it is hard to see why anybody would open an umbrella; many conspiriologists have suspected that the Umbrella Man, as he is called in the literature, was giving the signal for the shooters to open fire.

The House Select Committee on Assassinations interviewed a witness, Louis Witt, who said he was the Umbrella Man and had brought the umbrella on a rainless day to "heckle" the president.

Asked to explain that, Witt said he had heard that the president disliked umbrellas.

Conspiriologists reject Witt's story, because the *Zapruder film* does not show him doing anything with the umbrella that could remotely be considered "heckling." I reject it because I can't believe that anybody who heard Kennedy disliked zebras would have brought a zebra.

A more sinister cast was given to this absurd story when Charles Sensey, a CIA weapons developer at Fort Detrick, Maryland, testified before the Senate Intelligence Committee in September 1975 and described an umbrella poison dart gun he had made. He said it was always used in crowds with the umbrella open, so it would not attract attention. Our third source below argues that in the Zapruder film Kennedy reacts as if paralyzed by such a weapon just before the first rifle shot is heard.

See also:

James Jesus Angleton, Albert Guy Bogard, *NASA, Nazis and JFK*

References:

Umbrella Man—

http://users.southeast.net/~bgoldman/

Witt—

http://users.southeast.net/~bgoldman/witt.html

Umbrella dart gun—

http://www.ratical.com/ratville/JFK/ToA/ToAchp10.html

The UMMO Letters

Since about 1967, certain UFOlogists, scientists, philosophers, and various others have been receiving letters from a variety of addresses (every continent but Antarctica seems included), alleging that the senders are members of an extraterrestrial race called

UMMO who have come here to educate us. All are signed by the glyph:

)+(

The fact that the UMMO documents come from all over Earth is not the only thing that distinguishes them from most Outer Space communications "received" by psychics or channelers. Almost all other "wisdom" thus received is, in scientific terms, very low in information; that is, UFO revelations usually say the sort of thing you see on Hallmark cards. UMMO is, on the contrary, high in information (new concepts, new perspectives) and has fascinated a number of quite intelligent persons.

In fact, such prominent scientists as Juan Dominguez in Spain and Jean-Pierre Petit in France accepted UMMO's revelations as a more advanced physics and cosmology than Earth's. Dr. Petit even developed some of UMMO's ideas into his own parallel universe theories. Another French physicist, Teyssandier, although not that enthusiastic, said he had carefully analyzed all available UMMO communications and found no scientific errors in them. Even the skeptical Dr. Jacques Vallee describes the letters as equivalent to the work of a few dozen bright Ph.D. candidates.

Psychologist Jose Luis Jordan Pena recently confessed to devising the entire UMMO saga, which he intended as a demonstration that mental illness is far more widespread than we generally realize. (He says 79 percent of us are "paranoid.") A lady named Trinidad Pastrana confirmed Pena's story and said she traveled all over the world posting the letters, to create the impression that UMMO is well established everywhere on our planet.

Many UFOlogists reject these confessions, arguing that the original UMMO sightings could not be faked by any known technology and that Pena lacks the scientific knowledge shown in the letters. Others, accepting fraud, still say we do not know the full story, and suggest that some massive disinformation war between the CIA and KGB was behind it all.

See also:

Excluded Middle, Gods of Eden, Madrid UMMO Sightings, Voronezh, UMMO Visit

References:

Revelations: Alien Contact and Human Deception, by Jacques Vallee, Ballantine, New York, 1991, passim

"The UMMO Experience," by Scott Corrales, *Excluded Middle,* No. 7, Los Angeles, Calif.

http://www.loop.com/~exclmid/

Gary Underhill

Gary Underhill of the Center for International Studies at M.I.T. told friends in 1964 that a group within the CIA had master-minded the *John F. Kennedy assassination* and that he was going to expose them. According to William Torbitt, it was only "a few days later" that Underhill was found dead, shot through the head. The bullet entered behind the left ear, and Underhill was right-handed.

See also:

James Jesus Angleton, Sam Giancana, Kennedy Death Links, MMAO, Marina Oswald

Reference:

NASA, Nazis and JFK, by William Torbitt and Kenn Thomas, Adventure Unlimited Press, Kempton, Ill., 1996, p. 98.

Unsolved

Unsolved: The Mysterious Death of God's Banker, by Paul Foot and Paolo della Torre, was one of the first books in print about the strange death of **Roberto Calvi**, president of **Banco Ambrosiano**, close financial associate of the Vatican Bank and key figure in the **P2 conspiracy**. Foot and della Torre were also the first to offer a solution to the mystery. Calvi, the authors argue, laundered drug money for the **Mafia** in addition to his other irregularities; this seems rather well documented by now. Somewhere, Calvi either shortchanged the Mob, or accidentally caused them to suspect that he had done so, and the Mob ordered a contract on him. Hanging him where the rising tide covered his dead body—a traditional punishment for Freemasons who have betrayed their vows—was intended to point suspicion at Calvi's Masonic colleagues and away from the Mafia.

Although many other theories about Calvi's death have been proposed (see *"The Calvi Affair"*), it appears now that Foot and della Torre got it right on the first guess. Francesco di Carlo, a member of the real Corleone Mafia family,[1] has confessed to strangling Calvi and hanging him from the bridge. Being only a soldier in the hierarchy, di Carlo never asked or was told why the Mob wanted Calvi dead.

References:

London *Times*, June 20, 1996

Unsolved: The Mysterious Death of God's Banker, by Paul Foot and Paolo Filo della Torre, Orbis, London, 1984.

[1]The fictitious Corleone family, in the *Godfather* films, have no link with this real Sicilian family. Author Mario Puzo based them on the Gambino family. The real Corleones entered the Mafia only recently.

Usury

Veil

Veil: The Secret Wars of the CIA: 1981–1987, by Pulitzer Prize–winning journalist Bob Woodward of the *Washington Post*, documents some of the lawless tactics with which William Casey ran the CIA during the Ronald Reagan presidency. Aside from showing that the CIA is not bound by ordinary laws or ordinary morals, i.e., that it acts like any other intelligence agency in the world, *Veil* emphasizes in particular that the attempts to govern the Agency via the Senate Select Committee on Intelligence failed totally because Casey simply lied to the senators about his wars and warlike activities in Latin America, none of which Congress had authorized and some of which they had forbidden. The chairman of the committee, Senator Barry Goldwater, finally grew so angry, when the extent of Casey's deceits was discovered, that he wrote Casey a blunt letter stating in undiplomatic language that he was "pissed off."

Senator Goldwater was also annoyed at the CIA's unauthorized mining of harbors in Nicaragua, which he called "the dumbest fucking idea I ever heard of." And he was even more irate that the electronic bugs found in his office at least twice could not definitely be traced to either the KGB or the CIA. (See *Fedora* and *Yuri Nosenko*.)

Basically, Woodward shows that the CIA, at least under Casey, made up its own rules, unconfined by either Christian morals, international law, or senatorial "oversight," but he does not inquire into the allegations of CIA/Mafia links or CIA drug smuggling. His major demonstration is that the CIA often used other intelligence agencies of friendly countries (e.g., Israel, England, Saudi Arabia) to perform "dirty tricks" that Congress had prohibited; this at least gives some substance to the kind of international conspiratorial plots that paranoids believe in. *Veil* also presents evidence that the CIA has intervened in U.S. elections, and although this remains "plausible" rather than "proven," it is quite frightening. Sometimes, Woodward's evidence suggests, the paranoids are right.

See also:

James Jesus Angleton, Collier Brothers, John Hull, Mafia, News Election Service, P2 Conspiracy

Reference:

Veil: The Secret Wars of the CIA, 1981–1987, by Bob Woodward, Pocket Books, New York, 1987

Von Hapsburg Family

See:

Beethoven as Illuminatus, Church of Mary Magdalene, Knights of Malta

Voronezh UMMO Visit

On April 24, 1989, in Cherepovetsk, Soviet Union, a man named Ivan Vesalova reported a craft of enormous size, bigger than any airplane, about a thousand feet above ground. On June 6, in Konantsevo, several children saw, or claimed they saw, a luminous sphere land in a meadow and a headless person climb out. On June 11, a woman in Volagda reported a fiery sphere crossing the sky, visible for 17 minutes. All that, however, was prologue to the Voronezh "landings," or whatever they were.

For several days in October that year, hundreds of citizens in Voronezh, an industrial center with a population of about one million, saw a spaceship, or something like a spaceship, land in a public park. Gigantic humanoids (12 to 14 feet tall) got out and walked about the town, perhaps sightseeing. The citizens also reported "paranormal" events, including seeming teleportations, people vanished from one place and reappeared in another. In one sighting, about 500 people watched an unidentified craft hovering over their neighborhood.

Another craft flew over the nuclear power plant and sent down a ray of some sort, which left a burn mark in the ground.

Several Soviet scientists investigated and failed to convince themselves that all this was hallucination.

The witnesses claimed that the giant visitors had three eyes and that their craft and their uniforms were all marked with the symbol of UMMO:

)+(

See also:

Gods of Eden, Hono Intelligence Service 1901, UMMO Letters

Reference:

Revelations: Alien Contact and Human Deception, by Jacques Vallee, Ballantine, New York, 1991, pp. 214–24

Marilyn Walle

Marilyn Moon Walle, also known as Delilah, worked as a stripper at Jack Ruby's Carousel Club in Dallas. She planned to write a book exposing the inner secrets of the *John F. Kennedy assassination,* but was shot to death on September 1, 1966.

See also:

Hale Boggs, John F. Kennedy Death Links, Buddy Walthers

Reference:

The Big Book of Conspiracies, by Doug Moench, Paradox Press, New York, 1995, p. 13.

Father Edmund Walsh

Father Edmund Walsh had been a mentor to *Carroll Quigley* at Georgetown University and founded the Georgetown School of Foreign Service in 1919.

Father Walsh had been an adviser to Sen. Joe McCarthy during the 1950s' anticommunist fervor and had a long career in right-wing politics. *A-Albionic* cites Walsh's career as evidence against the John Birch Society's theory that Quigley was a member of the *Insiders* (Anglo-American banker/intellectual) conspiracy and as support for their own thesis that Quigley was part of the Vatican/ *Knights of Malta* conspiracy.

See also:

Gnomes of Zurich, *Yankee and Cowboy War*

Reference:

http://a-albionic.com/a-albionic.html

Buddy Walthers

Moments after the *John F. Kennedy assassination,* Dallas deputy sheriff Buddy Walthers found a .45 slug in the grass around Dealy Plaza. Walthers gave the fragment to a man who identified himself as an FBI agent, and it was never seen or heard of again. Walthers spoke of this strange .45 slug and its stranger disappearance frequently, saying that it never came from a 7.65 Mannlicher-Carcano. He was slain in a gunfight in 1969.

Reference:

The Big Book of Conspiracies, by Doug Moench, Paradox Press, New York, 1995, p. 14

The War on Some Drugs

According to Establishment rhetoric, the U.S. government is engaged in a War on Drugs. Pharmacological conspiriologists regard this terminology as deliberately misleading: If you go out your door and drive a few blocks, they say, you will find at least one store boldly declaring that they sell DRUGS, although some say PHARMACY, which can only be deciphered by those who know Greek roots; and in these stores, hundreds of drugs are available. Nearby is a supermarket where you can buy cigarettes, containing nicotine, a drug more addictive than heroin, according to former Surgeon General C. Everett Koop. Next door is a BAR where you can buy dozens of varieties of C_2H_3OH, a heavily addictive narcotic statistically linked to wife and child battering, divorce, and violent crime.

The government, thus, is not making war on all drugs, but only on some. The government asserts that the drugs on their taboo list are the worst ones; critics say they are merely the ones that are either (a) cheap and effective, such as herbal medicines, and/or (b) not easy to monopolize, such as marijuana, or (c) better than the higher-priced drugs manufactured by the large pharmaceutical corporations that financially support both political parties.

It all depends on whether you believe the cynical proverb "Laws are like sausages: You have much more respect for them if you haven't actually seen how they're made."

See also:

Food and Drug Administration, Hemp Conspiracy, Minneapolis Massacre, Newark Crash-In

George Washington

See:

American Dynasty, Christians Awake AIDS Theory

Washington Experiment

In 1968–69, the CIA experimented with the water supply of the Food and Drug Administration, injecting a chemical substance. No harmful effects were noted, and this case seems harmless except that Nuremberg rules were violated in that the subjects were not warned and not provided with information about the name or properties of the chemical used.

The experiment intended to test the possibility of poisoning drinking water.

See also:

AIDS Conspiracy Theories, Tampa Bay: Chemical Warfare, Tuskegee Syphilis Study

Reference:

http://home.earthlink.net/~bkonop/GermIncidents2.html

A.J. Weberman

A.J. Weberman maintains what is probably the largest website devoted to the *John F. Kennedy assassination*—certainly the largest site we've been able to find. In this megabyte colossus you can find virtually anything you might want to know about the John F. Kennedy case and its critics, together with long rebuttals of all defenders of the orthodox Warren Commission version of those events.

The same website contains a whole history of the CIA—or at least, a history of everything the CIA denies or doesn't want you to know about.

In an interview, Weberman claims to have read 20,000 pages of CIA documents and 100,000 pages of FBI documents. Look at his website and those figures will seem believable.

See also:

Robert Kennedy Assassination, Fletcher Prouty, "The Whole Bay of Pigs Thing"

References:

http://weberman.com

Interview—

"Interview With A.J. Weberman," *Popular Alienation: A Steamshovel Press Reader*, IllumiNet Press, Lilburn, Ga., 1995, p. 174

Nesta Webster

See:

Illuminati, *World Revolution*

Adam Weishaupt

See:

Ewige Blumenkraft, Illuminati, *World Revolution*

Orson Welles

George Orson Welles (1915–1985) was born in Kenosha, Wisconsin, and recognized as a child prodigy quite early, performing as stage magician, painter, violinist, actor, and cartoonist before he was ten. In his teens he concentrated mostly on painting and writing, but when this didn't earn much, he boldly walked into the Gate Threatre in Dublin, Ireland, at the age of 16, and announced that he was a Broadway actor of huge success, age 22, and eager to study Irish acting methods. The managers of the Gate (actor-director Michael MacLiammor and actor-producer Hilton Edwards) were so impressed that they hired him at once.

Or so Orson always told the story. According to MacLiammor, he and Edwards knew at once that Orson was a fake, but they recognized a real theatrical flair and decided to give him a chance.

Before he was 20, Orson had returned to the United States and had a busy career adapting, directing, and acting in classics on the New York stage and writing, directing, and acting for radio. His passionate devotion to his related profession, stage magic, influenced his attitude toward all these other arts, and hence he remains the most controversial theatrical innovator of our century. Audiences seem to either love his odd mixtures of drama and magic or else they find the magic element so unreal as to make him seem more showman than artist.

On October 31, 1938, Orson directed a radio production of H.G. Wells' *War of the Worlds,* in the form of a documentary. He discovered at once that a large segment of the American public had no training in critical thinking and would accept anything "documentary" as real: he provoked mass panic and became the most famous radio star in history. This led to his lifelong fascination with mixing documentary elements into his work, and this, together with the magic element, made him a huge success on the stage and in Europe, but his movies all suffered mixed reviews and small audiences.

In an Orson Welles production, you never know what is realism or why it turns surreal in a flicker, or what is intended as humor or intended as tragedy, who is supposed to be the hero, if there is one, or most of the things mass audiences want to know. Twelve years after his death, Orson Welles seems the model of the postmodern artist, and his works, endlessly ambiguous and ironic, have the dark flavor of conspiracy theories mixed with detached self-satire.

See also:

Buckaroo Banzai, Jean Cocteau, Elmyr, *F for Fake,* OM

"The Whole Bay of Pigs Thing"

In the Watergate tapes, President Richard Nixon makes the following remarks to Bob Haldeman on June 23, 1972:

> *When you get in, when you get in. . . [unintelligible]. . . people say, Look, the problem is that this will open the whole, the whole Bay of Pigs thing, and the President just feels that, ah, without going into details—don't, don't lie to them to the extent to say there is no involvement, but just say this is a comedy of errors, without getting into it. . . the President believes this is going to open the whole Bay of Pigs thing again.*

Later, conspiriologist **A.J. Weberman** presented evidence that Nixon used the code phrase "the Bay of Pigs thing" when he wanted to refer to the ***John F. Kennedy assassination***. According to conspiriologist Paul Kangas, this was confirmed by John Ehrlichman, another Watergate conspirator, who admitted Nixon did indeed use the code phrase "Bay of Pigs" to refer to the John F. Kennedy assassination.

It is far from clear how a full investigation of the Watergate burglary would open the John F. Kennedy assassination again, and this remains an unsolved mystery. Nonetheless CIA officer **E. Howard Hunt** was involved in Watergate, and many researchers believe he was also involved in the Kennedy hit.

On or about November 30, 1973, Hunt began to ask the White House for money, saying he had information that would "blow the White House out of the water" and "impeach the President." Many conspiracy buffs believe Hunt was one of the *Three Tramps* arrested on the grassy knoll immediately after the Kennedy assassination and then quickly released. Nixon agreed to pay Hunt $1 million in return for silence.

See also:

Hale Boggs, Flight 553, Mary Pinchot Meyer, Murder of Marilyn Monroe

References:

The Yankee and Cowboy War, by Carl Oglesby, Berkley Medallion Books, New York, 1977, p. 47, 227, passim

http://www.weberman.com/htdocs/22/22–4.htm#top

"The Role of Richard Nixon and George Bush in the Assassination of President Kennedy," by Paul Kangas, *The Realist,* No. 117, Summer 1991

Wicca

Wicca, from the old Anglo-Saxon root that gave us "witchcraft," is a neo-pagan religion based on—well, that depends on which witch you believe. Some say that wicca, as a goddess-centered religion, was passed on within certain families all through "the burning time" (the Holy Inquisition) and only now feels secure in resurfacing openly. Others say modern wicca was partly re-created out of old books, and partly invented, by an English eccentric named Gerald Gardner, with some help from *Aleister Crowley*. Still others admit that Gardner played a large role in re-creating the wiccan tradition, but don't care to admit his association with Crowley.

Witches, like Freemasons, call their rites "the Craft" and use the archaic Masonic expression "So mote it be" in concluding many rites. This may be explained, perhaps, by the fact that Gardner and Crowley were both Masons.

Wherever it came from, modern wicca is largely based on traditional Celtic festivals and old Celtic goddesses and gods, sometimes with their old Gaelic names and sometimes with modernized names. Dancing is part of the ritual in all covens; getting drunk or stoned only in some, mostly Californian covens. The rites all celebrate the seasons, the Moon, and the Great Mother Goddess.

Many wiccans are extremely litigious and will quickly start legal action against any Fundamentalist who claims that they are really a Satanic cult and engage in human sacrifice. At present, some Fundamentalists still say that, and the wiccans are still quick to sue.

See also:

Guardians of the Grail, Ordo Templi Orientis

Reference:

http://www.witchvox.com/wvoxhome.html

The Widow's Son

Hiram Abiff is often called simply "the widow's son" in Freemasonic speech, and charitable acts by Masons are said to be "for the widow's son." This refers to the one mention of Hiram in the Old Testament, namely 1 Kings 7: 13–14.

> *And King Solomon sent and fetched Hiram out of Tyre. He was a widow's son out of the tribe of Naph-ta-li and his father was a man of Tyre, a worker in brass: and he was filled with wisdom, and understanding, and cunning to work all works in brass. And he came to King Solomon and wrought his works.*

In Masonic lore, Hiram was killed by three sinister figures with the symbolic names Jubela, Jubelo, and Jubelum.

Parcifal, a major figure in some magick/Masonic orders (e.g., the *Ordo Templi Orientis*) was also a widow's son; but some who have been there and come back tell us that both Hiram and Parcifal are allegorical figures representing *Jacques de Molay*. An even more interesting theory about the widow's son appears in *"Holy Blood, Holy Grail."*

References:

History of Secret Societies, by Akron Daraul, Pocket Books, New York, 1961

Morals and Dogma of the Ancient and Accepted Scottish Rite of Freemasonry, Supreme Council of the Southern Jurisdiction, Washington, D.C., 1871

Light on Freemasonry, by David Bernard, Vonnieda and Sowers, Washington, D.C., 1858

World Finance Corporation

The World Finance Corporation of Miami, Florida, reputedly had an intimate relationship with the Cisalpine Bank of the Bahamas, part of the *P2 conspiracy's* drug-money laundering network. In 1982, the Dade County district attorney attempted to prove that at least seven officers of the World Finance Corporation were present or former CIA "assets" and that they engaged knowingly in laundering cocaine money. The D.A. also charged that the CIA was deliberately blocking and sabotaging his investigation; nonetheless, he proved that not only drug money but drugs themselves frequently passed through the WFC, which went bankrupt while three officers stood trial. Many other banks, including the respected Chase Manhattan, were part of the laundromat, but it could not be shown that all of them knew or even suspected that they were in the dope business.

See also:

Banco Ambrosiano, John Hull

Reference:

In Banks We Trust, by Penny Lernoux, Anchor/Doubleday, New York, 1984, pp. 100–142

World Revolution

World Revolution: The Plot Against Civilization, by Nesta Webster, presents one of the most scholarly and also one of the most unique of the theories in anti-***Illuminati*** literature. Although, like most 20th-century anti-Illuminists, Webster sees this order as the main promoter of the French Revolution (they took over the ***Grand Orient Lodge of Egyptian Freemasonry,*** the largest Masonic brotherhood in France, which included and influenced nobles, merchants, and even workers), she also shares the common view that they created communism, socialism, anarchism, and radicalism in general. But, uniquely, she tries to prove that all this is secondary to their real purpose. The Illuminati, she claims, was taken over very early in its career by the Prussian nobility and the German intelligence service, and Illuminati lodges spread left-wing ideas only to weaken other countries and make them easier for Germany to conquer. In short, where most others in this area of speculation see the Illuminati as an atheist plot or a Jewish plot, she sees it as basically a German plot.

Webster also tries to prove that the revived Illuminati founded in Dresden in the 1880s was as powerful as the original Illuminati of Weishaupt and played a major role in the history of socialism and communism. (See ***Illuminati Copies or Revivals.***) A classic example of her ability to find real links to hang her theories on is her question, "Was it. . . a mere coincidence that in July 1899 an International Socialist Congress decided that May 1, the day on which Weishaupt founded the Illuminati, should be chosen for an annual International Labour demonstration?" (p. 245).

See also:

Ewige Blumenkraft, Nazi/Illuminati Theory, P2 Conspiracy

Reference:

World Revolution: The Plot Against Civilization, by Nesta Webster, Constable and Company, London, 1921

World War II Deniers

Going one step further than the *Holocaust Deniers*, at least two writers have argued that World War II itself was entirely faked in every detail.

Donald Holmes argues in *The Illuminati Conspiracy: The Sapiens System* that the *Illuminati*—regarded by him as superior intelligences, perhaps from outer space—control the governments and media of this planet. World War II, the most terrifying example to date of how much harm humans can do to one another, never happened: By special effects, stage magic tricks, fake journalism, etc., the Illuminati made it *appear* to happen so that we would become so frightened of our destructive powers that we would establish a happier, more gentle society all over the planet. (They are, evidently, still working on that project.)

Similarly, in *Illuminati Lady*, a privately published poem by *Kerry Thornley*, it is proposed that World War II was faked by incarnate Illuminati, led by Mohandas K. Gandhi, in collaboration with discarnate Illuminati, led by Madame H.P. Blavatsky (the Illuminati Lady of the title). The purpose, again, was to frighten us into becoming pacifists.

See also:

American Hero, Creation Science, Charles Fort, George I. Gurdjieff

Reference:

The Illuminati Conspiracy: The Sapiens System, by Donald Holmes, New Falcon Press, Scottsdale, Ariz, 1988

X

The character of "X" in Oliver Stone's film, *JFK*, is based on *Fletcher Prouty*, one of the first government officials to dissent publicly from the Warren Commission version of the *John F. Kennedy assassination.*

Reference:

http://www.astridmm.com/prouty

Xists

See:

Anti-"Bob," The Con, Planet X

The Yankee and Cowboy War

One of the most intelligent and well-documented books on conspiratorial activities in modern America, *The Yankee and Cowboy War: Conspiracies from Dallas to Watergate and Beyond,* by Professor Carl Oglesby of Boston University, argues that our ruling Elite is divided into two groups ("Yankees" and "Cowboys"), who only cooperate when threatened by internal or external foes but more often compete, sometimes violently and murderously.

The Yankees in Oglesby's model are a brotherhood of wealthy old New England/New York families (the *Insiders* in *John Birch Society* theory) who have relatively "liberal" and "internationalist" values (except when this interferes with profits) and owned almost everything in the United States until fairly recently. The Cowboys represent new Western wealth, owning more than the Yankees like, and holding views that run the gamut from conservative to reactionary to neo-fascist; they suspect the Yankees of plotting against them, of ruining free enterprise by establishing government-backed monopolies, and of amoral willingness to cooperate with communism and other alien ideologies when this advances their interests.

David Rockefeller represents the archetypal Yankee and *Howard Hughes* the archetypal Cowboy; the legal and financial battles between Rockefeller and Hughes over control of Trans World Airlines represents an open, less clandestine side of the Yankee-Cowboy conflict, and is treated in great detail; this epic, although well documented, almost reads like a satire by Ben Jonson or Jonathan Swift, especially in Oglesby's cool treatment of Hughes' growing suspicion that the Rockefellers owned all the courts. The more controversial parts of the book attempt to revise the standard conspiratorial views of the *John F. Kennedy assassination* and Watergate, arguing that the Cowboys were ultimately behind the killing of Kennedy (whatever the role of the *Mafia* and CIA as agents) and the Yankees manipulated Watergate to destroy Nixon, the Cowboy's favorite politico.

Oglesby explicitly denies that the Yankee-Cowboy model explains everything, or that only two conspiracies are at work in our world. "A multitude of conspiracies," he argues, are always fighting over the territorial-economic Top Dog status; the Yankees and Cowboys are merely the two most powerful coalitions in the United States at this time.

A major sub-theme of this book concerns the evolution of the strange relationships between the CIA and three clandestine forces examined by other conspiriologists: (1) the "round table groups" established by *Cecil Rhodes* to guide Anglo-American foreign policy in a direction appealing to liberals and profitable to bankers (the Insiders, again); (2) the Mafia, which began its relationship with the U.S. intelligence community during World War II and has steadily developed a symbiosis with it; and (3) the neo-Nazi underground, headed by *General Reinhard Gehlen,* who managed the transition from Hitler's top intelligence officer to a CIA asset very quickly and brought lots of other Nazis with him.

The present author's reading of Oglesby's data is that the CIA thinks it is using each of these groups and each of them think they are using the CIA and everybody involved is terribly duped part of the time.

See also:

American Dynasty, James Jesus Angleton, Licio Gelli, "The Whole Bay of Pigs Thing," and for contrast A-Albionic and *Irish Wisdom*

Reference:

The Yankee and Cowboy War, by Carl Oglesby, Berkley Medallion Books, New York, 1977

Yin and Yang

The universe and everything in it, according to Taoist philosophy, always contains yin and yang. Yin represents a "female" force, darkness, passivity, water, flowing, mellowness, the shady side of a mountain, etc.; yang is "male," bright, shining, active, fiery, explosive, creative, the sunny side of a mountain, etc.

Some have identified yin and yang with the negative and positive forces in quantum wave mechanics. Others have identified them with the right and left hemispheres of the human brain.

In the Discordian revelation, the yin and yang are partial aspects of hodge and podge. Hodge contains yin but also includes chaos, practical jokes, anarchy, rebellion, etc., while podge contains yang but also law and order, bureaucracy, militarism, regimentation, mindless obedience, etc. In the Sub-Genius faith, all these opposites reduce to Something and Nothing, and the art of life is to attain *Slack,* the perfect balance in between, which allows you to get Something for Nothing.

These dualities appear continually throughout James Joyce's *Finnegans Wake* in such battling twins as Cain and Abel, Jacob and Esau, Shem and Shaun, Mick and Nick, Mutt and Jute, Mercius and Justius, Glugg and Chuff, Butt and Taff, Muta and Juva, Shakespeare and Bacon, Swift and Stern, Brown and Nolan, etc.

See also:

Aeon of Horus, Giordano Bruno, Sacred Chao

Yog Sothoth

Yog Sothoth is the most potent and most mysterious of the interstellar beings or forces that threaten this planet. Like the Hidden Variable in quantum mechanics, Yog Sothoth transcends both space and time, since "past, present, future: All are one in Yog Sothoth," and he and his kind exist "not in the spaces we know but between them."

See also:

Abdul Alhazred, Kenneth Grant, H.P. Lovecraft, *Necronomicon*

The Zapruder Film

On November 22, 1963, Abraham Zapruder took a motion-picture film of what he expected to be a minor historical event—a president passing through Dallas. Instead, he captured the most controversial assassination in American history.

The Zapruder film clearly shows that at the first shot, John Kennedy's head *snaps backward*. According to the laws of physics, when a projectile (such as a bullet) hits an object, that object moves in the direction of the projectile: Thus, if Kennedy's head snapped back, that bullet came from in front, e.g., from the grassy knoll. Defenders of the Warren Commission reply that this Newtonian law is only true of inanimate objects and that when an animal or human is hit by a bullet, inner neurological spasms may cause the body to snap in any direction. The experts on both sides seem equally learned, and the debate between physics and neurology still continues.

Leaving the experts to debate expertly against each other, David Lifton, author of *Best Evidence* (book and video), has highlighted two suggestive, even sinister, facts about the Zapruder film:

1. *Time-Life paid Mr. Zapruder $150,000 for the film (a price equal to a million dollars today, Lifton claims) and yet never showed the film anywhere—not in theaters, not on TV, nowhere.*

2. *The Warren Commission never once mentions this crucial fact about the film (the backward snap, which has inspired more than 35 years of controversy), indicating either that they were very hurried and sloppy or that they deliberately didn't want to face the implications this raised. On either assumption, Lifton says, we cannot trust the Commission or its verdict.*

See also:

Best Evidence, Lee Bowers Jr., E. Howard Hunt, Kennedy Death Links, Three Tramps, A.J. Weberman

Reference:

http://mcadams.posc.mu.edu/arrb/index38.htm

ZOG

Not a creature from the *"Necronomicon,"* although just as frightening as any of them, the *ZOG* is our Zionist Occupied Government, in the language of many far-right militia groups.

Some think the ZOG intends to kill all the Christians any day now, but others think it merely intends to turn us over to the *New World Order* to become slaves of the United Nations.

I would like to live in a world where all the conspiracy theories are as absurd as this one.

Reference:

Every Knee Shall Bow, by Jess Walter, HarperCollins, New York, 1995